Praise for
A Bohemian Dream

A Bohemian Dream is a fascinating family history!
—A. Young, Arkansas

One thing this story did for me is that it made me want to research my ancestors. I've been wanting to do this for a long time, and it just made me crave to do it even more. I think it will affect many other readers the same way, more than a story—it is an experience.
—T. Morlock, *Red Flag Conversations*

I thoroughly enjoyed reading *A Bohemian Dream*. Gwen's research was amazing. All the letters written over the years added a feel of actually being there witnessing and even partaking in the story as it unfolded. I am a descendant of the Karellas. So, it was even more interesting looking into the lives and the toils my ancestors went through to get us where we are today. I was at my aunt's funeral, one of Ambrose's daughters, and met a cousin from five generations back. It was interesting talking to a very distant cousin I had never seen before and having a conversation. I live within twenty-five miles of where most of the latter part of the story takes place. I know a lot of people who are decedents of my descendants and didn't know I was related to them. It was a wonderful read and really gives me an insight to my history and the strong family who made up part of my being. I would have been entranced with *A Bohemian Dream* even if I wasn't related. It is just well written and holds your interest but still gives a wealth of history about early America, the struggles, and some of the reasons people wanted to come here.
—Jim Ridder, Nebraska

te one's family history in story form makes for an enjoyable ntertaining read. The writer has intertwined historically t information of the political climate, which gives her s insights on why the proud Bohemian Karella family o America, where they settled, and how they ultimately ered in America.

—Ann Vukich, California

Bohemian Dream is both captivating and breathtaking at the ime time! Knowing that Vaclav and Antonia actually lived hrough these times makes the story even more compelling! If book one is this good, I can't wait to read the rest of the trilogy! A literal page-turner and a must-read!

—Kevin Karella, *Olivia's Hope*

A Bohemian Dream

GWEN KARELLA MATHIS

A Bohemian Dream

Library of Congress Control Number: 2020913370

Cover Design: Debbie O'Byrne
Interior Design: JetLaunch

ISBN Hardcover: 978-1-64184-451-2
ISBN Paperback: 978-1-64184-452-9
ISBN ebook: 978-1-64184-453-6

Printed in the United States of America

If you'd like information on bulk discounts, please contact the author at casaredondapv@gmail.com.

Dedicated in Loving Memory to:

My father, Ambrose James Karella, and his dream of writing the Karella family history

Imagination Ex-Press

Contents

Acknowledgments ix

Prelude: Important People to Know xi

Preface: A Beer, a Bohemian, and an Old Bottle xvii

1   Discoveries Beyond an Old Bohemian Bottle 1
2   Life in Bohemia with the Karella and Nemec Families 34
3   The Karellas of Kutna Hora 1863–1874 101
4   Voyage to a Bohemian Dream 1874–1875 127
5   A Family Reunited in America 179
6   The Long-Awaited Journey to Nebraska 1878–1889 210
7   The Bohemian's Dream Continues in Nebraska
    1890–1894 248
8   Karella Weddings, Births, and a New Century
    1895–1900 285
9   A New Era for the Nebraska Karellas 323

Appendix-1-A: St. Leonard's Grave Plot of the Ancestral
       Karellas in Madison, Nebraska 386
Appendix-1-B: Complete Outline on Historical Bohemia 387

Appendix 2: Genealogy Records Covering Generations
    1, 2, 3; The Births of the 4th Generation of
    Karellas; and Nebraska Family Groupings   412
Appendix 3: Research Data and Material References   422
Appendix 4: Bohemian Recipes   443
Appendix 5: Build Your Own Family Tree   449
Appendix 6: Examples of Genealogy Resources and
    Places to Begin Your Personal Search
    for Data   450
About the Author   453

Acknowledgments

Sister Margaret Mary Bean and Mary Karella Voborny, who gathered much of this historical information and interviews with Bessie Holy Finkral, and other relatives capturing memories of the Holy-clan's crossing to America in 1888, along with relevant historical material

Carol Robertson, Curator of the Madison County Historical Museum, for preserving so much of the photographic and material history of the settlers of Madison County, Nebraska

Mildred Karella Ridder, Rosemary Karella Macko, Florence Karella Roggenbach, and Andrew Rossow, for family documents and photos. Cathy Karella Ward, Darlene Helinski Cipra, Jim Ridder, and Anne Mathis Vukich for encouraging me and giving me valuable proofreading and editing advice

My husband, Steve Mathis, for his support, editing, and proofing skills

And acknowledgment of those rare souls who shared Alaska with Andy and Betty's family and who directly or indirectly taught their children so much about hope, love, life, and living in faith with the Lord

Important People to Know

The Patriarch, 1900s Karella Family— Ambrose Jerome Karella

The old Nebraskan Bohemian liked to wear his hair in a butch cut because it was too much bother to wear it longer. With a sturdy build topping out at 5'8", his name was Ambrose Jerome, but everyone called him Rusty. Born with a creative and analytical mind, Rusty could not only come up with good ideas or invent a tool, but he also instinctively knew how to put them to practical use. Nothing went to waste around Rusty. Faithful to those he loved and believed in, a father dedicated to his eight children, Rusty had been blessed to see all of them grow up. A dependably good man who wore his heart on his sleeve, Rusty had survived the Dust Bowl era, brought his family through the Great Depression, and lived through the worries of World War II. After 31 years of marriage, with their children grown and gone, he and his remarkable wife, Delora, moved to the Frontier Territory of Alaska in 1956. They would begin a new phase of their lives as they helped their eldest son, Andy, run his mail and delivery business.

The Matriarch, 1900s Karella Family—Delora Lucy Holt Karella

A 5'3" redheaded spitfire of a woman, Delora Lucy Holt Karella found Rusty to be a shy, moral man she could trust and believe in. Marrying him when she was very young, he called her Bitty because she was so tiny. That tiny woman became the mother and commander of four sons and four daughters. Delora matured into a woman people did not want to cross. She made a formidable foe who always got payback in subtle ways. Although she did not believe in sugar coating the truth, she made a faithful and compassionate friend. Perceptive and intelligent, she learned to be a nurse on the job during the war years and dedicated her life selflessly to the family she loved and to her calling as a nurse. Regardless of life's twists and turns, her heart never forgot how to have fun or enjoy an adventure.

The Karellas' Firstborn Son—Ambrose James Karella

Although his name was Ambrose James, nearly everyone called him either Andy or AJ. At 6'2", the handsome charmer with the jaunty wave in his hair towered over his father. This size difference in no way diminished the respect he had for the wonderful man who raised him. Being a first-born son, Andy was expected to take on a leadership role with his seven siblings. That rank naturally made him think he was right because he was the eldest. That misconception resulted in being overbearing and quick-tempered when challenged. His wife, Betty Le Rossow, also a first-born child, understood Andy. Romantic at heart and a dreamer, Andy's emotions ran deep. He possessed an uncanny psychic intuition and made most of his decision based on gut feelings. Though his gut feelings were often right, Betty preferred to have a few facts to back them up. Out in the wilds of nature, Andy found peace and renewed balance where he felt close to God. Through his parents, he learned about the things worth believing in, family, and dedication to country. Andy added friendship to that list. He and his best friend, Chauncey, had been inseparable as boys in Nebraska and never lost that closeness. Not even after Andy married his amazing wife, Betty. She became a sister to Chauncey. Andy treated people he met with respect, and most people who knew him liked him. Andy always yearned for adventure. Though he didn't know it at the time, his greatest adventure began at age 17 when he met Betty during a brief time at college in the fall of 1943. In January 1944, he and Chauncey became Marines in World War II. When the war ended, the real adventures began. Betty said yes, and Andy married the love of his life in the spring of 1948.

Andy's Wife and Soulmate—Betty Le Rossow Karella

A striking brunette with natural red highlights, Betty learned about style and grace from her well-spoken and fashionable mother, LeOra Rossow. She gained a love of facts, world history, and cultural tolerance from her German father, Frederick Rossow, though everyone called him Fred. Betty was her mother's only daughter and a son to her father for seven years before her little brother, Charles, was born. Betty was encouraged to question what she was told and make her own decisions. She had an orderly mind suited to good planning based on facts and an unrelenting drive to execute and achieve her goals. In college, her friends came from all over the world, and she planned to see as much of that world as possible after she graduated. Betty was Andy's match in every way. When the diminutive 5'2" beauty set her mind to something, she rarely missed her target. Her success had nothing to do with luck. She based her decisions on fact, not intuition. Consequently, there were times when she and Andy were at odds. To make her point, she used practical logic and facts. If that didn't work, sometimes she went head to head with him. Through persistence, tenacity, and natural honesty, Betty would bring Andy around to her way of thinking. Sometimes they found a compromise. Despite being beautiful, Betty was grounded and realistic, and her head was not turned easily by a compliment. Open to new information, Betty could modify her position on a subject. Once she was convinced, she remained dedicated and faithful to what she believed in. Betty was not a follower; she studied and chose her direction. She did not like being stuck in the house or doing housework. Given the chance, she would willingly drive a truck or dig a ditch and was not afraid to trade her skirts for a pair of pants. And she made pants look good! The people who knew Betty loved her. She was a person and friend you could count on no matter what. Betty and Andy were star-crossed lovers and proof that opposites attract. Their life together was a great adventure from the first moment, and their love and dedication to each other lasted all the years that she lived.

The Ancestral Mystery Researcher—Sister Margaret Mary Bean

Sister Margaret Mary loved her personal hobby, the study of genealogy, and was determined to solve the mystery of the Karella family's heritage. Being one of Andy's many cousins, she was also from Nebraska and became a Benedictine nun after graduating high school. Seven years older than Andy, Margaret Mary grew up with siblings and loving parents whom she admired. Sweet-tempered, she took great pleasure in helping others even as a little girl. Margaret Mary possessed an orderly and creative mind. Like many of her family members, she had a good memory. She loved to tell a great story but never stretched the facts or the truth. Margaret Mary possessed natural discipline and was not afraid to dedicate herself to a good cause. She greatly admired one of her schoolteachers, a Benedictine nun, who showed a 10-year-old Margaret Mary a way to thank God for her gifts of compassion and love of service. Through the nun's friendship and her examples of faith, Margaret Mary chose the Benedictine sisterhood where she embraced a life that allowed her to share her gifts with the world.

A Beer, a Bohemian, and an Old Bottle

U.S. Territory of Alaska, 1956

The fall hunting season of 1956 had arrived in the territory of Alaska and was colder than usual, even this far north. It did not take Andy long to learn why Alaska is called *The Last Frontier*. If you didn't succeed in gathering enough meat and fish before winter set in, your family could literally starve before spring. Today, they all thanked God for a successful hunt. Andy, his father, Rusty, his brother-in-law, Bill, and his mother, Delora, were coming home to the mining town of

Bull Moose, from Andy Karella's 1950s photos

Fairbanks with enough moose meat to feed their families through the coming winter.

The hunters were already exhausted and wanted to get cleaned up. But taking care of the meat always came first, so they drove to the garage. Colder than outdoor temperatures inside the garage, there were rafters high enough to hang the moose meat so it could tenderize. After winching the meat into the rafters, they were ready to relax. As they enjoyed a cold beer, Andy's dad related an odd fact about Budweiser Beer so surprising it awakened Andy's curiosity regarding Bohemia, the land of his ancestors.

Andy had heard old Bohemian adventure stories all his life and respected them for what they were—a part of his parents' and grandparents' history—he had never really been interested in old history, not as an American boy growing up in Nebraska in the 1930s.

Up until now, he had been even less inclined to be curious about old adventures, when at 28 years old, he was living new adventures every day. His amazing, beautiful wife, Betty, was brave to want to live in a territory town in Alaska. She proved her bravery over and over again giving him four rambunctious children. She also helped him operate their own delivery business, which covered over two hundred miles, including Fairbanks and outlying bush villages. They believed their life proved success was due to focusing on the future, not the past.

Yet now, as he sat at his father's kitchen table and stared at the old Bohemian beer bottle in his hand, Andy willingly admitted he was changing his mind. There was relevance in old history, and he had just heard a mysterious fact related to his Bohemian past that made him want to know more. Excited about this revelation, Andy could hardly wait to get home to share his new discovery with Betty.

Rusty (Ambrose Jerome) Karella and wife Delora Karella with son-in-law Bill Frost, GKM

Leaving his parent's house across the street from his own, Andy caught a glimpse of Betty through the living room window. Hurrying across the road, he walked through the front door.

When Betty heard him, eager to hear about Andy's hunting trip, she called out from the kitchen, "Andy, what took you so long? I've been waiting since I put the kids to bed."

As he walked into the kitchen, his wife held up a cold beer and a hot mug of coffee, asking, "Which one do you want?"

He grinned and replied, "I'll take the Budweiser."

Not in the mood to wait any longer, Betty said, "S-o-o-o, tell me about the trip!" Smiling at her impatience, Andy sat down next to her and rested his elbows on the emerald green kitchen countertop and began his story.

"We shot two bull moose this morning out by Murphy Dome. I figure they averaged about 1,500 to 2,000 pounds apiece. As soon as the moose were down, Mom and Dad went back to camp to make food and get the trailer ready for the meat.

"It took us all day to get the meat, hides, and racks back to camp and loaded on the trailer, and by then, we were filthy from head to foot. Though we were dog-tired, after five days without a bath, no one wanted to camp out one more night."

Pausing to take a sip of beer, he continued, "I think we turned into the neighborhood about 6:30 this evening, and Mom couldn't wait to get out of the car. We dropped her off at the house first and then drove over to the garage to unload the moose.

"Just when we thought we were through taking care of the meat, Mom brought us three cold Budweisers. She told us she'd have another one waiting for us up at the house after we brought her a chunk of stew meat and a bucket of ribs. Cutting up the ribcages took another hour." Andy paused to give his wife a tired smile

Czechoslovakia
1930 (Bohemia). ©
Czechoslovakia1930linguistic.jpg

before resuming his story. "As soon as Bill and I put the meat in Mom's kitchen, she asked us to sit down with Dad and gave us the beer she promised. Now, this is where the story takes an unexpected turn.

"After Dad takes a drink from his bottle, he says, 'There's nothing like a good Bohemian beer after such hard work.' I looked that label over carefully, and thought, *Dad's got that wrong!*

Betty gave her husband a stern look, and immediately, Andy clarified his statement by saying, "That's not what I *said* to him, Betty." Betty looked relieved as Andy went on with his story. "What I said was 'Dad, this is not a Bohemian beer. It says, made in the U.S.A., and I think the name is German, isn't it?'

"Can you believe it? Dad actually frowned at me, and we both know what that look means. Then, in his crankiest tone, he says, 'Son, you have a lot to learn about your own Bohemian history!'

"I told him I meant no disrespect, but I genuinely wanted to know what made him believe the beer was Bohemian. At first, he just stared at me, and I didn't think he was going to explain. He must have changed his mind because what he told me next came as a complete surprise.

Bottle at Bohemia pub, GKM

"According to Dad, Budweiser was originally a Bohemian-made beer named Budvar and was brewed in a town called Ceske Budejovice, south of Prague. In the old days, Prague was Bohemia's capital city. Anyway, Dad went on to remind me that all our Bohemian ancestors were born and raised in small towns close to Prague. He said my great-grandfather used to save those glass bottles to reuse when they bottled their own home brewed beer. While Dad was telling me all this, he walked over to a cupboard, took out an old beer bottle, and handed it to me. The bottle's faded label read, 'Czech Premium Lager, Budweiser Budvar.'

"I couldn't help shaking my head at seeing the proof with my own eyes. Dad was right. It was just like he could read my mind, too, because Dad actually smirked at me and asked, 'How's that for an interesting fact from our Bohemian Heritage?'

"It really surprised me and made me think. Seeing something I thought of as so American, I would never have guessed it had Bohemian roots like me! It really made me curious too. Now, I do want to know more about Bohemia and our family history."

Betty's eyes twinkled with amusement as she listened to her husband. She knew how much Andy disliked being proven wrong, particularly when he was sure he was right. To distract him, she hugged him and wrinkled her nose, saying, "You do need a bath. I'm going to

Betty Le Rossow Karella, wife of Ambrose James Karella

turn on the hot water in the tub for you *right now.*" His laughter followed her out of the room; the sound of it made her smile.

Outside a Bohemia Pub Wall, GKM

Ambrose James (Andy, AJ, Jr.)
Karella, 1927–1989

Betty Le Rossow Karella,
1925–1963

CHAPTER 1

Discoveries Beyond an Old Bohemian Bottle

The revelation Andy experienced as he looked at the old Bohemian Budweiser bottle changed his opinion about the relevance of his family's heritage and Bohemia. He found himself really curious and interested in the old family stories and decided to learn as much as he could about his Karella heritage in the land of Bohemia.

Left: Margaret Mary Bean, Graduation
Right: after becoming a Benedictine Nun,
1920–2009

1

Launching his investigation by contacting family in Nebraska, Andy discovered one of his cousins, Sister Margaret Mary Bean, had the same interest. Sister Margaret Mary's connection to the Karella lineage was through her mother, Helen, the eldest daughter of Anton and Anastasia Karella. Margaret Mary chose her hobby when she entered the sisterhood and had been researching Karella family genealogy ever since.

Columbus, Nebraska, Benedictine Convent

Sister Margaret Mary had just finished reviewing her latest notes and entries on the Karella genealogy chart. As she ran her hand lovingly over the names of her ancestors, Wenceslaus and Antonia Karella, at the top of the family tree, she got a little misty-eyed, thinking, *It's because of you two that we are here.* Smiling, she wiped away her silly tears just as her telephone rang. Sister Margaret Mary was astonished to hear her cousin, Andy, on the other end of the telephone line.

Fairbanks, Alaska

"Hi, is this Sister Margaret Mary?" asked the voice.

"Yes, it is," she replied.

"This is your cousin, Andy Karella, the one that lives in Alaska. Do you remember me?"

"Why, yes, Andy, I do! What a delight to hear from you," Margaret Mary replied.

"How are you doing? Do you have a minute to talk?" Andy asked.

"I am fine—thank you for asking. What is on your mind?" Sister Margaret Mary replied. She was delighted to hear of Andy's interest and told him about her recent discoveries in Bohemian and American Catholic Church archives.

"I'm curious, cousin, although this is really exciting, can you tell me how you got interested in genealogy?" Andy asked.

"I have always been curious about the mystery of our family's past because of all the languages spoken by family members. Plus, I was fascinated by the bits and pieces of the stories I heard over the years. But I could never find a logical connection between them, and it was a mystery I wanted to unravel," Sister Margaret Mary replied.

"Funny you should describe it that way because I do too. How did you get started?" Andy asked.

"First, it was Mother Superior's idea that I pick a hobby when I joined the sisterhood. Then, it took years of hunting through family stories for the right names. After that, it was hunting through church archives to find the oldest Karella ancestor who had a written birth record. Once I had that document, I had the facts I needed to begin our family's genealogy.

"Since making that key discovery, I have compiled important data from church records beginning in 1839 for both Wenceslaus Karella and his wife, Antonia Nemec Karella. I also found the names of the towns where they were born and the wedding records from the town and church where they were married. I've expanded my search to include the town they lived in after they got married. In that town, I found the birth records for Wenceslaus and Antonia's first three children born in Bohemia. This is the group of Karellas we are directly descended from.

"Antonia Nemec Karella was the first person in our family tree that came to America in 1875. Her husband, Wenceslaus, and their three children followed her to America in 1877. I also found the birth record for their fourth child, a boy born in America in 1878. Though we have verbal stories about Karella and Nemec generations that lived before Wenceslaus and Antonia's time, our genealogy records begin with these two because we can verify the facts through documentation. My chart begins with Wenceslaus and Antonia, and below them, I listed each of their children and their marriage partners. Below them comes the children born to those marriages, and I go on listing those children's children and so forth. I now have four generations recorded."

"What a superb accomplishment! I would love to see that chart! Have you had any time to do research on Bohemia itself or write about the family stories you've gathered?" Andy asked.

"Not really. Mostly, I've been concentrating on extracting dates and names from the stories to use for timeline research. I did recently enlist cousin Mary Karella Voborny to help interview some of the older Nebraska relatives. She is going to begin with Aunt Bessie Holy Finkral. Mary will focus on capturing Aunt Bessie's memories of her family coming to America by steamship in 1888. Bessie was one of our grandmother Anastasia's sisters. Did you know Bessie is 99 years old now?" Sister Margaret Mary asked.

"I hate to admit it, but I've lost track of many of the Nebraska relatives. I would love to help with this project, and you make a good point about our older relatives. I do feel an urgency to help keep their memories alive by gathering their stories and writing them down before we lose them. Their information will help us chronicle our ancestor's lives and the Karellas' relocation from Bohemia to Nebraska," Andy replied.

"That is exactly what I have been thinking, Andy. I'll put together a packet of information for you with a copy of my genealogy chart, a list of facts about our people, and the names of the key towns our people came from. You will be able to use those places and dates as historical references to begin your investigations. Look for the packet to arrive next week. It's going to be fun working with you, Andy."

Sister Margaret Mary, Columbus, Nebraska, Benedictine Convent

Sister Margaret Mary hung up the phone grinning. She felt almost as thrilled about her cousin's help as she had when she first discovered the records of Wenceslaus Karella. As a team, she and Andy could gather more information through family interviews and verify facts and details for the genealogy. With all that material, they could create a framework to tell the whole family story. Looking down at the chart in front of her, she read, "Wenceslaus Vaclav Karella, born 1839, Caslav, Bohemia; died Madison, Nebraska, USA, 1922." Next to it was another line on the same level that read, "Antonia Nemec Karella, born 1839, Nechanice, Bohemia; died Madison, Nebraska, USA, 1900." A secondary note in the right-hand margin read, "(Married 1863, Church of the Holy Guardian Angels, Nechanice, Bohemia)." Her eyes softened as she thought, *Yes, I remember that long-ago day when I first wrote your names at the top of this family tree; I couldn't stop smiling.* Sister Margaret Mary ran her hand over all the names she had added over the years and found it easy to talk to her ancestors in her thoughts, as she did now.

Wenceslaus and Antonia, Andy and I are so excited about this genealogy. I look forward to meeting you the day I walk through the pearly gates of heaven. I can't wait to hear what you think of our project. I'll bet you never imagined the huge family of Bohemian descendants your dreams would give birth to here in America. Because of your dream for us, neither the Karella name nor your story will be forgotten. I thank you both for all you did for all this family from the future you never knew.

Sister Margaret Mary's mind came back to the present, bubbling with excitement as she began thinking about her plans for the work ahead. *I will concentrate on getting more details about the marriages and the generations of children for the genealogy listing. At the same time, Andy and some of the other cousins will focus on recording family stories on our history and our roots in Bohemia. Once we combine our work, hopefully, we will solve the mystery of why our family came to America. Knowing the stories behind the facts will make the Karella family journey more like an adventure—a legend to capture the imagination, and it will be something the children of the future will enjoy reading.*

Glancing at her watch, Sister Margaret Mary thought, *Oh mercy, it is late!* Quickly but carefully, she refolded the large paper and tucked it back into the drawer. Turning out the light, Margaret Mary said her prayers, which included thanking God for her convent's Mother Superior who insisted her nuns have personal hobbies.

Mother Superior was right, Margaret Mary thought. *My personal hobby has brought balance to my life and brought me closer to my roots. From what I've learned of my ancestor's choices so far and the actions they took, I have begun to understand a universal truth. All people face struggles of one kind or other. Yet my ancestor's faith in God continually brought comfort and strength, and it inspired them to keep looking for solutions to their problems. Their faith in action reinforces my commitment to God. I have gained a better understanding of real life through my family's history. This kind of knowledge makes me better prepared to understand issues most people face in the day-to-day world outside of my convent. Everything I am learning fortifies my commitment to my spiritual calling and makes my work more rewarding.* Making the sign of the cross, she added, *And thank you, Lord, for directing Andy to me so we can work together on this family project.* Sister Margaret Mary fell asleep with joy in her heart.

316 Dawson Street, Home of Ambrose James Karella, Fairbanks, Alaska

Andy hung up the telephone and said, "God bless you, Sister Margaret Mary!"

How I've changed, he thought to himself. *She has inspired me as much as that old bottle did. I hate to admit how uninterested I was in our family history when I was young. Gosh, back then, I really didn't care about old history. The world was changing as we survived the Great Depression, and I was changing and making plans for my future. When World War II broke out, I wanted nothing more than to become a Marine and help save my country and the world from Hitler. I did wonder how Dad could expect me to spend time thinking about the past when planning and thinking about my future was so much more important and exciting.*

Today, I thank God for Dad's love of Bohemian history and Sister Margaret Mary's too. How remarkable learning something about Budweiser Beer could make me feel so different about my Bohemian Heritage. Now I know the past is not only relevant, but my Bohemian history may also be as important as anything I have learned or accomplished in my 28 years, except for marrying Betty!

The thought of his wife, Betty, switched the gears in Andy's mind as he remembered their history together. *My life really began the moment I met her. We were in a writing class at Norfolk Junior College in Nebraska. It was 1944, and I was 17, waiting for my enlistment date for the Marines. Betty was an upperclassman, and a beautiful older woman of 19 with a captivating smile. She had an adventurous spirit. A charming woman and very intelligent, she was unlike any girl I'd ever met. Betty understood what she wanted and didn't want in her life, and she wasn't afraid to state her position on any subject. I think I fell in love with her right then and there. I was so relieved when she said she'd write to me when I left college to join the Marines. After World War II ended and I got back to Norfolk, we started dating again. It was like I had never been away. Of course, I was nervous before I asked her to marry me. She said we'd have to wait until after she graduated from college, but all I heard was that she said yes.*

May 29, 1948, Betty made me the proudest man in the world when we got married. We both dreamed of adventure, and that's why we got jobs and worked at Yellowstone National Park in Wyoming through our first summer together. The following winter, we worked at the Sun Valley ski resort in Idaho. In the spring of 1949, as we drove back to check in for our summer jobs at Yellowstone, we decided we needed a new adventure and drove to Alaska. It took us three months on a dirt road that had only been open to civilian traffic less than a year. That road took us across Canada and the Yukon Territory before we reached the mining town of Fairbanks in Alaska. I have always admired her spirit! I don't believe she has ever been afraid of anything, Andy thought. *She proved it to me all over again when she agreed to build our Alaskan Dream with me in the rugged frontier Territory of Alaska.*

We started our mail and delivery business together in 1950, and even at eight months pregnant, Betty would go on a mail run to the airport. *We wanted a family. Now, we have Cathy, Deena, Freddy, and little Gwennie, and we are building a future for them. Even after all this time, Betty and I still find the daily challenges and adventures in Alaska exhilarating.* Shaking his head at his next thought, he admitted, *We have learned living in a wilderness territory comes with a list of problems that can be harsh. At times, that list seems never ending. Food is always at the top of that list. The selection of groceries in Fairbanks markets is limited, and the items they carry are very expensive. Living on a tight budget still takes imagination even if the Alaskan wilderness provides an abundance of fish and wild game to supplement our diet. Betty and I don't feel unprepared, though; we learned how to stretch a dollar from our parents, growing up during the Great Depression.*

Andy's thoughts jumped to a memory of when he and Betty were building their home at 316 Dawson Street in Fairbanks. *How excited we were about building a natural cold room in the basement at 316 Dawson. Just a simple dirt-walled room with shelves made from wooden crates we'd salvaged from behind the Piggly Wiggly grocery store. We were so proud the cold room didn't cost us a cent to keep cold. That might have been one of the few times we were happy about the permafrost in the ground around Fairbanks. Now, we can be happy it keeps the ground frozen year-round only six feet under the surface. Our burlap bags of potatoes and onions last a long time in there, and it makes a perfect storage place for the canned foods and jellies we prepare each year.*

With only three months of summer, everyone in Fairbanks picks and cans rhubarb, raspberries, strawberries, wild cranberries and blueberries, and anything else that grows in 24 hours of daylight, like cabbage, carrots, and zucchinis. Come the fall of the year, Dad and I do the serious hunting and fishing for the freezer. On a good year, in addition to moose and salmon, sometimes we get a caribou, bear, or buffalo to share. Living off the land dramatically reduces grocery costs, and we can use wild foods for barter and trade with friends for other things we might need anytime of the year. The whole family looks forward to camping, fishing, and berry-picking under an Alaskan summer sky that never gets dark. Even though these trips are primarily food-foraging expeditions, they are fun too. And there is nothing like the smell and taste of Betty's blueberry pancakes and bacon in the mornings to make us want to crawl out of our warm sleeping bags.

Andy smiled as he realized everything that came to his mind eventually steered his thoughts back to Betty. He suddenly had an idea he wanted to share with her regarding how to approach his dad about his and Sister Margaret Mary's project.

Advice from Betty

"Andy, do you really want my opinion?" Betty asked. Andy nodded that he did. "Well, if I were you, I would just start asking questions and then sit down and take the time to really listen to your dad and Uncle Shorty. Let them tell you their stories and just write them down and put them together with Sister Margaret Mary's work. Then, present it as a finished product. Your actions will do more to prove you've had a change of heart than talking about a subject that has been painful for all of you."

Andy hugged his smart wife and kissed her warmly on the lips before going over to his desk and typewriter to work on an outline. Armed with new purpose, Andy decided he wanted to surprise his father with the work he and Sister Margaret Mary were doing. He had always had a close relationship with his father except when it came to the old stories about Bohemia. Betty was right—it would mean more to his dad if he just demonstrated his interest, so he followed Betty's sound advice.

After the first week of his experiment, Andy sent a prayer of thanks to heaven that his dad was responding to his questions about Bohemia and did so without making one dig about all the years Andy had ignored him. Absorbing the information like a sponge, Andy listened to every detail of his father's and Uncle Shorty's memories. They were an assortment of recollections that came from random years in the past; Andy found it all entertaining and interesting.

Across the Street, 317 Dawson, Home of Ambrose Jerome Karella, Fairbanks, Alaska

While Ambrose Jerome Karella was proud of his Bohemian heritage, he had gone by the nickname *Rusty* for most of his adult life and never thought of it as rejecting his Bohemian name. At one time, he had thought Andy was rejecting his Bohemian heritage when he asked his teachers to call him Andy instead of Ambrose in high school. His son had explained his reasons for going by Andy or AJ, and Rusty had accepted his son's decision, but it had taken a long time to do so graciously.

Rusty eventually came to realize pushing his son to show interest in family history was not going to work. He had to wait until Andy felt interested enough to ask about it. In the last week, Rusty thought he detected a real change in his son's attitude regarding the family stories. He felt sure this change was more than a passing curiosity. Andy had been paying close attention to details during the telling of the old stories. He had been going out of his way to encourage both him and his brother, Shorty, to talk about their family history. His son not only listened intently, but he also asked additional questions about the early lives of the Karellas in Bohemia as well. Rusty grinned, shook his head, and smiled happily, thinking, *Miracles do happen.*

Benedictine Convent, Nebraska

Being Catholic and a nun gave Sister Margaret Mary access to a vast network for gathering information from different Catholic parishes. She spent hours writing and establishing contact with church pastors and nuns both in America and Europe in her search for information. Sister Margaret Mary's brothers and sisters in faith were happy to help her find her family's vital statistics. Once the list of people and places key to her genealogy was complete, Sister Margaret Mary focused on gathering dated documents and photographs. Like she had done with her genealogy, Sister Margaret Mary searched for evidence of Wenceslaus and Antonia's personal history regarding their journey from Bohemia to New York, then information about their move from New York to Nebraska.

As time passed, she discovered four photographs that became her prized possessions. There were two of Wenceslaus between the ages of 60 and 75 and a third, which had been taken shortly before he died in 1922. But in all her searching, she only found one portrait of Antonia. Antonia looked to be in her early 30s. Her age suggested the portrait had been taken just before she boarded ship to America in 1875.

Fairbanks, Alaska

Andy realized this project with his cousin had taken on an exciting and entirely new meaning for him. The only problem impeding his progress was finding the time, peace, and quiet to study. Betty helped a great deal keeping their four kids busy when he was home. She answered the office telephone, scheduled mail runs, managed local business pickup and deliveries, and made sure his food was warm whenever he got home. Yet it still seemed his normal activities required almost every moment of the day. Andy always looked forward to moments when he got to work on his project, determined to fit research in whenever and wherever time permitted him to do so.

Flying Saucer Delivery Service

Owned and operated by Andy and Betty Karella, *Flying Saucer Delivery* was a Federal Government contracted mail and parcel service within the city of Fairbanks. Andy and Betty privately expanded their business into a delivery service to outlying areas within a 200-mile radius of the city of Fairbanks. Being a United States Territory until 1959, Alaska's mail was handled differently than in the lower 48 states. The U.S. Government provided incoming and outgoing mail drops to the main airport in the large Alaskan cities. Then, the postmaster issued federal mail carrier contracts to private citizens to bring the mail and parcels from the airport to a distribution center or post office in the nearest town or city. That carrier also had a contract for pickup and delivery of outgoing mail and parcels to the airport going back to the lower 48.

In addition to the Karellas' mail contract, Flying Saucer Delivery privately contracted pickup and delivery service to several businesses in town and outlying areas around Fairbanks. The mix of Federal and private contracts for pickup and delivery kept Andy and Betty busy from early in the morning until suppertime in the evening. All work was scheduled around the Federal mail runs between the airport and the downtown post office six days a week. Every once in a while, a pickup and delivery was scheduled at night. That usually meant a film must be picked up at the Lacy Street Theater and delivered to the airport in time to catch the last flight to the lower 48.

Fairbanks, Alaska, Two Weeks after Andy's Conversation with Sister Margaret Mary

Andy turned off the radio on the long drive between the movie theater and the airport. The quiet gave him a chance to think about his genealogy project as the stars shone brightly in a clear, dark sky, and the temperature plunged to 30 below zero. Andy's good humor disappeared as the temperature dropped, making him regret being out in the bitter cold, although he had no choice in the matter. Today's film had been damaged during the matinee and had not been ready for pickup when Andy made his normal stop. Once Jack got

1957, Lacy Street Theater, downtown Fairbanks, Alaska

it repaired, he called Flying Saucer Delivery and left a message. After lunch, Andy called the theater, and Jack answered the phone.

"AJ, thanks for calling back so quickly. Sorry I missed your scheduled pickup at the theater today—couldn't be helped. But I still need you to pick up the film I fixed from the weekend. I'll send the one that finishes playing tonight with you as well, so you won't have to stop by tomorrow. The canisters will be ready at 9:30 sharp. Sorry to keep you out so late, but they've got to be on that last flight back to the states tonight, or corporate will charge me another day on 'em."

"No problem, Jack. I'll be there at 9:30 sharp, and the canisters will get on tonight's flight."

"Thanks, AJ! You know I'll make good on this favor. See you tonight."

Doing Jack a favor earned a privilege. Andy knew the next time a children's movie finished its run at the theater, Jack would let him keep it overnight and show the film at home for free. It was a special privilege only for his kids that came with one condition. The film had to be on the first flight out of town the next morning. When his kids saw a movie canister, their squeals of laughter and excitement compensated for cold nights like this one. He and Betty agreed the happiness produced by a movie night at home was well worth the discomforts of a late-night pickup and the trip to the airport.

Smiling at the thought of a movie night, Andy remembered the last time he called to warn Betty he was bringing home a film. She ran over to the Piggly Wiggly grocery store to buy apples. After dinner and the dishes were done, he set up the movie screen and projector while Betty popped corn and

Betty Le Rossow Karella, 316 Dawson Street, Fairbanks, Alaska, on a movie night cut up apples. The kids ran to get their pillows and blankets and piled up like puppies on the floor, mesmerized by the lights on the movie screen and musical overture even before the movie started. He and Betty snuggled on the couch behind the projector and had more fun watching the expressions on their kids' faces than watching the movie. *Memories like that make it worth braving the cold on a night like this,* he thought.

Andy pulled to a stop at a traffic light, and the old memories were forgotten as his mind turned to his current issue with time. When his mom and dad moved to Fairbanks in the fall of 1956 to help with the business, he and Betty hoped they would have more free time. So far, that had not been the case. Andy knew he could only count on using late-night hours, like tonight, for his research project. In a flash, his bad mood disappeared when he realized the very lateness of the hour guaranteed he'd have some time to call his own. Everyone at home would be in bed by the time this run was done.

Alaskan winters are tough on truck engines, particularly when temperatures drop below zero. Alaskans use electrical engine heaters to keep the oil warm and the radiator water from freezing. Andy installed poles with electrical outlets next to where he and his drivers parked the delivery trucks so they could plug them in during the night. When he was out late, like tonight, he would drive by Alaska National Bank on Cushman Street. His

316 Dawson Street, Karella home, with streetlamp above the Flying Saucer Delivery sign—three Karella girls, Cathy, Deena, and Gwen Karella Family Photo.

goal was to see what their neon thermometer sign posted for the current temperature, and tonight, it read 35 below zero. Ten minutes later, Andy turned onto Dawson Street and parked next

14

to the electric pole under the Flying Saucer Delivery sign and reluctantly left the warmth of the truck.

As his boots crunched over a newly formed layer of ice, he grumbled, "Dang it! Late September is never this cold." As he spoke, his breath froze into a fog right in front of his face. The moisture in the fog immediately solidified into frost that clung to his eyelashes. The frost already formed little blobs of ice that tried to glue his lashes shut as Andy leaned over to plug in the truck's heater cord. After flipping the switch on the pole, he waited for the little light, which indicated electricity was flowing, then Andy hurried toward the house. Even through gloves, the bitter cold bit into his fingers and rendered his lightweight jacket useless before he reached the enclosure around the back porch. Leaving his boots and jacket on the porch, Andy opened the door to welcoming warmth and entered the house as quietly as possible.

The back porch led directly into Betty's canary yellow and emerald green kitchen. Each time he stepped through that door, the bright and cheery place perked up his spirits. That colorful bit of comfort was especially welcoming during the long, dark nine-month winters.

Touching the side of the coffee pot on the stove, Andy found that it was still hot and realized Betty must have recently gone to bed. After pouring a cup, which he could drink at any time of day or night and still sleep, he took his mug and sat on a stool at the kitchen counter. Thumbing through the stack of mail in front of him, he spotted a large manila envelope from Sister Margaret Mary.

The envelope contained a letter and a portion of her genealogy research. Excited by what he saw, Andy read the letter immediately.

Dear Andy,

I can't express how excited I am to be working with you on our family history. Enclosed is an outline that might help keep us on track. I suggest main-
taining the momentum of
the work by dividing up
the research as much as
possible. Take a look and
let me know what you
think.

Packet envelope from Sister M.M. Bean

As you are living in Alaska and my convent is here in Nebraska, let's start by split-ting up the work geographically. You do the interviews with your father and his brother and the cousins up there for any stories and names of the Karellas they remember, and I'll do the same here in Nebraska. List family connections as well as the parents and all their kids by full name and birthdate—I'll need that information for our charts.

I also thought you could start the geographic and historical research on our Bohemian cities. You mentioned that you have access to the local library and the university library. They should have reference books that will help give you an idea of what the land was like and more about the individual cities where our people came from. Starting with 1839, please keep your data and notes organized by city and date.

There was a note on Wenceslaus' records from Bohemia that said he worked for the Governor of Bohemia, Count Chotek. Wenceslaus also made boots for the Kaiser's army. We have dates regarding when this was happening, but we need to know more facts about Count Chotek and the Kaiser during the 1800s.

Meanwhile, I will continue to gather family papers and photographs. I have noticed our ancestors had a tendency to use the same names in subsequent generations. Please list people you are researching this way:

1) Full name of husband; 2) full name of wife with maiden name; 3) all of the children's full names; 4) places of birth; 5) birthdates: day, month, and year.

With this additional information, we'll have an easier time verifying the correct people.

Don't be discouraged about misspellings of the Karella name if you run across any. I have already run into this issue prior to finding Wenceslaus. However, I found that using all the other details I specified above for your research, I was able to match the correct persons to the correct time in our family genealogy.

The research will get much easier once we are studying our people in America. In America, we have more resources to check for details, such as federal and state agencies that store public records and Catholic Church records. We can also hunt for land deeds and published Nebraska business listings to trace our family's journey.

Some of your aunts in Nebraska are already searching U.S. Census data and checking records at St. Leonard's Catholic church in Madison, Nebraska. We have found notations about Karellas in state and county farming publications. I have a new lead at the Antelope Land Office in Neligh, Nebraska. I hope to be able to find copies of the Karella homestead land deeds there. I'll keep sending you the details we find, and I look forward to seeing the story you build around them. I'm going to say something that you might find odd since I'm from the Bean side of the family tree, but Andy, this story must follow the Karella name. We're off to a good start!

Good hunting, cousin.

Thank you for sharing this adventure with me,
Sister MMB

His cousin's letter made him smile. Though he hated to admit it, he had felt a bit intimidated by the scope of their project and had not known what his next step should be. With such clear guidelines and direction—dates and facts—Sister Margaret Mary had cleared away his doubt. Now, he felt he could make a substantial contribution to their project.

Within months, Andy had accumulated a long a list of important details. It included information about many ancestors and the towns where they had lived in Bohemia. He had even found some information about the Catholic churches the Karellas attended in Bohemia. Thankfully, his family had been Catholics for many generations. Being Catholic had been fortunate as the priests of the Catholic Church, throughout early European history, were the keepers of vital records of their time. As Sister Margaret Mary had discovered, the information the priests amassed included family names, wife's maiden name, and complete list of children by name, birth dates, and birth towns. Dates of major events such as baptisms, weddings, first communions, confirmations, and deaths were also included.

After Andy recorded all the stories and facts he could gather during family dinners and visits in and around Fairbanks, he started looking for information at the libraries. Andy had a good laugh at the answer he got from a literature professor at the University of Alaska Fairbanks when he asked about Bohemia.

The man misunderstood his question and explained that being called *Bohemian* usually described an avant-garde personality interested in art, music, or literature. These people often lived unconventional lifestyles and ignored traditionally acceptable ways of behaving. "In fact," he said rather pompously, "one could say we who choose to live in Alaska are living a Bohemian lifestyle."

Smiling at the misunderstanding, Andy replied, "No, professor. I am Bohemian."

"You are?" the professor replied with a confused look, which made Andy laugh.

Andy found librarians had the most accurate information he needed or knew where to find it. Two of his good friends were librarians: Babs worked at the Fairbanks public library, and Martha worked at the University of Alaska Fairbanks Library. So, Andy began spending every bit of extra time he could in one place or the other.

Public Library—Fairbanks

One early afternoon, Andy had dropped off his last load of packages and mail for the day at the airport post-office dock. As he prepared to leave, the postmaster asked him to deliver a set of Encyclopedia Britannica to the George C. Thomas Memorial Library. The idea had been in the back of Andy's mind all week to stop at the library to work on his project. This delivery gave him an official reason to stop there. Once he completed the delivery, he could spend a few hours searching for historical information on Bohemia.

Andy parked his truck in the lot behind the library; it was an old square log building built in 1909 and located on First Street across from the Chena River. The weather had warmed up again, hovering at 30 degrees above zero. The sand-salt everyone used to melt ice had made the wooden steps wet with briny puddles. Andy used a hand truck to pull the stack of boxes up the stairs to the wraparound porch and wiped his feet. Babs, the librarian, saw him coming through the window and trotted over to hold the

George C. Thomas Memorial Library, Fairbanks, Alaska, GKM 2017

19

door open. Smiling, she said, "How good to see you, AJ. What have you got for me today?"

"Encyclopedias from Britannica, Babs—several boxes of them. But I also need some information. Do you have a moment to spare after we check in your books?"

"Absolutely! What do you need information on?" Babs asked as Andy rolled the stack of shipping cartons over to the front desk.

"I'm looking for information on Bohemia before it became part of the Republic of Czechoslovakia," Andy replied.

Babs smiled broadly and replied, "You're in luck. Our library happens to have a lot of reference materials and books on that part of the world. How much time do you have?"

"After I haul the rest of your books in here, all you need today," Andy answered.

Once the delivery was checked in, Babs crooked her finger at Andy, indicating he should follow her.

"Babs, if it gets late before we finish, please remind me to give Betty a call so she won't worry," Andy requested.

"I'll set my cooking timer on the front desk. It will give off a good loud ding in two hours. If it goes off before we're done, you can use the phone on the front desk to call home," Babs replied.

When they got to the reference section at the back of the library, Babs started pulling books off the shelf and stacking them in AJ's arms. They were hefty volumes, and by the time he was holding six or seven of them, he started laughing and said, "Whoa, Babs! Come on now. I think we have enough books to get started, right?"

By the grin on Bab's face, Andy realized she had been teasing him, waiting for him to start grumbling about the weight, so he teasingly replied, "Now I get it! You were just trying to see how long I was going to stand there like a dope and let you pile books on me."

Babs laughed and replied, "Well, I did wonder how many books I could get you to hold before you started complaining."

Andy started to put the heavy stack down, and Babs said, "Don't put them down, AJ. We actually need the books I've handed you. But you're right—we have enough books to get you started. Let's sit down over at the reading tables, and I'll show you how to find the information you're looking for."

Two Hours Later

Totally engrossed in his studies, Andy did not hear the loud ding go off in the background and went on compiling his notes. Babs had been paying attention, though, and tapped him on the shoulder, then pointed at the phone.

Although Andy nodded, his thoughts were instantly re-captured by the information he had found on Bohemia. The books Babs selected had maps of Europe that included the country of old Bohemia. Andy searched the tiny print on the map for the names of towns in northern Bohemia he had received from Sister Margaret Mary. Twenty minutes had elapsed since Babs tapped him on the shoulder. He had been so captivated by his search that Andy jumped when Babs laid her hand on his shoulder for the second time.

Czechoslovakia 1930 (Bohemia). © Czechoslovakia1930linguistic.jpg

"Andy, did you call home yet?" Babs asked. She could tell by his red face he had not, and this time, she insisted he get up and call home. Andy felt even more embarrassed that Babs had interrupted her work twice to remind him, so he got up immediately to make his call. He told Betty he was just leaving the library and would be home soon. Hurrying back to the study table, he started stacking up the books so he could put them away. Babs waved him off with a smile and said, "Go home, Andy. I'll take care of the books this time."

Grateful, Andy whispered, "Thank you" and dashed out the door.

On his way across town headed toward his neighborhood, Andy thought about what he had learned. Bohemia had been a small, ancient, and important kingdom in central Europe. The area had been named Bohemia by the original Roman Empire in the first century BC. As a country, Bohemia had existed until right after the end of World War I, but by that time, Bohemia had been under the control of the Austro-Hungarian Empire for years. Once the war was over, the victorious allies redrew the borders of the lands which had been controlled by the Austro-Hungarian Empire. The allies made the land that had been Bohemia the core of a new country called the Republic of Czechoslovakia. This new republic also included the lands that had formerly been known as Moravia, Silesia, upper Hungary, present-day Slovakia, and Carpathian Ruthenia and put them under the control of a single Czechoslovakian government.

Turning onto Dawson Street, Andy glanced at his watch and thought, *I hope Betty isn't mad at me for being so late. It would be nice to talk to her about what I discovered today, and I think I should write an update for Sister Margaret Mary too.*

Betty had the kids fed and tucked into bed by the time she heard the truck stop on the street. She had put Andy's dinner in the oven to keep it warm after he called from the library. When Andy walked into the house, Betty smiled and kissed him. He gave her a quick hug and said he'd be right back as he set his books and papers on the counter and went to wash up.

"Andy, I'm putting your food on the table. Please don't take too long, or your food will get cold," she called out as she set his food on the table next to a letter from Sister Margaret Mary. Andy hurried out of the bathroom and sat down as Betty brought him silverware.

"Will you sit with me a moment?" he asked. Betty nodded. But as soon as she sat down, her eyes drooped. "Are you mad at me ... or just tired?" Andy asked softly.

"Just tired," Betty replied, too tired to put much effort into her smile.

Lately, due to Betty's pregnancy, Andy noticed his wife would fall asleep if she stopped moving, exactly like Betty was doing right now sitting at the table. The early onset of cold weather and long workdays were tough on both of them but especially for his pregnant wife. Andy gently shook her awake, saying, "Honey … let me walk you to the bedroom. You need rest. Your bed is a better place for sleeping than sitting at the table with me while I eat my dinner." Betty let Andy put her to bed without complaint and had fallen into a deep asleep before he was out of the room. Returning to the kitchen, Andy sat down to eat and read the letter from his cousin.

Dear Andy,   *Columbus, Nebraska*

Enclosed in this packet are the additional names, dates, and places you asked for. This information will help you with the Bohemian history you are writing about the Karella family.

I have also enclosed a copy of the family tree, specifically for Wenceslaus Vaclav Karella and his wife, Antonia Nemec Karella. It lists their children who lived to adulthood. When you look at the list, you will see four children were born in Bohemia. Unfortunately, the first girl child (Stanislaus' fraternal twin) died in Bohemia. They named her Antonia after her mother, and she lived for one year. The fifth child, Emil John, was born in America during the time when our Karella family was moving from New York to Nebraska.

The names below are the parents of Wenceslaus and Antonia.

- *Parents: I have only their names with no further documentation on Miklaus Jerome and Eliska Ambrosia Karella, parents of Wenceslaus Vaclav Karella*

  - *One son, Wenceslaus Vaclav*

- *Twin daughters, Masynda and Julienka (both died in 1877)*

- *Parents: I have only their names with no further documentation on Nicolas Stanislaus, Marketa Ivana Nemec, parents of Antonia Nemec-Karella*

  - *One daughter: Antonia*

I have found only a few photographs of Wenceslaus and only one portrait of Antonia, which I have included in this packet. I feel inspired when I look at them. I see their souls in their eyes, and it makes me want to know more about them as people. I am thrilled about your research!

Looking forward to hearing from you,
SMMB

The family of Wenceslaus Vaclav and Antonia Nemec Karella

Wenceslaus, born in
Caslav, Bohemia

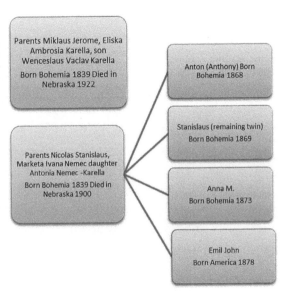

Parents Miklaus Jerome, Eliska Ambrosia Karella, son Wenceslaus Vaclav Karella

Born Bohemia 1839 Died in Nebraska 1922

Parents Nicolas Stanislaus, Marketa Ivana Nemec daughter Antonia Nemec -Karella

Born Bohemia 1839 Died in Nebraska 1900

Anton (Anthony) Born Bohemia 1868

Stanislaus (remaining twin) Born Bohemia 1869

Anna M. Born Bohemia 1873

Emil John Born America 1878

*Antonia
*Born in Nechanice,
 Bohemia
*Married in Nechanice,
 Bohemia
*After marriage, lived in
 Kutna Hora, Bohemia,
 and their first four
 children were born in
 Kutna Hora Bohemia

October, 316 Dawson Street, Fairbanks, Alaska

As Halloween approached, Betty's schedule got crazy busy, and she felt a little anxious about her to-do list. *I still want to work my shifts at Sanisystems Dry Cleaners to make a little extra money for Christmas. I need to make time to help Cathy, Deena, Freddy, and Gwennie with school projects and Halloween costumes. I must make time to rearrange the dining room to make more space for the packages being dropped off for the Flying Saucer Christmas package wrapping and mailing service. That bit of madness was my idea, so I can't complain about that,* and her list went on and on.

She felt a little guilty she had shown so little interest in Andy's history project. But in her defense, even the normal mail runs were increasing with holiday packages being sent out of Alaska early. Everyone hoped they were beating the rush and the stuff would arrive at its destination on time for Christmas. She had even taken on a few mail runs herself so Andy could take a break to eat. Her activities left little energy to sit still and hear about Andy's progress in the evenings after dinner and the kids were in bed. As soon as she sat down or Andy started talking, she would fall asleep. She used to love it when Andy read to her. Now, she just hoped she'd have more energy when she stopped working at Sanisystems because the baby was not due until the end of January.

Betty was not the only one feeling overwhelmed with the workload. Andy and his dad were swamped keeping the mail trucks running, hiring another driver, and keeping up with the ever-increasing holiday mail-run volume. He had not even had an opportunity to tell Betty about the information he had collected on Bohemia at the Fairbanks city library. That required two people being awake at the same time. Between their schedules and time the kids needed, it was nearly impossible to spend a moment with Betty just to talk. He hoped they'd get a break in the Christmas work rush before Thanksgiving. Perhaps next week after he did some research at the UAF library, they could sit down together, and he could show her what he had discovered.

University of Alaska Fairbanks (UAF) Library

To find specific information on Bohemia, Andy focused on history books and geographic materials prior to World War I. The first books explained Bohemia had been a country controlled by the Austro-Hungarian Empire from 1806 to 1918. Andy found maps from the 1800s showing the capital city of Prague at the center of Bohemia. The countries surrounding Bohemia were Austria, Germany, Poland, Moravia, and Hungary. His father said their family's ancestors were from small towns close to Prague. Sister Margaret Mary's genealogy listed them as the towns of Nechanice, Caslav, and Kutna Hora. With a magnifying glass, Andy found all the Karella family towns near Prague including Ceske Budejovice, the town where Budweiser Budvar

Bohemia countryside, GKM 2015

Bohemian Countryside-2, GKM 2015

Central Europe, showing old Bohemian borders

was made. Turning to the post-World War I map of the Republic of Czechoslovakia, Andy was amazed to discover all his ancestral towns still existed. Next, he looked up Caslav, Bohemia, and the more he read, the more questions he had.

As Andy's writing professor in college used to say, "To understand a subject, you must trace it all the way to its roots." To understand the book references about Caslav, Andy had to dig into its history farther back than when Wenceslaus lived there. That was the only way he might get a feel for what motivated his ancestors to leave their families and the country of their birth. He needed more information on the religious, political, and economic realities of the times. Questions flooded his mind, and the answers he found were as thought provoking as they were exciting. Hours later as he walked out of the university library, Andy could hardly wait to talk to his dad and Betty about what he had discovered.

317 Dawson Street, Home of Ambrose Jerome and Delora Karella (Rusty & Bitty)

Rusty's little black cocker spaniel, Tuffy, had to be the smartest cocker he'd ever raised. Besides learning every trick lickitisplit, the dog's favorite thing to do was to look out the dining table window and raise a ruckus whenever anyone was near the gate or the house. It was nearly dinner time when Tuffy alerted Rusty that someone had stopped in front of the house. Rusty walked to the door and saw it was Andy. He had expected his son hours ago and wondered where he had been all afternoon.

"Hey, Dad," Andy called as he climbed out of the truck and walked up the driveway. "Do you have some time to sit down with me and have a cup of coffee? I have something I want to share with you."

Nodding his agreement as he motioned Tuffy to his side, he said, "Let's go to the kitchen. I just made a fresh pot of coffee. Your mom will be home from work soon, and I need to start supper while you tell me what's on your mind."

Andy was a little nervous as he sat down at his father's kitchen table but also excited as he dove into what he wanted to say. "Dad, I have been doing some research on our family history.

Now, before you say anything ... I will admit ... you were right. I know my interest in our heritage is long overdue."

Rusty smiled warmly at his son and replied, "I'm pleased, and I would love to hear what you have discovered."

Andy knew it would help him organize his thoughts if he began with a basic description of Bohemia. "At its pinnacle of power, Bohemia covered approximately 53,000 sq. km, which is about two-thirds of today's Czech Republic." Rusty nodded, and Andy kept talking. "The powerful kingdoms surrounding Bohemia were Germany, Austria, and Hungary, and they all coveted Bohemia's land for its strategic location as well as it's natural resources. The kingdom of Bohemia lost its independence within a few hundred years and was under the control of many different monarchies over the centuries. I found it interesting that even though Bohemia's existence as an independent country had been brief, its capital city of Prague still survives to this day. Over the centuries, no matter what country claimed Bohemia's land or how the borders and countries changed around it, Prague remained untouched. Which, to me, is remarkable. By all accounts I've read, Prague is so beautiful it even became the seat of government for the Holy Roman Empire for a time. Today, it remains as famous for its beauty and architecture as London or Paris."

Rusty did not interrupt—he just nodded in agreement, pleased with his son's enthusiasm for his subject.

"As you told me, Dad, our Karella ancestors came from small towns around Prague. Sister Margaret Mary sent me a list of those towns, and I found them all in the north-central region of Bohemia. The central region of Bohemia has two different types of topography. The northeastern section is mostly lowland used for farming and has large tracks of pine forest. The northwestern section is wooded, mountainous, and has five major rivers flowing through it.

"Studying Europe during World War I, I found maps depicting the countries controlled by the Austro-Hungarian Empire. That is where I found a detailed map of Bohemia. Dad, not only did

I find our ancestors' towns, but I also found Ceske Budejovice, which is in southern Bohemia below Prague."

Rusty enjoyed watching the triumph of discovery on his son's face, and it warmed his heart.

At that point, Betty knocked on the door and called out, "Dad? Are you in there?"

"Yes, Betty, please come in," Rusty replied.

"Betty!" Andy exclaimed. "I'm so glad you are here. Do you have a minute to sit down with us? I was just telling Dad about what I've learned about Bohemia."

Smiling, Betty nodded and replied, "Let me get a cup of coffee and a couple of those cookies in the kitchen. Then, I'd be happy to sit down for a while, and I'd love to hear what you've been up to."

"When I was at the university library, I found a book with a section on the early history of Caslav, Bohemia, and the Bohemian kings. I came across a marvelous story about the first King of Bohemia. It surprised me to discover that my great-great-great-great-grandfather Wenceslaus was named after Bohemia's first and most beloved king, Good King Wenceslaus!"

Betty's eyes lit up with excitement as she guessed the connection and asked, "As in the *Christmas carol* we sing?"

"Yes! That's him! Good King Wenceslaus. Incredible, right?" Andy replied.

Betty started laughing. "Andy, this is amazing. First, it was the Budweiser Budvar Bottle and now a Christmas carol? How many other things in our American culture do you think might have Bohemian influence at its roots?"

Statue of Good King Wenceslaus I, Prague, GKM 2015

"I don't know, but it is going to be fun looking for them," Andy replied with a grin.

Rusty felt proud as he witnessed how the history of their ancestors was pulling his family in Alaska and Nebraska closer together. To see Andy and Betty's enthusiasm regarding Karella heritage warmed his heart.

316 Dawson: Home of Andy and Betty Karella, Two Weeks Later

Andy walked into the house and found Betty in the kitchen. She had been making lunch and barely had a chance to hug and a kiss him when he started speed-talking nonstop in his excitement. "Betty, you won't believe what I've found out. You remember I mentioned Caslav a while back?" Betty nodded. "It is one of the important towns in our Karella history. King Ottokar II of Bohemia is the guy who built Caslav, or rather the new Caslav in 1250.

"Ottokar had great aspirations for himself and his family line. He planned a strategic alliance by betrothing his eight-year-old daughter to the son of the Holy Roman Emperor Frederick II. For several reasons, that arrangement didn't work out. Nor did the second arrangement when Ottokar tried to marry the same daughter off at 23 to another King. When his daughter finally discovered how her father was trying to use her to gain power for his throne, she joined a convent.

"I think Sister Margaret Mary is going to love this bit of history, don't you?" Betty only nodded because Andy kept talking. "When Ottokar failed in his attempts to use his daughter for his political gains, he needed another way to stand as an equal among the great kings of Germany, Hungary, and Austria. On a visit to the central region of Bohemia, he decided to build a fabulous new city."

Betty smiled, thinking she could guess where Andy was headed with this bit of information, but she did not say anything and thought, *It is a wonder Andy can breathe he's talking so fast.*

31

"Ottokar decided to construct the most beautiful and modern city in Bohemia, making it second only to the city of Prague."

Betty grinned and finally spoke up quickly, saying, "Let me guess! This new city was Caslav?"

"Yes!" Andy replied enthusiastically. "The place where our Karella ancestors lived and where Wenceslaus was born and raised. Basically, Caslav went from being a historic village to the equivalent of a metropolitan city. Ottokar erected a huge government complex in the city center. Then, by royal summons, the Bohemian nobles were required to build winter castles in Caslav in order to attend regular parliament meetings.

"Sister Margaret Mary's research was able to clarify that the Karella's of Caslav were leather craftsmen, and Wenceslaus' father, Miklaus Jerome Karella, worked for the Governor of Bohemia, Count Karel Chotek. She also found a record that said when Wenceslaus got older, he also worked for the House of Chotek. And he made boots for the Kaiser's personal guard. So, not only did Ottokar's ambitions make Caslav an important destination for government and business for centuries; the nobles and government officials were a good source of revenue for all the craftsmen of the city including our Karella ancestors. That's as far as I've gotten. But now, I know our Karella story begins with the birth of Wenceslaus Karella 589 years after King Ottokar built the new Caslav."

"First, let me say, Andy, I'm impressed with what you have learned about your family's history. And second … I think this Ottokar was a jerk! I'm glad his daughter caught on to his shenanigans and had the chutzpah to stop him."

Andy grinned at Betty, knowing she was not a woman who tolerated being manipulated or relegated to a role simply because of gender. Andy thought, *My wife has real chutzpah, too, and I'm proud that she is not shy about showing it. It's a big part of what I love about her!*

Time to Begin

With the material references he had received from his cousin and his own research, Andy felt ready to begin piecing together the story of their ancestors' lives. Using the oldest dates from his dad's stories and Sister Margaret Mary's notes on Karella-Bohemian history, the story would begin to unfold.

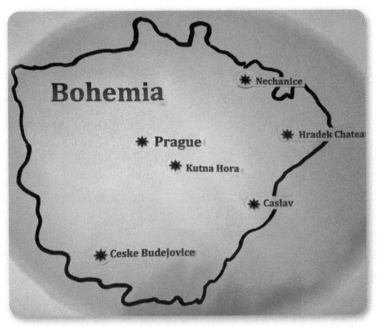

Cutout of Bohemia and important cities to the Karella family, manufactured by GKM

CHAPTER 2

Life in Bohemia with the Karella and Nemec Families

"Hello, AJ! I have been seeing you here at the university a lot lately," Professor John McBride said.

AJ grinned and held out his hand to shake John's hand and replied, "I've been doing some research on Bohemia. That is, after I drop off mail and packages on Tuesdays and Thursdays."

John laughed. "I'll admit, the last time you mentioned Bohemia to me you caught me by surprise. Have you found out anything new?"

"Yes. I have found three towns located in today's Czech Republic where my ancestors were from. I'm still looking for more information, but I am making progress."

"Let me know if I can help. I know the university library well, and I do love puzzles." Looking at his watch, he said, "I have a class in ten minutes. Gotta run."

Andy sweet-talked the librarian at the university into letting him check out a few books. Normally, only students and faculty had that privilege. Martha said, "Andy, your contract with the UAF is good enough for me, and I trust you will return the books in a timely fashion?"

The charmer nodded with a grin and replied, "Yes, ma'am, I will!"

316 Dawson, 10:00 p.m.

The unusual quiet was due to the lateness of the hour. As Andy sat at his kitchen table holding a cup of coffee, he browsed through a new book on Prague that described the surrounding area. Despite all the wars that had taken place in Eastern Europe over the centuries, Andy learned Prague had never been sacked, destroyed, or even damaged. Bohemia never had an army, except at the very beginning of its history under Good King Wenceslaus. After losing its army, when an enemy threatened to attack, the city fathers of Prague merely opened the gates and said, "Come in—we surrender! Just don't break anything!" Evidently, this tactic worked. Not only did Prague survive as the center of Bohemia prior to World War I, but it also became the center of the new republic when the country of Czechoslovakia formed after World War I.

Wenceslaus was born and raised in the city of Caslav, and Antonia was born and raised in the village of Nechanice. Trying to choose which place to read about first, Andy laid the chart he had received from Sister Margaret Mary in front of him. Looking at the photographs of his great-great-great-great-grandparents, Andy thought, *Thank you, Wenceslaus and Antonia, for all you did for the family. I wish I could talk to you.*

Andy Dreams about How Life Began for Wenceslaus Karella in Caslav, Bohemia, 1839

Andy's long day caught up to him. Leaning his head back on the chair, he closed his eyes and thought, *Caslav … Nechanice … where should I start looking next?* He imagined the beautiful forests in far-away Bohemia … the rolling fields … rivers … and cities built of golden sandstone that put him in mind of castles in children's fairytales. As his mind drifted, close to sleep, he heard his great-great-great-great-grandfather whisper, "You'll find me in Caslav where I was born."

In 1839, the beautiful, thriving city of Caslav attracted a large population of noblemen and royalty who supported a sizable number of businesses and master craftsmen. Among those craftsmen was a Master Cobbler named Miklaus Jerome Karella. He produced custom leather items in his shop such as saddles, bridles, and household clothing. He also made items for black-smiths like shin guards and

Bohemian City of Caslav, GKM

farrier tool belts, but his specialty was footwear. Miklaus spent years building a reputation for excellence in all the products he produced. He made clothing and horse tack because it was necessary. He made shoes because he enjoyed it. However, he had a passion for designing exquisite military riding boots, which paid very well.

The summer of 1839 had been a warm one. At that moment, Miklaus' temper was frayed to the breaking point. August should be cooling off, yet it was still as hot as a smithy's forge. The unbearable heat was not the only reason Master Miklaus was distracted and cross. In frustration, he threw down his leather cutter and thought, *Lord have mercy! Working the most difficult piece of leather is far easier than waiting for a child to be born!*

All the distraction, fretting, and worried pacing were forgotten on September 1, 1839, when a healthy baby boy announced his arrival with a loud cry. Miklaus Karella and his wife, Eliska Ambrosia, chose a famous name for their son. They named him after the first and most beloved King of Bohemia, Good King Wenceslaus.

The Karella family belonged to St. Mark's Parish, part of the Catholic Archdiocese of Prague. The baby's baptism was set for a month after his birth. On that day, applause filled their church along with Wenceslaus' wailing. Miklaus smiled. *My son has good strong lungs,* he thought and proudly rocked the boy. Meanwhile, the congregation enthusiastically welcomed its newest baptized member, Wenceslaus Vaclav Karella.

Only three months later, another young Catholic Bohemian couple, Nicolas Stanislaus and Marketa Ivana Nemec, also rejoiced because of a birth. They lived in the village of Nechanice about 40 km away from Caslav and celebrated the birth of their daughter, Antonia Nemec, on December 1, 1839.[11] What none of them could know was that 24 years into the future, this baby girl would become the wife of Wenceslaus Vaclav Karella.

Between the town of Caslav and the village of Nechanice sat a grand and

Above: Chateau Hradek, gothic romantic period chateau near Nechanice, summer residence of the Harrach family, GKM 2015

Below: Johann Nepomuk Graf von Harrach, 1828–1909

---

[1] City is also spelled Nechanic

beautiful chateau constructed between 1839 and 1857. Chateau Hradek U Nechanic was the summer home of Count Harrach and his family. During the childhoods of Wenceslaus and Antonia, this 74-acre estate employed a large number of people from the nearby city of Caslav and small villages like Nechanice. The steward of the estate took up residence after the guardhouse was completed around 1840. Steward Cyril made business trips to both Caslav and Nechanice, seeking the best craftsmen to supply goods and services for the count and his family. Within a couple of years, a steady stream of craftsmen and laborers were traveling to and from the chateau weekly.

Future Ancestors Meet

Marketa Ivana and her husband, Nicolas Nemec, were the best master bread and pastry bakers in the area. Because of this skill, Mrs. Nemec had the honor of delivering fresh-baked goods to Chateau Hradek every morning.

Eliska Ambrosia, wife of Master Cobbler Miklaus Karella of Caslav, normally met with Steward Cyril at the chateau two times per week. On such visits, she picked up leather items in need of repair, delivered new and repaired items, or collected additional orders.

On a morning in 1868, the two women drove their wagons into the courtyard at the same time. One of the count's prized stallions had gotten loose and was creating havoc in the court-yard. Steward Cyril stood in the middle of the yard directing stablemen and groundskeepers on how to capture the animal. While the steward was preoccupied, the two women parked their wagons. Each directed house staff to fetch in the goods they were delivering. Rather than waiting in the yard, the two women went to the steward's office across the hall from the kitchens. Steward Cyril was a stickler for punctuality. Both women knew he would come to his office once order was restored.

Waiting on the vendor's bench in the hall, Eliska smiled and said, "The bread that passed me on the way into the kitchens smelled wonderful."

"Thank you," Marketa replied. "My husband is the best Master Baker in Nechanice."

"I'm Eliska Karella. My husband is the best Master Cobbler in Caslav." The women looked at each other for a moment with proud grins on their faces, and then both burst out laughing. They liked each other instantly.

"I see you are just as proud of your husband as I am of mine. I like that. My name is Marketa Nemec. I've seen you here many times, but there has never been a proper moment to introduce myself."

Eliska smiled and replied, "I've seen you as well. So, perhaps it's a good thing the steward had to chase a horse today. His problem provided the opportunity for us to meet."

From that day on, Marketa and Eliska made time to talk whenever they found themselves together at the chateau. The women enjoyed sharing stories about their children, Antonia and Wenceslaus, who were both born the same year and were now five years old. The two families shared many customs and beliefs. They were tradesmen of Bohemian descent, Catholic, stalwart believers in education for their children, and equally devoted caretakers for the graves of their departed ancestors. Caring for family graves was an important task because blessed ground was in short supply. Old graves not taken care of by family members were cancelled by the church. Meaning, the bones of the dead were exhumed and stored elsewhere to make room for those who had recently died. The Nemecs and Karellas were ensuring their relatives stayed where they were laid to rest.

When Antonia's parents tended the Nemec family graves at the old *Vojenský hřbitov,* the Catholic Abbey cemetery outside of Nechanice, they would have a picnic afterward. One of their favorite spots was a beautiful meadow near the turn-off to Chateau Hradek. The Nemecs and Karellas also met in this meadow a few times per month for a picnic after Mass. Their children were playmates. As time passed, the friendship between young Wenceslaus and Antonia grew. Both families encouraged their bond, and the mothers saw to it that Antonia and Wenceslaus attended each other's birthday celebration every year.

Caslav, 1853

By age 14, Wenceslaus had grown into a tall and strong lad. Though dedicated to learning a man's trade from his father, his mother still called him by his babyish nickname, Vaclav. His papa stopped calling him Vaclav when he became serious about his craft training. By age 16, everyone at the Karellas' workshop knew him as Apprentice Wenceslaus.

Nechanice, 1853

Like Wenceslaus, Antonia decided to join her father's trade. After school, her first lessons were cooking and learning to bake sweet pastries from her mother. During these lessons, Mrs. Nemec worked tirelessly to mold her exuberant daughter into a proper young lady who could take care of a household. After mastering the kitchen and household tasks, Antonia began to study with her father. She learned about the bakery business and the art of making bread in the family's bakeshop.

1863, Nechanice Church of the Holy Guardian Angels, GKM 2015

Nechanice, same church, Church of the Holy Guardian Angels, GKM

A Bohemian Dream

For Antonia's 16th birthday on Saturday December 1, 1855, she made a special request. She asked that Wenceslaus be permitted to stay overnight in Nechanice and go to church with them on Sunday. At morning Mass, the young people sat side-by-side. They whispered incessantly to each other until Mrs. Nemec gave them a *look* that silenced the teenagers immediately. After Mass, before reaching the church doors, Antonia leaned close and whispered in Wenceslaus' ear, "I'm going to get married in this church someday." After making that bold statement, she pulled her shawl about her shoulders and ran out the doors. She did not look back at Wenceslaus.

Antonia's announcement surprised and confused Wenceslaus. His mind quickly jumped from one fragmented idea to another until he arrived at the conclusion that his friend was going to drive him nuts. Even having little sisters who were twins did not help Wenceslaus understand the way Antonia's mind worked.

Wenceslaus' sisters, Julienka and Masynda, were identical twins and much younger than he was. The older one, Julie, tended to be the instigator of mischief while the younger one, Masy, followed her sister's lead. He loved them even though they tried his patience at times. He also liked them. Having that relationship with his sisters made Wenceslaus feel that he could also admit he liked Antonia's friendship. He certainly didn't think of Antonia as one of those silly, giggling village girls. Antonia was smart and liked to learn. She also knew how to have fun. Antonia never seemed afraid of anything and was quick to help with even the messiest work task and loved a good challenge. Her fearlessness gave him cause to rescue her on several occasions over the years.

The one that came to mind took place during a family picnic in the meadow near Chateau Hradek. Antonia wanted to ride their wagon horse. He had told her the horse was too big and that she would never be able to get on him. "Just watch me!" Antonia called out as she ran. The huge draft horse stood unharnessed next to the side of the wagon. Before Wenceslaus could say anything, Antonia had climbed up on the wagon and slid onto the Percheron. Their Percheron wagon horse was not a saddle horse.

Antonia's presence on its back surprised and spooked him. Just before Wenceslaus reached the pair, the horse jerked his head up, and the loosely tied halter rope came free. Wenceslaus dashed toward the huge animal prancing and shivering violently. Between those two actions, the horse easily dislodged Antonia. Wenceslaus caught her right before she hit the ground.

Coming back to the moment, Wenceslaus stared after his friend. She seemed to be changing right in front of his eyes. Unlike the carefree little girl he had known for years, today, her dress was tidy, and the red-brown braid hanging down her back was smooth and orderly. He smiled at another memory.

Antonia's mother had been complaining about the state of her daughter's hair. It had been a snarled mess. Strands of stray hair had pulled free from her braid and were hanging down around her face.

Suddenly drawn away from old memories, his attention was caught as Antonia stepped into a ray of sunshine. His reaction was instantaneous, and he thought, *She's pretty!*

Caught off guard and disconcerted by such an odd notion about his childhood companion, Wenceslaus pushed the thought away immediately, but the idea came right back. *Pretty? What kind of nonsense is that? She's my friend! Why did she mention marriage?* A mixture of thoughts and feelings whirled about in his mind uncomfortably.

Wenceslaus shook his head to rid himself of such absurd reflections. He quickened his pace to catch up with Mr. and Mrs. Nemec and thanked them for their hospitality. Then, he said good-bye to Antonia just as his father brought their wagon to a halt close by.

Caslav, 1855

Almost six months had passed since Wenceslaus began the second stage of his apprenticeship in September. At that time, his father promised he could start running the shop when he was away on business trips. But to gain that privilege, Wenceslaus had to do well in his school studies, complete the second level of leatherwork training and accomplish all this before the spring season arrived. By the middle of January, he felt time was running out.

Wenceslaus knew his craft training and school curriculum required all his mental focus. Unfortunately, Antonia's comment about getting married kept creeping into his mind. The idea bothered him.

Why was she thinking about getting married? Who was she thinking of marrying? Those questions irritated him for some reason and made him feel strange.

When Wenceslaus realized how these feelings and thoughts about Antonia were disrupting his concentration, he wanted to put an end to them. But then, he would start wondering again.

Had Antonia somehow become one of those giggling village girls? How could his friend change so radically? He used to think he knew her and could trust her!

When Wenceslaus realized how much time he wasted pondering about what Antonia said, thought, and did, he determined to stop such foolishness. Pushing all thoughts of Antonia away, he told himself he had important things to do. To achieve his goals, his work and studies required his undivided attention.

Wenceslaus Plans His Future

Becoming an apprentice leather worker and living up to that commitment required six years of total dedication. After completing his apprenticeship, the next stage was *Journeyman Leatherman.* With three more years of study and practice, he would attain the rank of *Cobbler,* which would allow him to make and sell his unique designs without the stamp of *Master.* At that point, he could submit his work for final guild approval. If his workmanship passed the Guilds' rigorous inspection, he would attain the rank of *Master Cobbler* and receive his own *Craft-Master Seal.* With that rank and a master's seal, he could run his own business and sell his work to the wealthiest clientele, including the nobles of royal houses! *Such grand ideas,* thought Wenceslaus. Smiling, he shook his head remembering, *When I first started my workshop training, all I was allowed to do was sweep floors and stiffen soles for boots.*

The Three Stages of Training for Apprentice Leather Workers

During Wenceslaus' *Apprenticeship*, he learned to measure a customer's foot, make patterns for inner soles, measure and cut the leather for the upper portions of a shoe, use the punch to make matching lacing holes, and attach the hooks for laces on ladies' boots. Assembling various shoe types was the last stage of apprentice training and the hardest to master.

He had the leather craft lessons under control. But his father specified his school studies had to be excellent as well to become the manager at the shop when he was away on business. Wenceslaus took his father's promise seriously and began to look at school like an apprenticeship, which merely taught him to use a different set of tools. Reading, writing, and mathematics were skills that allowed him to understand the fundamentals needed, to manage his father's business. He practiced his skills by volunteering to record daily transactions in the shop ledgers. Every afternoon, he assisted his father by taking notes on customer requirements, writing up and filling orders, and scheduling his father's work appointments for Saturdays. By the following summer, Wenceslaus was managing the Karella workshop when his father was away on business.

By age 16, Wenceslaus had exceeded the skill of an apprentice craftsman, and his father began to teach him how to make journeyman-level military boots. Thrilled to learn such advanced techniques so young, Wenceslaus would be ready for *Journeyman* status at 19. Then, he could *design* his own shoes and boots! Wenceslaus didn't mind that his father would continue to inspect his work. Or that his father had to mark his finished goods with the *Master's Seal* before they could be sold. As a Journeyman, Wenceslaus would make a larger percentage of the sale and have a lot more artistic freedom in his work.

Between Wenceslaus' work and schooling, months and years passed swiftly, leaving little time to spare for Antonia or his friends in town.

Journeyman Wenceslaus, a Leatherworker

Under his father's tutelage, Journeyman Wenceslaus diversified his skills. Miklaus arranged for Wenceslaus to work two days a week with the master of horse for Count Chotek. The count was Master Cobbler Karella's most important client in Caslav, and the count's *master of horse,* Lucas, was pleased and motivated by Wenceslaus' desire to learn about harness and horse trappings.

Master Lukas taught Wenceslaus how leather items should fit a horse's body properly. After each lesson, Wenceslaus applied the concepts he learned in his father's workshop. The results showed. His saddles, bridles, and horse harnesses were not only beautiful, but they were also perfect in their function.

A Journeyman Leatherman had to be proficient in making a variety of items besides horse tack and shoes. That list included articles of clothing such as blacksmith aprons and leggings, sword belts and quivers for arrows. Though Wenceslaus completed this segment of his training, and his products were completed with excellence, this work did not satisfy his creative side. Wenceslaus preferred the art of shoe and boot making, and important people were noticing the detail in his craftsmanship.

Within a year of achieving his rank of Journeyman, Wenceslaus' superb designs significantly increased the monthly revenues of the cobbler shop. In recognition of such excellent work, Miklaus spoke to his wife, Eliska, and proposed buying an unusually expensive gift for Wenceslaus's 20th birthday. The gift of a riding horse would improve their son's future business opportunities, and Eliska agreed wholeheartedly.

After gaining his wife's support for such a large expense, Miklaus made a visit to his friend, Master Lukas. "Lukas, gifting Wenceslaus with a horse will allow him the freedom to make business trips to neighboring towns and cities and begin showing his own work now that he is a Journeyman. Will you help me pick one out for him?"

Master Lukas was more like an Uncle to Wenceslaus and as proud of the boy as if he was the boy's father, rather than a friend and business associate. Master Lukas liked Miklaus' idea so much he wanted to be an equal partner in the gift. "Please let me go in on this gift with you, Miklaus."

"I'd be honored Lucas, and glad of your help," replied Miklaus.

"I already have a solution that will allow us to buy this gift in late August. I have an equine review scheduled for Count Chotek's guard. Instead of buying two horses, I can bargain for three. Then, I can have the animal delivered to Chotek's stable just in time for Wenceslaus's 20th birthday. What do you think of that plan?" Lucas asked. Miklaus was delighted, and the men agreed to keep their plan a secret, making it an exciting and happy conspiracy between old friends.

Wenceslaus Karella's 20th Birthday

For months, Lukas and Miklaus looked forward to completing their plan for Wenceslaus's 20th birthday. Their excitement grew as the end of August of 1859 approached. Master Miklaus watched as Master Lukas inspected five, two-year-old geldings. Though Master Lukas easily selected two

Master Lukas selects riding horses, GKM

replacement horses for Count Chotek's guard, he surprised the stockman by saying he was interested in a third.

Master Lukas dickered fiercely with the stockman for being given the privilege of selling him three horses instead of two. Lukas took his time selecting the third horse. Then, he said to the stockman, "You give me your best individual price based on my buying three horses, and I promise you will get future horse sales from the house of Chotek." That promise sealed the deal. Miklaus could not help being impressed with Lucas's incredible negotiating skills!

A week later on Thursday, September 1, 1859, Mrs. Karella had the kitchen humming with activity making many of Wenceslaus' favorite foods for his birthday dinner. "Julienka, Masynda," Mrs. Karella called out to the twins, "please set the table for nine."

Julie asked, "Mama, who else is coming?"

Masy answered the question before her mother could. "Antonia, her parents, and Master Lukas."

An hour before their guests were to arrive, Wenceslaus and his father, Miklaus, came in from the workshop to get cleaned up for dinner. Excited, the younger man hurried through a quick wash and donned fresh clothing while his belly growled ravenously. Moving quietly and following the delicious aromas, Wenceslaus entered his mother's kitchen. The young man managed to snag a taste from several pots before his mother caught him. She could not help laughing, even as she waved her wooden spoon in the air with a warning, "Wenceslaus! Please do not spoil your appetite!"

Wenceslaus could not stop sampling the delectable food. His mother had to physically push the grinning rascal out the kitchen door. At the door, he turned and hugged her and dropped an adoring kiss on her cheek before strolling away. Eliska beamed tenderly as she watched her son disappear around the corner.

The magnificent dinner put huge, satisfied smiles on everyone's face, though that did not fully account for the extra twinkle in their eyes. It was time for presents! Nicolas Nemec cleared his throat, and everyone turned to look at him. Ceremoniously, he handed a large, oilcloth-wrapped bundle to his daughter, Antonia, and she presented it to Wenceslaus. Opening the soft fabric bag, Wenceslaus' eyes lit up with appreciation as he extracted a beautiful set of soft leather saddlebags. Antonia leaned over to Wenceslaus and eagerly whispered, "Papa and Mama paid for the leather, and I baked bread for your parents for the last three months in barter so your papa would make them."

Wenceslaus gave Antonia a quick hug of thanks and then turned to her parents and told them the saddlebags were perfect. Then, he added, "I look forward to using them the next time I borrow my father's horse for a trip to come and see all of you."

Wenceslaus' comment elicited giggles and smiles from around the table and then his father stood up and asked, "Wenceslaus, would you accompany me to the barn?" Wenceslaus nodded at his father and noticed the mood around the table had suddenly changed. He wondered what was going on but did not have time to sort it out. Looking at his mother, Wenceslaus thanked her for the wonderful dinner and then excused himself, got up from the table, and followed his father to the door.

Master Lukas stood up quickly and said, "I feel the need to stretch my legs as well. I think I'll join you." Together, the three men walked out of the house toward the barn. Within minutes, everyone else from the table followed quietly behind them. The three men entered the barn side by side, and when the two older men stopped walking, it went unnoticed by Wenceslaus.

Wenceslaus had been in the barn a thousand times and knew every animal that had ever been stabled there. Yet now, he was staring at a gorgeous horse he had never seen before. Almost reverently, he asked, "Whose horse is this? I've never seen him before."

"That horse belongs to you," Miklaus replied in a calm voice that belied his excitement.

Momentarily stunned silent, Wenceslaus turned in wide-eyed astonishment to face the two most important men in his life, and whispered incredulously, "He's mine?" The two older men nodded their heads enthusiastically, grinning from ear to ear.

Totally astounded at the idea, Wenceslaus turned his gaze back to the two-year-old bay-colored horse with black stockings, mane, and tail. Dazed by such an idea, he whispered, "How is it possible? How could such a magnificent horse belong to me?"

Excitement filled his father's voice as he explained, "Son, this is your birthday gift from me and Master Lukas. But Lukas picked out this spunky gelding especially for you."

"It's hard to believe this beautiful creature is really all mine." While he spoke, he slowly placed his hand below the horse's nose and mouth, allowing the beautiful animal to catch his scent. Wenceslaus slid his other hand along its forelock and then down its soft nose. The horse murmured and lipped Wenceslaus's palm in response to the gentle caress. Turning to face his father and Master Lukas, he said, "I don't know how to thank you both for such an extravagant, and spectacular gift."

At that moment, the horse shoved Wenceslaus with his nose, expressing how he felt about being ignored and everyone laughed. Wenceslaus turned back to the indignant animal and said softly, "Now, Kristof, show some respect." Antonia, Julienka, and Masynda had crowded in close during the gift giving because they wanted to pet the horse.

Antonia heard Wenceslaus speak to the horse, and asked, "Is that what you are going to name him? Kristof?" Wenceslaus just nodded, too overwhelmed to speak.

"That is not all of your surprise, son," said his mother as she lifted a blanket off a haystack. On top of the hay sat a handsomely tooled saddle and bridle. Overwhelmed at his good fortune, Wenceslaus tried to convey his gratitude to all these wonderful people. He truly believed nothing could make him happier than he was at that moment.

Within minutes, Wenceslaus realized he was wrong. In addition to all the amazing gifts he had received, his father invited him to go on his first trade trip to the city of Kutna Hora. Full of excitement, Wenceslaus felt a surge of elation caused by the invitation from his father. Before that idea could sink in, his father also suggested that instead of taking the wagon, a Craft Master and his Journeyman should ride their saddle horses. The emotion Wenceslaus felt pumping through his heart and body left him speechless.

Wenceslaus' First Trade Trip

A week later on the morning of their departure from Caslav, Wenceslaus and Miklaus outfitted each horse with large, two-sided satchels strapped behind their saddles. The inventory they packed that completed orders from an early trade trip were ready to be delivered to Kutna Hora. The men could barely tie the satchels shut, stuffed as they were with boots, shoes, and specialty items.

Having sat up late the night before going over travel plans, they estimated that even at a steady pace, it would take them a day and a half to reach their final destination. Being an excellent time manager and planner, Miklaus reviewed their work schedule as they rode.

"The morning after we arrive, our first visit will be to the castle of Count Chotek." Hearing that name evoked fond memories of Wenceslaus' childhood, which is why the rest of what his father said went unheard. A soft smile stretched across Wenceslaus' face as his mind wandered back in time reliving old boyhood memories.

How things have changed since I first heard that name. I sure used to get into a lot of mischief. Of course, that was before I started my apprenticeship, he thought.

In his mind, he relived the thrill of skipping school to sneak off to the town square near the government buildings. He loved to watch the noblemen dressed in their fine clothing, walking between the buildings. Wenceslaus remembered making a game out of trying to identify which of them were wearing his father's

Rohliky, Bohemian crescent rolls

boots or shoes. Suddenly feeling a bit embarrassed, he also remembered the times he pilfered leather shoestrings from his father's workshop and traded them for things he wanted. Most often, he bartered them for hot rohlikys covered in black poppy seeds. He knew the baker thought he was taking the rolls home to his mother, but he ate them all himself. Even now, it was hard to feel totally guilty over such a sin, when the mere thought of those hot moon-shaped rolls made his mouth water.

Despite his errant behavior, he had been accepted as a full-time apprentice by his papa after he turned 14. Humbled by the faith his papa had in him, Wenceslaus chose to change his ways. He remembered praying and asking God to help him make better choices. God must have believed in him, because with that change of heart, he no longer felt tempted by those juvenile behaviors. That was when he became serious about everything, and fully committed himself to his apprenticeship and his schooling.

He learned to watch quietly and listen carefully and then refined those talents into skills. When Wenceslaus was not at school, he spent most of his time in his papa's presence. His father could change demeanor without saying a word. Even as a boy, he began to understand his father was a master of many faces. For instance, with a browsing customer, he might present himself as a helpful but anonymous clerk. In a lesson, he became a calm mentor and diligent teacher. With the entrance of a client, he could become an attentive shopkeeper or turn into the aloof and most sought-after Master Cobbler, with many people vying for his attention all at once.

Wenceslaus honed his skills as he watched and worked with his papa and vividly recalled the first time he connected Count Chotek's name with a face. He was about 15 and was watching his papa assemble a shoe when a well-dressed

Count Chotek, Governor of Bohemia, 1800s

man walked into the workshop on a Saturday. As his papa looked up, his demeanor changed to that of the Master Cobbler. Miklaus immediately stopped what he was doing and walked over to the man. Always polite and quick to acknowledge a customer, Miklaus was doubly so when he presented himself as the Master Cobbler.

Wenceslaus also remembered noticing more respect in the Master Cobbler's manner with this particular man. As he observed their comfortable greeting, it suggested they knew each other well, and their conversation progressed rapidly. Neither man seemed to notice they were being watched as Apprentice Wenceslaus straightened up the workbench. Picking up a few tools, Wenceslaus moved to the tool wall, and from that location, he could listen to their conversation without detection. The Master Cobbler called the man Count Chotek, and he remembered being impressed that a count would come to talk with his papa.

From that day on, two things changed. Although Wenceslaus still thought of Miklaus Karella as his papa at home, in the workshop, he began to think of the man with more dignity and called him Father or Master out of respect. Second, whenever the count visited the shop, Wenceslaus made sure the Master Cobbler was undisturbed during their long conversations.

Learning to be invisible during such visits allowed Wenceslaus to hear most of what was being said. Sometimes, the two men talked about footwear, and other times, they spoke about current events related to the count's duties as Governor of Bohemia. Those snatches of overheard conversations intrigued him and Wenceslaus began to take a greater interest in his history lessons in school.

His teachers were fond of saying education and language were a commoner's survival skills and that education and language were the only weapons a man had, who was not an aristocrat by birth with inherited rights of protection. This awareness made Wenceslaus ask questions about Bohemia's government, the count's work, and the workings of the royal family.

He paid more attention to his father and mother's conversations at home. He learned of the political unrest within Bohemia and about issues his parents faced resulting from a lack of civil rights or protection under the law. As he became a man, he grew to understand what they were talking about, but at that age, Wenceslaus did not always grasp the full meaning behind their words.

Wenceslaus' mind skipped to another memory that included Count Chotek. This memory was one of the proudest moments in his life as a craftsman. He had recently turned 17 when the count made this unexpected visit to the Karella shop to buy a Christmas present for his eldest son. When the count selected the first pair of knee-high riding boots Wenceslaus had designed and made for sale, his father introduced him to the count. Master Miklaus told the count the boots were his son's craftsmanship. That day, Count Chotek really looked at him for the first time and seemed both surprised and impressed. Then, he spoke directly to him, saying, "I look forward to seeing more of your designs in the future young man." Wenceslaus remembered nearly bursting with pride and would never forget what happened later that afternoon. The Master Cobbler allowed him to deliver the boots and collect the payment from Steward Cyprian at the Chotek Estate.

Upon Wenceslaus' return to the workshop, his father allowed him to keep 30% of the sale. As his father handed him the coins, it was with a reminder that a successful businessman makes sure every cost is covered before the craftsman takes his percentage. Those coins had made him feel like a real craftsman for the first time.

Reminiscing About Caslav

Wenceslaus' mind continued to wander through a sampling of different memories from long past Caslav summers. His first summer season as an apprentice leatherworker was rather dull, as most of the elite and wealthy citizens left Caslav for their summer homes in the mountains. His second year in the shop was much different because his father began leaving him in charge when he took business trips to the summer palace of Count Chotek. Wenceslaus remembered being exhilarated to be managing the workshop on his own. But all too soon, the excitement wore off, turning into long hours of sitting and waiting without much to do. Yet today, he found himself thankful for those boring summers. The nobility's need for cool mountain weather created this opportunity for him to travel to one of the most famous cities in Bohemia. Not only would he see Kutna Hora, but he and his father would also be calling on the royal family at Chotek's summer palace!

Drawn back to the present, Wenceslaus slowly became aware of the soft clop of horse hooves on the dirt road, and by the murmur of his father's voice. Startled to find his father's mount walking next to his, Wenceslaus quickly looked to see if his father had noticed his lack of attentiveness. His father's next question confirmed his fears when Miklaus asked, "Well, son, what do you think?" And was obviously waiting for an answer.

Embarrassed and thinking to disguise his lack of attention, Wenceslaus simply said, "I agree."

That reply seemed to satisfy his father, and Miklaus continued with his description of the Cirkvice Inn, saying, "It may be small, but it is also the best inn between Caslav and Kutna Hora, and the cost of a night's stay includes a room, food for us, and fodder and stabling for our horses."

As soon as his father stopped talking, Wenceslaus asked if they could stay in Cirkvice for the night. Miklaus looked at him strangely for a moment and then replied, "Wenceslaus, we already agreed to do that."

Self-conscious for getting lost in daydreams, Wenceslaus apologized for the confusion, blaming it on the fact that his back and rump ached terribly. Miklaus smiled and replied, "I feel the same way, son. I wonder if anyone ever gets used to 50 kilometers on horseback in one sitting."

Cirkvice Inn, on the Road to Kutna Hora

Both men were relieved to see the yellow flames of the village oil lamps, shining through the darkness up ahead. Saddle-sore and hungry, the Karella men had barely dismounted in front of the inn when a stableman appeared and greeted Miklaus by name. Thankful to be off his horse, Wenceslaus just stood where he had dismounted while his father spoke to the man.

As he listened, Wenceslaus could tell there were years of trust between them; otherwise, his father would never have relinquished the reins of his horse so easily. When Wenceslaus received a nod from his father to do the same, he did so immediately. Taking both sets of reins in one hand, the stableman pointed with the other hand toward a door, and said, "Go inside. You'll find hot food and the hotel clerk."

Wenceslaus' next discovery came as quite a shock. When he tried to take his first step toward the inn, he was stunned by the pain that shot through him. Aching fiercely, he could barely move, let alone walk. The excruciating jolts running through his body made him instantly aware he had much to learn about riding horseback on long journeys. His previous experiences with horses and wagon rides hadn't prepared him for this.

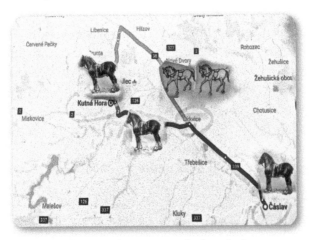

Road map, Bohemian towns by horseback—
Kutna Hora, Cirkvice, and Caslav

That night, Wenceslaus thanked God for hot food and more importantly, for the soft bed right before his aching body fell into a deep and exhausted sleep. In the morning, Wenceslaus hobbled like an old man back and forth across the room, trying to work the stiffness out of his backside and legs. He sat stoically through breakfast and could not suppress a groan of pain upon rising to leave the table.

His first attempts to mount his horse were humiliating, and the saddle seemed inordinately hard once he got seated. During that first hour on the road, Wenceslaus determined riding was less painful when standing stiff-legged in the stirrups. That riding position allowed him to keep his rump off the saddle. He regularly used this technique to ease the pressure on his backside and to stretch his leg muscles. The pain-ridden young man silently blessed his father for not teasing him. In return for that kindness, Wenceslaus made a courageous effort not to groan or complain during that long day's ride, although he sincerely wished to.

City of Kutna Hora, Bohemia

The Karellas arrived in Kutna Hora at sunset. Primarily, the reason the trip took so long was because the men had let their mounts walk most of the day. Wenceslaus, too uncomfortable to look at the city sights, merely followed his father directly to their lodgings. The Dark Duchess Inn sat on the hillside located near the *Cistercian Monastery*. At the front desk, Miklaus asked for the owner. Philip, the proprietor of the inn, had been a friend for years, and Miklaus knew he could make a few requests without being questioned. He immediately ordered a hot bath to be prepared for his son in a private sleeping room. The old friends traded grins as they watched the young man hobble after the maid carrying bath towels. Sitting up late into the night, Wenceslaus' honorary Uncle Philip and Miklaus enjoyed a hearty local brew and laughed about their first journeys on horseback and being saddle-sore.

Wenceslaus slid gingerly into the steaming hot water. The relief it brought was indescribable, and he didn't even mind missing dinner. After soaking in the bath until it was barely warm, his legs still refused to work properly. He would be forever grateful that no one witnessed him crawling out of the tub and over to his bed on hands and knees. Rolling himself onto the bed, Wenceslaus felt as weak as a babe and dropped into sound sleep the instant his head hit the pillow.

The following morning, Miklaus was glad to see his son's stiff legs were functioning, even if they still seemed a bit wobbly. While waiting for their breakfast, Wenceslaus reported the bath made a tremendous difference. "I'm going to soak in the hottest water I can stand each evening while we remain in the city," Wenceslaus said.

Miklaus listened with twinkling eyes and nodded in agreement. Long ago, he also discovered walking was a good remedy for easing soreness out of riding muscles. Whenever it was an option during the next several days, Miklaus insisted they walk to appointments. Both men privately hoped that by the time their business was concluded, their bodies would be ready for the long ride home.

The first day in Kutna Hora tended to be the longest according to Miklaus, and was reserved exclusively for the count, his family, and the master of horse. The time and additional attention spent to complete or deliver an order regularly translated into more coin. The first and most important rule the *Master Cobbler* taught his *Apprentice* was that a smart businessman never rushed a royal. Wenceslaus was reminded of this axiom as they headed toward the palace.

Fortunately, Count Chotek's needs were fairly predictable. The first visit of the summer, the count and his two sons generally ordered one or two sets of lightweight riding boots. The countess always needed at least two pairs of new shoes, several sets of soft slippers, and at least one pair of dress boots with matching gloves to go with her latest summer and fall wardrobes. Since the Master Cobbler knew the family so well, he could also suggest new items based on different types of leathers or leather colors he had in stock. On each visit, when the Master Cobbler was finished with the royal's fittings, Miklaus mentioned should there be anything else the steward needed, he would be at the Dark Duchess Inn for two more days. Though this trip was mainly for delivering the spring orders, Wenceslaus found his master's sense of timing and business technique impressive.

That night, over bowls of thick, wild boar stew, dumplings, and a plate of hot rohlikys, Wenceslaus volleyed questions one after another at his father. All of them had something to do with making these annual business trips profitable. Pleased with his son's interest, Miklaus reiterated the first day was strictly reserved for maintaining recurring business, and explained, "Son, over the years, I have learned the count's steward, Auberon, is much too busy making sure all goes well with his employer's fittings each year, to assemble a personal order.

"Additionally, every other year, Auberon orders new footwear for the count's butler, the countesses' lady in waiting, and sometimes he adds shoes for the household staff as well and appreciates being reminded about these items. Therefore, by the second or third day after my first business call on the palace, Auberon generally sends a note to The Dark Duchess. If I receive a note, it is a request that I pick up a secondary order comprised of household leather items and shoes.

"Because I have earned the steward's trust, and because of our diligence and flawless work, the steward exclusively awards the supply of leather products for the count's family and household to us.

"As for the second day in Kutna Hora, I set this day aside for distributing other completed orders and collecting payment. The third day, I usually dedicate to generating new business." During the next two days, Wenceslaus' father explained where to look for additional business. "First, there is Philip, the proprietor of the inn, who can be tempted into placing an order each spring because of the quality and craftsmanship of our products. Then there are several businessmen in town worth calling on, because they liked to brag about wearing shoes or boots made by the count's Master Cobbler."

Miklaus also told his son never to forget to call on the Chotek's Master of Horse Dominik while staying in Kutna Hora. Master Dominik was in charge of all the count's saddles, bridles, and parade regalia used for royal processions during the summer season. There was an excellent profit to be made on these items.

Impressed with his father's business sense, Wenceslaus gained a new level of respect as he observed his father's salesmanship and strategies in practice. Over breakfast on the third day in town, Miklaus received a note from the Chotek steward requesting that he pick up a second order before leaving town. Wenceslaus beamed at his father saying, "It is a brilliant strategy, Papa, and it turned out just as you predicted! One day, I'll use what I have learned from you to build a successful business of my own."

Pleased with his son's perception, Miklaus smiled, thinking, *What more could a man want in a son?*

Then, Miklaus replied, "Excellent plan, son. Now, once you have finished eating, it's time to get the horses ready. We'll make our stop at the palace before heading home."

Caslav, Bohemia, Winter of 1859

After returning from their fall delivery trip to Kutna Hora, Wenceslaus helped inventory the workshop supplies. His father decided a buying trip to the guild stores in Prague would be necessary before the holiday season began. The two men worked diligently through September completing their existing orders, as well as catching up with a few client requests that had come in during their trip to Kutna Hora. Eliska had a list of repair projects that needed to be done between the shop's daily business requests. Those projects did not get completed until the beginning of October, and the Karellas still had to repair the workshop roof before the winter rains set in.

One morning, as Wenceslaus walked to the barn to feed the horses, he could smell rain. It was nearly the end of October, and the cooler weather brought overcast skies and more rain than usual. They were out of time and needed to make a buying trip to Prague soon. The longer they waited, the more complicated the trip would become due to muddy roads. Wenceslaus mentioned this worry to his father at dinner, and Miklaus agreed with his son.

"Please check the list of materials we made when we got back from Kutna Hora. Add the items we've made note of over the last few weeks and anything else you believe we'll need for Christmas projects. Son, please make sure the quantities we buy of each item will be enough inventory to last until spring. Don't forget the extra bolt of treated black leather for officers' boots and an extra skein of sheepskin for trim on ladies' gloves and boots."

Winter Buying Trip to Prague, Bohemia

Understanding the urgency, Wenceslaus made quick work of revising the purchase list. Orders usually began piling up in the shop by the end of October, and product demand continued at full pace through the middle of December. The timing of this trip was frustrating to Wenceslaus, but it was also unavoidable. Some of the materials on their list were needed immediately to finish several sleigh-harness repairs that had been put on back-order until they made this trip.

Calculating the volume of supplies to be purchased, Wenceslaus knew his father would have to take the bigger, heavier wagon. It would make the trip much slower than usual, and he felt obliged to mention this and went in search of his father. "I have prepared the list you asked for, and the quantity of goods is substantial. You will need the big wagon, and I think you should leave for Prague by the first week of November. That will give us plenty of time to finish Christmas orders when you return."

Pleased with his son's evaluation, Miklaus nodded and replied, "I think you are correct, son. That is why I need you to come along and help. We need to make this trip as quick as possible."

That evening, the men planned their travel time, calculating three days to reach Prague. After arriving, they needed another seven days to collect supplies. Once their work was completed, they could afford to spend two additional days selecting Christmas gifts. It would take another five days to get home because of the extra weight in the wagon. If all went well, they should be able to make the entire journey in less than 20 days.

Prague, castle complex above the oldest part of the city, GKM 2015

Only one thing worried Wenceslaus; he wanted to be back in Caslav and get to Nechanice by the first day of December. It concerned him enough to ask his father exactly when they would get back to Caslav.

Miklaus smiled, knowing his son's question had something to do with Antonia Nemec. He and his wife were happy about the attachment that had been forming between the young people since they were children, so he replied, "As long as the weather stays dry, and we have no issues on the road, I believe we can be home well before the first of December." Reassured by his father's words, Wenceslaus felt confident he would be

Cobbled Street- Prague, Bohemia, GKM 2015

Prague Castle Bridge, GKM 2015

attending Antonia's 20th birthday celebration on December 1, 1859.

While on the road to Prague, Wenceslaus had time to think about what he had accomplished in the last seven years. The pinnacle of those achievements had been reaching the rank of Journeyman Cobbler. There were many people to thank for supporting him and helping him reach this goal, like his parents, Antonia, and Master Lucas.

Prague Puppet Historical Theater, Prague, 2015

The luxury of having time to think about these things made Wenceslaus realize he had seen very little of Antonia in the last two years, except for a few summer picnics and their birthdays. The memory of his marvelous 20th birthday celebration still made him smile. Antonia had worked hard to plan his surprise, in addition to the hours of work she had put in to pay for his beautiful saddlebags. It would be her turn to celebrate her 20th birthday soon. Going on this trip could not have come at a better time. After deciding to buy a special birthday gift for Antonia in Prague, he felt pleased with his plan and began

Life-size marionettes, Don Giovanni's, Prague, GKM 2015

to relax and enjoy the wagon ride and the scenery.

The Ancient and Beautiful City of Prague

The magical city of Prague was a place they seldom had the pleasure to wander through without a specific purpose. Warm afternoon sunlight bathed the beautiful cream-colored buildings, and the brickwork streets felt smooth under their feet, as father and son finished the last piece of business on their list. Miklaus looked at Wenceslaus with a grin and asked, "Son, how about we go and get some dinner and see a show at Don Giovanni's?"

Stairs leading to castle complex, Prague, GKM 2015

Wenceslaus' face lit up with delight. He had not seen a puppet show at Don Giovanni's theater since his grandfather had taken him when he was a boy. The theater was built in 1787. Don Giovanni had performed with his marionettes before kings and queens in that same theater.

Miklaus broke into Wenceslaus' thoughts, saying, "We can't visit Prague and not see the best marionette show in Bohemia, can we?"

Grinning from ear to ear, Wenceslaus responded, "No, Papa, we can't. What a wonderful idea! What's for dinner?"

"I'd say dumplings with sausage and sauerkraut, hot rohlíky and a Budweiser Budvar. What do you say to that?"

"I bow to my master's wisdom. Lead on, good sir, I am your humble servant," replied Wenceslaus, laughing with delight. It turned into a fabulous evening between father and son.

Wenceslaus ordered Antonia's birthday gift and Christmas present the first day in the city. Those gifts would be ready for pickup on the day they left Prague. His mother had told him she already had Miklaus' gift. What remained on their list was gifts for his mother and sisters. The next morning over breakfast, the two men split up the search. Miklaus would select a gift for Eliska while Wenceslaus found something for the twins.

Marionette store in castle complex, Prague, Bohemia, GKM 2015

What should I get for them? Wenceslaus wondered. *Julienka and Masynda are young…they still love to play-act and tell stories.* Suddenly, as he looked at the ticket stub from the Don Giovanni theater, Wenceslaus got an idea.

3-H. Dragon from marionette shop— Prague, Bohemia, GKM 2015

That's it! he thought. "Papa, I'm going over to the high street area. I'll be at the marionette shop in the castle complex. I know just what to get for Julie and Masy!"

Miklaus' eyes filled with pride as he watched his son's excitement. The boy practically flew out of the door on his way to buy Christmas gifts for his sisters.

Wenceslaus stared through the shop-window at countless wooden faces with hundreds of bright marble eyes staring back at him. Entering the shop, a brown-eyed angel attracted his attention, as did a three-headed green dragon that seemed to be looking down at her.

Angel marionette shop— Prague, Bohemia, GKM 2015

He examined the craftsmanship of wood, carving, paint, and strings and then worked the marionette handle controls to check for the correctness in the puppet movements. Wenceslaus felt the spirits within these two small images beg him to take them home. *Yes, you'll be perfect for my sisters! The twins will love you*, he thought.

On the Road Back to Caslav, Bohemia

With the wagon loaded and covered for traveling, the Karellas headed for the store where Wenceslaus would pick up his gifts for Antonia. He had chosen a pair of fleece-lined gloves of the softest leather and had them dyed and embroidered to match her favorite coat. He also bought leather of the same color and fleece to make a matching set of boots for her Christmas present. The idea of surprising Antonia made him smile *She is going to be thrilled with them,* he thought.

The Karellas left Prague on schedule. The weather remained fair, and the roads were dry for three days. They were making such good travel time that Miklaus believed they could be getting home earlier than expected. Their optimistic outlook collapsed when one of the wagon wheels broke. With such valuable cargo on board, the Karella men had no choice; they had to camp with the wagon in the village of Kolin, until the wheel was repaired. Once the blacksmith got the part he needed, they would be forced to unload the wagon while it was being repaired, and then reload it. Miklaus sent Eliska a message not to expect their arrival until the following week.

During his absence, a birthday invitation arrived for Wenceslaus from the Nemecs. After receiving the message from her husband, Eliska send a note to the Nemecs explaining why Wenceslaus would not be in Nechanice for Antonia's birthday.

When the Karella men did finally get home, they immediately began to unload the wagon. Until the inventory was put away, everything else had to wait. Eliska and her daughters were not able to put hot food on the table for the exhausted men until well after dark. After finishing his supper and before Wenceslaus went to bed, he announced he would leave at first light. He was going to Nechanice and would be gone for at least two days, maybe three. It all depended on his friend's mood.

Preparing for bed, Wenceslaus reflected on what he was going to tell Antonia. He knew he had hurt her feelings by missing her special birthday. Most people had no idea his friend had a formidable temper. Thankfully, that temper was rarely aimed at him. After missing such an important event, he did not expect Antonia to be reasonable. Nor did he believe he would escape feeling the bite of her temper, even if he did have a good reason for missing her birthday.

The darkness was lifting as Wenceslaus made his way to the barn to saddle Kristof. Early morning sunbeams backlit the steam rising off Kristof's back. It turned the horse's breath into filmy white clouds as he snorted, full of spunk and energy after a month without exercise. The gelding pranced under his rider, yet Wenceslaus held him to a walk until they were through the city and came to the crossroad where they would turn toward Nechanice.

Kristof tossed his head and tugged at the reins until Wenceslaus leaned over his neck, close to his ears and whispered softly. At the sound of Wenceslaus' voice, Kristof arched his neck and slanted his ears back toward his rider, listening intently. The horse snorted again and pawed the ground while his shoulders quivered with excitement, but he waited. With only the softest touch of his rider's heels, the horse leapt forward and Wenceslaus let him choose his own pace. After ten minutes at a breakneck run, Kristof slowed to a trot with sides heaving and breathing deeply through flared nostrils. With his initial excess energy spent, the horse settled into an easy canter, and his strong legs ate up the kilometers that lay between Caslav and Nechanice.

During the ride to Nechanice, Wenceslaus remembered to stand in the stirrups periodically and he enjoyed his hours in the saddle. Starting in Caslav at dawn, Wenceslaus was impressed with his horse's strength and speed as they arrived in Nechanice by mid-afternoon. This had undoubtedly been the fastest trip he had ever made to Antonia's home.

Home of Antonia Nemec, Nechanice, Bohemia

Having visited the Nemecs many times over the years, Wenceslaus went straight to the barn. His father had been adamant—a man always took care of his horse first and then himself. This lesson had become deeply engrained, and before today, it had always been his father's horse he unharnessed or unsaddled and rubbed down, not his. Wenceslaus enjoyed taking care of Kristof and took extra time to settle his gelding in a clean stall with a full trough of hay. The act of grooming Kristof usually calmed Wenceslaus, but not today. It was odd being excited and feeling a bit daunted at the same time. Wenceslaus shook his head, admitting to himself he was using his work with the horse to delay the lash of temper he was expecting from Antonia.

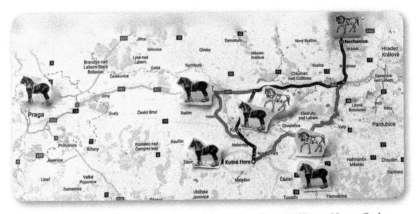

Horse Map—showing the Karella world, 1800s—Prague, Kutna Hora, Caslav, and Nechanice, Bohemia, GKM

Wanting to be as presentable as possible, Wenceslaus brushed the horsehair off his pants and wiped his hands. Opening one of the saddlebags, he took out Antonia's gift. The box had suffered no harm, and though it was unnecessary, he took the time to re-tie the ribbon decorating the package. Setting the gift on a bale of hay, he checked to see if his boots were clean and brushed off his pants for a second time. Wenceslaus chided himself for deliberately stalling, again. "Get on with it! What are you afraid of?" he shouted to himself. Taking a deep breath and straightening his shoulders, he picked up the gift and resolutely walked out of the barn toward the Nemecs' house.

Like a shield, Wenceslaus held the gift he brought for Antonia in plain sight. He passed the Nemec Bakery and knocked on the front door of the Nemecs' home. Within moments, the door swung open. Wenceslaus stood thunderstruck, frozen in place and speechless. The beautiful girl standing in front of him merely grinned at his stunned expression. She glanced at the package he was holding. Losing her grin, she looked back up at his face and said, "You're late! My 20th birthday was almost a week ago!"

Astonished at the change in his friend, Wenceslaus' befuddled brain tried to calculate how long it had been since he had last seen Antonia. How could she have changed so much in a few months? Wenceslaus had no idea how long he stood in the doorway without saying a word. The fog in his brain lifted enough to hear Antonia invite him in. Walking through the door, he absently closed it and followed her down the hallway.

As soon as Antonia told Wenceslaus to come in, she turned quickly toward the center of the house, careful not to grin until she knew he could no longer see her face. Antonia continued to walk as she spoke over her shoulder saying, "My parents are still in the bakery next door and will join us later."

Wenceslaus stared at Antonia's back, and it seemed she did not walk but floated through the house. Reaching the sitting room, late afternoon sunbeams streamed through the window and made flashes of red dance in her dark hair. He noted Antonia did not wear her customary braid. Instead, auburn curls cascaded over her shoulders and swished back and forth right above her tiny waist. Unexpectedly, he noticed her dress seemed overly tight in places, too, revealing parts of her body he never remembered seeing before, and suddenly, his cheeks felt uncomfortably warm.

Antonia composed her face before turning gracefully to sit on a chair facing him. Wenceslaus remained standing, looking as if he were in a trance. Antonia abandoned her mock anger and let him see her playful grin. With real laughter in her voice, she asked, "Are you going to sit down? Or are you just going to stand there all afternoon staring at me?" Her comment snapped him out of his embarrassing thoughts, and his cheeks turned a shade redder as he sat down.

Without thinking, he blurted out, "What happened to you? You are a vision."

"What happened to me?" Antonia repeated once again with mock anger. "Honestly, I think you were better company without opening your mouth." Then, softening her tone, she added, "I suppose it is lucky for you that you also called me a vision, and that you came with a gift. So, I guess I will forgive you."

Astounded to hear their daughter's raised voice, Nicolas and Marketa rushed into the room. They wanted to know what could have caused Antonia to chastise the one person she had been so anxious to see since her birthday. Relief washed over Antonia's parents when they found the young people smiling at each other, and heard Antonia tell Wenceslaus he was forgiven.

A bit self-conscious because of his clumsy words, Wenceslaus quickly handed Antonia the gift he had forgotten he held. He enjoyed watching her delight as she opened it. Excited and surprised, she touched the supple leather gloves tenderly. They were stitched beautifully and dyed her favorite shade of blue. With sparkling eyes and a dazzling smile, she whispered, "They are lovely, Wenceslaus, and worth waiting for. Thank you." Aware her parents stood behind her, Antonia looked over her shoulder and said, "Mama, Papa, come and see what Wenceslaus brought me."

Wenceslaus Returns Home to Caslar with News

All the way home, Wenceslaus could think of nothing but Antonia. Powerfully struck by the truth somewhere between Nechanice

and Caslav, Wenceslaus thought, *I'm in love with her! I think …
I have always been in love with Antonia!*

It had been a difficult truth to recognize because they'd known
each other since they were five years old. They had been playmates
… then friends … but somehow, the girl he had always thought
of as his friend had grown into everything he felt a young lady
should be. Now, he found himself utterly in love with the woman
she had become.

Wenceslaus did not remember the miles disappearing beneath
his gelding's hooves. The past hours disappeared like smoke.
Wenceslaus was surprised to find Kristof was standing in front
of his own barn, quietly waiting for his rider to dismount. With
great determination, he made quick work of putting his horse
away. Then, he sought out his parents. Thinking they would be
shocked, he announced, "Mama, Papa, I'm going to ask Antonia
to marry me."

Wenceslaus thought it odd that his parents did not act surprised. He did pause to gauge their reaction, and when none
came, he continued, "It is going to be a long engagement." That
statement did get a reaction. First, it was a look of surprise, which
turned to a look of confusion, and finally into one of disapproval.

Holding up his hands to forestall any argument, he said,
"Please wait a moment and let me explain my reasoning. Mama,
Papa, I need the rank of Master Cobbler and the income I can
earn with it so Antonia and I can afford a home of our own when
we get married. That's going to take some time to accomplish."

Given that explanation, Miklaus nodded in understanding.
Eliska replied, "Son, we do admire your goals, and of course we
will support your decision."

Privately, Wenceslaus' parents hoped Antonia would feel the
same way after he explained his plan to her. This union was something they had wished and prayed for. It looked as though their
hopes and dreams were going to come true, as long as Antonia
said yes to Wenceslaus' proposal.

Later that night, snuggling together in bed, Miklaus and
Eliska talked about Wenceslaus' engagement, "We must stop

thinking of these young people as children. Neither Wenceslaus nor Antonia can be considered children by anyone except doting parents like us," Eliska said. She pulled away from Miklaus' arms to turn and look at him when she added, "Do you realize at age 20, Antonia is old enough to be considered an old maid in her village? She might not be so agreeable about waiting. I fear our son may meet resistance if she accepts his proposal and then hears his plan."

Miklaus pulled his wife back down to his shoulder, thinking, *She is probably right,* but replied, "Let's pray it all works out."

Soon, his breathing indicated Miklaus had fallen asleep. As Eliska lay wrapped in her husband's arms, she kept wondering what she could do to help Wenceslaus. An idea came to her and made her smile. In the morning, when Miklaus heard Eliska's idea, he liked it very much and suggested she should talk with Wenceslaus about it after breakfast.

Having finished his breakfast, Miklaus caught his son's eye and bobbed his head toward his mother and said, "Wenceslaus, you can meet me in the shop when your mother is finished with what she wants to say to you." Miklaus kissed his wife on the cheek as he stood up from the table, saying, "I'm off to the workshop, my love. "

"Thank you, Miklaus. Have a good day." Turning to Wenceslaus, she said, "Please wait here at the table a moment" and left the room. Returning quickly, Eliska carried a small, ornately painted box and sat back down across from her son. Opening the fragile container, she removed a ring. Eliska held it out to her son. As he opened his hand, she laid the small gold band set with a brilliant red garnet on his palm. The soft lamp-light made the garnet sparkle. Wenceslaus stared at the beautiful object as his mother explained, "It was your great-grandmother Nemec's wedding ring. Your grandparents and I would like you to have it for Antonia."

Closing his hand to protect the heirloom, Wenceslaus stood up and pulled his mother into his arms, whispering, "Thank you, Mama! It is beautiful! I know Antonia will be as honored as I am by this gift."

Nechanice, 1859, Home of the Nemec Family

Filled with hope, it amazed Wenceslaus how nervous he felt as he waited for Antonia. Her parents had been surprised to see him at their door so soon after his last visit, and even more so when Wenceslaus formally requested to speak to Antonia alone. Both Nicolas and Marketa suspected what this request meant as they asked him into the parlor. Wenceslaus sat down to wait. When Antonia arrived, her parents excused themselves immediately.

Surprised yet pleased to see him, Antonia said, "I'm glad to see you, though it is unexpected so soon after my birthday." Wenceslaus stood up as Antonia sat down. Nervously standing in front of her, he did not know how to say what he wanted to ask. His odd behavior concerned Antonia. "Wenceslaus, is everything alright?"

Full of emotion, Wenceslaus nodded distractedly and answered, "Yes ... my parents ... my sisters... everything is fine." Then, dropping to his knee, he blurted out, "Will you marry me?"

Antonia sat motionless. Silently, she looked deeply into Wenceslaus' eyes. She had dreamed of and hoped for this moment for so long, Antonia was not sure she had truly heard him say it. With her heart beating fast and trying to remain calm, she asked slowly, "Wenceslaus ... did you just ask me to marry you?"

Wenceslaus could only nod with love in his eyes as he offered her the precious heirloom from his great grandmother Nemec. Antonia leaped from the chair into his arms, nearly knocking him over as he caught her. She hugged him tightly around the neck. His arms closed around her immediately. Elated, she whispered into his ear, "Yes! Yes! I will marry you!"

Wenceslaus nearly crushed her as he stood up, pulling her feet off the ground. In relief, his body trembled with emotion as he thought, *She said yes! She will marry me!*

Laughing joyously, Antonia wiggled her dangling feet and said, "Wenceslaus, please! I can hardly breathe!" He immediately loosened his grip and set her on her feet.

"May I have my ring now?" Antonia whispered breathlessly. Only then did Wenceslaus realize he still held the ring in his hand. "Antonia, will you sit down with me so we can discuss our engagement?" Antonia nodded as he gently took hold of her hand and slipped the ring onto her finger. It fit perfectly, as though it had been made for her.

Feeling confident now that everything had gone so well, Wenceslaus was sure Antonia would see the logic in his plan. "Antonia, you are the most intelligent girl I have ever known." She nodded her head, accepting the truth of his compliment. "You understand business and how expensive everything can be. So, I know you will understand how important it is for me to have a Master Cobbler's rank."

Antonia nodded again but did not interrupt. "Once I attain that rank and the income that comes with it, we will be able to afford our own home." He smiled, nodding his head, expecting her to agree.

"Yes, I understand that is important Wenceslaus. I know you will work hard to achieve that goal, and of course, I will support those efforts. Until then, where will we live after we get married?" Antonia did not wait for Wenceslaus' reply. Following a logical chain of thought, she continued on, "I assume we will live with your parents because you work with your father."

Shaking his head, Wenceslaus realized he had not explained his plan very well. "No, Antonia, what I … I … meant to say … was … is … I think we should wait until I have that rank and income before we marry. I don't want us to live in my parents' house. I want to give you a home of your own *when* we get married."

Now it was Antonia's turn to shake her head in disagreement and remained silent for a long time. Very unlike her normal demeanor, Antonia's silence began to make Wenceslaus nervous all over again. "Wenceslaus, I understand what you are saying. I do like the idea of having my own home. But I am not convinced you need the rank of Master Cobbler before we marry. I really must think about this," she said, still shaking her head.

Wenceslaus was shaken. He had not anticipated any resistance to his wedding plans. *Antonia said she wants to marry me! But she does not agree with my plan to wait … and now … she wants time to think about it? What, does that mean?* Bewildered, with his heart pounding fiercely, he wondered, *What do I do now?* The look on Antonia's face was not promising. Nor did she seem to be in a mood to be reasonable and talk about it. When she remained silent, Wenceslaus realized all he could do was wait and try to explain himself better. When Mr. and Mrs. Nemec came back to the house, they were taken aback by the somber mood of both Wenceslaus and their daughter. They became alarmed when Wenceslaus excused himself and went home.

Rough Beginnings for an Engagement

It had been an irritating two weeks of visits from Wenceslaus with the same proposal. "Mama, I don't want to wait!" Antonia announced in an infuriated tone.

"My dear," her mother replied understandingly, "do you believe you can change his mind about this?" Marketa asked.

Antonia shook her head. "No! And don't think I haven't tried!" she replied as more tears of frustration ran down her cheeks.

Marketa hugged her daughter and asked, "You love him, don't you?" Antonia nodded that she did. "So, my darling, you need to support his decision. In doing so, you can get a few concessions of your own."

That notion stopped Antonia's tears immediately. She had not thought of asking for conditions of her own. Now, her mind was moving fast. She could not change Wenceslaus' point of view, so she would accept his wedding plans, which came with a four-year engagement … on one condition. Antonia sent a note to Wenceslaus, asking him sweetly to come as soon as possible to discuss their wedding plans. Wenceslaus arrived on her doorstep the day after her note arrived at his home in Caslav.

Seated comfortably in Antonia's home in Nechanice, Wenceslaus listened intently as Antonia began to speak, "Wenceslaus, I have decided to agree to your entire plan for our future. That is, as long as we set our wedding date, today, for September 28, 1863. That will be shortly after your twenty-fourth birthday. I must have your promise that we will be married on this date with or without the Master rank." Wenceslaus smiled in relief. With considerable joy, he accepted Antonia's condition immediately.

As they held hands, the young couple announced their official wedding plans to Antonia's parents. Wenceslaus asked, "Antonia, will you and your parents come to Caslav tomorrow with me so we can officially share this great news with my parents as well?" All graciously accepted Wenceslaus' invitation, and then Wenceslaus kissed Antonia on the lips.

After two anxious weeks, Antonia and Wenceslaus' hearts were overflowing with happiness. They quickly got lost in the bliss of their kiss, forgetting there was anyone else in the room. Nicholas quietly took Marketa's hand and whispered in her ear, "We should give our daughter a few minutes alone with her fiancé." Marketa nodded, and they quietly left the room.

Christmas Day, Caslav, 1859

The holiday season of 1859 filled everyone with excitement. Following Antonia and Wenceslaus' official engagement, Antonia and Wenceslaus' parents began planning many joint celebrations. The first one they celebrated together was Christmas in Caslav.

Christmas morning, both the Nemec and Karella parents fondly watched Antonia open her gift from Wenceslaus. With a radiant smile, she held up a lovely pair of boots that matched her beautiful gloves and her coat perfectly. Miklaus told his seven-year-old twin daughters, Julie and Masy, that they could open their presents too.

Breathless with excitement, Wenceslaus' sisters instantly fell in love with their marionettes. Miklaus made his daughters a wooden box stage—a replica of the kind of stage real puppet masters use. Both girls received several lengths of white fabric from their mama. When they looked confused, Eliska explained she would help them cut the fabric, and make curtains and backdrops for their puppet stage. She also promised to help paint the backdrops with different scenes and explained, "You will be able to change the backdrop scenery depending on where your story takes place."

Portable marionette stage, GKM

Julie and Masy immediately picked up on the idea and joyfully began to plan the first backdrop for their Christmas story. Excited and talking at the same time, Julie asked, "Mama, can we paint a hillside … with rocks … and evergreen trees?"

Then, Masy suggested, "And some humps of snow with grass showing through … oh and at the top of the backdrop, maybe just a tiny bit of blue sky with little puffy clouds? What do you think, Mama?"

Eliska smiled, loving her daughter's enthusiasm and nodding her head in agreement, replied, "I think it sounds perfect."

Using Time Wisely

During their four-year engagement, Antonia never begrudged the long hours Wenceslaus spent in his father's shop working to achieve the rank of Master Cobbler. Antonia stayed busy using the time to deepen her relationship with Wenceslaus' sisters and mother. In return, the women helped plan Antonia's wedding, assisted Mrs. Nemec in the sewing of Antonia's trousseau, and both families showered the young couple with items for their future home.

Wenceslaus and the City of Kutna Hora

After turning 22, Wenceslaus began traveling to Kutna Hora alone, reducing the time his father spent away from home and his workshop. Wenceslaus' adventurous side saw his trade trips as an opportunity to learn more about the history of Kutna Hora.

During his latest visit to Kutna Hora, as Wenceslaus sat waiting in the hall for his appointment with Chotek's steward, Auberon, he heard voices approaching the office door. Auberon opened the door, then waited for a monk to proceed him into the hall. Catching sight of the young man outside his door, Auberon said, "Ah, Wenceslaus, how good to see you. Let me introduce you to Abbot Ansell of the Cistercian Monks of Kutna Hora. Ansell manages that huge monastery and cathedral that sits above the city."

"I am honored to meet you, Father. Your cathedral is magnificent. I remember my father took me to see the cathedral on my first trip to Kutna Hora. Each time I visit the church, I get a deep sense of faith and purpose in that holy place," Wenceslaus said respectfully.

The Abbot smiled, thinking, *What a well-spoken young man.* "Where are you from? For it does not sound like you are from Kutna Hora."

"I am from Caslav, Father."

"Ah yes, another beautiful city. Although it has no mountains to compare with ours, does it?" Wenceslaus shook his head in reply.

Steward Auberon said, "Abbot Ansell, this is Journeyman Cobbler, Wenceslaus Karella. His father is Count Chotek's Master Cobbler and has worked for the Count's family for years, both in Caslav and in Kutna Hora."

The abbot raised his eyebrows in surprise and asked, "Do you come to Kutna Hora often?"

"As often as I can," Wenceslaus replied with a grin.

Abbot Ansell looked at his friend, Auberon, and observed, "It appears we have another soul who loves this city as we do." Then Ansell excused himself, saying, "I must be off, but I do hope to see you again, Wenceslaus. Maybe the next time we meet, I will have a chance to tell you some of Kutna Hora's history."

"I will make an appointment to see you on my next visit," Wenceslaus replied.

"See that you do, young man. I look forward to it," answered the abbot as he walked out the side entrance to the courtyard, next to the castle kitchen.

Friendships in Kutna Hora

After that first meeting, whenever Wenceslaus planned a trade trip to Kutna Hora, he added a fourth day to his routine. On those days, Steward Auberon and Wenceslaus often met with Abbot Ansell at the monastery. They would sit in the magnificent library for hours while Wenceslaus enjoyed listening to Auberon and Ansell try to best one another with knowledge of the town, and the history of its royals. The information fascinated him, and he encouraged their discussions.

However, Wenceslaus would soon learn that Abbott Ansell never tired of talking about his beautiful city. He could ramble on for hours about his brother monks who founded Kutna Hora in 1142 or that Kutna Hora had been an important destination city for over 700 years.

The Cistercian Monks Come to Bohemia in 1142

Once again, Wenceslaus and Auberon had been invited to Abbot Ansell's library at the monastery. Today, they listened to Ansell recount the history of the Cistercian monks in Bohemia. "In 1140, some of the Cistercian monks of Waldsassen, Germany, were requested to come to Bohemia by a nobleman named Miroslav of Cimburk. Two years later on land donated to them by Miroslav, our monks founded our first Romanesque-style monastery in 1142. The monks were given enough property to raise the necessary crops to brew beer and ale for sale, which allowed them to remain self-supporting in obedience to the charter of our brotherhood."

"So, this was not the original cathedral or monastery? And did they plan to farm in these mountains?" Wenceslaus asked.

"The answer to your first question is no. That building and church is not even close to what it is today. And secondly, these Bohemian nobles had their own reasons for bringing our monks to this mountainous region, besides religion. The land donated to our brotherhood was strategically located in a remote area along an important travel route. Because our brotherhood is self-supporting, once Miroslav donated the land, he incurred no further costs to support our monastery. So, the answer to your second question is yes. This brotherhood always farmed or better said, always raised certain grain crops wherever they had a monastery."

Wenceslaus nodded but did not interrupt. He thought, *Miroslav had made a wise investment bringing these monks to his mountains. Especially if he had no further support costs to worry about.*

Abbott Ansell continued on without noticing that he was the only one talking. "Our monks hired the builders they needed for our first monastery and chapel, and that construction was completed within two years of receiving the land. That first monastery immediately became a safe-place for nobles to break their travels between Prague and destinations along the Danube River and ports along the Black Sea.

Wenceslaus whispered quietly to Auberon, "I've always wanted to see the Black Sea." Auberon nodded but did not say anything.

"Historically speaking," Ansell continued, "aside from construction workers brought in to build the monastery and church, the town of Kutna Hora grew very slowly until 1260. That is when German miners discovered a rich vein of silver on our property. During the 13th century, several more silver mines were opened, and the miners also unearthed several deposits of blood red Bohemian garnets. At that time, mining went into full production here in Kutna Hora."

Auberon had heard this story more than a few times and yawned discreetly, then interjected, "The Count's wife has many jewels set with Bohemian red garnets. They are lovely to behold."

"Yes, well, that may be true. But I was talking about *history*," Ansell said pointedly. "Now, where was I? Oh yes, each of the Bohemian royal families received revenues from the silver and gem mines. Before long, all the royals were building palaces here in Kutna Hora, where they could stay during their visits. They also stored their wealth at these palaces before transporting it to Prague or Caslav. The nobility spending time in this area attended Mass at our old Romanesque church. Eventually, they wanted the old church replaced with something a little grander. The steady growth of mining revenues allowed our monks to acquiesce, and we remodeled our entire complex in the Baroque style you see now."

"So that is when this complex was redesigned. How long did that take?" Wenceslaus asked.

"Well, dear boy, that is a good question, isn't it? The new plan for the complex included our magnificent cathedral, a larger monastery, this library, and a new vineyard, so it took many years to create what this complex is today," he finished.

"It is impressive, Father," Wenceslaus replied.

"We named our cathedral after St. Barbara, and we put some unique frescoes on the walls that honor the working people. Auberon and Wenceslaus, please come with me—I want to show them to you." Ansell stood up and motioned for Wenceslaus and Auberon to follow him. The abbot led them from the library, out of the monastery, and into the cathedral.

Abbot Ansell pointed at the walls, saying, "You see, the biggest of our frescoes give glory to God, as they should. Now, look over there. See the workingmen depicted in the midst of their crafts. Now, see the images standing near the craftsman? They are patron saints and guardian angels protecting and helping the craftsmen as they work. These images are very different from other churches."

Auberon and Wenceslaus looked confused, and Wenceslaus asked, "Could you explain what you mean, Abbott Ansell? I'm not sure I understand."

Smiling at Wenceslaus for his honesty, the Abbott obliged his young friend. "I'm delighted that you ask. As I said earlier, my brotherhood believes in a life dedicated to God, but also to self-support. We do not live off mandatory tithing or parish donations. That fact makes us unique among other Bohemian Catholic orders with monasteries and cathedrals."

Suddenly, Auberon grinned, deciding to tease his old friend a bit. "My that sounds a bit arrogant or perhaps just a little too prideful. I wonder! Do you think that line of thinking qualifies as a sin, Father?"

It was hard not to laugh because Abbott Ansell's face turned bright red. "Some have said as much, and everyone has a right to their opinions," he replied gruffly. "But in my defense and in my experience, those orders that operate by means of mandatory donations also bargain for financial funding from rich patrons, sell indulgences, and a form of public recognition for those donations. I believe these practices are reflected in the content of the paintings and frescoes found in their cathedrals. Next time you happen to walk through a different Catholic Church, take a close look. After the images dedicated to God, you will notice most of the other images on the walls are kings, nobility, or benefactors who have donated large sums of money to that church. I do concede one might also find a couple of prominent saints or martyrs too.

"However, I believe our frescoes of people at work are more fitting. Since they are the craftsmen who toiled to build these holy places of God. They are also the people who make up the largest portion of the congregation who attend Mass in our churches and cathedrals."

Trying to keep a straight face while nodding solemnly, Auberon replied, "Yes, I see your point, Ansell. I do agree with your beliefs." The Abbott calmed down, and his face returned to its natural shade.

"Wenceslaus, I think it is time for lunch. Perhaps we ought to let the Abbot get back to his work," Auberon suggested.

"Nonsense," the Abbott replied." You don't have to leave! We can have some lunch with my brothers while I finish telling you the rest of our history." Auberon tried to signal Wenceslaus, hoping he would say he needed to get back to work or leave for Caslav. Apparently, the lad was not in a hurry because he did not take the hint about leaving. Resigned to hearing more history, Auberon motioned for Wenceslaus to follow the abbott.

The three men walked to the dining room in the monastery. As they selected food from a buffet where other monks were serving themselves, Abbott Ansell continued his story about the town of Kutna Hora. "The workmen we employed for the construction period of the original church and monastery established the town of Kutna Hora in the 1100s. Eventually, mining revenues drew members from all 15 royal families of Bohemia to Kutna Hora. Remarkably, each of those 15 families had been given a license to mint their silver into their own coins. Those coins were used as official Bohemian money, and they minted those coins right here in Kutna Hora," Ansell said.

The Italian Court Castle, 13th century, Kutna Hora, GKM 2015

Finally, the abbot hit on a subject that interested Auberon. But before he could say anything, Wenceslaus said, "I heard King Sigismund lived in Kutna Hora when he was emperor of the Holy Roman Empire during the Hussite wars."

"True, but the emperor's real purpose for living in Kutna Hora was to guard his silver horde stored in the *Italian Court Castle*," Auberon replied.

Abbot Ansell, not to be outdone, said, "Emperor Sigismund was not the only royal motivated to live in Kutna Hora for the protection of his wealth. Even after they built their own palaces, the royals appropriated the Italian Court Castle from its hereditary owners in the 13th century. They justified that appropriation because it was the most secure place to store all their silver and gems. The royals turned the castle into their treasury house and also minted each family's coins in its courtyard.

Bohemian Coin—minted 1310–1346 in Kutna Hora—owned by GKM 2015

"I can get an invitation for all of us to visit the Italian Court castle," said Auberon. Both the abbot and Wenceslaus were excited about that opportunity and said it would be interesting to see it!

"Fine, I'll coordinate that visit with your next trip to Kutna Hora, Wenceslaus. When will that be?" Auberon asked. The Steward made good on his boast in two months' time.

After an unforgettable visit to the Italian Court Castle and the old mint-works, Wenceslaus made a point to closely examine all the Bohemian coins he received. To his amazement, many of them had been minted in Kutna Hora.

Count Chotek's steward in Kutna Hora had been impressed with Wenceslaus from their first meeting. As the years passed, his admiration for the young man grew. Steward Auberon observed Wenceslaus maturing into a man who demonstrated excellence in his profession, always met his commitments on schedule, and showed a keen interest in Auberon's city. Those qualities made the steward suggest that Wenceslaus start his own business in Kutna Hora once he achieved the rank of Master Cobbler. Wenceslaus found the idea extremely appealing. During the four years of his engagement, Wenceslaus told Antonia all about Kutna Hora, and asked if she thought she could be happy living in such a place.

Antonia was not only thrilled with the prospect of being married, but she also thought it would be delightful to raise her family in a big city. Only two thoughts worried her, and both concerned their families. First, how would Wenceslaus' father feel about his son leaving home, leaving Caslav, and leaving the family business? Second, she fretted over how her family would feel about living so far away from their future grandchildren. Wenceslaus shared Antonia's concerns, and they prayed for guidance.

A Goal Achieved

Wenceslaus' dedication and hard work turned him into an exceptionally skilled Master Cobbler during his four-year engagement to Antonia. The news regarding the quality and beauty of his shoes and boots spread quickly, which brought a constant stream of new customers to the Karellas' workshop in Caslav.

During that time, Steward Auberon wrote to Miklaus to convey an idea he had about appointing a Master Cobbler to live and work in Kutna Hora. Miklaus wrote back asking Steward Auberon if it was appropriate for Wenceslaus to handle all the cobbler business for the Chotek Castle in Kutna Hora, after his wedding. The final letter between the old friends outlined an agreement that would help ensure a solid future for Wenceslaus and Antonia if they chose to move to Kutna Hora.

1863, Kutna Hora

By the mid-1800s, Kutna Hora had approximately 6,000 permanent residents and many successful businesses. This was true even though the mines no longer produced silver or gems, and the mint-works had been moved to Prague. The city prospered for many reasons. A large part of the town's success evolved around the monastery's productive vineyard and wine and ale sales. Then there were the royal events held throughout the summer season, and the magnificent cathedral drew many visitors to the city as well. The aristocrats and their guests who came to the city played an important part in Kutna Hora's economic stability. These people not only spent summers in their palaces, they also spent money in the town.

Months before Wenceslaus' 24th birthday and wedding day in September of 1863, Miklaus and Wenceslaus sat down for a father-to-son talk. "Son, you are ready to start your own business. I think Kutna Hora holds the best opportunities for you to build a successful cobbler trade of your own. I think you should build your business close to Count Chotek's summer home," Miklaus advised.

Wenceslaus felt greatly relieved that his father brought up this subject and told him about his conversation with the Chotek steward in Kutna Hora.

Smiling, his father replied, "I know about that conversation, Wenceslaus. Auberon and I have been friends a long time. He wrote and asked if I would mind him making that suggestion to you. I hope you agree because I intend to give you the Chotek business account once you are married."

Humbled and honored by his father's and Steward Auberon's confidence in him, Wenceslaus was thrilled to learn he would have the Chotek business to support his new family. He thanked his father for such generosity. Wenceslaus felt a great pressure lift off his shoulders knowing his father supported the idea of him and Antonia moving to Kutna Hora. It made their decision an easy one.

Seeing the relief in his son's eyes, Miklaus added, "You have our blessing, son. Your mother and I want you to make the move to Kutna Hora once you and Antonia are married."

Wenceslaus hugged his father, saying, "Thank you, Papa." Then, he asked, "Could I have tomorrow off. I want to talk to Antonia."

Miklaus replied, "Take two days and enjoy the trip."

Wenceslaus could not wait to share this amazing news with Antonia. Now that they had his parents' backing, he was sure Antonia's parents would accept their decision.

The Nemec-Karella Wedding Approaches

As Wenceslaus and Antonia prepared to start a new life together in Kutna Hora, Wenceslaus shared all the things he had learned about their new city. "Antonia, Abbot Ansell told me about the 1700s in Kutna Hora and how the city had been ravaged by war and then by floods that closed down the mining operations. Yet the city not only survived these devastations, it thrived. The abott said his monastery had always been the largest consumer of local products. However, he believed it was the day-to-day requirements of the townspeople that stabilized Kutna Hora's economy. Antonia, he believes as I do, we will do very well in Kutna Hora."

For Antonia and Wenceslaus, it was exciting to plan and dream about their future together. Their life-long friendship and love deepened as they kept their minds and hands as busy as possible while they waited.

Eliska Karella and her ten-year-old daughters, Julienka and Masynda, visited often with Marketa Nemec and Antonia. The five of them designed and sewed the new clothing Antonia and Wenceslaus would need as they started their new life together. As the wedding day approached, the women carefully packed the clothing, household items, and heirlooms that would be taken to Antonia and Wenceslaus' new home.

Church of the Holy Guardian Angels exterior and interior for wedding, Nechanice, Bohemia, 1863

Antonia could hardly contain her excitement as the day of her wedding finally approached. Wenceslaus and his family would arrive in Nechanice the very next day.

Antonia did not remember falling in love with Wenceslaus. All she knew was that she had been in love with her Wenceslaus for as long as she could remember. Now, she found herself breathless with excitement. Her dream of marrying him was about to come true.

Wenceslaus had been so completely focused on attaining the rank of Master Cobbler that he expected to feel calm after achieving his goal. To his bewilderment, after attaining the goal that would enable him to provide for Antonia and the family they hoped for, he was edgier than ever. That is when he discovered he had not recognized his feverish work pace for what it truly was. As his wedding day approached, and as the men helped him pack up hardware and the workshop items, he was all too aware of how mentally, emotionally, and physically obsessed he was with Antonia. It would be a great relief when the waiting was over, and he could make Antonia his wife in every way.

The Karella-Nemec Wedding, Nechanice, 1863

Just as 16-year-old Antonia Nemec had predicted, she became Mrs. Wenceslaus Karella in the Church of the Holy Guardian Angels in Nechanice on September 28, 1863.

Wenceslaus whispered to his radiant bride, as they stood side by side receiving the loud applause of congratulations from their families, "Antonia, My Heart, are you ready for our adventures to begin?" With sparkling eyes, she smiled up at her husband, her dear Wenceslaus, and joyfully nodded yes.

The day after the wedding, both Nemec and Karella family members loaded wagons hitched to huge percherons that stood calmly in harness. Fortunately, the French draft horses were bred for strength and stamina. The wagons were loaded so heavily that normal horses would never have been able to pull the weight. The first wagon stood filled to overflowing with wedding gifts, furniture, and household items as well as the clothing trunks for the newlyweds. The second wagon transported Wenceslaus' shop tools, benches, and workshop supplies. It also carried bales of hay, oats, and horse tack. When the men were finished loading the second wagon, it may have looked less full, but it was as heavy or more so than the one stacked high with household goods.

Wenceslaus drove the first wagon with his wife and Mrs. Nemec. His father, mother, and Mr. Nemec drove the second wagon. Two uncles rode along on their own saddle horses.

Percheron 1800s draft horses in harness

Wenceslaus' father planned to stay in Kutna Hora a week longer than the rest of the family. He volunteered to help Wenceslaus set up his workshop. Consequently, his saddle horse walked alongside Wenceslaus' gelding, tied to the back of the shop wagon.

A Quick Trip for the Relatives

Both Marketa Nemec and Eliska Karella had business deliveries scheduled in the following week and would be returning home with the wagons right after the newlyweds were settled. Everyone was happy the temperatures stayed warm and the roads remained dry. Though they had agreed to stick to a strict travel schedule, Wenceslaus called for a brief stop at Vojenský hřbitov, *the old Catholic Abbey cemetery*, right outside Nechanice. Antonia wanted Wenceslaus to see where her Nemec ancestors were buried, and he graciously honored his new wife's request.

Grave marker for Nemec family, Vojensky hrbitov, abbey cemetery
outside Nechanice, GKM 2015

Abby Cemetery, Nechanice

Antonia walked quietly by her husband's side, "Wenceslaus, I used to come to this graveyard as a child. I remember bringing beautiful flowers to plant and helping my parents pull weeds from each plot. One time, I asked Mama why it was so important that we come every other week to this place. Do you know what she told me?"

Taking hold of Antonia's hand, Wenceslaus replied, "Probably the same thing my parents told me. If we didn't, our ancestor's graves might get cancelled and then their bones would be dug up and stacked in the churchyard somewhere. I remember being horrified by the idea, and I never complained about going to the cemetery again."

Vojensky hrbitov outside Nechanice,
Catholic abbey cemetery, GKM 2015

Antonia nodded solemnly. "That is exactly what my mother told me." Antonia stood silently by each grave and then laid several blossoms by the headstones—flowers she had saved from her wedding bouquet.

Nearing the gate, the newlyweds stopped for a last moment of silence. When Antonia made the sign of the cross, Wenceslaus knew his wife had finished her prayers, and they quietly left the cemetery.

Leaving Antonia with her mother, Wenceslaus went to consult with Miklaus and Nicolas. They estimated it would take two full days from sunup to sundown to get to Kutna Hora but also agreed to stop for the evening in Cirkvice, which made Wenceslaus happy. The Karellas and Nemecs collaborated on secret arrangements at the Cirkvice Inn and could hardly wait to surprise the newlyweds.

Pulling the wagons to a halt in front of the stable, Marketa and Eliska said they would bring in the overnight satchels. The older men waved Wenceslaus away, saying they would take care of the livestock.

"Wenceslaus and Antonia, will you go inside and secure four rooms?" Miklaus asked. Wenceslaus nodded as he helped Antonia down from the wagon and headed toward the inn.

Giving their names and the room requests to the clerk, the owner stepped up to the counter. "You are Mr. and Mrs. Wenceslaus Karella?"

"Yes," replied Wenceslaus.

"Congratulations on your recent marriage. We have a private room ready for you with a bathing tub, and dinner will be served in your room after you've had time to freshen up," the manager informed the astonished couple. "Please follow the maid."

Refreshed and Ready to Travel

Antonia and Wenceslaus rose early feeling refreshed and were still astounded by the accommodations they had enjoyed the night before. When the newlyweds walked into the dining hall, they found everyone at breakfast smiling and chatting as they consumed a hearty meal. Wenceslaus and Antonia said good morning, and everyone returned their greeting with happy smiles. The men had finished their meals and told Wenceslaus to take his time while they got the wagons ready.

Wenceslaus looked at Eliska and Marketa and said, "Antonia and I were amazed when the inn manager knew who we were yesterday, and that we had just gotten married. The room, the bath, and the dinner were all delightful and very much appreciated after our day on the road. But how do you suppose he knew about us?"

Marketa and Eliska stood up, smiling, and both started to leave the table, and Eliska said cryptically, "Good news travels fast?"

"Maybe one of your wedding guests mentioned it while they were passing through?" added Marketa with a grin. Then, she took hold of Eliska's arm and the two women hurried out of the room. Antonia looked at Wenceslaus and he seemed just as puzzled by their mothers' behavior as she was.

Wenceslaus stopped at the front desk to pay for their stay. Instead of a bill, Wenceslaus was handed a note. The beautiful handwriting said:

Please accept the past evenings stay and dinner as a wedding gift.

Overwhelmed by the kindness and generosity shown to them, Wenceslaus looked around the room, not knowing exactly whom he should thank for such a generous gift. The front desk clerk who had handed him the note ignored him, and he did not see the manager he had spoken to the night before. Wenceslaus was determined to find out who paid for the all the arrangements so he could eventually thank them properly. However, at this time, they had a long day's drive ahead of them and needed to get going.

Fortified with rest and good food, everyone felt rejuvenated and ready for a long day of travel. Looking up at the sky, Miklaus said, "If it stays nice, we might even get into Kutna Hora sooner than anticipated."

Antonia surprised everyone by asking if they could take their midmorning break at the *Bone Church*. Ignoring the odd look from Antonia's mother, Wenceslaus agreed to his wife's request.

Antonia had heard stories about this place. She also learned about the time of the Black Death and Hussite wars from her schoolteacher. From those lessons, she knew that during those olden times, there was never

Walls around the Bone Church, Bohemia, GKM 2015

enough blessed ground to bury all the dead. The priests and monks solved part of this problem by digging up the oldest graves to make room to bury the newly dead. In ancient times it was common to see human bones lying out in the open in churchyards. But not where she grew up.

Bone Church ossuary wall, GKM 2015

When Wenceslaus first told her he had seen the *Bone Church* while traveling to Kutna Hora, Antonia remembered the stories her mother had told her when they took care of family graves. She never wanted to see her family's graves canceled. But she did want to see this bone church for herself. Now was her chance. She almost doubted it was true. It was hard to imagine such a thing.

As requested, the group stopped, and everyone went into the church to say a prayer. A plaque inside the church estimated 40,000 to 70,000 human skeletons were stacked below them in a crypt called an ossuary. Disquiet filled the faces of the family. Wenceslaus saw that he needed to give them an explanation for what they would see.

Wenceslaus repeated what he had learned from Abbot Ansell. Gathering everyone together he whispered, "This collection of bones below includes deceased people from the local area, past wars, and times of plague. In ancient times, monks in charge of abbey graveyards had to stack exhumed human bones in piles on blessed ground inside enclosed churchyards. Because they lacked blessed space for new burials, they began by can-celing the oldest graves first.

Chandelier made of human vertebra and skulls in the ossuary of the Bone Church, Bohemia, GKM 2015

That did not make enough room, and so the churched continued to slate the oldest graves for cancellation.

"Eventually, the piles of human bones began reaching critical proportions. At this location, at the beginning of the 1500s, the abbey underwent major reconstruction to create the upper-level church and a lower level chapel with an ossuary beneath the church. The idea behind creating the ossuary was to create a holy place to respectfully store the human remains from the cancelled graves. According to the Cistercian abbot, this church and ossuary were completed in 1511, and the existing skeletons were stacked below, and more skeletons were unearthed.

"The Catholic Church continued to approve the exhumation of old skele-tons, so this ongoing work of stacking new skeletons in the Bone Church was assigned to a half-blind Cistercian monk, whose name is no longer remem-bered. It was that monk who

Kutna Hora, Bohemia, 1800s

came up with the idea of how to decorate the ossuary. He felt assembling the bones in a respectfully decorative manner enhanced the sacred site as well as maximized consecrated storage space."

Even with such an informative explanation, only Antonia and Wenceslaus went down into the ossuary to have a look. Antonia thought she knew what to expect. Yet as she made her way down the stairwell, she could not help shivering as she stared at walls made of shoulder bones and skulls. She gripped Wenceslaus' arm tighter. But when she saw what was hanging above her head, it nearly paralyzed her. The chandelier hanging from the ceiling was made of human backbones and skulls. Hoarsely, she whispered, "I've seen enough." Anxious to leave the unnerving ossuary, Antonia urged Wenceslaus to take her back up to the chapel, whispering, "Lord have mercy, I'm glad we helped keep our relative's bones from coming to a place like this!"

Arriving Safely in Kutna Hora

Two heavily ladened wagons rolled through the narrow cobbled streets of Kutna Hora just before sunset. Thinking ahead, Wenceslaus and his father visited the new house in Kutna Hora two weeks earlier. The purpose of the visit was to sketch a location plan for the heavy furniture and larger items in hopes of moving those items only once. The rest could be sorted out as the family unpacked trunks and baskets. Now that they had arrived, the tired group of people worked steadily

Kutna Hora, Bohemia, GKM 2015

to unload the household goods, and the sky grew dark before everything was secured in the house. The uncles unhooked the percherons from the empty wagons, and holding the horses with halters, they waited for Miklaus, Nicolas, and Wenceslaus to show the way to the stables. Leading the saddle horses down the street, the wagon horses followed making a slow, heavy clip-clop … clip-clop on the cobblestones with their enormous hooves.

A short distance from Wenceslaus' new home, the stable owner awaited his new client's arrival. As the parade of horses approached, the man opened the wide wooden doors and stood ready to take the reins from Wenceslaus. He led the saddle horse directly to the stall Wenceslaus had already rented. Returning to the waiting group the stableman proceeded to take the other animals one at a time until all were penned.

Cobbled street and barn door, Kutna Hora, GKM 2015

Wenceslaus negotiated an overnight payment to cover the cost of the additional saddle horses based on his monthly rate. However, the stableman insisted on a slightly higher fee for the wagon horses. "They will require extra oats and hay," he explained, and the Nemec and Karella men nodded agreement, sealing the deal with a handshake.

By the time the menfolk returned to the house, the women had candles burning in the lamps, hot mulled wine simmering on the stove, and plates of hard cheese and bread waiting on the table. The initial excitement of being in her new home began to ebb giving way to exhaustion, as Antonia sat quietly with Wenceslaus and the family. Tangy cheese and sweet bread had sated appetites, and the warm wine worked quickly making everyone sleepy. Fatigued from the past few days of excitement, travel, and work, no one complained about sleeping on the floor.

The women handed out blankets and pillows, and lying down, everyone instantly fell asleep.

A New Life Begins for Wenceslaus and Antonia

Apart for Miklaus, the Nemec and Karella relatives departed for Caslav and Nechanice after breakfast. After saying goodbye, Miklaus and Wenceslaus began setting up the cobbler shop. On the second morning, Antonia asked the men to come to her kitchen to build extra shelving in the pantry for her bakery pans and tools. When they asked Antonia to check what they had built, she thanked them for giving her more room on the floor for large flour sacks alongside the regular food supplies.

After lunch, Wenceslaus handed Antonia the satchel with her recipe boxes, and she immediately began to shuffle through them to select three items to bake and sell in the market. Leaving Antonia happily working in her kitchen, father and son finished assembling the workshop. On Monday, Miklaus would accompany his son to the Chotek Palace for Wenceslaus' first appointment as the count's new Master Cobbler. It would be a proud moment for both men.

Bohemia Was Changing

Wenceslaus and his father had many conversations about why the land of Bohemia, under the Austro-Hungarian Empire's control, had been troubled for as long as either of them could remember. The country suffered from a mixture of political unrest, disputes over the national language, and the lack of civil rights.

By 1863, Wenceslaus and his wife had lived all their lives with no personal rights, no protection under the law, and no voting privileges. As married adults starting a business in Kutna Hora, Wenceslaus and Antonia read about these ongoing issues without too much alarm. Those conditions and issues had been creating conflicts for years.

However, the newspaper stories about the Industrial Revolution felt completely different. Wenceslaus could see the philosophy, which supported and promoted this Industrial Revolution, represented a huge economic shift in Bohemian culture. With each additional story, uneasiness grew in his mind. As automated factories spread across central Europe, the Karellas of Kutna Hora worried about the impact those changes were going to make on their lives.

Mother Nemec wrote letters with disturbing news from Nechanice. She had spoken to a local weaver named Zelda Horák who had been making cloth in Nechanice since Antonia was a baby.

Marketa wrote, *Zelda says she can no longer afford to weave cloth that a machine makes and sells cheaper. The family has closed their weaving business and left Nechanice.*

Wenceslaus heard from friends at church about several men who moved their families from Kolin to Brno, Bohemia. "My brother and a couple of cousins told us they read about factories in Brno. The factory advertised good wages and would train people to run their new machines. A couple of the families moved to the Brno factory town, and no one in Kolin has heard from them, and that's got us worried."

Image of 1800s European factory

Such disconcerting information, added to what the Karellas read in the newspapers about the Industrial Revolution, increased their uneasiness. Wenceslaus' businessmen associates discussed these problems, although they had not seen any evidence that Kutna Hora had been affected by it yet. Weavers in Kutna Hora still did good business in the market, and neither Wenceslaus nor Antonia knew anyone who wanted to work in a factory.

Wenceslaus and Antonia considered themselves blessed to have a nice home and a growing clientele, which generated sufficient income to make them feel secure. They chose not to become obsessed with bad news, although they did keep track of the changes happening around the country. It did them no good to worry too much about things happening elsewhere, which they could not change. Instead, they focused on their immediate future—building up his cobbler business while Antonia developed her baking business.

Newspapers Spread the Word About Industrialization

Textiles were the first mass-produced factory product in Bohemia. People flocked to the towns built near these factories to fill machine operator jobs. Unable to compete, village weavers lost their incomes when low-priced factory cloth began to flood the retail markets.

Automation vs. Handcraft

Newspapers reported industrialization as a positive change. Factories reported they could employ a wider range of people and more of them. In addition to creating a larger workforce, it was said that machines made work more efficient, and factory workers could be trained quickly to do one task. That concept differed greatly from handcrafts, where a master took on one or two apprentices at a time and trained those few apprentices for years to perform many tasks.

The Craftsman's Dilemma

Machines were doing tasks that only an artisan had been able to accomplish. Tradesmen and craftsmen saw the grim long-term business realities. They could not compete with the prices, production time, or volume of machine-made goods. The success of the weaving factories predicted change in other handcrafted products as well. Newspapers wrote about new jobs that came with mass-produced items, but they did not write about the skilled craftsmen and artisans whose skills had become obsolete and had lost their livelihoods.

Bohemia's Dilemma

In the early stages of industrialization, a company building a factory did not consider how much air, water, or land pollution would be caused as a result of its production processes. The wretchedness within the slum towns that grew up around the factories created more problems for the rural-minded people who had risked everything to relocate and live near the factories.

As hundreds of people poured into factory towns, work conditions within the factories began to decline as fast as the town's labor pool increased. The towns themselves were nightmares of overcrowded, unsanitary housing and living conditions. The unprecedented number of rural people living in close proximity with one another had no experience dealing with the health problems produced within slums.

A Society of Rural Minded People

On the eve of the *Industrial Revolution*, less than 10 percent of the population of Europe lived in towns or cities. For Bohemia, that meant 90 percent of the country's citizens had lived scattered across the land or in small villages. Even though most of these citizens were literate, they were still simple people who spent their lives farming or in barter trades. Bakers, shoemakers, butchers, weavers, and candlemakers traded their skills and products for what they needed to live. If a farmer could not sell his surplus food in a nearby town or village, he rarely grew more than what the family needed. Rural Bohemians were creative and understood hard work. They made most of their own cloth, clothing, furniture, and tools from raw materials produced on a farm or from the forest.

Bohemians Begin Leaving Their Homeland

By the mid-1800s, pre-existing problems resulting from past border and civil wars, ongoing ethnic, language, and civil-rights issues added to the desperation caused by this new and ever-growing economic threat to their traditional livelihoods. These conditions forced a great number of Bohemians to believe there was no future for them in the country of their birth. Large numbers of Bohemians began relocating to faraway lands in search of a better life.

A Brief Time of Happiness for the Newlyweds

Kutna Hora would not be able to escape the changes or issues being felt by the rest of the country. But In 1863, when Wenceslaus and Antonia were moving into their new home in Kutna Hora, their city was still relatively untouched by economic changes taking place in other parts of Bohemia and in western Europe.

Wenceslaus and Antonia still had exciting years ahead that would be blessed with peace and a happiness. This happiness in the years to come would include children they had prayed and waited for.

CHAPTER 3

The Karellas of Kutna Hora

1863–1874

Time moved rapidly for the newly married couple as they focused on their businesses and getting settled into their new life in Kutna Hora. Antonia loved her home. A kitchen and five rooms on two floors made up the Karella's home and work spaces. The two connecting front rooms with a main street entrance served as Wenceslaus' workshop, customer salon, and office. The small room off the kitchen doubled as a pantry for Antonia's baking supplies and larder for their daily meals. The bedrooms were on the second floor.

Word spread rapidly regarding the talented new Master Cobbler, and before long, the volume of orders coming in required a strict schedule to get them finished on time. Antonia helped in the afternoons with the small jobs like laying out a roll of leather on the worktable, organizing work orders, rewinding shoestring, or putting away tools. She made an adept assistant dedicated to completing any task, that helped Wenceslaus close the shop before supper.

At first, Wenceslaus had been concerned for Antonia, wondering how well she would adjust to living in a large city with thousands of people. By comparison, there might have been 100 country folks living in and around her village where she grew up. In fact, most of central Bohemia was made up of farms or small villages just like Nechanice. Prague, Caslav, and Kutna Hora were exceptions to that rule and had been important destinations

Stone buildings, cobbled streets, and arches, Kutna Hora, GKM 2015

of kings and noblemen for centuries. Wenceslaus grew up in a large city and understood these thriving centers of commerce. With great relief and considerable pride, he discovered his Antonia adjusted to city life splendidly.

Wenceslaus proudly admitted his reputation for excellent footwear had almost been eclipsed by Antonia's growing reputation as an outstanding pastry baker. The difference between them was in their business approaches. Unlike his desire to own and operate his own business, Antonia did not want to be tied to a cukrárna, which is what they called the permanent sales stalls in the market square. Instead, she established relationships with the owners of several cukrárna, and those pastry and sweet shops bought all Antonia's inventory each morning, six days a week.

Antonia planned her work schedule flawlessly. She prepared the fruit fillings and pastry dough for her new orders in the early afternoons of the previous day. Once those preparations were completed, she let those items rest overnight and joined Wenceslaus in the workshop.

After breakfast each morning at 6:00 a.m., Wenceslaus would kiss Antonia and go to his workshop, and she would begin her baking. Not a minute wasted, Antonia's timing and baking schedule spun out smoothly. She had done so much baking with her mother that she no longer needed a recipe for most things, but she had written down a few favorites. Everyone made rohliky a little differently, and she loved her father's recipe the best.

Master Baker Nemec, Rohliky

1) *1-cup milk*

2) *1/4-cup sugar*

3) *1/4-cup water*

4) *2 1/2 teaspoons dry active yeast*

5) *1-teaspoon salt*

6) *1 (beaten) egg*

7) *1/4-cup lard, melted and cooled*

8) *3 1/4–3 1/2 cups flour and re-measure (sift two times as Papa says it makes them fluffier)*

9) *Brush with sweet butter while hot and sprinkle with black poppy seeds*

   Nicolas' note: alternate method of preparing the dough in advance

10) *Prepare dough, cover in crock, knead once before bed and let set overnight*

The three items Antonia selected to bake and sell in the market were rohliky, sweet kolaches with berry filling, and oatmeal-walnut-raisin cookies.

As Antonia started her baking schedule, the first job was to knead and flatten the rohliky dough and then let it rise again.

Next, while that dough was rising, she hand pressed a lump of kolache dough, tearing it into 24 round pieces. Using a spoon, she prepared an indentation in each piece of the kolache dough to hold a dollop of her fruit compote after they were baked and cooled.

While the kolache dough baked for 20 minutes, Antonia used a rolling pin to flatten the rohliky dough again, then cut it into thin strips and rolled the triangle strips into three-dozen moon shaped rohlikys. She removed the kolaches from the oven and set the pan of rohliky to bake for 15 minutes.

While the rohlikys baked and the kolaches cooled, Antonia portioned out lumps of oatmeal-walnut-raisin dough with a spoon, dropping each spoonful on a baking sheet. She would get three-dozen cookies per batch. The cookie trays went into the oven after she removed the golden-brown rohlikys.

While the cookies baked and while rohlikys were still hot, Antonia brushed the rohlikys with butter, then sprinkled the melting butter with black poppy seeds, which stuck in place as the butter cooled. Once she was finished with the rohlikys, Antonia filled the kolaches with her berry compote. As she finished the kolaches, the oatmeal cookies were ready to come out of the oven, and she set the cookies on the table to cool.

Antonia stored her handcart in the small garden outside her kitchen, which had its own gate to the main

Cistercian Abbey and Cathedral, Kutna Hora, GKM 2015

street. Her baker's cart had been designed and built by her father. It contained three shelves inside an enclosed frame, which could be kept warm without coals, and it held her three large baking trays perfectly. Loading the cart was part of her baking schedule. As the cookies cooled, Antonia took the first two trays of kolaches and rohlikys out to her cart and slid them into place. Returning to the kitchen, the cookies would be cool enough to cover, and after sliding that tray into its slot, she put Wenceslaus' rohlikys in the oven. Antonia would stop in the shop for a moment to say she was off to the market and reminded Wenceslaus not to forget his snack in the oven.

The cart was perfectly balanced and required very little effort to push even fully loaded. Her father had installed a small version of a carriage spring between the frame and the axle. Because of this clever suspension system, she never had to worry that her pastries would jiggle off the trays as she rolled the cart over the cobbled streets. Every time she used the pushcart, she happily blessed her father's ingenuity.

As an apprentice, Antonia learned two essential rules in her father's bakery and lived by them. First, a baker must be organized and develop perfect timing to become successful. Second, be first to market with fresh items at a fair price. By following these rules, a baker reduced the chances of losing money or wasting merchandise.

Antonia delivered her pastries to the cukrárnas every morning—except on Sundays—by 8:00 a.m. After her deliveries were completed, she would clean her empty cart and smile at the pouch full of coins she had received in exchange for her baked goods. It made Antonia proud to help her husband and supplement her family's income using her baker's skills.

Kutna Hora, 1868, a Year of Celebration

The Karellas of Kutna Hora felt blessed. Life was good, and while they were extremely busy with their growing businesses, four years passed by without Antonia bearing any children. Naturally, Wenceslaus and Antonia talked about children. They wanted to have children. During their early years together, they wisely did not fret over the issue, taking each day as it came, hoping and expecting that miracle to happen. After the first year remained childless, they prayed regularly about it. As the second and third year came and went childless, they secretly began to doubt they would ever have children. As the fourth year began without a baby, their hopes faded away. Knowing they were middle-aged and nearing their 30s, they began fear a family would not be part of their future. Nonetheless, the couple tried not to let that possibility destroy their happiness.

During those years of waiting and hoping, Wenceslaus honestly believed he would be prepared to receive the news he was to become a father. When 29-year-old Antonia finally announced she was pregnant, the news so overwhelmed Wenceslaus with emotion, he could barely respond coherently.

Joyful letters raced back and forth between Nechanice, Caslav, and Kutna Hora during the Christmas season of 1867, and the whole family made plans for a visit. Wenceslaus received several letters from his twin sisters. At 17 the girls were thrilled about becoming aunties and volunteered to come to Kutna Hora to help out. He wrote back saying that he might just take them up on their offer.

Bohemian-style wooden cradle

Exhilarated with the idea of being parents, Antonia and Wenceslaus rearranged their living space to make room for a baby who would be born in the spring. On May 22, 1868, almost five years after their marriage, Mr. and Mrs. Wenceslaus Karella welcomed their first child into the world and named him Anton.

A great celebration took place for Anton's baptism. Both Karella and Nemec relatives traveled to Kutna Hora to welcome this new child into the Catholic faith. Everyone brought wonderful gifts for Antonia, Wenceslaus, and the baby. Grandfather Karella brought a handmade cradle that had been Wenceslaus', and Miklaus was eager to see how it fit his grandson. Aunties from both sides of the family gave Antonia baby clothes, and Eliska and Marketa collaborated on a matching set of linens and blankets for the cradle. They also made a second set of matching linens for Wenceslaus and Antonia's bed.

Wenceslaus and Antonia could scarcely believe how much joy, extra work, and chaos came with having a baby in the house, but they loved every minute of it.

The spring of 1868 was momentous for a second reason. The Chotek steward recommended Wenceslaus to another important client. This new client was the purchasing agent who traveled with Kaiser Wilhelm I of Germany and his son, the Crown Prince Wilhelm.

Wenceslaus, excited about the introduction, said, "I studied about this family in school, Antonia. Kaiser Wilhelm's son is next in line for the German throne. He will become the next German Kaiser and King of Prussia. He is also the eldest grand-child of Great Britain's Queen Victoria! These royals are related by bloodline to most of the monarchs throughout Europe, and I'm going to meet them personally." Jittery with excitement, he said, "I must sit down and write to Papa." Antonia smiled; it was almost too much to take in.

The Kaisers' son, Crown Prince Wilhelm II, had become friends with the sons of Count Chotek. The Kaiser and Count Chotek often mixed business with family outings during their summer visits to Kutna Hora. During these annual visits, begin-ning in the summer of 1868, Wenceslaus spent a good deal of time making boots for the Kaiser's regimental guard and officers who visited Count Chotek's palace each summer.

Most Bohemians resented being forced by law to use German as their national language. However, reading, writing, and speaking German was mandatory in Bohemian schools. As a professional, Wenceslaus was thankful for that requirement. German was the language spoken in the most influential business circles through-out Bohemia. Speaking multiple languages gave both Antonia and Wenceslaus a great advantage in their professional lives, and that ability had become essential in Wenceslaus' trade.

Kutna Hora, Anton Karella's First Christmas

Both Karella and Nemec grandparents made extended visits to Kutna Hora during the holidays of 1868. None of the family believed it was possible to be happier than they were as they shared baby Anton's first Christmas. Four months later, they were proven wrong. Just before Anton turned one year old, Antonia surprised everyone by announcing she was pregnant again.

1869 was a year of significant events. The first of those events was an unexpected death. All of Kutna Hora mourned the loss of Count Karel Chotek and Wenceslaus was especially saddened by his passing. He had known the count since he was a boy and liked and respected the man. A week after this news, Wenceslaus received a note from Steward Auberon to come to Chotek palace. Wenceslaus hoped for a chance to pay his respects to the family after his business with Auberon was concluded.

Master Cobbler Wenceslaus arrived for his appointment to find the palace staff in a frenzy of activity. Standing at the service entrance, Steward Auberon's eyes settled on Wenceslaus immediately. Motioning to Wenceslaus, Auberon began to leave the room, and as Wenceslaus caught up to him, the steward said, "The two young masters of this house have summoned me to the library. Stay close and keep silent."

Wenceslaus spoke to Auberon softly as they walked, "I'd like to convey my condolences if there is an appropriate moment." The steward gave him a single nod to indicate he'd heard Wenceslaus' request.

Abbey main altar—windows and celling,
Kutna Hora

The eldest son, the new Count Anton Chotek, and his younger brother, Bohuslav, stood looking out the window behind their father's desk in the library. Over the years, Wenceslaus had spent a good deal of time with the young masters of the Chotek palace and liked them. Upon entering the library, Wenceslaus stood quietly and listened as Steward Auberon confirmed travel arrangements for their mother. She planned to move back to Caslav after the new count's inauguration ceremony.

Main altar, Cistercian Cathedral, Kutna Hora, GKM 2015

"As I am now Count Chotek, I am required to go to Caslav to fulfill my governmental duties. However, it is my intention, Auberon, to be the master in residence here in the Kutna Hora palace. Our mother, the dowager countess, will return permanently to the Caslav palace. My brother will travel between our two estates regularly. He will need to schedule travel plans with you Auberon," Count Anton said.

"Very good, Count Chotek, I will see to it," Auberon replied.

The steward bowed slightly and turned to Wenceslaus and

Frescoes, Praga, Bohemia, GKM 2015

nodded at him. That was his cue to speak, and he said, "Count Anton, Master Bohuslav." Hearing the Master Cobbler's voice, the young men looked directly at him, waiting in silence. "I am sorry for your loss. Your father was a great man," Wenceslaus said quietly.

The young men bowed their heads slightly in acceptance and seemed to appreciate his kind words. Auberon tapped Wenceslaus on the arm and bobbed his head in approval. Then, he indicated with his eyes and another head movement that they should leave.

Steward Auberon lead Wenceslaus from the room but waited at the door. Once Wenceslaus passed into the hall, the steward turned to face the count, and bowing respectively, he said, "Count Anton, Master Bohuslav," then he pulled the double doors closed with a soft click.

As Auberon escorted Wenceslaus back to the courtyard, he said, "Well done, Wenceslaus. Now, the reason I called you here was to let you know that Count Anton and his brother will need your services far beyond normal this year. As they take on their official duties, they must be outfitted according to their new ranks." Auberon handed Wenceslaus a list of items needed for upcoming events, including Anton Chotek's inauguration. The list included boots, gloves, and sword scabbards for the count's uniform as well as his brother's ceremonial uniform. The brothers would also need new parade tack for their horses. The first sets would be for the inauguration. The second and most resplendent sets of tack would be for the annual formal parades held throughout the year in Kutna Hora. As Wenceslaus perused the extensive list, Steward Auberon said, "I know this is a lot of work. If you prioritize by when we need the items, I think you'll find the requests are reasonable." Pointing at the paper, Auberon said, "We will need these items in 60 days for the count's inauguration."

Nodding, Wenceslaus could see Auberon was correct. Timing was the key to everything and replied, "All will be ready in the order that Count Chotek needs these things."

The second surprising event of 1869 brought great joy to the Karella household.

Kutna Hora, the Karella Family Prepares for a New Arrival

The Karellas of Caslav and the Nemecs of Nechanice could hardly wait for their new grandchild to be born. The anticipation was nearly overwhelming for Wenceslaus and Antonia as they attended their business commitments, took care of their infant son, Anton, and prepared for the birth of their next child.

By November of 1869, Antonia could tell her pregnancy was far different than her previous one. She tried not to complain, but she felt as big as her father's draft horse. Her belly seemed twice the size it had been when she delivered Anton, and the baby was not due for another month. As requested, the doctor came and checked Antonia's condition again. "Wenceslaus, you must try to keep Antonia calm. The baby's heartbeat is strong, and the movement of the infant is normal. Be happy you will have a big strong child, and the baby should be born in early December." The unusual conditions of this pregnancy remained a mystery to everyone until Antonia gave birth to twins on December 4, 1869. Their son, Stanislaus was born first, followed quickly by his twin sister, Antonia. The children's grandparents joyfully volunteered their assistance and made extended visits to Kutna Hora. Marketa and Nicolas helped Antonia with her baking business, Eliska helped with the babies, and Miklaus helped Wenceslaus with the Chotek orders.

Kutna Hora, Birth, Death and Heartbreak 1870

Over the next 11 months, toddler Anton and baby Stanislaus thrived and grew stronger while their baby sister grew weaker. In late November of 1870, with tears and heavy hearts, the Nemecs and Karellas journeyed to Kutna Hora to attend the funeral of baby Antonia. The infant passed away before she turned one year old.

Life is fragile, and tragically, Wenceslaus and Antonia learned it is possible for parents to be filled with hope and drowning in sorrow at the same time.

Praying for a Deceased Soul

Wenceslaus remembered that he and Steward Auberon had smiled as the abbot talked about the craftsmen painted on the walls of his cathedral. Wenceslaus was not smiling now. He sat in the cathedral hoping to find comfort in the quiet surrounding him. His eyes traveled along the magnificent walls. Slowly, they came to rest above the pew where he sat. He found the image of the cobbler and his guardian angel, St. Crispin. Kneeling down, Wenceslaus folded his hands, not know-

Frescoes of the working man and guardian angels, alcove off main church, Cistercian Cathedral, Kutna Hora, GKM 2015

ing what to say to God. The sorrow in his heart made it difficult to think straight. In his mind, he kept seeing the loss etched in his wife's eyes, a sad reflection of the pain he felt too. Recently, he and Antonia asked the abbot if the pain of losing a child ever went away. His words of counsel had provided little comfort on the matter of loss, when he told them to focus on the rewards of going to heaven.

Looking up at the altar, stained glass windows, and the vaulted ceiling, Wenceslaus thought, *All my children were baptized in this church. It is a good place to come to pray for the soul of my little girl. Lord, please take good care of her.* Within minutes, Wenceslaus made the sign of the cross and stood up. He stepped into the aisle and respectfully genuflected, putting his knee to the floor. His mind kept returning to the same thought—*How unpredictable life is.* He tried once again to concentrate on what he wanted to say to God before he left the church and thought, *Lord, help me remember the blessings in our life so that peace can fill our hearts.*

As if in answer to his prayers, he remembered his mother shouting at him, "Yes! Your daughter went to heaven! But God also blessed you with two healthy sons who are right here on earth with you!"

The memory of her voice was so vivid and clear, Wenceslaus thought she might be standing right next to him. He even looked over his shoulder to see if she was there. But of course, she wasn't. Turning toward the front of the church again, his eyes came to rest on the compassionate face of Jesus' mother, Mary. He felt a presence in his soul, looked up at the cross above the altar, then back at mother Mary, and slowly, comprehension filled his face. He closed his eyes and whispered, "Yes, Lord. I understand what you want of me." He said in a choked whisper, "You and your mother will take care of our little girl while Antonia and I take care of our little boys. Thank you for answering my prayers," Wenceslaus whispered and bowed his head.

When he left the church and stepped into the sunshine, the smile that started on Wenceslaus' lips penetrated all the way to his heart.

Through the Eyes of a Child

Anton and Stanislaus' cheerfulness and natural curiosity kept Wenceslaus and Antonia so busy when they were not working, that they had little time left for sorrow. When the boys got a little older, they were the ones who decided their little sister Antonia had become their guardian angel. That loving thought eased everyone's heart.

On one of his many visits, Abbot Ansell smiled when he heard the boys refer to their deceased sister as a guardian angel. Inspired by the idea behind Anton and Stanislaus' thoughts, the abbot used their imagery in one of his homilies. He reminded the adults in his congregation to imitate the faith of children. "In their innocence, they know God is a loving parent who sets guardian angels to watch over and protect us." Then, he quoted, "It is as Jesus said, 'Out of the mouths of babes you will hear truth.'" All heads nodded at such wisdom, and each one of the Karellas from that day forward thought of little Antonia as the angelic soul who watched over their family.

The Future in a Rapidly Changing Bohemia

With the dawn of 1870, the Karella family of Kutna Hora no longer felt insulated from change. Wenceslaus spoke to his father about his fears for the future during family visits and in reply his father, said, "Son, everything was so different in your grandfather's time, and even for me. Life was much simpler for me as a younger man."

Mr. Karella continued to explain about how things had been different before the Industrial Revolution began to spread across Bohemia.

"For centuries, Bohemia was a country built around traditional trades with highly skilled craftsmen, many farms, small villages, and very few cities. Some goods were produced in guild shops, but the guilds strictly controlled those items. Guild-crafted items like fine clothing, hardware, jewelry, leathered armor, silverware, and weapons were highly sought after in cities like Kutna Hora or Prague. Guilds generally received orders and requisitions for their products directly from aristocrats.

"The guilds did not trade beyond the borders of the big cities unless they were using their products in payment for raw materials being shipped to Bohemia from England or America. Nor did they compete with small village businesses. They did use their finished inventory to barter for farm-raised food and personal items like wine or beer."

"I agree with you, Papa. We've done business with guilds, particularly the Tanner Guild for their specialized leathers. I never thought of them as a threat to my own business; they were a resource. But these new factories are totally different, and I fear the future they represent."

Miklaus nodded and said, "Son, we cannot afford to believe that our lives are set and secure anymore. Nor can I tell you that these new factories and their machines will not change our craft because I fear they will. Maybe not today, but in the coming years, this change will be something we cannot stop."

Focusing on the future, Wenceslaus wondered, *How am I going to protect my family? I believed my craft would create a stable future for us. My livelihood could be destroyed by these new factories. It might not happen tomorrow, but I cannot help the anxiety I feel when I read what is being predicted in the newspapers.*

The Creation of Automation Hails the Demise of Entrepreneurialism in Bohemia

Wenceslaus' instinct to look ahead had been developing since he became apprenticed to his trade 17 years earlier. His boyish attitudes had disappeared, and he had become serious both at work and in school. Overhearing many conversations between his father and Count Chotek, he reaped an awareness and maturity beyond his years. He remembered that even at age 16, the scholars at his school treated his questions about history and business with respect. The answers he was given were always fascinating and enlightening. His teachers were excited to explain the history of trade in Bohemia.

"In the 1700s and early 1800s apart from the guild's market, most of Bohemia's manufacturing took place in rural areas. Laborers were scattered all over the countryside, which created a unique niche for a special kind of merchant known as an *entrepreneur*.

"These businessmen employed workers in several adjacent villages. Within those villages, whole families worked together making contracted products from raw materials supplied to them by the entrepreneur. The contracted products produced by villagers varied. Some made food items such as sausage, bread, or pies. Other contracts were made for sewing clothing or making bulk woven materials or items made of wood. The key factor was that these products were handcrafted. Now Bohemians did have water wheels that generated small amounts of power, but that was used primarily for grinding grain.

"The lesson I want you to understand about business dealings, Wenceslaus, is that the entrepreneur distributed raw materials to workers, then collected the finished products. He paid the villagers for the labor. But the entrepreneur owned the finished product outright and took the risk of finding markets where those finished goods could be sold. Major cities like Caslav, Kutna Hora, or Prague were large permanent population centers where the entrepreneur sold his finished products."

Wenceslaus remembered telling his papa about this lesson with his teachers and what he thought. "I think being an entrepreneur is really a state of mind. It is a smart way to think, always looking ahead. A good businessman must keep track of details and above all watch for new opportunities."

His papa had praised him, saying, "Many older men never figure out such things. Keep thinking that way, son. It will serve you well."

About the Monarchs and Royals Who Ruled Bohemia

Wenceslaus and Antonia grew up in a time when all European countries surrounding Bohemia were ruled by monarchs who owned all the land and wielded all the power. The royals distributed some of that land and power to negotiate alliances with rich merchants and land barons to remain in control of their countries. Rulers even made deals with specific important members of the Church to maintain control of their kingdoms. Craftsmen, laborers, farmers, and peasants had no power or voice in government, and the existing laws and new laws being passed were put in place to protect the aristocracy and their interests, not the common man.

Trades, Product Taxes, and the Value of Education in Bohemia

The listening skills Wenceslaus developed as an apprentice cobbler paid off during lectures with his educators. He became intrigued with the changes taking place in business and in government policy being discussed in parliament. Sometimes what he heard was confusing and he would ask his father to explain.

"Wenceslaus, most Bohemian lives revolved around a cycle of raising livestock for meat or barter, and the agricultural seasons of cultivating, planting, harvesting, and processing.

Before the Industrial Revolution began to spread across Europe, life changed very little from one generation to the next. A man's son generally became apprenticed to his father's craft or trade or profession, just like you did.

Trade businesses grew up around groups of farmers and stockmen who needed craftsmen to supply services or to provide items they could not or did not make themselves. These businessmen and women brought valuable skills wherever they set up shops and made villages stronger. Everyone worked hard, and although people might not have had a lot of coin, they could live off the land they worked, even though they could not own the land they worked."

"Why, Papa? Why couldn't they own the land they worked?" Wenceslaus had asked.

"There is no option to buy land in Bohemia. All the land is owned by the royals and is governed and controlled by the Austro-Hungarian Empire. The government makes its money off every citizen that works the land. Or in our case makes and sells a product.

"We pay to live on the land or work the land. A Bohemian farmer pays rent for the land he works either in coin or in goods he produces. Tradesmen like us rent our shop space and pay a tax on every product we sell. If a man defaults on his rent or taxes, he and his family can be thrown off the land so it can be rented to someone else.

"This is part of the reason your mother and I are so adamant about education. What you learn will help you survive. Reading, writing, mathematics, and the languages you can speak are valuable tools that cannot be taken away. These tools can help you earn a living, avoid being cheated in business, and create opportunities for you. Change is a part of life, son. These tools and skills prepare a person to adapt to changes that can affect your future."

Wenceslaus came to understand practicality ruled Bohemian life. Few citizens enjoyed large incomes. Those that did were aristocrats who had inherited their land as a birthright, held public office like Count Chotek, or had a successful side business that brought in extra money. Wenceslaus believed most of the population in Bohemia worked hard. But after paying rent and taxes, a family had to live on what was left. Few people had extra money to invest in what did not generate an immediate return. That concept brought to mind Wenceslaus' 20th birthday gift. He had been given an expensive saddle horse as an investment in his future. Master Lukas and his father had known Kristof would pay for himself by taking Wenceslaus to business opportunities too far to reach on foot. They had also taught him that what the horse saved him in travel time could be reinvested in work to generate profit.

Bohemian Political Climate and Its Effect on Wenceslaus Karella and His Family

As Bohemia entered the 1870s, the new decade did not inspire confidence in the Karellas of Kutna Hora. A foreboding feeling had been building in Wenceslaus and Antonia since the death of Stanislaus' twin sister. As they continued to read disturbing stories published about increasing problems related to factory automation, their sense of foreboding became a constant anxiety.

Change dominated the news. The current trend of business and government policy did not bode well for the craftsmen politically nor would they have any protection for their crafts under civil law. The Austro-Hungarian Empire showed no concern for what industrialization was doing to Bohemia's trade system, and there was no evidence that the government would make any changes to improve the situation.

The future Wenceslaus' children faced in Bohemia looked bleak. Bitterness nearly overwhelmed him at times. His family's future was being threatened, and he could not protect them against the economic and social catastrophe growing in Bohemia. It made him feel helpless, and Wenceslaus prayed, "Dear God, guide me. Please help Antonia and I find the answers we need to keep our family secure."

The Karellas of Kutna Hora Welcome a Baby Girl

During the Christmas holidays of 1872, the Karella's were given a joyful distraction from their worries. Antonia announced she was pregnant again. With that wonderful news, the whole family's mood brightened. Wenceslaus decided he had to stop letting fear dampen his hope and excitement for the future.

It had been four years since the death of little Antonia, and now happiness grew each day. Everyone eagerly awaited the birth of this fourth child. The united Nemec and Karella families prayed for the safety of Antonia and the health of this new baby. Heaven overflowed with a flood of thanks when on July 24, 1873, Antonia delivered a healthy baby girl whom they named Anna.

Fantasy, Solutions and Dreams of Land in America

As rapidly as the country of Bohemia was growing weaker, the four Karella children were growing stronger. A new protectiveness forced the maturing couple to begin searching for solutions instead of worrying. They needed solutions that would lead to a better future for their children. Even if that future lay beyond the borders of their homeland.

Wenceslaus and Antonia felt real optimism as they read about the opportunities in America. They gobbled up every newspaper story they could find about the railroad expansion occurring in the American Midwest, and about owning land. Such exhilarating headlines seemed unbelievable to people in Bohemia. Yet over and over again, the newspaper articles stated land was being made available in America. Land that could be purchased by anyone.

Until now, the idea of owning land was a fantasy to Bohemians. The opportunities that lay across an ocean filled their waking hours with hope and dominated their nights with dreams of creating a legacy for their children.

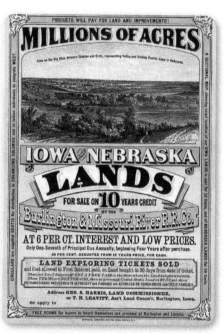

Nebraska Land Sale Poster © 1872

Fortunately, for the Karellas, American railroad companies spent a significant amount of money abroad advertising land for sale. It was through railroad representatives sent to Europe to speak about land sales that the Karellas began to get the answers to some very important questions. These representatives explained in detail how to purchase land in a place called Nebraska. With this information, the Karellas began to think seriously about moving to America. A place where their dreams of a secure future for their children might come true.

Kutna Hora, Antonia Brings Home Exciting News

While delivering her baked goods to Petra's cukrárna, Antonia overheard a conversation between Petra and an American. After the American left, Antonia questioned Petra regarding what she had overheard. Being a longtime friend, he took no offense to her eavesdropping. Smiling at her enthusiasm, Petra gave Antonia one of the handbills the railroad man had left on his counter to be given away. Antonia thanked her friend and hurried home. Wenceslaus was nearly finished with a pair of riding boots for a visiting Austrian prince staying at the Chotek palace.

Rushing into the workshop, Antonia set down her market satchel and excitedly said, "Look what I found today." She put the handbill nearly on top of the boot sole Wenceslaus was working on. Then, pointing at a line on the paper, she said, "It says the railroad in America has millions of acres of land for sale in Iowa and Nebraska."

Wenceslaus looked up happy to see the joy back in Antonia's eyes, and for a minute, he sat smiling at his lovely wife's enthusiasm. Coming back to reality, he softly said, "Darling, please let me finish this pair of boots first. The Prince's footman will be here with Steward Auberon in an hour. There will be extra coin in it for us if I am finished when he arrives. After I am done, I promise we will sit down together, and we will read the leaflet you brought home. Then, you can tell me all of what you heard in the market today. Will that be alright with you?"

While Antonia had been talking to her husband, her two sons, four-year-old Stanislaus and five-year-old Anton, had been playing with pieces of leather and some of their father's tools in a corner of the workshop. Now they were hanging on her skirt trying to get her attention. Looking down, she gently said, "Boys, please let Mama talk to Papa." Her gentle request was enough to make them stand quietly by her side for the moment, but she knew her sons' acquiescent attitude would not last.

Nodding her head, Antonia replied, "Yes, you are right, Wenceslaus. My news will be just as exciting later. I'm going to check on the baby. I'll take the boys with me so you can finish up without being interrupted."

Seeing Antonia motioning for the boys to follow her, Wenceslaus smiled and replied, "Thank you, My Heart. Little Anna has been sleeping since you left. I have not heard a sound out of her."

It pleased Antonia to know Anna's papa had been listening for his daughter's cries, so she replied cheerfully, "I'll have lunch ready in an hour. After the footman leaves, we can all eat together." Now focused on making lunch, Antonia headed toward the kitchen with Anton and Stanislaus trotting along right behind her.

Wenceslaus voice followed her through the door as he replied, "Yes, my darling. That will be perfect."

Waiting would not dampen the effect of her wonderful news. Antonia's mind buzzed with excitement. However, she did agree the boots were more important at the moment. Antonia had a healthy respect for the money her husband made with his skills. Many people living in Kutna Hora were not so fortunate, and money was not as plentiful as it had once been.

Slightly over an hour later, Wenceslaus sauntered into the kitchen with a satisfied grin on his face. Sitting down beside his sons, he proudly set a good-sized stack of coins on the table near Antonia's cup. Then, he announced, "I'm hungry, Mama!" Winking at Anton and Stanislaus, patiently waiting at the table for food, he asked, "Who's ready to eat?"

Instantly, two high-pitched voices squealed, "We are, Papa!"

That playfulness continued throughout the meal as he teased his sons and his wife. Wenceslaus enjoyed their smiles and the teasing they gave him in return. After Antonia cleared the table and put the children down for naps, she sat down next to her husband. Her excitement had been building while they ate lunch, and it was time to show Wenceslaus the handbill. Laying it on the table so they could read it together, the printed message gave them hope. "Wenceslaus, could this be the place of our dreams? Could our future include owning land? What I am reading makes me believe it could all be possible," Antonia whispered breathlessly.

"Land that could be ours ... farmland we could work that could support this family. Land we could pass on to our children," Wenceslaus whispered back.

They shared a common exhilaration about such wonderful ideas ... yet Wenceslaus also felt a bit of trepidation. As the primary provider and planner for his family, he worried about the sacrifices they would be forced to make, for such a dream to become a reality. *But to have a new future and to own land,* Wenceslaus thought, *the sacrifices made and the risks taken would be worth it.* Owning land no longer seemed like a fantasy or an impossible dream. But the Karellas needed an action plan before they could pursue these ideas. "Antonia, we must gather as much information as we can about this land in America, and about the Railroad selling the land in Nebraska," Wenceslaus said, and Antonia nodded her head in agreement.

Kutna Hora, Karellas Learn of Progress and the American Railroad

What Antonia and Wenceslaus discovered was that in 1865, the Union Pacific Railroad in the United States began building railroad tracks extending westward from the city of Omaha, Nebraska, with the goal of connecting with California. Within two years, those tracks traversed the entire state of Nebraska. The United States Government wanted the western region of America settled and to be connected with the east. It was the consensus of the military and government that traveling and shipping goods by train would be the best and safest method. The settlers traveling on these trains were going to be Americans, businessmen, and farmers with families who would secure land as part of the future of a united America. The United States Government encouraged the extension of the railway lines but would not monetarily fund the enterprise. To motivate the railroad companies to finance their own expansion across the west, each participating railway company received specific land grants from state and federal agencies. These grants gave the railroad owners legal title to tracts of land along their rail paths, which could be sold to offset construction costs.

Advertising campaigns to sell this land saturated the east coast of America in the hope of selling parcels of land to new immigrants arriving in New York and along the east coast. When sales were not realized as quickly as the railroads needed to recapture their investment dollars, they created an alternate plan. The plan was to attract more immigrants to American shores who had the goal of buying land from the railroad before they even sailed to American shores. To accomplish this, the railroad companies sent representatives to Europe with handbills full of glowing promises about the farmland in Iowa and Nebraska for sale. Wenceslaus and Antonia believed the words they heard as they attended lectures on the ease of buying railroad land in America. The Karellas of Kutna Hora became Bohemians with a dream. The more they read and learned about land in America, the more their dream became hope for their future and for the future of their children.

A Visionary Becomes an Ally and Helps the Railroad Forge the Future of Nebraska

Another promoter of the state of Nebraska and an influential Nebraskan during this time period was career newspaperman, J. Sterling Morton. He migrated west with his family from the wooded state of Michigan to homestead in the rolling, treeless plains of Nebraska in 1854. Instinctively, he knew Nebraska needed a wood resource before the state could realize any notable business progress. Without harvestable forests for building, it would be extremely difficult to draw settlers to its farmable land.

Morton established Nebraska's first newspaper. As editor of the newspaper, he became an influential journalist, and in time was drawn into politics. His forestry project was always in the back of his mind and to set an example he and his family planted hundreds of trees around their home and property.

The obstacles mentioned in most of the discussions he had with other Nebraskans were the same problems—the lack of fuel, shade, windbreaks, or wood for building. Settlers who did stay and live on the land made their homes out of prairie sod and burned buffalo chips as their only source of heat. Despite these problems, Morton encouraged settlement of the state extensively through his Newspaper and wrote, "Beneath the tall prairie grass covering much of Nebraska is rich, fertile soil waiting to become someone's wonderful farmland." Opposing Morton's glowing descriptions, other writers called Nebraska and the Midwest "the great American desert." During the mid-1800s, Morton extended his campaign about Nebraska, placing ads in prominent eastern newspapers full of glowing imagery. "Come build your home from Nebraska marble." Early settlers that did go west and buy land as a result of Morton's ads discovered Nebraska marble was actually prairie sod.

The railroad companies could not have been more pleased to see Morton's news articles. The naysayers printing opposing opinions proved that Morton's words were influencing the public, and Morton's message directly supported their goal of selling land along their railroad tracks in Nebraska. Pleased to see bad press did not discourage Morton, the railroad men planned to imitate Morton's example. They created a similar sales campaign of their own using printed handbills to describe Iowa and Nebraska land they had for sale. Then, they sent the advertising and salesmen to Europe to explain how to buy American Railroad land.

Morton, totally focused on Nebraska, had an idea for a tree-planting campaign he would call Arbor Day. The concept was simple; he must get everyone living in the state to plant trees. He presented a proposal to the Nebraska State Board of Agriculture (NSBA) in 1872. In the proposal he outlined a tree-planting contest to be implemented as a new holiday. To perpetuate the event and get more trees planted every year, he also asked for the plan to be accepted as an annual holiday in Nebraska called Arbor Day. To gain the participation of as many people as possible, he recommended it be administered as a contest with rules and prizes offered to the counties and individuals who properly planted the largest number of trees on that day.

The NSBA committee unanimously voted to accept the proposal and establish the holiday, the contest, and the planting prizes. Nebraska held its first Arbor Day on April 10, 1872. The event was hailed as a resounding success as noted by NSBA contest managers who estimated more than one million trees were planted on that day. Morton's pride in the success of Arbor Day is reflected in this famous quote. "Other holidays repose upon the past; Arbor Day proposes for the future."

Kutna Hora, Bohemia, A Crossroad, and a Choice

Wenceslaus checked on the children and found them warm and asleep despite the cold weather outside. Slipping back into the bed, he pulled his wife into his arms.

"Oh Wenceslaus, your feet are ice cold!"

"And you, My Heart, are warm!" he said as he tried to put his cold feet on her warm legs.

Antonia giggled as she snuggled close and suddenly the playfulness left her voice. "Wenceslaus," she whispered.

"Yes, My Heart?" He replied.

"We must make a decision soon. Are we going? Or do we stay in Bohemia? If we stay, are we going to be alright living here in Kutna Hora? Or should we move closer to your parents or mine?" Antonia asked.

On the end of a heavy sigh, Wenceslaus replied, "My mind says we must leave Bohemia, and America is the right place to go. I don't think we have a choice about that. But the consequences, Antonia … for the family we will leave behind … my heart is finding that choice very hard to live with."

CHAPTER 4

Voyage to a Bohemian Dream

1874 –1875

Kutna Hora, New Years, 1874—Wenceslaus and Antonia stood watching their children play in the courtyard outside the kitchen. The children's breath froze in the air like a dense fog in the fading sunlight. That fog seemed as magical in that moment as everything they had learned about America in the last six months. Wenceslaus and Antonia were excited about the future for the first time since moving to Kutna Hora.

They had recently attended a lecture held by an American railroad sales representative. Now, they understood how to buy land in a place called Nebraska. As extreme as it sounded, moving to a foreign country seemed to be the solution they had been searching for. A way to avoid the dreadful future their children would inherit if they stayed in Bohemia. To set such a plan in motion, there were hard decisions to make. Opportunities in the land of America provided promises for a new future they could not afford to ignore.

Kutna Hora, Frightening Statistics Regarding Ocean Travel

One of the major obstacles in their plan was sailing across the Atlantic Ocean. As the Karellas investigated ocean passage, they discovered some frightening facts. Sailing vessels—whose average length of voyage was six weeks between Liverpool and New York—listed mortality rates over five times greater than that of the new steamships. They heard it said by a Kutna Hora shipping agent that it was not uncommon for a sailing vessel to report a passenger death toll of up to 50%. In comparison, a similar size steamship reported less than a 10% passenger death toll.

Risk to life was not the only consideration. Aside from the ticket price, steamships crossed the Atlantic Ocean in two weeks instead of six. Should they decide to go to America, they would only travel by steamship. If a higher passenger fee enabled them to reduce the risks they faced during the crossing, it would be worth postponing departure until they could afford steamship passage.

Wenceslaus and Antonia felt fortunate to be able to make such choices about their future even if this gamble meant leaving all they knew behind. It was not only the unknown that inhibited them but also the anxiety and heartache of leaving their parents forever. As a result, the summer and half the winter of 1874 disappeared without a solid commitment to go or give up the idea and stay.

It had been a full year since Antonia and Wenceslaus began considering moving to America. As January of 1875 arrived, they committed themselves to a decision. In the spring, the family would go with Antonia as she traveled 1700 kilometers to Liverpool, England. From there, she would go on alone and take a steamship to America, which would dock in New York.

As a married couple and as parents, sacrifices had to be made to create the future they hoped for. Despite how well Wenceslaus and Antonia planned this new journey, they understood some danger would be unavoidable for all of them.

Wenceslaus continued to struggle with the idea of his wife going to America alone even after the decision had been made. It took all Antonia's strength to convince her husband this choice of action was correct.

Antonia's concerns were different than Wenceslaus'. They did not include being in America alone nor was it the money she had to save to reunite her family. She was worried that when the time came, Wenceslaus would be traveling to America with three young children by himself. The fear she felt for her family's safety held her back. Until that issue was resolved, she was not leaving.

Making a trip to Caslav, Wenceslaus had a heart-to-heart talk with his parents and then with his sisters. He asked the twins to come help him with the children in Kutna Hora and then to travel with them to America once Antonia sent the money.

Julienka and Masynda were thrilled with the idea of moving to Kutna Hora. It was an exciting city, and they loved their niece and nephews. They never dreamed they would have the chance to go to America. The two young women could hardly sit still while their brother explained the seriousness of the commitment they were making.

Watching the eyes of his mother, Wenceslaus regretted forcing her to make this sacrifice. Allowing him to enlist his sisters in his plans, knowing she might never see any of them again was both courageous and heartbreaking. He did not wish to cause his parents pain. But Wenceslaus' fear for his children and Antonia outweighed the desolation he saw in his mother's eyes.

Eliska Karella stood holding her husband's hand as they watched their son ride away. Miklaus looked down at his wife's sweet face and saw the tears forming in their depths. He squeezed her hand and whispered, "We understood the reality of this situation before he made this visit, my dear. We knew a time might come when we would have to say goodbye to them."

"Yes, I know," she whispered back. "I made peace with knowing Wenceslaus and the children would be leaving. But not all of my children and my grandchildren! If they all cross the ocean, this goodbye might be forever." With that statement, her whisper turned into a sob.

Miklaus held her in his arms. His tears dropped into her hair, and he knew he had to be strong for both of them. In a soft voice, he replied, "My Dearest Heart, you and I have been blessed with them for many wonderful years. Our lives are nearing the end, but theirs are only beginning. We must let them go and take comfort in knowing they have hope for a good and happy life. What more could we ask for them? We will keep them in our prayers, and they will always be in our hearts. We still have a little more time with them, my love. This is not goodbye yet."

Once her sisters-in-law had moved in with them in Kutna Hora, Antonia was more committed than ever. Wenceslaus' solution had been the answer they needed to move forward with their plans to go to America. Filled with anxious energy, Antonia was ready to get started. Several times a day, she repeated to herself, *I'll find a job. I'll save $40 for Wenceslaus and the children—and the $20 we need for Julie and Masy too. I can do this! I will do this!*

When doubts about going to America threatened her resolve, she would retaliate by thinking, *How difficult could it be? I speak German, Bohemian, and French, and I have a fair command of English, thanks to having a British headmaster.*

It had been difficult for her in school, learning to speak all the languages of the most powerful royal houses of Europe. Headmaster Kent had always told his students they would need these skills one day. Antonia remembered his words and was thankful. *Headmaster was right. My language skills are a blessing and a strength on this journey. I will be able to speak to many people in America. I have confidence in my baking skills. Living in this big city and working with my husband, I have learned how to improvise. If there is not a baker's job available, I'll find some other kind of job, and I'll make our plan work. I must!*

Antonia voiced none of her doubts out loud fearing Wenceslaus would change his mind. The time for indecision was long past; it had to be her, and it had to be now. She regretted that it would be harder on Wenceslaus without the extra money she added to their weekly income. Yet that hardship was unavoidable. The truth was he could take care of the children with his income alone, plus save a few coins to fund their new business endeavor in America. Her baker's income would never be enough alone. Antonia kept telling herself her family would be all right. Wenceslaus and his sisters would take good care of one another and her children until they could be reunited. Antonia had become close friends with the twins over the years. Saving the extra travel money would be a way to thank them for helping protect her family. She was happy they were coming to America, too, and looked forward to Julienka and Masynda living with them.

Now, the most pressing decision to be made was deciding which sailing company to engage for this journey.

Kutna Hora, Researching Steamship Competition

Steamship passage to New York from Liverpool, England, was 2 lbs. sterling or $10 US

Continuing his inquiries about travel to America, Wenceslaus discovered the truth behind improved ocean passage conditions for immigrant travelers. The Chotek Steward said the improvements were due to fierce competition between Lloyd and Hapag, two German steamship companies. The Americas represented such a wealth of business for these huge shipping companies sailing out of Bremen, Hamburg, and Liverpool that they competed aggressively for the transportation of travelers from all over Europe. According to Steward Auberon's sources, the competition between the companies ultimately lowered ticket prices. When Wenceslaus went to buy Antonia's steamship passage, the price for a single passenger was two-pound Sterling or ten American dollars from Liverpool to New York.

Liverpool, England: Antonia's Voyage to a New Land, Spring 1875

After the long overland journey with her family, the day of Antonia's ocean departure from England had arrived. She hugged and kissed each of her children, and into each child's ear, she whispered, "Mama loves you now and always. Please be good. Help your papa and listen to your aunties." After hugging Julie and Masy, she asked them to take the children back to the carriage. She did not watch them go. She took hold of her husband's arm, and they walked side-by-side down the pier. Filled with a mixture of sadness and excitement, Antonia found the emotions confusing. With all her heart, she wanted this new life for her family, and the only way to get it was to take this leap of faith into the unknown.

The closer the time came for her departure, the more fear began to eat away at her resolve. She did not want to leave her husband and children.

No matter how slowly they walked, they eventually reached the end of the pier and found themselves standing at the bottom of the gangway. Antonia knew she had to be strong and tried to lift Wenceslaus' spirits by saying, "Darling, if competition continues to drive down the prices of steamship tickets, that would be a blessing, don't you think? It would mean I could save the money we need that much faster." In her heart, she knew nothing would ease the pain she felt at leaving her husband, children, and family behind. But she still had to be strong for her husband.

Wenceslaus made a valiant effort to smile at her words, but it did not make saying goodbye to his wife any easier.

As husband and wife, they had spoken all the love words the night before in the privacy of their room at the inn. What was left was a deep ache inside while they clung to each other. As the minutes passed, Antonia realized standing there in misery was not helping either of them. With an unusual show of affection in public, she stood on her tiptoes and kissed her husband on his lips as tears escaped from her eyes and rolled down her cheeks.

Demonstrating great courage, she took her hand from her husband's arm. Placing one foot on the gangway, she forced both feet to continue that heart-wrenching climb to the ship's deck where a crewman asked to see her papers. She was the last passenger to board because the men withdrew the gangway immediately after her papers had been matched to the steward's list.

Ropes were being stowed, and everywhere, men were busy preparing for the ship's departure. Most of the passengers had already left the railings. Then, the ships steward directed her below, telling her to stow her satchel at the end of her bunk before the ship left the pier. Before she left the deck, Antonia could not resist one last look at the love of her life still standing on the dock below. She raised her trembling hand in farewell, and to help them both, she turned and went below where she could cry in private.

About the Steamship and the Voyage to America

Though Antonia's time aboard ship would be reduced to a predictable two weeks and she faced less than a 10% chance of dying during the voyage, there were still risks. Even with the improvements steam vessels afforded travelers in steerage, the ocean voyage would not be easy. The compartments were divided into units of four to six beds that were two-feet-wide and stacked three levels high. Each compartment had an open latrine, without walls, shared by six passengers. Each bunk bed in the compartment had a number, and every passenger had an assigned bed number on their passage papers.

When Antonia found her assigned compartment and bunk bed, she detected a tinge of rancid body odor and vomit beneath the strong smell of disinfectant they used to clean the compartment. Sanitation would be difficult in rough seas, and many people would not eat for days because of seasickness. It was fortunate Wenceslaus and Antonia had not read the following information sent anonymously to the New York newspaper about passenger food rations during the ocean crossings.

New York Daily Times Newspaper article printed on October 15, 1851

"From Liverpool each passenger receives weekly 5 lbs. of oatmeal, 2 1/2 lbs. biscuit, 1 lb. flour, 2 lbs. rice, 1/2 lb. sugar, 1/2 lb. molasses, and 2 ounces of tea. He or she is obliged to cook it the best way they can in a cook shop 12 feet by 6. This is the cause of so many quarrels, and many a poor woman with her children can get but one meal done, and sometimes they get nothing warm for days and nights when a gale of wind is blowing, and the sea is mountains high and breaking over the ship in all directions."

Antonia's Voyage 1875

Antonia was issued food rations aboard ship once a week. When the quartermaster issued the weekly supplies, he laid down a few rules with strict instructions. First, each steerage passenger was responsible for securing their own rations, cooking their food, and only had permission to use the small cooking area with tables and chairs on their own assigned deck. Second, steerage passengers were expected to stay on their own deck. Third, steerage passengers had the privilege to spend small amounts of time in the open area of the main deck but were to return to their own deck when they heard the deck bell toll the hour. The last challenge of living aboard ship she learned for herself; if and when she did eat, keeping that food in her stomach became her biggest struggle.

Time dragged slower than normal during the two-week voyage across the Atlantic Ocean. During her waking hours, Antonia could not rid herself of the sorrow she had seen in Wenceslaus' eyes. During her restless sleep, she relived the pain of watching the tears roll down her children's faces as she said goodbye. The fear that she might never see them again only penetrated her thought during brief nightmares. Upon waking each day, all negativity would be forced away as Antonia refocused her mind on why she was traveling so far away from all she knew.

Each day as the air below deck grew heavy with the smell of seasickness, Antonia escaped into the frigid air on the main deck. She only returned to her bunking area when the weather forced her to do so or a deckhand told her to.

During those hours above deck, she met an elderly German couple by the name of Wolff. Instantly trusting the young woman who spoke beautiful German, the Wolffs told her they were traveling to join their son, Johann. They explained their son had been living in New York for many years and that he owned and operated a butcher shop. He had done so well he had been able to marry, and now, Johann had invited them to come live with him. "We are beside ourselves with excitement," Mrs. Wolff said with bright eyes. "You see, Antonia, we are going to meet our grandchildren for the first time." "How exciting! I am so happy for you both," Antonia replied.

During the next two weeks, the Wolffs proved to be a source of useful information about New York and the community, which the couple had gleaned from their son's letters. Antonia listened and encouraged them to tell her all they knew about New York City and America. Despite having the company of the Wolffs to keep her distracted, the 14 days aboard ship seemed like forever.

When the announcement finally did come, Antonia experienced immense relief and a jolt of nervousness upon hearing the ship would be docking in New York in two days. That evening, there was no time to think about anything except what she was going to do once she left the ship. She did not have much of a plan when she fell asleep.

The early morning light revealed a lone woman sitting on a bench on the main deck. Gusts of wind kept trying to snatch the hat from her head as she nervously gazed across the water, lost deep in thought. Antonia jumped when a hand touched her arm. Looking up, she found the Wolffs smiling down at her. "May we join you, Antonia?" Mrs. Wolff asked. Motioning them to sit on the bench next to her, the three of them huddled close in an effort to block the cold wind blowing across the deck.

"I hope it will be warmer after the ship docks tomorrow," Mr. Wolff grumbled.

Within minutes, Antonia found herself humbled by a generous offer. The Wolffs told her they would speak to their son on her behalf and that they would help her find a safe place to stay. Upon hearing the concern in their voices, Antonia hugged them with relief. As her parents would have done, the Wolffs held her hands, patting them to comfort her while telling her not to worry. In the morning, she would not be leaving the ship or going into a strange city alone.

My Dearest Wenceslaus,   *New York, May 1875*

I arrive in New York tomorrow. Though I have only been gone from your arms and those of my sweet children for two weeks, in my heart, it already feels like torturous years. Now I promise you, this is the last time I will indulge in self-pity through my letters, as I know you suffer just as greatly.

My darling, let us look to brighter things as I also write of good news. I have met an older couple who reminds me much of our parents. Mr. Wolff bears a great

1875 U.S. Postage Stamp

resemblance to your papa, and Mrs. Wolff reminds me of my mama. They already have family in New York and have promised that their children who live in the city and own a butcher shop will help me find safe lodging to rent and per-haps a job as well. At the very least, you need not worry that I am alone. I will fare well with friends to help me avoid the dangers of being a solitary woman in such a city.

I will write as often as possible, and I implore you to please do the same. The Wolffs have said I can receive your letters through their son's business until I find a permanent place of my own. Please use the address I have written on this letter until I send another.

Husband, seeing your words on paper you have touched will make me feel less lonely and at the same time, closer to you. My darling, I send my full devotion to you and the children. Kiss them for me and know that I will work as long and hard as need be so we can be together again soon.

May God bless you and keep you all safe, your devoted wife, Antonia

True to their word, once the ship docked, the Wolffs waited for Antonia near the gangway and stood in line together until it was their turn to disembark. As soon as they set foot on the pier, Antonia was startled by a young man who swept Mrs. Wolff off the ground into an enthusiastic hug, which she returned with equal fervor. When she demanded to be put down, the young man refused until Mrs. Wolff gave him a kiss on his cheek. Blushing yet overjoyed, Mrs. Wolff delivered the kiss and then found her feet back on the pier. Then, Mrs. Wolf took a few steps to stand next to Antonia and proudly whispered, "Antonia, that is our son Johann!" Nodding yet speechless with astonishment, Antonia thought, *The Wolffs seemed like such normal-sized people. But their son is a giant!*

Mr. Wolff fondly watched the scene with his wife and son with amusement. As Johann put his mother down, he turned to his father and gave him a welcoming bear hug too.

After the joyful greetings subsided, Johann Wolff turned to look at the woman who appeared to be about his age or maybe a bit younger standing close to his mother. He could see she was *with* his parents, so he asked, "Did you two have another daughter while I have been in America?"

His mother's face blushed bright red at her son's words while his father grinned shaking his head at such impudence. With mock sternness, Mr. Wolff replied, "No, Johann. This is our dear friend, Mrs. Antonia Karella. Antonia, this is our son, Johann." Grinning up at the laughing young man, Mr. Wolff said, "Now, no more teasing, son."

Depiction of New York, New York, in 1875

Immigration Process—New York City, 1875

America was the land of dreams for many people like the Karellas and Wolffs. However, these two families were not the first Europeans to send a family member ahead to America to make the money to bring the rest of the family to this new land. As life became more difficult across Europe in the late 1700s and through the 1800s, the number of passengers traveling on money sent to them by a relative already living and working in America increased rapidly. By the mid-1800s, records state at least 35% of all European immigrants traveled to America on pre-paid tickets or on money sent to them from relatives already living in America. Antonia Nemec Karella was the first of her family to set foot on American soil. She entered America through the Castle Garden Immigration Center gate in Battery Park, New York. It is estimated that approximately eight million European immigrants passed through the Castle Garden gates before the

Ellis Island immigration depot of New York was established fifteen years after her arrival.

Antonia Starts Her Life in New York City, 1875

Though the Wolffs wanted to invite Antonia to stay with them in New York, it was impossible. They were to live with their son, his wife, and two children in a three-room apartment above the butcher shop. The Wolffs did ask their son to help Antonia find temporary lodging. Johann introduced Antonia to Peter and Margot Kraus who had a two-bedroom apartment and no children. A seamstress by trade, Mrs. Kraus made clothing for Johann and Maria's children and used the second bedroom in their apartment for her sewing and alterations work. Peter Kraus worked for a large cigar factory in the city near their neighborhood.

Taking Antonia by the hand, Mrs. Kraus assured her new friend that she and Peter could make room in their home for her until Antonia could find housing. Hugging Margot tightly, Antonia released one of her worries. With a sigh, she whispered a heartfelt "thank you" and sent a prayer of thanks to God for letting her meet such good people.

Antonia was to use Margot's sewing area for a bedroom. The workspace furnishing consisted of a small bench-style sofa under a big window, a small round worktable with one chair, an armoire, a few trunks, and a modified coat rack.

Peter placed Antonia's luggage at the end of the sofa, which she would use as a bed while Margot went around the room boxing up her sewing supplies. When she was finished, she set the box on the chair.

Next, Mrs. Kraus went to the armoire to remove a pillow and a few blankets. Seeing what Margot was doing, Antonia went to help. Taking the sleeping items first, Antonia set them on her makeshift bed and then handed Margot the box of items from the chair. After putting the sewing things into the armoire, Margot looked around the room. Nodding her head in satisfaction, she wished Antonia a good night's rest, leaving her in peace to get settled in.

In the morning, Antonia's sleeping clothes and blankets went into the armoire, and she made sure all Margot's sewing items were restored to their original locations. By the time Antonia sat down to breakfast, her bedroom had been transformed, once again, into a sewing workspace.

When Peter joined the women at the breakfast table, Margot suggested he show Antonia around the neighborhood before he went to work. Peter nodded his agreement as he filled his plate with food.

Antonia's Hunt for Work Begins

Later that morning, Peter Kraus pointed out the street signs and explained the numbering system in their part of town. "Use the corner market across the street as a landmark."

The sign in the grocer's window said *Larson's,* and Peter went on to explain that every neighborhood had a store like it. Looking down the street, Antonia noted many buildings had businesses on the street level with several floors of apartments above. It reminded her of the Wolffs living above the butcher shop.

Peter interrupted her thoughts, saying, "Those corner shops make deliveries in the neighborhoods and know the city. If you get lost, find the nearest corner market, and they can give you directions on how to get back to our street." She nodded in compliance and asked Peter where Margot shopped for their bakery items.

Pointing, Peter said, "Last shop on the next block on this street. A place called Pickering's."

"Thank you," Antonia replied. With a nod, Peter turned and headed off in the opposite direction.

That day, Antonia discovered the baker's trade was not a practical source of income in New York City unless she owned the bakeshop. The most she could earn as an assistant baker would be similar to the extra money she had made in Bohemia, which was not enough to accomplish her goals. Antonia had to rethink her plan.

She fell into a comfortable routine during her initial week in the Kraus household, which included helping Maria clean up after breakfast each morning. Antonia would leave the apartment right after Peter each day to resume her job hunting before Maria started sewing. Often going without lunch, Antonia returned to the Kraus' in time to help Maria with dinner preparations.

Each morning began with the same hope—*Today will be the day I find the right job.* Antonia could only afford to take a position that paid enough to buy lodging, food, and still leave some to save for her family's passage. Methodically, she went from shop to shop, street by street, and neighborhood by neighborhood without success. Antonia did not speak of her anxiety. Instead, she made a concerted effort to disrupt the Kraus' life as little as possible and thought she was hiding her emotions. However, the Kraus' could see her growing worry.

Antonia maintained her grueling schedule every day of that first week until Saturday evening when Margot and Peter invited her to attend Mass on Sunday. When Antonia hesitated, Margot took hold of her hands and said, "My friend, you need this break. You are not inconveniencing us. Furthermore, we were told to bring you to the Wolff's home after Mass for our lunch gathering, and none of us will take *no* for an answer." Having dispelled her fears, Antonia smiled at Margot's words. She accepted the invitations and looked forward to going to Mass and spending the day with all her new friends.

A Letter Arrives from Bohemia

My dearest wife,   *Kutna Hora, Bohemia, June 1875*

*It is impossible to express how
relieved I am to have received your
letter. I cannot thank God enough
that you not only arrived in America
safely but that you met such wonderful people as the Wolffs aboard ship.
However, I am not surprised that
these people have treated you kindly
and have come to look on you as a
loving daughter. It is your sweet and
tender nature that attracts people to
you.*

Bohemian postage stamp

*I would have you know many of your friends here in Kutna
Hora ask about you every week, and they wish me to say they
send their prayers for your safety and good health. It fills my
heart with peace to know you have friends in that faraway
place and that you will not face the coming winter alone.*

*My dear Antonia, the children include you in all their prayers
every day and want you to know they miss you. But also,
Anton says to tell you he is being strong and is making a great
effort to help me with the younger children. He wants you
to know he is being a good big brother. My darling, our son
wants you to be proud of him, and I tell him that you are.
Please write as often as you can and give my thanks to the
Wolff family for taking care of my precious wife and mother
of my children. Your family misses you, and we want you to
know we love you with all our hearts. Until we are together
again, know that we think of you every minute of every day.*

Your devoted and loving family, Wenceslaus, Anton,
Stanislaus, and little Anna

New York

As time passed, Antonia's new life slipped into a predictable pattern. In addition to her ongoing search for employment and assisting Margot with household tasks, once a week, she made use of her small candle and a precious piece of lettersheet to write to her husband and children. The lettersheet was unique in that she could write her letter on one side of the paper. Then, it folded to form its own envelope where she put the address and attached the postage.

She could only afford to write her parents once a month. The ink, wax seal, and lettersheet she brought from Bohemia had to last until she got a job. But once she had an income, the first luxuries she would buy would be more candles and writing materials.

As a guest, Antonia never failed to tell Peter and Margot how grateful she was to live in safety in their home and for their friendship. However, when she wrote to her husband and parents and shared the same message, she added side notes about her cramped living space and the uncomfortable settee she slept on. Yet in her optimistic fashion, Antonia's next sentence turned those hardships into blessings.

My Dears, I actually find the discomfort beneficial in that it
motivates me to rise early and continue my job search four days
a week.

In the same letter, she was also pleased to let Wenceslaus and her father know she had found a way to help offset the expense of her room and board. During her second Sunday with the Kraus', Margot and Peter tasted some of her baking at the Kraus and Wolff group lunch. Afterward, both the Kraus and the Wolff families agreed to purchase whatever supplies Antonia needed if she would continue to bake for them. Their reaction warmed Antonia's heart and she found that after a satisfying day of baking she loved to write letters to her family.

Now I can enjoy making fresh bread and pastries every Tuesday and Friday. Maria and Margot always split the cost of the baking supplies and put a little extra in the pouch for me. Though I tried to refuse their generosity, they insisted. Saying it was worth the coin not having to leave their homes to buy breads and that mine taste much better.

While I am baking, I allow myself to pretend I am at home baking for you, the ones I love. You are in my heart as I work. I miss you, and you continue to be my inspiration.

After Mass each week, the women divided up preparation tasks for the weekly gathering. Antonia's contribution was supplying her special sweet kolaches and rohlikys. This day of faith and sharing helped and hurt Antonia equally. The gifts of acceptance and love were priceless, yet the memories these family gatherings evoked were painful. Antonia crawled into bed on Sunday nights tormented by homesickness that bordered on grief. On these nights, she let silent tears flow unchecked until she gained freedom from her feelings in sleep.

It had been forty-five days of non-stop activity since Antonia's arrival and the commencement of her determined search for the right job. As the days fled, her failure to find work saddened her. She lost her appetite, and all she wanted to do was go to bed when she returned home. Margot and Peter worried and could see some of her despair. They made a point of insisting Antonia share their supper each night. Antonia understood they wanted to help her, but she had no desire to talk about the disappointments of the day over dinner. After helping clean up the dishes, Antonia would wish the couple good night and retire to her bedroom.

Most evenings, Antonia's grueling daily routine brought on deep sleep from exhaustion. Once in a while, unlike homesickness, loneliness escaped her control and chased away sleep. On those abysmal nights, she felt true moments of weakness. Only at these times did she allow herself to admit that New York and the incredible challenges she faced each day were frightening despite having good friends and protection. Yet even on those nights, fatigue would eventually shut down her mind, allowing her to rest.

Antonia learned something important about her faith. While physical rest brought relief to her body, Sunday Mass helped heal her spirit. The peace Antonia found through faith allowed her body to relax and rest. She began to understand it took both rest and faith to erase her deepest doubts and reignite her hope. Starting each week with Sunday Mass, Antonia's faith renewed her strength and made her feel ready to continue her search for the right job.

New York and a Village Named Morrisania

June was almost over, and still, Antonia had not found a suitable position. As she and Margot finished making dinner, they heard heavy footsteps coming up the staircase, and then, the apartment door burst open. Short of breath, Peter announced, "I just recommended Antonia for a full-time cigar roller job in a factory in Morrisania!"

Margot and Antonia shouted with delight.

"Oh, thank heaven," Margot said.

"Please tell me about it!" Antonia urged, excited to learn the details.

Holding up hands that were still dirty from cigar wrappers, Peter said, "Let me wash up and come to the table. Then, I'll tell you all about it."

Margot filled a plate and placed it in front of her husband. However, the women were too full of excitement and couldn't wait to hear the news. They forced Peter to begin his explanation between mouthfuls of food. Consequently, all Antonia gleaned from his garbled responses was that he had recommended her for a job like his, hand-rolling cigars. After dinner, Peter's explanations made more sense.

"Antonia, I met this foreman, Mr. Kulich, at the home of a mutual German friend. Margot, it was at Günter Schmitt's home a few months back—do you remember him?" She nodded but did not interrupt, wanting Peter to proceed with his story.

"During my conversation with Gunter, he introduced me to Mr. Kulich and said the man worked as a foreman at a cigar factory in Morrisania. Today, on my way home, I happened to recognize Kulich and Günter walking into the pub just down the block. I followed them into the pub to say hello. They asked me to sit down, and we started talking. During the conversation, Mr. Kulich mentioned his factory was going to start hiring more rollers. He said he wanted people who could speak both German and English, and I immediately thought of Antonia. Since I knew Kulich already, I felt comfortable recommending Antonia for a job." Looking at Antonia, he continued, "Mr. Kulich said he will see you at 10:00 a.m. at the factory on Monday of next week."

Antonia was speechless with excitement. Margot jumped in quickly to ask more questions. Peter answered those questions as fast as he could while the women cleaned up the kitchen. When they were finished, Peter asked the women to sit down with him. Putting on his most serious manner, Peter recommended several things to Antonia, and as she listened, her hope sored to new heights.

"When you go to see Kulich on Monday, I suggest that you introduce yourself in German and then finish your interview in English. As I said, the fact that you speak both languages is valuable to him. This fact will be important to any foreman or shift boss you might meet for the same reasons. I can't tell you anything about the wages or the shift hours that far from the city center. I'll find out what I can from the men I work with tomorrow."

By the next evening, none of the issues Peter cited before bothered Antonia one bit. Since the men in Peter's factory had no intention or desire to move to Morrisania, they told Peter everything they knew. The most important fact was that there were more than 100 cigar factories in Morrisania, and several of those factories were ready to hire full-time workers.

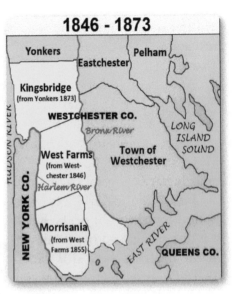

Nine of the original twelve counties of
New York State

Upon hearing this additional news, Antonia was confident one of them would hire her. Being very grateful for Peter's help, Antonia would start her search at the factory he recommended. If that one did not produce the right job for her needs, she would go from one factory to the next until she found one that did!

Feeling satisfied with her prospects for securing the right position, Antonia's mind jumped to her last problem—lodging. As she mentioned this, Peter smiled at his wife and then looked at Antonia, saying, "I know I didn't mention this yesterday, but I've important news about that subject too." Peter instantly had Margot and Antonia's undivided attention. "During my conversation with Mr. Kulich, I asked him about housing and rent."

"'Peter,' he said to me, 'rent's much cheaper in Morrisania than it is in New York City.' Then, I asked, 'What about safe lodging for a single woman?'

"And he replied, 'I actually know of several boarding houses near my factory with rooms for rent, which I can recommend.' Anticipating my next question, Kulich added, 'And there is no need to worry about crime. It's practically non-existent in those village neighborhoods.'"

Sitting across the table filled with joy, Antonia could not stop grinning at her delightful and wonderful friends. Overwhelmed with this incredible news, she reached across the table taking hold of Peter and Margot's hands so they formed a circle. Giggling and squeezing those hands, Antonia whispered, "Thank you. Thank you so much."

Antonia could hardly wait until Sunday, and after Mass, she told Johann and Maria about the factory job in Morrisania and her appointment with Mr. Kulich. Excited for their friend yet cautious, Johann and Maria insisted on taking Antonia to Morrisania for her interview. "We will pick you up on Monday morning at 6:30 a.m.," Johann said.

Johann and Maria were waiting in the wagon as Antonia walked out the door of the Kraus' apartment building. The sun was just rising, and the windows of the business were still dark. The only other people up were the lamplighters making their rounds turning off the gas street-lights. Antonia climbed up to the wagon's front seat with her friends. Johann clicked his tongue, snapped the reins on the horse's rump, and the Wolff's wagon rolled steadily through the empty streets of the city. The long ride gave Johann a chance to tell his wife and Antonia what he knew about Morrisania.

Governor Morris, source of the name Morrisania

"Antonia" said Johann, "you probably have not seen a map of New York. So, I'll tell you that Morrisania is located on the mainland of the state, a little east of the Harlem River across the Willis Bridge. The Willis area extends from First Avenue and East 124th Street in Manhattan to Willis Avenue and East 134th Street in the Bronx. The Willis Bridge is called a lift-gate bridge because it opens at its center. It rises up and out of the way, creating a clear passage, which allows cargo barges and tall chimney-stacked steam-ships to move up the river. In 1874, the villages of Morrisania,

West Farms, and Kingsbridge became part of New York when the city annexed the three large villages into the city's outer limits."

Willis Lift Gate Bridge, New York City, 1870s

Johann's information had been so interesting that before they realized it, the wagon was rolling through the streets of Morrisania. Johann pulled up in front of Kulich's factory, and Maria hugged Antonia, saying, "Don't be nervous—you will do fine." Then, she added, "Antonia, if you don't mind, to save time, Johann and I will evaluate the boarding houses and rental costs in the area while you are with the foreman."

Antonia smiled and accepted their generous offer. Just before the Wolff's shooed Antonia off to her interview, they asked, "If it's alright with you, we will select and hold the best place we find." Antonia waved and replied, "Yes, please do!"

Dearest Wenceslaus,   *Morrisania, June 1875*

Thank you for your wonderful letter, and I hope this letter finds you and the children well. I am in good health and have some exciting news to share.

Johann and Maria Wolff took me to a village outside New York City called Morrisania and waited for me while I interviewed for work. Yes, my love, I found a job in a cigar factory! We are one step closer to being together and fulfilling our dream of land in Nebraska.

Though I have been blessed to stay in the home of the Kraus' for more than a month, I have finally moved to my own one-room, cold-water flat. It is close to the factory so I can walk to work. I am so relieved that I now have a job and a place of my own.

I started working last week. The shifts are long. Twelve hours each day except for Sundays. Do not worry. You know I am an early riser, so I am lucky to start my work shift at 6:00 a.m., and I come home at 6:00 p.m.

The Wolffs helped me move into my flat two days before I started at the factory. The little room has a bed on one wall and a three-drawer clothing chest that sits next to the bed. I have a potbellied stove for heat, which also has a small flat top for heating water. There are clothing hooks on the wall by the door, and I share a toilet on the same floor as my room. I have a sink with running water, which is enough for cooking and cleaning. I feel fortunate I was able to get settled before my long workdays began as I have much to learn. I will set up a savings account at the bank with my first wages and will save every bit I can.

Johann and Maria were very generous, giving me some cookware and utensils for my kitchen and two wool blankets. I don't think I mentioned it before, but Margot Kraus taught me to knit in the evenings. Knowing I would not have much time to make my own, she made me some warm mittens and also gave me a sturdy cloak that she no longer had use for. She said it was moth-eaten, but I could find no holes in it. Margot also gave me two sets of sheets and another thick wool blanket. My darling, I am brought to tears by the generosity of our new friends. I cannot wait for you to meet them.

Our new village is on the outskirts of New York. It is much quieter here, and I feel safe. My neighbors tell me I need to start preparing for the cold season. Right now, the weather has been mild, mostly sunny. This week, it rained in the evenings.

I am quite tired when I return home from work, and I have been sleeping better since finding my job.

Dearest Wenceslaus, I find my eyes are growing heavy, so I will close for now. May God bless you, my love, and keep you and the children safe until I can hold you all in my arms once again.

I love you most tenderly, your devoted wife, Antonia

The New York Cigar Industry 1875, People vs. Automation

Peter's information had been correct. Antonia learned that in 1875 100 mid-size and two large cigar factories were operating right in Morrisania. In contrast, Peter and Margot Kraus lived close to 123 medium-size and 12 large cigar factories in the heart of New York

Morrisania area as viewed from Harlem, 1870s

City. In 1875, a typical work shift for hand-rolling cigars ranged as long as ten to 12 hours per day, and many factories operated six days a week. Antonia learned the combined factories within the state of New York manufactured millions of cigars for American use as well as for export. Antonia thought it an odd coincidence that just as industrial innovation had made handcrafted weaving obsolete in Bohemia, industrial innovation was causing problems for the American cigar makers too.

She had occasion to overhear the bosses talking. Four years earlier, an inventor had sold a semi-automated system for manufacturing cigars to a few of the larger companies. The medium and small-sized companies were afraid they would be forced to adopt this new and expensive system to stay competitive. Yet most of the smaller companies continued to resist the change. By stalling for time, the cigar manufacturers who refused to invest in technology unexpectedly profited. By waiting, time itself delivered an unpredicted solution to their problem.

1872 Flooded New York City with Bohemian Immigrants

Antonia learned from Peter that prior to her arrival in 1872, a substantial wave of immigrants from Bohemia arrived in New York. They provided the cigar-manufacturing companies with an eager source of low-cost labor. The factories that had resisted modernization not only avoided investing in new manufacturing changes, but they were also able to reduce wage costs. The factory management accomplished this by hiring laborers willing to work for very low wages.

It saddened Antonia to discover it was the arrival of some of her own countrymen that had limited her wage prospects in America. Because of them, low wages would lengthen the amount of time she would be separated from her family. After discovering this information, she remembered the time she had wasted due to indecision and regretted not coming to America sooner.

Considering what she knew now, the dinner conversations with Peter Kraus made more sense to Antonia. Peter had said his friends in the workplace were enraged with new arrivals for accepting subsistence wages that were well below the normal rate of pay for factory workers. When she questioned him about it, he explained this new rate was significantly less than the standard $2.00 per day gross income. He had bitterly complained that it was hard enough to make ends meet at $2.00 per day with all their expenses. He sure didn't need the added pressure of competition for his job either.

Since moving to Morrisania, Antonia had also overheard conversations on the factory floor. Disillusioned new arrivals complained they had falsely believed coming to America would make life easier. "Two dollars a day might have been an acceptable wage back home," an old woman sitting at the table next to hers complained in German. "But no one mentioned rent and food would be so high. Thieves are what they are! How can they charge 10% to 15% of an old woman's wages just to keep a roof over her head? Heaven forbid these food prices. It is plain robbery charging nineteen cents for a small pot of butter! For a few slices of bacon, they want ten cents, and they demand 15 cents for a dozen eggs! Heartless they are, asking ten to 15 cents for *one small fowl.* I could have bought a whole flock of chickens at home for that! How am I to eat with costs running over a dollar per day? Who can afford that? I can't—not on what this factory pays me!"

"Shush, Gunta," came urgent whispers from several directions. The elderly woman frowned but quit her muttering. She had been so loud Antonia was afraid one of the foremen might hear and ask her to interpret what the old woman had been saying.

Antonia's language skills had earned her a bit of favor with the supervisors. She regularly helped smooth out altercations between the workers who did not speak English, which helped keep production running smoothly. Nevertheless, she did not want to be put into a position of explaining what her fellow workers were saying. Thankfully, Gunta ceased her complaints before she drew any attention, and Antonia sighed quietly in relief.

She could not blame Gunta for her feelings; she understood these complaints all too well, keeping a strict eye on every cent she spent. The first 30 cents Antonia made each day paid her rent. After that, she had to make a dollar per day cover food, coal, wood, candles, clothing, postage, ink, lettersheet, and all the essentials she needed to live. Yet it was critical for her to hold back five to ten pennies per day to put toward her family's passage. That is why she and many people like her lived on bread alone with no meat for weeks at a time. When she had to do without, she found comfort in her thoughts. *I can wait. These pennies will help bring my family to me and fulfill our dream of owning land in Nebraska. With God's help, I can do this!*

The ever-growing labor pool in New York put the power in the hands of management. Desperate people signed on to work for nothing more than the cost of food and shelter. The definition of subsistence wages in 1875 was about $1.30 a day. The workers who did have jobs, particularly the ones who made better than subsistence wages, were afraid the bosses would try to replace them with cheaper labor. In reaction to that knowledge, Antonia learned to be quiet unless she was asked a question. She was never late to work, kept her mind on her own business and worked hard each day. On the job, she used her language skills to help her supervisors when asked, never complained, and carefully fulfilled the duties of her job. Antonia never missed a day of work. She understood excellent performance was the only way to protect her position and income.

New York Wages and Antonia's Goals

Antonia's objective to save the incredible sum of $60 in U.S. currency for the passage costs for her husband, three children, and two sisters-in-law was daunting.

Women's wages were lower than men's, and their jobs often came with longer work shifts. Subsistence wages for most jobs could be half the normal going pay rate. Subsequently, despite Antonia's dedication to saving money and the many hardships she personally faced to save every penny possible, it took two years to accumulate the required passage price for all six of her family members.

Antonia Concentrates on Facing One Day at a Time

Letters sent between America and Bohemia traveled slowly over the miles that separated Antonia and Wenceslaus. Her letters could be written quickly and delivered to a posting station in Morrisania, but then the waiting began. It had to be taken to the shipping dock in New York harbor. After that, depending on the mail-ship schedule, letters could sit at the dock a week or more. Once the mailbags were loaded on a steamship, it took another 14 days between American and European seaports. The final stage of a letter's journey, an overland delivery route of approximately 1,700 kilometers by coach was required before a letter could reach the towns of Kutna Hora, Caslav, or Nechanice. Antonia estimated the time to send a letter and be received was at least a month or more from the time it was posted. Yet these small fragments of news from home, which came as frequently as time and money permitted, were nearly all that kept her going.

My dearest wife,   *Kutna Hora, Bohemia, July 1875*

I pray this letter finds you well. First, congratulations on your job. I confess I do worry that you will not use enough coin to take care of yourself. I know you, Antonia. Once you set your mind to a goal, your thoughts only focus on that single purpose. Please, My Heart, for the love of your family and our future together, spend the coin you need to stay fed, warm, and healthy. America would have no meaning for us if we lost you. Now, I must beg your forgiveness for my need to say these things that weigh heavy on my mind and heart. It is the distance that preys upon my mind and that I cannot be there to take care of you myself. My brave wife, I do trust in your judgment, so I will say no more on this subject.

I am happy to tell you the cobbler business has been steady, and I have been able to start saving money for our business and our dream of land in Nebraska. My reward after a long day in the shop is to simply eat dinner with our children. Julie and Masy have been a great help, preparing meals and keeping the children busy. The house is rather crowded now, but the twins entertain the children and make them laugh. My sisters did find jobs for a few hours work each week, and they insist on using that money to help pay for food. They wanted to let you know they are doing some baking and take care of the laundry as well. We all go to the market once a week. But the

*girls enjoy making quick runs to the market for items we run
out of. Today, they brought home another handbill about land
in Nebraska. It made us all very excited to know you are so
close to this new land of our dreams. The bakery owners in the
market told my sisters to tell you all their customers miss your
rohlikys. But none of them could miss your baking as much as
I do.*

*Julie and Masy take turns watching our little Anna. She has
become a whirlwind. Even her brothers find it hard to keep up
with her. She plays in a corner of the shop in the afternoons,
and it is all Anton and Stanislaus can do to clean up after
their baby sister. She is curious and pulls leather off the shelves
to look at, and unspools my shoestring and then joyously scat-
ters my tools as soon as I turn my back. Anton calmly follows
her around re-rolling and storing the leather items while
Stanislaus retrieves my tools and puts them away for me. You
would be proud of how gentle they are with her.*

*All the children miss their mother, but our Anton is a wonder-
ful older brother and comforts his younger brother and sister.
I've heard him say that we will all be going to see Mama
very soon in America. Julie and Masy send their love, and my
dearest Antonia, we all want you to know we all believe in
you, and we are proud of you.*

*As for me, my darling, I so miss sleeping beside you or seeing
you come into the shop just to say hello. I miss your sassy grin
and the sparkle in your eyes when you have something on your
mind, something you cannot wait to tell me. I miss your tender
kisses. My dear wife, I miss all the small and wonderful things
that are you. I yearn for the day when we are all together
again, and I can wrap my arms around you and keep you safe.
Until then, I ask God to bless you and keep you safe for me and
never forget we love you more every day.*

A BOHEMIAN DREAM

Your devoted husband and loving children, Wenceslaus,
Anton, Stanislaus, and little Anna

P.S. Julie and Masy also send their love

Wenceslaus rarely mentioned the political situation at home or wrote of trouble. Her father and mother infrequently mentioned the unrest developing in Bohemia but did not dwell on the subject, and she was wise enough not to ask. It was easy enough to read between the lines, particularly when her father closed his letters by making it clear how glad he was that she was building a future for her family in America. She knew he missed her terribly, but his words clearly conveyed he'd rather miss his only daughter than have her suffering with them in Bohemia. Antonia forced herself not to worry about them; she had enough to deal with each day.

For a similar reason, Wenceslaus concentrated on encouraging Antonia. He shared his concern for her, wrote about their children, and wrote about how much he missed her and how they all longed to be with her again. In return, Antonia made an effort to be as cheerful in her letters to Wenceslaus as possible. She spent part of each letter explaining she felt safe, even on her own in a foreign place. She wrote about her daily tasks and how quickly she had made friends with community shopkeepers and the hawkers at the vegetable market, and even the neighborhood baker. In one letter, she wrote that in tiny ways, Morrisania reminded her of the life in Nechanice when she lived with her parents. Of course, she hoped writing about these inconsequential matters would keep Wenceslaus from worrying about her.

She never touched on the subjects that would hurt him, such as how hard she found the world without him or the difficulties she endured knowing he suffered as well. Instead, she focused on writing about how his love and that of her children meant everything. It was their love that helped her get through each day. Because of that love and their faith in her she was inspired to keep working hard toward their dreams. Antonia made an effort to close each of her letters with an encouraging thought:

My dearest, remember with each sunset we both suffer through alone: we are a little closer to being together again and achieving our wonderful dream of owning land in Nebraska.

Kutna Hora: Christmas, 1875

The holidays approached, and Master Cobbler Karella found it difficult to be cheerful, and desperately tried to hide that fact from his children. Having Masy and Julie living with them made everything easier. The girls never seemed to run out of joy. They were certainly filled with Christmas spirit. Julie baked cookies, and Masy made sweet breads with the children during the week. Each night, the twins made a game out of setting the table for dinner and cleaning up afterward.

Despite the extra house space their baggage required, when Masynda and Julienka moved to Kutna Hora, they refused to leave the marionettes or the theater behind. They also made Wenceslas promise to let them bring it all to America as well. As time passed, Julie and Masy put their theater and puppets to good use. His sisters were blessed with limitless imagination, and their stories and plays were wonderful.

To dispel the sadness, on many evenings, Masy and Julie would put on a show. Each story was different, and the girls developed several voices to create different characters that interacted with the puppets. The fun and magic always transported the onlookers to a happier place for a brief time.

Knowing the first holiday season they were facing without Antonia would be hard on everyone, the sisters planned a special puppet production for Christmas Eve. After supper, Masy and Julie sat the children down facing their little stage. Wenceslaus built up the fire in the fireplace at the back of the room and lit two candles, setting one on each side of the stage.

Wenceslaus mused, *I'm so happy they made a family tradition of using their marionettes to tell Christmas stories. It warms my heart that the presents I gave them so long ago brought the family such joy. Now, as grown women, they are sharing that joy with my children—what a gift.* Wenceslaus found himself as eager for the story as his children. His sister's plays often drew the audience into their performances in some charming and unexpected way, and each story usually contained a wonderful message.

Both sisters had collected the extra props they would need to play their roles, and one of those items was a wooden statue of St. Nicholas, which had been beautifully painted. In his right hand, he held wrapped gifts, and in his left, he held a lantern as though he searched for something or someone.

* * * The Play * * *

Standing to the left of the stage holding a candle, Masy opened the show with her narrator voice. "Good evening! Welcome one and all to the Karellas' annual Christmas show. The story is about to begin."

While everyone watched Masy ... Julie slid St. Nicholas into position, stage left. Then, she hurried to take her place with her dragon stage right.

Masy set her candle near the left side of the stage where it suddenly caste light on St. Nicholas.

Wooden image of St. Nicholas—
Christmas puppet show

The children gasped, pointing and whispering, "Look, it is St. Nicholas."

- Narrator: "As you know, St. Nicholas spends all year searching for good children who deserve a small gift at Christmas—a reward for being good helpers at home. One Christmas Eve very near our town, when it wasn't more than a tiny village, St. Nicholas found himself up in our mountains. He was high in the woods where the mist clings to the trees, and the woods were silent with a fresh blanket of snow.

- Narrator: "St. Nicholas stopped and listened, quite sure that he heard weeping. He looked into the darkness but could not see who was crying. As he prayed to discover who needed help, he saw a bright light had floated down from the treetops."

- Masy lowers her angel slightly left of center stage, and the children gasped again. "Look, it is little Guardian Angel Antonia," the children whispered in hushed voices.

Marionette, Guardian Angel Antonia—
Christmas puppet show

- Angel: "Yes, it is I, Guardian Angel Antonia."

- St. Nicholas: "Guardian Angel Antonia, do you know who is crying?"

- Angel: "Why yes, St. Nicholas, I do."

- St. Nicholas: "It sounds like a little boy. I can't see him; do you know where he is? Why is he so sad?"

- Angel: "S-h-h-h-h!" Angel Antonia put her right hand up to her lips and she whispered, "To see him, you must be very quiet. Now, look straight into the trees over there to the right." The Angel's left hand raised up and looked like it was pointing, and the children followed the hand pointing to the right.

3-H Daegan the Dragon, Christmas puppet show

- Julie had quietly lowered her dragon onto the far-right side of the stage while the children focused on Angel Antonia and St. Nicholas stage left. As they followed the direction Angel Antonia had pointed, suddenly the children gasped for a third time. Where only trees had been, they could now see a green, three-headed dragon sitting there.

- "He can make himself invisible," whispered the children. "That's why we couldn't see him before."

- St. Nicholas: "There you are! What is your name?"

- Dragon: "My name is Daegan," the three-headed Dragon replied, snuffling back his tears.

- St. Nicholas: "Thank you for letting me see you, Daegan. I only believed there were trees where you are now. How nice to see you! Please tell me, Daegan. Why are you so sad?"

- Dragon says with a sniff, "I went to the village to buy presents for my forest friends with silver and gold I had buried in this mountain."

- St. Nicholas: "I don't understand. Why would that make you sad? It's very kind of you to buy gifts to make your friends happy."

- Dragon: "No, you don't understand." Dragon's heads drooped to the forest floor. "I wanted to buy honeycomb for Bjorn, but when my first head breathed out the word *honey,* a flame leapt from my tongue and started the shop-keeper's broomstick on fire. With my second head, I tried to blow the first fire out and only made the flames grow higher! When I ran into the street shouting *help! Help!* with my third head, I snarffled just a bit and poof! The roof of the store was on fire! The villagers chased me away even though I meant no harm. They would not listen; they were too alarmed. Now I have no gifts for my forest friends, and I fear Christmas is near. No matter what I try, my fire won't stop, so I cry." He sobbed.

- St. Nicholas: "That is a sad problem. Oh, what can we do?"

- Angel: "Pssst, I have an idea." Angel Antonia called out as she waved her arm at St. Nicholas. She flew over to him. The children could see her tiny wings as she moved her hand up by St. Nicholas' head to whisper something in his ear.

- St. Nicholas: "Do you think *He* could? You will go and see if *He* would? If He can, may I help with the plan?"

- Angel Antonia nods her woodenhead up and down. She points at Daegan and said, "You wait with Daegan, and I will go and see." Then, Angel Antonia floated away up past the trees and out of sight.

- Daegan the Dragon flew over to Saint Nicholas, and they stood side by side.

- Angel Antonia floated back down and announced with happiness, "The Lord said yes! He will do it! But we are to remember to make a dragon understand requires both time and rhyme."

- St. Nicholas clapped his hands with joy and said, "Daegan, we have a plan. Because you were willing to share your silver and gold, your heart will never be cold. Now, open your mouths wide, and God will blow out the fire inside."

- Daegan readied himself to do as Angel Antonia and St. Nicholas instructed.

- Angel Antonia, "Open mouth one!" The angel yelled and Daegan's first head quaked and swayed and then dropped to the floor. "Open mouth two!" Daegan's second head quaked and swayed and then dropped to the floor. "Open mouth three!" Daegan's third head quaked and swayed and then dropped to the floor.

- Then, all of Daegan's heads rose up in the air. He shook his body, and then released a shout, "Thank the Good Lord! My fire, it's out! I can't feel it! Not even in my snout!"

- St. Nicholas: "Now, you must be quick and fetch your gifts before your fire is reborn on Christmas morn."

- Angel Antonia: "Time to go before the bells chime, to bring good cheer without fear. Jesus is smiling—he loves your kind heart; he's granted you time, so please depart! Be quick with your shopping and get back to the forest without stopping." Angel Antonia waved as Daegan flew up and out of sight.

- Angel: "I have one more request, St. Nicholas."

- St. Nicholas: "How may I help?"

- Angel: "I know three children whose names are Anton, Stanislaus, and Anna. They have a wonderful papa named Wenceslaus and two aunties named Julie and Masy. They all miss someone very dearly, and her name is Antonia. She lives far away in America. When you see her tonight, will you tell her that her family has been very good and that they miss her?"

- St. Nicholas: "I most certainly will, and I will also tell her that they will all see her soon in the light of the Christmas star under God's full moon."

- Angel Antonia turned to look at the children in the room. Her warm brown eyes glowed green-gold in the candlelight.

Suddenly, Wenceslaus realized they looked like his Antonia's eyes. He knew they were made of glass, but they looked so real at this moment in this light. Perhaps that is what had attracted him to this little angel so many years ago. Drawn back to the present, he heard the Angel ask another question.

- Angel: "Now, children, I will see your mama tonight in her dreams. Is there anything you would like me to say as I pray for God to bring her blessings?"

Leaning forward, Anton whispered, "Yes, please tell Mama I'm being a good big brother as she asked me to."

Clasping his hands together, Stanislaus whispered, "Please tell Mama that I'm being good, too, and helping Papa with little Anna."

From behind the children, their papa's voice whispered, "Please tell Mama we love her and miss her, and we are sending her warm Christmas hugs and kisses from each of us."

- Angel Antonia nodded her head and said, "Remember, no matter how sad you are, a prayer sent to heaven with a little faith has the power to flower in most unexpected ways. The Christmas star is near, and I can hear angels singing. Hallelujah, Jesus is born on Christmas morn, and *He* gives a gift to bring you cheer. *He* has promised that I, your

Angel Antonia's eyes, Christmas puppet show

guardian angel, will always be near." With that, Guardian Angel Antonia flew out of sight.

- St. Nicholas: "Christmas blessings to one and all; I have places to be and gifts to haul. Be good, dear children, and hurry to sleep. It's very important that you don't peek. My job is clear; I must bring you cheer. And so, I'll start in your heart. I'm weaving dreams into moonbeams that float straight into your soul, dreams to warm you without using coal. You'll dream of one you miss, your mama, as she sends you her sweet Christmas kiss."

With the word kiss, Masy and Julie blew out the candles near the stage

Sitting in the room with shifting shadows cast by flickering flames, all was quiet except the sputtering logs burning in the fireplace. The children had been totally entranced. They never noticed the strings that moved the angel's head, hands, feet, and wings. Nor the fact that St. Nicholas never moved, and they truly believed that Daegan the green, three-headed dragon, had been invisible and then magically let them see him.

The children cheered and clapped their hands. After drinking a glass of warm milk, they hurried to their beds. With a kiss and hug for each child, their papa left them to their dreams while he walked down the hall with his sisters. Leaving them at the door of their room, he said, "Mama and Papa will be here tomorrow." Kissing each of his sisters on the forehead, he said, "Thank you. Your play was wonderful. May God keep bringing more sweet ideas to your imaginations."

Kutna Hora, Bohemia, 1875

Touched by his children's faith and his sister's heartwarming and gentle imaginations, he sat at his desk in the stillness of the night to write by candlelight.

My Dearest Heart,   *Christmas Eve 1875*

I wish you had been here tonight. My eyes filled with tears as my sisters weaved magical moments with their puppets. I will do my best to recreate the enchantment they spun. The very air that surrounded us was filled with your presence …

First Christmas in America, Christmas Eve Night, 1875

The Kraus and Wolff families insisted that Antonia spend Christmas in the city with them. Everyone would attend Christmas Mass together, and then they would share a traditional German Yuletide feast.

Knowing how devastated they would feel without their families, they would not let Antonia refuse. Johann drove the wagon out to Morrisania to pick her up on Christmas Eve. Upon their return, the women kept Antonia's hands busy baking while they chatted and prepared the food for a late supper and the Christmas day feast.

The baking had distracted Antonia with something she loved to do. Later that evening, she even smiled and made an effort to take part in the dinner conversation. No one said anything about how often her eyes got teary nor mentioned the times she walked away to catch her breath to keep herself from crying. The family joy she was sharing hurt and helped in equal measure. Before midnight, Antonia went home with the Kraus', staying with them as she used to do.

Christmas morning, Peter and Margot noticed Antonia wore an unusual smile at breakfast. It was a relief to see. Antonia had been so sad when they had said goodnight to her. "What has you smiling so?" Margot asked softly.

"I had a wonderful dream," replied Antonia slowly. "I can't recall anything clearly, except Wenceslaus and my children were there and Julie and Masy too. Everyone was having fun, and they sent me kisses and hugs and told me they loved me and missed me. I don't know how, but it felt so real, and it still does. I'm just thanking God for it. To feel my family's love and the warmth of their care is the best Christmas present I could ever receive."

Kutna Hora, Late April 1877

Wenceslaus was thinking about Antonia's last letter as he worked late in the shop. She had hinted she would be sending news about a wonderful surprise for everyone very soon. He had watched and laughed as Julie and Masy danced around the kitchen shouting, "We are going to America! That's the surprise! We know it is, Wenceslaus!" He believed they were right and had been working late ever since, trying to put as much money away each week, as possible.

Julie caught a spring flu several weeks back, and he told her to rest in bed. When she developed a slight fever and a cough, he told Masy to concentrate on taking care of her sister. "You both need to be strong and healthy when it is time to travel." Wenceslaus had told them.

In the meantime, Anton happily took charge of the younger children. With Anton's help Wenceslaus made dinner and put everyone to bed each evening. Tonight, as he often did after the children were asleep, he would go back to the shop and work late. As Wenceslaus finished assembling a shoe the lamplight drew his attention to Antonia's latest letter lying on the workbench. He began mentally listing what the family should take with them to America. He had a strong feeling the news they were waiting for would come very soon. Otherwise Antonia would not have mentioned a surprise.

Suddenly the door leading to the house swung open and banged against the wall. He looked up and saw Anton rush into the room. "Papa, Aunt Masy needs your help now!" Anton shouted with fear in his voice. "What is the matter son?" Wenceslaus asked, immediately concerned as he set down his tools. "Aunt Julie can't breathe and Aunt Masy says to go get the doctor right away!" Anton explained, as he began to cry.

Wenceslaus rushed to the shop door leading to the street, and said, "Anton, lock the door behind me. I'll bring the doctor back into the house through the kitchen." Then hurried out the door and disappeared down the dark street.

America, First Day of June 1877

The season of summer had nearly arrived once again in Morrisania. Yet between the factory buildings, in shadowed streets, a damp chill still clung to the air after sunset. Nearly two years had passed for Antonia in America. During all that time, winter, spring, summer, and fall each of those days had seemed much the same to her. But not today. Antonia did not notice the chill as the sky darkened, she was too nervous and excited. Tonight, she would write the most important letter of her life, both as a mother and a wife.

Shortly after sundown, Antonia approached her neighborhood and encountered Mrs. Jacobson, the woman who collected her rent each month. The kind old lady smiled, waving enthusiastically, so Antonia was unable to avoid stopping and talking with her.

"I am so glad to see you. I have a letter for you that came two days ago. I am sorry, dearie. I have been so busy that I forgot to bring it up and put it under your door. I do have it with me now, though." As Mrs. Jacobson rambled on, she reached into her skirt pocket to retrieve the letter she mentioned and handed it to Antonia.

Instantly, Antonia recognized Wenceslaus' handwriting and said, "Thank you. I appreciate you collecting it for me. It always seems to be so late by the time I get home. Your thoughtfulness is a blessing."

Mrs. Jacobson felt pleased to be able to lift at least one burden off the younger woman's shoulders. Mrs. Jacobson did hope it was happy news. Antonia appeared to be sad most of the time. But not tonight. She seemed to glow with excitement, so Mrs. Jacobson asked, "What has caused such a radiant smile on your face? Surely, it is more than receiving a letter."

Antonia could not hold her emotion back. She had to share her delight with someone and whispered, "I have done it! I have saved enough money to send for my family. I need to write them a letter tonight, but I fear my hands are shaking so in my excitement that I will not be able to put the words to paper."

Mrs. Jacobson sweetly replied, "Oh, God be praised my dear. How wonderful for you." Then, the woman continued to chatter on endlessly. Trying not to be rude, Antonia finally begged her pardon, said a quick goodnight, and hurried up to her flat.

Filled with anticipation, she had no appetite. Instead, she struck a match and lit her precious candle. Before the match burned out, she placed it under the stack of dry kindling she always prepared in her potbellied stove. Flames leaped up immediately eating hungrily into the dry wood. Lastly, she tossed three pieces of coal on top of the snapping wood as the fire burned hot. Settled comfortably on her bed, Antonia opened Wenceslaus' letter.

My dear and beloved wife,   *Kutna Hora, July 1877*

Misfortune has struck with a heavy hand. It grieves me to burden you, but I cannot withhold this information. Let me begin by saying this summer has been rainy and cold, and many people fell ill in Kutna Hora. This region was hit with a particularly contagious influenza that brought on fevers, a cough, and made breathing difficult in the extreme.

Do not worry, Antonia; our children are fine and healthy. This tragedy concerns my twin sisters, Julienka and Masynda, who have been so good, helpful, and kind in your absence.

In recent months, your letters hinted that you would have a surprise coming to us very soon, which made my sisters giddy with excitement. They were sure it had something to do with making the ocean voyage and were exhilarated by their good fortune. They were filled with excitement at the idea of accompanying the children and me to America. My darling, they have missed you as much as we have and longed to be with you again.

With great sadness, I write to say Julienka contracted an influenza in April, and Masynda took care of her. Julienka died in the middle of May. Shortly after her twins' death, Masynda fell ill herself and died at the beginning of June. The doctor did not think Masynda was sick enough to die, but I am not surprised she did. She came into the world minutes after her sister and lived every day of their life together. I believe Masynda died of a broken heart more than the illness. She was an identical twin and had never felt alone as most people do. Julienka was like Masynda's own reflection. Like two halves of the same person. When her reflection disappeared, Masynda just faded away too.

My heart, my brave, brave darling, I am profoundly sorry you worked so hard for my sisters' passage, and now, it is all for naught. I am sorry that I will not be bringing the helpers I promised you. I miss them very much, but they came into the world together and left the world together. My heart tells me this is what they wanted; I don't think my parents will ever recover from losing both of them at the same time.

Please know that your children and I are praying for their souls and for you to be strong and not give up. We need you more than ever and want only to be with you again. Close your eyes, and you will find us in your heart. Please be strong for us. We love you and need you and miss you so very much. We wait, always hoping and looking forward to hearing from you, My Heart.

Your loving family forever, Wenceslaus, Anton, Stanislaus, and little Anna

As Antonia read the words, tears filled her eyes and then fell unchecked dropping onto the letter that shook in her hands. Under the assault of her teardrops, the carefully inked words began to bleed, one into the other, as their message cut deeply into Antonia's heart. Wenceslaus' younger sisters had been so lovely and full of joy two years ago.

Antonia had sailed away innocently believing they would not be parted for long. *It hurts to have been so close,* her mind wailed as she pinched out the fire on her candle. *One more month—that's all the time I needed to bring them to safety. Why could I not have achieved my goal a few months sooner? Now, my husband's sisters, my sweet little sisters, will never sail to America.* Filled with anguish and drowning in goodbyes left unsaid, she was tortured by the knowledge she would never see those beautiful young faces again. In pain, Antonia collapsed on her bed, sobbing in the dark and eventually fell into an exhausted sleep.

Antonia woke early as was her custom. Her eyes felt swollen and sore. Her body felt cold and stiff from sleeping on top of the blankets. She briefly wondered why she had slept in her clothing. Then, her eyes came to rest on Wenceslaus's crumpled letter still clutched in her hand. Memories flooded her thoughts. She could not allow sorrow to overwhelm her again.

She had to hear the words, so she said, "No, Antonia! This will only make you weak! You cannot change what is done; there will be time to help Wenceslaus grieve later. Right now, you must be strong. You cannot let this terrible news break your resolve!"

With that said, Antonia got off the bed and crossed the room. She lit her candle, quickly built a new fire in her stove, and sat down at the small table. The letter she wrote to her family was bittersweet. There were a few words of comfort, explaining how sorry she was to have failed his sisters by not getting the money to them sooner. But mostly, she wrote about the joy of her accomplishment.

Wenceslaus, the untimely loss of your beautiful sisters only reinforces the uncertainty of life. I urgently request that you and the children be prepared to travel to America no later than mid-September 1877. Look for the money soon. I will send the bank draft after I meet with the banker in two days.

She closed this important note by once again stating the urgency she felt about getting her family out of Bohemia and to America as quickly as possible. She expressed her love and devotion and also said she would be waiting anxiously with great joy for word on their pending arrival.

Bohemia—Caslav and Nechanice

It had been difficult preparing for this trip. Miklaus Karella felt old as he helped his wife into the wagon. The Nemecs would meet up with them in the village of Cirkvice, and they would all travel to Kutna Hora together. Both wagons carried precious gifts that would be packed to go with Wenceslaus to America.

Miklaus and Eliska Karella had thanked Nicolas and Marketa Nemec for staying with them after they buried Julienka and Masynda barely two months back. They would always mourn the loss of their daughters, but the four of them understood it was imperative to set all grief aside at this time. They needed to focus on the memories they could make now. These grandchildren were the one constant joy in all their lives. Every moment spent with them was priceless, and these precious moments would have to sustain them for the rest of their lives.

As Nicolas helped Marketa into their wagon, she sobbed, "Time! Nicolas, we are out of time!" Nicolas nodded at his wife's comment as he snapped the reins across the Percheron's rump. The huge horse understood the signal from the reins and started the wagon wheels rolling with an easy tug.

"Marketa," Nicholas said in a sad voice but then stopped talking. Once the wagon moved out onto the road, he went on to say, "I understand what you are saying. It's nearly impossible not to dwell on the fact that we are going to be forced to say farewell. But we must try to appreciate being able to say goodbye. We know they will live. Imagine how Miklaus and Eliska feel at this moment."

Marketa nodded as silent tears dripped from her eyes. "Yes, you are right." She cried softly. "Our family's greatest treasures live, and I will be happy with that gift, even though this will be the last time we see any of them."

Kutna Hora, a Farewell Visit

Kutna Hora's Master Cobbler finished his work early and took pleasure in preparing dinner for his children. As he worked, he was reminded of how much he missed his sisters, especially at dinnertime. Masy and Julie had made dinner and chores so delightful and fun. Streaks of light from the setting sun shone through the kitchen window. Wenceslaus glance at his timepiece. He was expecting his and Antonia's parents to arrive within the hour. It grew dark as the Karella family finished their dinner, and still, his parents had not arrived. Trying not to worry, Wenceslaus put his children to bed a little early and read them a story before he kissed each of them goodnight. Sitting a little longer with his eldest son, Wenceslaus spoke softly so he would not wake the others. He whispered, "Son, I know you are a little young for this, but would you like to stay up with me while I wait for your grandparents to arrive?"

"Yes, Papa, I would. I know it is time to say goodbye, and I promise I will not cry when it is time for them to leave."

"My son, it is never wrong for a man to cry. Particularly when you are saying goodbye to someone you love."

"Then, why did you tell us not to cry when Mama left?" the boy asked wide-eyed.

That innocent question brought tears to Wenceslaus' eyes, and blinking rapidly, he hoarsely replied, "Because we knew we would be seeing her again."

Anton's eyes widened with alarm as comprehension hit him, and then the boy nodded gravely in such a wise, adult fashion that it squeezed Wenceslaus's heart. He hugged his son quickly and then leaned back looking into his son's eyes and whispered, "Yes, I see you understand the difference. So, it will be alright to shed a few tears when we say goodbye to your grandfathers and grandmothers, yes?"

"Yes, Papa," the boy whispered back, "and I will tell the little ones it is alright for them to cry too." They both heard horses outside at the same time. Father and son stood up. Anton took hold of his father's hand and together they walked to the front door.

Bohemia, Packing Day in Kutna Hora

It had been an emotional visit on many levels, particularly the long talk with his father. Images of early morning fog and hunting birds in wet fields filled his mind as he carefully wrapped the long gun in oiled cloth to protect it from the corrosive sea air.

Long gun, 1800s rifle

Wenceslaus had tried to refuse this gift, but his father insisted, saying, "It would be of better use in America. I'm an old man now. I don't use it enough to justify keeping it anymore. So, please take it with you."

After that statement, Wenceslaus acquiesced, saying, "Thank you, Papa. I remember you taught me how to shoot with this rifle. You had me carry it when I became a journeyman and started traveling the road alone." Lifting the rifle, Wenceslaus chuckled softly, recollecting how the hefty weapon had knocked him flat on his backside the first time he had fired it.

One whole trunk was needed to pack the gifts for Antonia from her mother. In addition to those things, Wenceslaus had been entrusted with a few extremely special family items. When Mother Nemec handed him the poppy seed masher and a small wooden box with a hinged lid, she explained, "This is no ordinary treasure chest. It contains the best secret recipes of the Nemec family bakers, and here is a letter for my daughter as well. I

Poppy seed masher / grinder

trust these things will help our Antonia remember her childhood at home in Nechanice." Suddenly, his mother-in-law's voice quivered as a sob escaped her throat before she could leave the room, and Wenceslaus watched her go through watery eyes.

On their final evening together, the adults held the children long into the night even after they had fallen asleep. Wenceslaus found a lump in his throat each time he tried to find words to thank his relatives. Not only for the wonderful gifts they were sending to America but also for a lifetime of support and love. This was a family he and Antonia had always been able to depend on. Even now at this late hour, they bravely continued to try to make this parting as painless as possible. Sitting before a warm fire, they spoke of old memories.

Unexpectedly, Wenceslaus felt the need to apologize to his parents for past sins he believed no one knew about. While making his confession, Wenceslaus received a few indulgent smiles and nods from his parents. By their actions, he concluded his parents had known all along about the pilfering he had done in his father's workshop.

As a parent himself, he now realized what they had accomplished without reprimand. They had trusted him, believing with time he would see the difference between right and wrong. They granted him the opportunity to develop a conscience and choose to become a good boy and a better man. Only at the moment of his apology did he fully come to appreciate the depth of faith they had in him. Lastly, one after another, each family member recalled a particularly beautiful moment or experience they had shared, and everyone shed many tears before dawn.

America, and Antonia's Daily Struggles

Antonia's anxiety regarding her family was only part of what was weighing heavily on her mind. In addition to the personal strain, Antonia faced local turmoil at her job due to the ongoing battle between American and Cuban cigar companies. American manufacturers were struggling to keep American smokers exclusively purchasing American-made products.

To remind buyers to support American companies, the union affiliated with Antonia's employer provided labels that were to be affixed to every box of cigars they produced. It was a visible means of informing consumers of the product's origin. In the 1870s, even a company as important as Straiton & Storm was not recognized as the face of the products it produced.

For example, Straiton & Storm owned three large factories in New York and employed more than a thousand cigar-rolling workers. This company produced hundreds of famous cigar brands. The factory itself was not acknowledged; it was their products and the individual product lines that

Hands of a woman hand rolling cigars

made the impression on a buyer's mind. A man didn't say, "Give me a Straiton & Storm cigar." He would say, "Give me a Robert Burns or an Owl." Factory identity did not exist for most American cigar companies; conversely, this type of recognition was extremely important to the Cuban

Old family cigar box—from a garage sale found and saved by N. Mathis

companies who competed fiercely for American clientele.

Antonia could not do much about how her company fought its competitive battles, but she did make sure the union labels were prominently displayed on each box she filled with her hand-rolled cigars. Not because she was told to do so but because it also helped protect her job and the income she so desperately needed for her family.

America Symbolizes Freedom

Men and women from all over the world were becoming new American citizens. Embracing the ideals of freedom, they were choosing to become what they wanted to be. These were men and women who did not fear hard work and often elected a path of self-sacrifice to secure a better future. They were eager to build a different world than the one they had come from and achieve what had been impossible for their parents.

1880—American cigar industry union-made label

For example, a commoner in Europe could not own land. In America, for an immigrant who had been a commoner in Europe, to own land, was hugely symbolic. They were rejecting the old laws of Europe that had prevented them from bettering themselves. Land, like personal rights and protection under the law, had been reserved exclusively for aristocrats. The titled elite and royals who lived and ruled by birthright could purchase or inherit land and wealth, and they could gain titles through marriage.

In America, the class of their birth no longer limited men. They were free to pursue opportunities, build their futures, and achieve dreams. The ideals of freedom started an additional revolution in the women of America. Women also sought to breakdown limitations based on gender.

Cigar companies saw this awakening population of females as a viable resource. Women represented a new category of consumers, a new market that could boost product sales and make their factories more profitable.

In Europe, smoking had been traditionally only a man's prerogative. To achieve their goal of capturing this new market, cigar companies designed advertising campaigns for print media, which encouraged women to break free from old European taboos. Leading newspapers and magazines featured images of beautiful, fashionably dressed women smoking cigars.

America was the place people came to be free. That notion not only appealed to men, but it also spoke directly to women who yearned for more personal liberty. Many women were fascinated by the temptation of taking up a habit previously reserved exclusively for the male gender. One could even say they were demonstrating their emancipation and equality with men by choosing to smoke and doing so in their homes and in public.

Lotta Crabtree smoking cigar, 1868

CHAPTER 5

A Family Reunited
in America

Antonia's hand shook slightly as she signed the bank papers.
Mr. Charlton, the bank manager, was a friend of Johann
Wolff. At her meeting today, Mr. Charlton personally took charge
of her transaction and of sending the money draft directly to
Wenceslaus in Kutna Hora. It had taken slightly over two years
to reach this moment. She had accomplished a nearly impossible
task, and finally, it was a reality.

Depiction of bank draft from a New York bank, 1800s

Walking back to the Wolff's apartment, Antonia realized she had learned a lot about herself. It was about so much more than earning a living, taking care of herself, or saving the passage money for her husband and children. God had given her a test of faith and opened her heart to friendship. She had experienced real growth in personal strength and character and learned what real friendship is. At this moment, the Wolff and Kraus families waited to help her celebrate this victory.

New York City End of July 1877

The bank was only a few blocks from the Wolffs' butcher shop. As Antonia turned the corner, she could see the sign hanging above the door. The silhouette of a black Wolf with the words **Meat Butcher** below it. Antonia passed by the store entrance and climbed the stairs leading to the Wolff's apartment above the butcher shop. Her eyes moistened briefly as thoughts of Wenceslaus' twin sisters entered her mind. Knocking on the door and shaking her head to dislodge those images, Antonia thought, *I'll put that extra money to good use, and I will ask the Wolffs to help me.*

As Antonia finished that thought, the door swung open, and she received warm greetings and hugs from everyone. "How did it go, Antonia? Did you have any problems?" Johann asked cheerily. "I could have gone with you."

Antonia knew her friends had been just as anxious for this moment as she had. Smiling in response to Johann's concern, she replied, "Thank you, Johann. You did more than enough by introducing me to Mr. Charlton. Not to mention, you also taught me what I needed to know about making deposits and checking my account balance. I assure you—everything went very well today."

"Johann, shall we all sit down so everyone can hear what Antonia has to say? She can tell us about her bank visit while we eat lunch," Maria Wolff suggested.

With hearty agreement, everyone gathered around the table. After saying grace and the food was dished up, Antonia told them about her meeting with Mr. Charlton and that the money was on its way to Bohemia.

"Congratulations, Antonia! We are so happy for you. What are your plans now? Is there anything special we can help you prepare for your family before they get here?" Margot Kraus asked.

"As a matter of fact, there is," Antonia replied quickly. She had everyone's attention after making that statement. "You all know I saved extra money for Wenceslaus' sisters." Silently, all the people at the table nodded their heads. No one wanted to talk about those sad deaths, so Antonia hurried on with her request. "I want to find better lodging. With the extra money I have now, I hope to rent a place with plenty of space for the children to play and room enough to give me and Wenceslaus a little privacy. Will you help me do this?" Antonia asked.

"We would love to help," replied the Wolffs.

"We want to help too!" replied the Kraus'.

Johann took charge by saying, "Now, Peter, neither you nor Margot has free time during the day. You two can help once we find this new place for Antonia. I am sure whatever place we find will need some work. How does that sound?" Johann's suggestion met with approval from the Kraus'.

During the rest of the meal, Antonia's friends held a lively conversation about housing. She smiled, happy to listen to all their suggestions. Antonia felt secure in the knowledge her friends would make sure she found the best rental at the best price.

Morrisania, New York, August 1877

Now that the bank draft was on its way to Bohemia, Antonia found it hard to wait. All her thought and energy had been poured into achieving this goal and getting to this moment. Having accomplished it, she had to tell herself to be patient. And she had to keep repeating it to herself because her body did not seem to be listening. *Antonia, be patient! The money will not reach them for a month or more. Wenceslaus needs time to finalize travel plans… get all our belongings packed… and prepare the children for this momentous move.* Antonia always tried to avoid what came next. But the thoughts filled her mind anyway and made a sob catch in her throat. She closed her eyes and finished the thought—*And Wenceslaus has to say goodbye to our parents.* There was nothing she could do about the pain. It had to be endured before her family would be free to come to her. It was an impossibly difficult situation, wanting her husband and children with her, yet knowing it was going to break their parents' hearts.

They certainly understood, just as she did, this would probably be the last time they saw any of their children or grandchildren. Unfortunately, Antonia's thoughts regarding her parents immediately brought on a bout of tears and made her anxious all over again. After spending an entire day of wavering between hope and sorrow, Antonia finally scolded herself by yelling out loud, "Antonia! It is pointless to waste your time being so emotional. Do something!"

Each night after Antonia's work shift ended, she turned to knitting mittens or scarves. Once her knitting projects were completed, she turned to mending or patching her clothing. When those chores began to drive her completely senseless, she took to scrubbing the floor of her little flat. Despite her best efforts and using logic every waking minute, the waiting seemed endless.

It was the end of another long and frustrating day as she headed home at sunset. Almost two months had gone by since Antonia sent the money. Turning the corner leading to her street, she saw Mrs. Jacobson standing in front of her building waving a packet in the air.

As she drew near, Antonia heard the woman shouting, "Hurry, you have a packet from your family!" Generally, after a workday, Antonia did not have the energy to run anywhere. But run she did and grabbed the packet out of Mrs. Jacobson's hand. Before the older woman could say a word, Antonia shouted, "Thank you. I'll tell you the news later. I must go now!" Antonia kept running and did not hear Mrs. Jacobson's grunt of disapproval for being dismissed so abruptly.

Antonia did not stop until she was up the stairs and through her door. Once she was inside, she leaned against the door to close it. Her chest heaved and her heart pounded as she worked to catch her breath. With shaking hands, she turned the packet over and broke the seal.

A steamship advertisement fell out of the packet onto the floor, but Antonia managed to grab the letter as it slid free of the envelope. Bending down to retrieve the item that had fallen to the floor, she recognized it for what it was. It was a departure and arrival schedule with a date circled; it was an arrival date!

Tears of joy filled her eyes, and holding the papers to her heart, she closed her eyes and softly said, "They are coming! Thank You, Lord! Thank you for bringing them to me so quickly!"

1800s steamship advertisements

The following week was filled with anticipation, but now, time was something she could measure. Antonia planned to use it to her advantage. Fulfilling her six-day workweek at the factory, she spent her next day off making a trip into the city to visit the Kraus and Wolff families. Antonia's friends were almost as excited as she was about the impending arrival of her family. They were thrilled Antonia was ready for them to help hunt for a new place to live.

While Antonia spent her day at the factory, the Wolffs found a wonderful apartment located only three blocks away from Antonia's factory. It was a house converted to a rental building, and

Johann struck a terrific deal with the owner on behalf of Antonia. She would manage the rental rooms, and her rent would be free.

"It will be easy for you," Johann told Antonia. "There are only three rooms located on the building's second floor, and you will collect the monthly rent for each of them. A few secondary tasks will fall to you as manager. The first is to notify the owner of any problems you have with the building. Secondly, when needed, you will be expected to show the rooms to new renters. Fortunately, the second floor has its own outside staircase. That means your renters will not be walking through your first-floor apartment.

Antonia reached up and hugged the big man and then hugged Maria. She could hardly believe her good fortune and agreed instantly even before Johann had finished his explanation. Laughing with relief and excitement, Antonia said, "I know you, Johann. You will have looked at this situation from all sides; I trust your judgment. Thank you so much!"

"Wait! Let me finish there is more good news! The whole ground level will be your living space, Antonia. The rent for this apartment is part of your monthly compensation, plus you will receive a small salary as well. There will also be an additional bonus for you each month that all the apartments remained rented," Johann concluded with satisfaction. Antonia wore a happy grin and could not find enough words to thank the Woffs.

Johann, Maria, Peter, and Margot helped clean Antonia's new apartment and worked alongside their friend to make each room feel as homey as possible. The space seemed enormous. It had two practical-sized bedrooms, an entry, and a parlor that connected to the dining area adjacent to the kitchen. In the kitchen, there was a real cooking stove with an oven, running water, and down the hall from the kitchen, was an enclosed toilet.

The house also came furnished with a plank-style trestle table with ample bench seating. It would fit five comfortably, but there was also room for several guests. Where the entry, parlor, dining, and kitchen areas connected, it created an open floor plan that made a good-sized living space where the whole family could gather. There was even an extra pot belly stove for heating on the far wall of the parlor room, across from the main entrance into the house.

Tickled at discovering a third small room behind the kitchen, Margot said, "Oh, come look, Antonia! This would be perfect for your baking pantry." The wistfulness in Margot's voice revealed how much she missed Antonia's weekly baking.

Antonia smiled at her friend but shook her head. "I think I shall let Anton decide. He is quite grown up now. Perhaps he will want to have his own space away from his younger brother and sister. I can certainly make do with the spaciousness within my new kitchen."

Everyone nodded agreement at that remark, as Antonia's kitchen was larger than either of the Wolffs' or the Kraus' cooking spaces. Inspired by her new surroundings, Antonia insisted on hosting a Sunday gathering for the following week. A way to say thank you to everyone for their help, and she promised to bake all their favorite sweet rolls, bread and rohlikys. The agreement to her suggestion was immediate and extremely enthusiastic.

Between work, settling into the house, and learning as much as she could about the current tenants, Antonia kept herself too busy to think. She hoped being incredibly active would make time move faster. The days did, but the nights still seemed to be crawling by at a snail's pace.

Imminent Arrival

Suddenly, her waiting was almost over. The day of her family's arrival was tomorrow! As sleep claimed her exhausted mind, Antonia's last thoughts were, *Now, that is odd. I can't seem to remember the last two years of loneliness and hardship. Even the memory of it has vanished.*

Awake at dawn, barely able to grasp her miracle was about to happen, Antonia hugged her knees to her chest. She closed her eyes, and whispered, "Today, my prayers will be answered. Tonight, this empty house will be a home filled with my family. Thank you, Lord!"

Worries and Doubts

She wanted to look nice for her family, and now Antonia shook her head as she stared at her reflection. Was it her face or the mottled surface of the looking glass that made her look so old? She struggled with emotions, which ran from utter excitement to something akin to fear. The anxiety she could see in her eyes had been caused by questions creeping into her mind all morning. *What if my children don't recognize me? What if I've changed so much that Wenceslaus does not know me? My Anton is nine years old now, and Stanislaus is eight. How grown up my little boys must be. It is hard for me to comprehend my baby Anna will be five years old. It has been over two years since they have seen me. What if they don't understand why I have been gone? What if they don't need me anymore?*

1800s women's hair and hat styles

Actual 1800s brass hat pin

Nearly touching the mirror, she examined her image more closely, which did not improve her confidence. Once again, Antonia started shaking her head as she thought, *Oh dear, I have lost weight, and I have aged. Wenceslaus used to compliment me on my fiery auburn hair. Now, all I see is a dull brown color that has streaks of grey in it.* Looking away from her reflection and down at her hands, she grimaced. *My skin looks dry, and my fingers are stained from the cigar wrappings. What will my husband think when he sees me now?*

Worries and doubts kept nervously streaming through her mind as the minutes ticked by, and the arrival hour crept closer. The time had come to meet the ship, and thankfully, the fortitude and courage that had kept her going through the lonely years reasserted itself. In a no-nonsense tone she needed to hear out loud, she said, "Stop this, Antonia!" Then, looking deeply into the eyes of her reflection, she softly said, "Have faith in them. They have waited just as long as you have for this moment. This reunion will be full of love and happiness, and we will never be parted again."

Closing her eyes, she briefly sent a prayer to heaven. *Please, God, grant me release from my fears. You know I love them with all my heart. It has been your love and theirs that has sustained me through these lonely years. Help me feel only joy, now that the waiting is over.* She felt God answer her prayers as a sudden calm flowed through her mind and body.

Picking up her hat, Antonia fitted it snuggly over the soft bun on top of her head, then anchored it firmly in place with a hatpin. Throwing her long wool cape around her shoulders, she tied it closed and said once more with conviction, "I am ready for this." Antonia took a deep, steadying breath and resolutely walked out the door, turned, locked it, and headed for the coach that would take her to the harbor district in New York City.

Antonia's heart beat rapidly as she rounded the corner of the last warehouse. With the whole dock in view, she suddenly realized she had subconsciously doubted the timetable was correct and had been prepared for disappointment. But the ship was there!

As Antonia neared the throng of people on the dock waiting for passengers, the steam-
ship's anchor ropes were being secured to the dock-ing rings. Sailors on the ship's deck were methodically and quickly preparing for debar-kation. Like the rest of the crowd, Antonia seemed to be holding her breath as she watched the gangway extend toward the pier.

1875 steamship at dock, New York, New York

A commotion on deck drew everyone's attention. Passengers flowing out of a port door elicited a happy roar from the people standing on the pier below. The noise increased as those passengers began moving forward and started down the gangway.

The rampant emotions coursing through Antonia almost left her breathless. Her searching eyes finally came to rest on a tall man standing at the top of the gangway. She recognized his profile as he looked down at two young boys while holding a little girl in his arms. Her heart beat so loudly it drowned out the noise of the crowd around her. *It's him! That is my Wenceslaus!* Right at that moment, the man seemed to sense her presence and turned to scan the crowd below. Seemingly of its own volition, her hand shot into the air and waved. Incredibly, the man she had been staring at looked straight at her. Without looking away, he took the hand of the older boy who held onto the younger boy, and the whole troupe made their way down to the pier.

Steamship dock arrival area, 1800s

For a moment, she lost sight of them, then magically they were standing right in front of her. Antonia opened her arms speaking in little more than a whisper that sounded very close to a sob. "Anton, Stanislaus."

It was the most wonderful sound in the world to hear them yell, "Mama" in return as both boys wrapped their arms tightly around her waist. Elated, holding her sons close, Antonia's mind chanted joyfully, *They remember me! They missed me!* Overwhelmed with emotion, she closed her eyes as they filled with happy tears.

When she opened them, she looked briefly up at her husband. After kissing the forehead of each of her sons tenderly, she whispered something to them. In response, they let loose of her, though they did not move too far away, only enough for their mother to close the distance between her and their father. Antonia gently touched the cheek of their daughter who seemed rather shy as she laid her head down on her papa's shoulder. Finally, she looked deeply into eyes she had dreamed of for two years, eyes she could never forget.

Wenceslaus turned slightly, handing Anna to Anton and then stepped a little closer to Antonia. In a deep voice, he said softly for her ears alone, "I have missed you, My Heart." His eyes also swam with tears as he held out his hand to her.

Placing her hand in his, Antonia felt safe for the first time since she left her home in Kutna Hora. He drew Antonia's hand up to his lips and kissed it gently. She smiled radiantly and whispered, "And I have missed you, too, my husband. Shall we leave this crowd?"

Her husband nodded agreement and signaled Anton to hand Anna back to him. Anton stepped to his mother's side, and Stanislaus stepped to his father's side while Antonia slipped her hand through Wenceslaus' free arm. As they made their way through the crowd, Antonia's decorum was completely proper on the outside, but on the inside, she was giddy with delight. Her mind chanted, *My family! They are really here! I love them so much! I am never going to let them out of my sight again!*

Wenceslaus stopped and said, "Pardon me, darling. I must speak with the freight master for a moment." She nodded in response.

Antonia was content to wait with her children and took a few moments to send a quick prayer of thanks to God. When her husband returned from the shipping office, he said, "The freight master says it will be hours before the cargo is unloaded. I think Anton and I should come back with a coach to pick up the baggage later. He says all the cargo will be locked up and safe until I can return to collect it. In the meantime, I propose we go home. What do you think?"

The boys were excited, talking over each other as they supported their father's suggestion. Such exuberance and enthusiasm made their parents smile, and with great pleasure, Antonia captured her husband's attention, saying, "Yes, I agree with our children. Let us go home."

The Karellas Live in Morrisania

It had been a week since Wenceslaus arrived in New York. Antonia sensibly insisted that she continue to work at the factory at least until Wenceslaus got the children settled into school and he found work. Listening to Antonia's suggestions, he found them sensible, and having confidence in her judgment made it easy to agree with her proposals. They also talked briefly about their long-range plans of buying land. Of course, the first step in that process was making the money to move their family to Nebraska. Then, he would need time to open his business before they could afford to buy land. Wenceslaus told Antonia he still had hopes of making that move by late spring or early summer of the coming year. However, he freely admitted those plans might not be realistic. Once he had employment, many things would be easier to plan. He told his wife he looked forward to the time when she could stop working at the factory and stay home with little Anna. When her husband mentioned this, Antonia smiled and added that it might also be a good time to do some wholesale baking to bring in extra coin. It felt good to talk about their plans and dreams.

Antonia had always been a brave girl in Bohemia, but in America, she had grown into a much stronger woman. She had experienced taking care of herself and fulfilling a nearly impossible task for her family all by herself. Wenceslaus was deeply in love with his wife, but at the same time, the way Antonia's mind worked now, she seemed a little intimidating as well.

Nothing is Simple Between Men and Women

The fire in the stove burned low as Wenceslaus sat warming himself. Out of habit, he had gotten up to check on the children, letting Antonia sleep. Afterward, finding he was too restless to go back to bed, he went to sit by the fire.

As Wenceslaus stared into the flames, his mind mulled over the changes that had occurred in his life, particularly regarding his wife. Antonia had developed a new kind of strength in his absence. Part of him was relieved knowing she could understand his worries about the money they needed to pursue their dreams. Antonia understood those feelings having experienced them, and she had become an independent thinker.

Wenceslaus did miss how things had been between them in Bohemia. He wished it could be like it was; yet in his heart, he could feel they had both changed in ways he couldn't quite grasp yet. What Wenceslaus did know was that their lives were going to be different in this new land. He hoped Antonia would want to stay home eventually and spend her time with the children and let him take over the burden of supporting the family. Slightly unsure of himself, Wenceslaus wished he could speak with his father about his conflicting feelings regarding this new situation.

Since his arrival in Morrisania, Wenceslaus had not been idle. In the past week, he had gotten the boys settled in school, and now, he could concentrate on finding someone to watch Anna. Since he and Antonia still planned to move to Nebraska during the following summer, he did not want to open his own business in Morrisania. He'd have to find a local merchant to work for in town. Once he had employment, he knew he would feel more settled.

Sighing deeply, Wenceslaus stood up and thought, *I must find work!* Putting a few pieces of coal on the red embers, he wiped off his hands, closed the door to the stove, and walked back to the bedroom where his wife slumbered peacefully.

Sleep did not come to Wenceslaus' mind for hours as it continued to whirl with strategies. It made sense to him that if he had a job, it would make Antonia feel more secure. Maybe even secure enough to quit her factory job and be content to manage the apartments and fill her days with being his wife and mother to their children.

Another notion popped into Wenceslaus' head. *Perhaps I should do something special for Antonia to show her how much I respect, cherish, and love her. She has always possessed a tender heart. Once I have a job, I'll have extra coin, I could make her a few things for her new kitchen, like a baker's cooling rack. She would love that.* Pleased with the notion, he smiled and wrapped his arms around his wife. *It's a place to start,* he thought and fell asleep.

Wenceslaus Finds Employment

Wenceslaus arranged for Mrs. Jacobson to take care of Anna during the day while he began hunting for employment. His prayers were answered within a week when he accepted a position in a cobbler shop located two streets away from their home. Business hours were from 10:00 a.m. to 7:00 p.m., Monday through Saturday, which allowed Wenceslaus to organize a plan for keeping things going at home until Antonia could take over those tasks.

Each morning, Antonia had already gone to work by the time Wenceslaus got the boys off to school and took Anna to Mrs. Jacobson's. After school, the boys walked home. While Anton checked in with the renters, Stanislaus took care of household chores. Antonia picked up Little Anna on her way home from work, and once their mother and Anna arrived, the boys helped prepare supper. Wenceslaus would arrive home in time to eat with his family before the children went to bed.

With steady work, Wenceslaus felt like a new man. His family had begun to adjust to their new routines, and he hoped that soon he would be able to suggest other changes but did not want to rush Antonia.

From the time of his and the children's arrival in America, going to church with Antonia began renewing their connection with each other. They had all been struggling to adjust to living together again. Yet with each passing week, the tender bond between the five of them was growing steadily.

Sunday was a day the Karellas really enjoyed as a family. Being at Mass together and sharing the warmth of their faith in God felt wonderful. Each week after Mass, the Karellas took time to meet and chat with neighbors. Unless a Karella, Kraus, and

Wolff family picnic was planned—and then they were delighted to share an afternoon with friends.

Mass in America was basically the same as Mass in Bohemia. On this particular Sunday, the priest mentioned the Thanksgiving holiday Mass schedule would be the same as Sunday. Wenceslaus was unfamiliar with this holiday, and he asked Antonia about it on their way to meet the Kraus and Wolff families. She replied, "I would like Johann to clarify the meaning of this holiday and how it came into existence as he did for me. Would you mind waiting until we get to the gathering?" Wenceslaus nodded in agreement.

America's Thanksgiving Holiday

After the blessing had been said and the food had been served, Antonia asked Johann to explain about the Thanksgiving holiday coming up. Johann looked at Wenceslaus and asked, "Do you know anything about the pilgrims and Puritans who settled in America back in the 1600s?" Wenceslaus shook his head. In response, Johann started his explanation at the beginning. "Originally, the leadership of those groups proposed to do away with all 95 of the European church holidays when they settled in America. Particularly those that required people to forego work to attend extra days of church or make mandatory donations to pay for expensive celebrations. In the end, they voted to keep 27 of the existing church holidays and add two new ones."

Maria jumped in to say, "We really like the new ones. The first kind is called a *Day of Fasting*. Our priests call for one when our people or the country is in dire need of God's help. The other is called a Day of Thanksgiving to celebrate the abundance God has granted us."

Johann added, "In fact, it was President George Washington himself that proclaimed the first Thanksgiving celebration in America nearly 100 years ago on November 26, 1789. Washington wrote a proclamation that said, 'This is a day of public thanksgiving and prayer to be observed by all. Acknowledging with grateful hearts the many and single favors of Almighty God.' He was a very smart man," Johann concluded.

Upon hearing how passionate Johann and Maria were about the principles behind these two new American traditions, Wenceslaus reacted as Antonia had. He privately decided to accept them as his own. Antonia added her thoughts, "I must say I have gained a new appreciation for the meaning of prayer and fasting during the last two years. Now, I find great joy in celebrating all I have to be thankful for. I love having a special day reserved for being thankful." With misty eyes, Antonia looked around the table and continued, "Especially when I can share that special day of Thanksgiving with my husband, family, and our dear friends."

After a hearty round of agreement, Johann said, "I'm hungry. Let's eat!"

Late one evening in the first week of November after sending the children to bed, Antonia sat thinking that Thanksgiving, Advent, and the Christmas holidays would be upon them soon. When she prayed and thanked God for His blessings each night, she realized how impossible it was to list everything she had to be thankful for, though she could easily list the people who deserved to be thanked. Antonia wanted to invite the Kraus and Wolff families to share Thanksgiving and

Old fashioned Pot Belly Stove for heating

Christmas with them and asked Wenceslaus what he thought of the idea. As they stood in front of the warm heat radiating from the potbellied stove in their living room, Antonia had hopes that Wenceslaus would agree to her proposal.

"I think it is an excellent idea," Wenceslaus replied as he wrapped his arms around her and pulled her close. "These gatherings will give me the opportunity to show my gratitude to the people who watched over you when I could not be here to do it myself."

Exhilarated at being able to do what he loved most, Wenceslaus continued to hold his wife and placed a warm kiss on her lips. With a blushing face and a giggle, Antonia enthusiastically returned his kiss. Her eager response quickened his pulse with anticipation, and the loving couple was thrilled to realize they were the only ones awake in the house. Grinning and breathless, they held hands as they hurried to their bedroom and silently closed the door behind them.

First Thanksgiving and Christmas Celebration in America

On Thanksgiving Day, Johann told Maria to be sure the children had their heavy coats and mittens. He could tell the weather was going to turn, but he hoped it would stay nice until they reached Morrisania. Maria and Grandma Wolff helped dress the children while Johan and Grandpa Wolff loaded the wagon with a large chest and lots of food. The Wolff and the Kraus families arrived at the Karellas just as the first heavy snow of the year began to fall.

Antonia and Wenceslaus hurried out to greet their guests. Filled with excitement, the adults laughed as they unloaded the wagons. Once everyone had come inside the ladies hung the Wolff children's cold weather clothing on pegs by the door, and the men gathered by the warmth of the pot belly stove in the living room. Peter nodded his head at Johann, and they both grinned as they watched Grandma Wolff, Margot, and Maria call Antonia over to them and then began whispering excitedly.

Standing in front of the window in the early afternoon light, the children stared excitedly at the falling snowflakes and begged Wenceslaus to let them go out and play. Johann, standing with

Peter and his father, waved at Wenceslaus, catching his eye. Johann mysteriously shook his head and then nodded at the women.

Obviously, there was some kind of conspiracy going on, and the smiles on Peter's and Johann's faces indicated he should play along. Wenceslaus looked at his children and replied, "You need to ask your mother if you can go outside and play."

Across the room, Margot and Maria opened the large trunk they brought, which was sitting by the table. Before the children could ask to go outside, they were ordered to line up starting from the tallest down to the smallest child. Antonia and Grandma Wolff watched as Margot and Maria fitted each of the Karella children with winter overcoats, which they said their neighbor's children had outgrown.

As soon as the children were dressed, they asked if they could go outside. The Wolff children dashed off to put on their coats and joined the Karella children standing by the table. The adults could not help laughing as all the children began to complain, saying, "We are hot! P-l-e-a-s-e, can we go out and play now?"

"You have not even thanked Margot and Maria for your wonderful new coats!" replied Antonia.

Anton acted as the spokesman for his siblings and replied, "Thank you very much, Mrs. Wolff and Mrs. Kraus, for these warm coats and mittens."

Laughing, Margot and Maria replied, "You are welcome, young man. Antonia, let them go out and play," suggested Maria.

With that, Antonia granted them permission with one condition. "Children, dinner will be ready soon. We want no argument when we call you in to eat, agreed?"

"Yes! We agree! N-o-w can we go?" The women nodded in unison, and all the children except Anna dashed immediately across the room trying to get out of the house before any of the grownups changed their minds.

Anna stroked the material of her new coat and then smiling up at her mother, indicated that she wanted to take it off. Antonia knelt down to help her sweet little girl with the task and whispered, "Don't you like your new coat?"

Anna leaned close to her mother and whispered back, "Yes, mama, it's pretty and soft."

"Don't you want to go outdoors and play?" her mother asked.

Scrunching up her little face, she replied, "No, Mama, I don't want to get cold. Can I go sit with Grandma Wolff by the fire?" Surprised that Anna did not want to play in the snow, she nodded, saying, "Of course you can go and sit with Grandma Wolff."

Antonia laid Anna's coat on the trunk and turned to walk into the kitchen, and looking back at the two by the fire, she stopped. She could not help smiling for now she clearly understood why her little girl had no interest in the snow. Anna sat on the floor in front of Grandma Wolff close to the heat of the fire with a piece of saltwater taffy strung between her teeth and the fingers of both hands. Watching was an indulgent grandma, warning the little girl not to touch her hair with her sticky fingers. Wistful memories filled Antonia's heart. *Grandma Wolff does make wonderful taffy, almost as good as Mama's.* Realizing this train of thought would lead to tears, she quickly walked into the kitchen with the intent of setting out the food.

Instead of setting out food, she found herself hugging Maria and then Margot. Stepping back to look at them, she whispered, "Thank you both. This was so kind and generous of you."

"Hush now," Maria replied gently.

Then, Margot added, "If we did not have your children to use these things, the clothing would be wasted sitting in storage." Smiling and wiping away her tears, Antonia accepted their generosity with a grateful heart.

Thanksgiving dinner was the most wonderful affair anyone could remember. Each family prepared a favorite food to share, which reminded them of their old homes in Europe. Antonia could not remember when she had eaten so well or so much. Nor could she remember tasting such wonderful flavors since she had been a child in her mother's kitchen in Nechanice. The greatest gift of all was the love and laughter that filled the house.

While they sipped on Grandfather Wolff's wild berry cordial sitting near the potbellied stove, the grownups shared stories of their adventures long into the evening. Grandmother Wolff's salt-water taffy kept the children out of mischief, but eventually, the mother's noticed the quiet. All their young ones had dropped off to sleep. The convivial evening ended with mothers, fathers, and grandparents bundling the grumbling children into their warm clothing. After exchanging warm hugs, each family returned to their homes.

Wenceslaus and Antonia sat a while longer by the heat of the stove talking quietly about the day's events and enjoying the quietness surrounding them. Antonia spoke softly, saying, "Isn't it wonderful that Peter and Margot are finally going to have a baby? She was so happy today when she gave me the news. They have waited a long time. Last winter, she confessed she had begun to fear they would never have children. I told her that you and I had felt the same way. Then, we had three, so she should not give up hope." Antonia was quiet for a moment, smiling and staring intently at her husband. The look made his heart leap, and other parts were getting excited too. He returned her look with a heated smile of his own and whispered impishly, "What is going on inside that head of yours, wife?"

Suddenly, Antonia felt shy and dropped her eyes to the floor. His demeanor cooled instantly with that reaction. With great concern, he gently lifted her chin with his finger, so she had to look at him. "What is it? Is something wrong?"

She shook her head, her cheeks turned pink, and then looking up into her husband's eyes, she whispered, "We are going to have another baby too."

Wenceslaus had been walking on clouds since Antonia gave him the wonderful news. Now, he questioned whether or not their previous plan for the coming spring was wise. It might be better to postpone moving on to Nebraska—at least until after the baby was born and strong enough to travel. He and Antonia needed to have a serious conversation regarding the future before they made any more decisions. He would insist on having this conversation after the Christmas holidays were over.

On Christmas Eve, Wenceslaus brought home a little evergreen tree from the nearby grove. Antonia showed her children how to decorate it with colorful cloth bows. A tradition passed down in the Kraus home, Margot showed Antonia how to make the ornaments her first year in America. She gave Antonia leftover materials from clothing she made so Antonia could make decorations of her own.

With childlike joy Wenceslaus asked his children to wait for a moment. Bolting from the room he returned within moments proudly holding a small box of leather animal shapes and tiny wooden toys he had made in his workshop in Kutna Hora. Adding his ornaments to Antonia's the children and their papa took over the decorating and begged Mama to go back to the kitchen and finish her baking. Laughing Antonia knew they would all be begging for hot rohlikys as soon as they smelled them. She also knew she would not be able to say no and decided to prepare sweet *Kolache* rolls as well. Pulling out her mother's special recipe box she reviewed the Kolache recipe and came up with a new idea. She would break with tradition and fill them with her own wild blackberry and strawberry compote. These rolls she would save for Christmas morning.

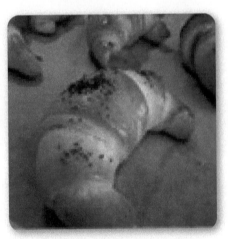

Bohemian rohlikys with black poppy seeds

Nemec family recipe for Bohemian kolache (sweet rolls)

Filling: Prepare a total of 2 cups stewed fruit (berry, cherry, prune, and lemon)

Dough Ingredients: for 14 to 16 rolls
  1/4-ounce active yeast
  1/4-ounce dry yeast
  1/2-cup sugar (divided in half)
  2 cups warmed milk, hot to the touch
  5-3/4 to 6-1/2 cups flour
  4 large egg yolks
  1-teaspoon salt
  1/4-cup butter, softened

Nemec prepares the dough the night before:

Instructions:
Next morning:
1 large egg white, beaten in a
  small bowl,
Dissolve yeast and 1-tablespoon
  sugar in warm milk. Let stand
  10 minutes.

Bohemian kolache—sweet roll with berry filling

In a large bowl, combine 2 cups
  flour, remaining sugar, egg yolks, salt, butter, and yeast/
  milk mixture.
Mix until smooth. Add enough remaining flour to make stiff
  dough.
Drop dough ball onto a floured surface and knead until smooth
  and elastic, about 6-8 minutes.
Add additional flour if needed to keep the dough from getting
  sticky.
Place dough in greased bowl, turning once to grease top.
Cover. let rise in a warm place until doubled in bulk, about 1 hour.

Punch dough down and allow it to rise again to the prior volume
On a floured surface, roll out flat to 1/2-in. thickness
Cut with large water glass to form 2-1/2-inch rounds.
On large greased baking sheets: place the rounds on sheet, let
rise until doubled, about 45 minutes.
Firmly press indentation in center and fill each roll with a heaping
tablespoon of compote.
Brush dough with lightly beaten egg white.
Bake at 350° for 10-15 minutes or until rolls are light, golden
brown.

The wonderful sounds of her family's laughter caused her to glance up from her baking periodically. She loved how festive the room looked as they put the finishing touches on the tree and the joy in her heart made her feel like the child she had been in her mama's house.

She thought her children had not been paying attention to what she was doing. As she started sprinkling black poppy seeds over the hot buttered bread, she found them lined up by the table with hopeful faces. When their papa joined them, the children began to plead, "Are they ready yet? We're starving. Can we please have some, Mama?"

Wenceslaus turned his head away from Antonia so only the children could see, and he winked at them. Turning to look at his wife, he pleaded wistfully, "Yes, please, Mama, can we have some?"

Antonia's laughter bubbled up and floated across the room. "How can I resist such famished gazes? Yes! You may each have two rohlikys, but the rest we must save for tomorrow."

By the end of the evening, the five of them had eaten most of the rohlikys. Relieved she had taken the time to bake kolaches for Christmas morning, Antonia shooed the children off to bed. She needed to put the berry compote in the cooled kolache shells and would have to wait for the filling to set up before she could cover them. She had been saving money for a special treat for her family for the past month. Filled with excitement, she could hardly wait for Christmas morning to come as she touched the compote in the kolaches to see if it had cooled enough to cover.

Wenceslaus came up behind her as she worked and tried to snag a kolache from the tray. Giggling, she tapped his hand and scolded him with mock anger. "Please, darling. Wait for them like the children. These are part of my Christmas morning surprise." He looked like he was going to cry and pretended to pout.

About the time Antonia was ready to give in and let him have one, he put his arms around her and whispered, "I'm only teasing you. I will wait and be just as surprised as our children in the morning." Then, he whispered, "Thank you, my darling, for all you have done for me and for our family. You brought us back together and made this place a home for us. But more than all of this, you have opened the doorway that will allow us to pursue our dreams. You are an amazing woman, and I thank God you are mine."

Antonia blushed. Her husband's words of praise filled her with love and a sense of fulfillment. All the hardship she had lived through was worth enduring because it had made this moment possible. Her smile came from the depths of her heart as she turned in his arms to face him and replied, "Husband, this is going to be the most wonderful Christmas ever. Being able to hold you and my children again is all I ever wanted."

"When will you be finished in here?" He whispered in her ear and hugged her a little tighter.

"Just let me cover these," she replied softly.

Antonia never heard Wenceslaus get up during the night nor the rustling noises that went on in the parlor and kitchen. When Wenceslaus returned to bed before dawn, his smile was tender, and he was bursting with excitement. He could not wait to see the looks on the faces of his family when Christmas morning arrived.

The Karellas' First American Christmas

Christmas morning revealed big surprises for the whole Karella family. On the kitchen counter was the biggest turkey Antonia had ever seen. It was already cooked in a roasting pan and stuffed with potatoes, carrots, and onions. Her mouth watered looking at it and Wenceslaus grinned as he whispered in his wife's ear, "We owe another thank you to Mr. and Mrs. Saint Nicholas Wolff."

A smile sparkled deep within her eyes, and feeling a bit awed by all she could see, she replied, "Yes, my dearest love, we certainly do."

Within moments, her children came running into the kitchen and began jumping up and down. Shouting excitedly, they tried to get a better look at the huge bird in the pan. There was so much laughter and anticipation over the supper they would have;

the children did not even notice the Christmas surprises waiting for them under the tree.

Antonia settled her children at the table with Papa and produced a little magic of her own. She had saved money to buy bittersweet chocolate and made a hot chocolate drink to go with her berry kolaches for this very special Christmas morning. The two younger children giggled, delighted with the special treat. Anton licked his lips dramatically and said, "Mama, Papa, this is the best Christmas breakfast I have ever tasted!"

Once the children's stomachs were full, they noticed the other side of the room. To them it was unbelievable. Brown paper packages tied with colored string had appeared under their tree. Joyful chaos erupted in the room. With squeals of excitement, one child after another scrambled from the table over to the little Christmas tree and knelt as close as possible to the packages without touching them. With big eyes, they looked back at their parents asking in an awe-struck whisper, "Did Saint Nicholas bring these for us?" Antonia and Wenceslaus smiled and nodded in response to their question. Pandemonium broke out in the room as the children jumped to their feet and danced around the room, shouting, "Saint Nicholas found us in America! Just like little guardian Angel Antonia said he would."

The three children had settled back down on their knees close to the tree. Sounding remarkably adult-like, Anton asked calmly and politely if he might distribute the gifts. His parents laughed at how grown up he sounded and nodded their approval.

All eyes were glued to the bundles as Anton took them one at a time from beneath the tree, examined it for a name, and then handed it to either Stanislaus or Anna. He put his packages aside until he had distributed all the gifts except the ones for his parents. Only little Anna began to open her packages without permission. Her brothers looked eagerly at their parents and received a nod of approval before tearing into theirs.

Each child found a soft pair of knitted mittens with a matching cap and scarf in their first box. In a second package the boys received new trousers and shirts while Anna's additional package revealed a lovely pink and white dress with a matching shawl and stockings. Antonia decided she needed to make a special trip to thank Mr. and Mrs. Saint Nicholas Kraus as well.

Curious, Anton touched a packet tied to a tree branch and asked, "What are these? We did not put them on our tree." His parents told him to open one and to the boy's delight he discovered a hard peppermint candy. Each child was allowed one piece, but the rest would have to remain on the tree until after Mass and their holiday feast.

Sitting proudly together at Mass, the whole family looked splendid in their new clothing. Nothing could dampen the Karellas' Christmas spirit—not even when a few parishioners whispered to Antonia that her children were singing a bit too loudly. She merely smiled and whispered back, "My family has a lot to be thankful for." Then, she sang the songs of rejoicing even louder than her children, wanting all of heaven to hear her celebrating the birth of the Savior. She thanked baby Jesus for bringing her family back together, for the gifts of love and friendship, and for the fabulous Christmas dinner that still sat waiting for them at home.

Walking in frigid air after church made the heat from the house feel wonderful as everyone bustled through the door, jostling one another in their hurry to shed coats and hats. Bubbling with laughter and excitement, the children enthusiastically set the table and then sat fidgeting with anticipation. Once the blessing was said, everyone was too busy eating to talk.

Hours later, amazed their children could want anything else to eat after such a feast, Wenceslaus and Antonia listened to all three children beg to continue the Christmas candy hunt. Receiving a nod of permission, the children scoured the branches of the tree until they had found and devoured every last piece of peppermint.

The holiday gatherings of 1877 were filled with some of the happiest and most emotion-filled celebrations of Antonia's life. Perhaps the increased sensitivity was caused by her pregnancy, yet there was no denying Antonia felt overwhelmed by the remarkable friendships she had made in America. She had also discovered a richer and more profound love for her husband and children. Quite often during their gatherings, Antonia's bouts of laughter mingled with bursts of tears. Smiling with understanding, her friends decided it was because she could scarcely contain all the joy she felt having her family together again.

Twelve Days of Christmas, 1877

Antonia learned as a child that starting December 25th, the following 12 days were referred to as the 12 days of Christmas. This was a custom across Europe, and they found that it was the same in America for this period leading up to the Catholic celebration of Epiphany. This is a liturgical feast-day that commemorates the three kings finding baby Jesus and presenting him with gifts of gold, frankincense, and myrrh.

Celebrating Epiphany with the Karellas

During the 12 days of Christmas of 1877, the Wolff, then Kraus, and finally the Karella family took a turn hosting a Christmas gathering. Everyone contributed to the dinner so no single family suffered a huge burden to supply all the food. Since the Karellas had the biggest space, they requested to hold the final gathering on the feast day of Epiphany.

Johann drove everyone to Mass in his wagon, and then upon returning to the Karella home, while the women worked in the kitchen, Peter took control of the children and helped Wenceslaus unload the food baskets. Johann stabled the horses and carried in the last large bundle wrapped in paper and set it on the table.

Peter and Wenceslaus had taken up their seats near the stove as they watched the women. The wonderful aromas coming from the kitchen made the men's mouths water. All the women took the time to examine each dish as they were uncovered and complimented each other on the different foods that had been prepared.

It had been decided that the gifts the families planned to share during the twelve days of Christmas celebrations had to be something made with their own hands. Everyone thought this would be a fitting way to end the holiday season. Margot presented Antonia with the first gift, saying, "I think this is the right time to open this."

The other women turned to watch Antonia unwrap the bundle. "Oh, Margot, how lovely they are!" Grandma Wolff and Maria were at Antonia's side instantly, and praised Margot for the beautiful linens she had made to fit the Karellas' table. All the women helped remove everything from the table so it could be reset with the lovely linens.

"Now, Johann, please set that package you carried in on the counter over there so you don't get the table linens dirty," Grandma Wolff directed.

During these gatherings, Peter, Johann, and Wenceslas liked to engage in some friendly competition with each other. Today presented a perfect opportunity for Peter and Wenceslaus to tease Johann a bit.

Johann unwrapped the bundle on the counter by the stove. Everyone could see it was a huge roasted goose. Peter and Wenceslaus began teasing Johann immediately, asking, "Are you going to tell us you made that goose with your own hands, Johann? If so, that's a good trick we'd like to learn."

Johann had a fast mind and a quicker tongue and rapidly hatched a clever idea of how to get the women to come to his defense with a few compliments. "See here, you slowcoaches," he said, laughing, "it seems to me it was your lovely wives doing the work by hand and not you two! Now, I cannot sew like our good Margot does. Those are truly lovely linens, Margot." Margot blushed and smiled at the compliment.

"Nor can I make such excellent mulled wine as my Papa does, nor make saltwater taffy like my Mama." His papa puffed out his chest, and his mama smiled broadly, enjoying the praise they received from their charming son.

If Johann had been a rooster, he would have been crowing with delight because everyone was smiling with pride at his compliments. His ruse was working! Continuing on, he said, "And no one can bake like our Antonia! As for me, what I can say is that I bloody well wrung this bird's neck and cleaned it with my own hands. My Maria stuffed it with her hands, and it was the oven that cooked it!"

Maria was nodding and looked like she was going to jump to his defense, so before his wife got really riled up, he said, "So, you two can quit your blathering because I don't see that you did anything with your own hands!"

Both Peter and Wenceslaus chuckled realizing Johann had turned the table on them! Even the women were grinning. Johann was winning the game. Scrambling for a proper response to the challenge, Wenceslaus chimed in and said, "Wait a minute! I brought in the coal for the stove that Antonia baked with."

Peter followed weakly, saying, "Well, I carried Grandma Wolff's basket of taffy into the house. Does that count?" Johann shook his head. Glumly, Peter admitted, "Ok, Johann, you're right. You win." Johann grinned, Peter looked pitiful, and all the adults started laughing.

The children had been patiently waiting since before Mass, and now their stomachs growled. They did not understand the game the adults were playing nor what they found so funny. Anton, being the oldest of the children, looked around the room as though the grownups were acting childishly. Speaking for the Wolff and Karella kids, he suddenly sounded very grown up and asked, "Is it time to pray yet? I'm thinking all of us children are hungry." His stuffy-sounding attitude actually made the adults burst into another round of laughter. Anton merely rolled his eyes and frowned at them.

Smiling at him, Anton's mother held her hand up and cleared her throat, which hushed everyone. With twinkling eyes, she said, "I think Anton is right. Let us pray."

During the next few months, on many evenings after the children were in bed, Wenceslaus sat quietly and listened as his wife told him about the last two years. She could not help but mention how amazed she still felt that perfect strangers took her in and offered her love and comfort. Often during these private moments, tears flowed. Wenceslaus would hold her as she spoke of how their kindness helped her survive those years of hardship and loneliness and how she appreciated their support. It amazed her all over again and left her humbly grateful seeing how they had welcomed her family with open arms and showered them with astonishing generosity.

Once Antonia's tears subsided, exhausted, she would lean heavily on Wenceslaus' shoulder saying, "Dearest, these Americans and the loneliness of those years taught me some important lessons. We must never forget to honor a kindness, assist those in need whenever we can, and never be too proud to accept help from a friend."

At which point, he hugged her warmly and whispered, "Rest is what you need at this moment. I am so proud of you, my darling. You are an amazing woman. Sleep. You are safe. I am here now to watch over you, My Heart."

CHAPTER 6

The Long-Awaited Journey to Nebraska

1878–1889

Time Transforms Relationships

Wenceslaus soon came to the realization that everything was different in America. He felt the differences as he walked through the streets of Morrisania. He noticed it in conversations with people he met and even saw it in their clothing. He had become particularly aware of the differences in customer etiquette after he started work at the cobbler shop. One of the interesting differences he observed was the American habit of using nicknames. Wenceslaus asked Markus Pratt, the proprietor of the shoe shop, why Americans use nicknames.

Markus scratched his head and replied, "I hope it does not bother you, but I think Americans find foreign names hard to pronounce, spell, or remember. I've noticed when one of my customers is trying to get a clerk's attention, they sometimes pick a name that they associate with that clerk because of the way they look or in relation to what they do. My son was nicknamed Red because of his hair. One of my clerks was nicknamed Boots because he works on boots brought in for repair. They mean no disrespect by it, so don't let it bother you."

Wenceslaus thought about what Markus said and was surprised to realize he already had a nickname. His parents had called him Vaclav when he was a young lad and only went back to calling him Wenceslaus as a sign of respect after he achieved his Journeyman status.

The more he thought about it, the more he liked the idea. From that day forward, he encouraged his business associates, wife, and friends to call him Vaclav. This change gave him the feeling of being a little more American while it fondly reminded him of Bohemia.

During his hours at work, Wenceslaus thought about why it had taken time to adjust to living with his wife again and she with him. He decided it was because they had both changed considerably during their time apart. They were both more independent, and since being reunited, he now saw Antonia more as an equal. In the past, he had shared only his joys and hopes. In America, she joined him in planning for their future, and he did not mask his frustrations and fears. She had experienced those feelings herself and would not consider him weak for having them or showing them.

Filled with respect for what his wife had accomplished for them, Vaclav began asking her opinion on almost everything before making a decision. The reward for such consideration was her unstinting cooperation. Their first joint decision came shortly after moving into their home in Morrisania.

Long-Awaited Goals

Buying land in Nebraska had always been Vaclav and Antonia's dream, and they decided to push forward with their plans and move to the town of Madison, Nebraska, in the spring of 1878. To save money for the future, Vaclav chose to work for a local shoemaker rather than opening his own business. As Antonia had predicted, Vaclav's shoe and boot designs were a great success. In fact, that the shopkeeper promised Vaclav a percentage of the sales his designs generated in addition to his standard wage.

With each payday, Vaclav's confidence grew almost as fast as his concerns for Antonia. He could see the ill effect the long factory hours were having on his pregnant wife. He set out to convince her it was time to stay home and do something she enjoyed.

Vaclav revisited the idea of Antonia doing some baking. He promised to find customers to buy her goods. All she had to do was pull out the family recipes and start baking again. Remembering how happy she had been baking for the Kraus and Wolff families, Antonia smiled sweetly in agreement with her husband and replied, "Yes, I would be much happier at home."

With his worry for his wife's health lifted off his shoulders, Vaclav gladly went to work earlier each day to make up for the loss of Antonia's factory wages. He also convinced many of his clients to sample the baked goods he brought to work each day. Almost everyone who tried the pastries became Antonia's customers.

After the holidays of 1877, Vaclav received permission from Mr. Pratt to spend time on personal projects once the shop was closed in the evenings. During those late hours, he made a new pair of shoes or boots for each member of the Wolff and Kraus families as goodbye and thank-you gifts.

Time Was Passing Quickly

As spring neared, Antonia was torn by conflicting emotions. Excitement was in the air because she and her family were about to take the next huge step toward achieving their dream of owning land in Nebraska. At the same time, she could not escape the stab of sorrow she felt about saying goodbye to her dear friends. Though not blood relatives, they had given her love from their hearts. When she needed it most, God gave her an American family complete with brothers and sisters to help her stay strong. Their unconditional love reinforced how precious time was with family, and it reminded her that time should not be wasted. Come spring, saying goodbye would cause a lot of tears, but for now, she would cherish her time with them.

By the end of March of 1878, the Karellas accomplished their two main goals and had the beginnings of a third. The first one had to do with money. Between Vaclav's work and the supplemental income Antonia brought in from her baking and her rental manager's compensation, they had saved the train fare to Madison, Nebraska, four months house rent, and increased the savings fund for setting up Vaclav's business. Now any extra money they made was set aside to buy land when the time came. The second goal would allow Vaclav to show his appreciation to their American friends. Having completed the shoes and boots, he brought them home. He planned to wrap and present them as gifts to the Kraus and Wolff families. As the hour was late when he arrived home, he left them on the table in the kitchen before quietly going to bed.

Walking into the kitchen the next morning, Antonia admired Vaclav's skill and craftsmanship. She knew her husband would earn a good living with these skills in Nebraska just as he was doing in Mr. Pratt's shop. As she held the smallest pair of shoes up to the light, her talented husband came up behind her. Turning her around to face him, he asked if she would help him wrap and mark the packages with each person's name. Smiling, she nodded and then suddenly realized he intended to present these gifts like the wonderful Christmas gifts they had received. She whispered, "Darling, we will need lots of brown paper and a few dyes in different colors so I can make pretty tie strings for the packages."

Vaclav hugged her and said he'd bring the supplies home after work. As an afterthought and before he let her go, he asked, "Will you help me deliver these presents this weekend?"

Without hesitation, she replied, "Of course. I'd love to." Understanding the giving of these gifts was the prelude to partings and knowing this was going to be particularly difficult for Antonia, he was relieved by her quick answer.

Capturing her eyes with a gentle, questioning look, he asked, "Have you told our friends we are going to have a baby yet?" Antonia blushed and shook her head. Deciding to tease his wife a little, Vaclav said with raised eyebrows "You will not have to tell them now because I am sure they will notice." Her husband's silliness made her laugh. "I also think it is time to tell our friends we are leaving in April, don't you?"

Antonia's smile disappeared as she nodded, and her shoulders slumped. "Yes, it's time to tell our friends," she replied but thought, *It will be hard disappointing these dear people.*

As the weekend approached, Antonia's thoughts grew heavier, and she made excuses all morning as to why she should stay home. None of them worked. For every problem, her husband or son came up with a solution. Anton even insisted he could take care of the renters if anyone needed help. Her eldest son reminded his mother he had been watching his brother and sister for years and was capable of watching them while she went into the city.

Vaclav wisely stayed out of this conversation between mother and son. Keeping busy after breakfast, Vaclav loaded the rented coach they would use for this trip. When he came in to fetch Antonia, even though she took his arm to walk out the door, he could tell she was confused and emotional. His wife seemed on the verge of tears. Yet she was also excited about seeing her friends.

"I can't wait to see their joy and surprise when they open these unexpected gifts. I'm a little nervous about them seeing I'm going to have a baby, and I feel sad, because as we give these goodbye gifts, it's going to make leaving in the spring feel real."

As she spoke, Vaclav watched emotions play across his wife's face, and beneath those colliding feelings, he could tell she was also suffering from anxiety. Walking through the door, Antonia kept looking back over her shoulder at Anton standing in the doorway. Suddenly, Vaclav knew what it was worrying her. His brave wife was afraid of being separated from her children again. It did not matter they were only going to be away from home for the day. She was reacting like they were leaving forever. Antonia was trembling, and she had not even reached the coach yet. Vaclav stopped and gently turned her to look at him, saying, "It will be fine. I promise we will be home with our children before sunset."

Taking several deep breaths, she straightened her back and clenched her hands. "Of course, we will be back." Bewildered, Vaclav watched her walk back into the house as she said, "I forgot my shawl. I'll fetch it, and we can go."

As they drove away, Vaclav watched his wife look back at the house one last time through the carriage window. "Don't worry, darling. Anton feels very grown up and honored to be in charge of the renters while you are gone, and he enjoys taking care of his brother and sister."

She smiled, pleased with her husband's perception. "All true, but I still worry about leaving them."

Vaclav brought her hand to his lips, kissed, and said, "My Heart, we will not be gone that long, I promise."

It had been several months since Mrs. Kraus or Mrs. Wolff had seen Antonia, and neither one could hide their stunned expression at finding Antonia in an advanced stage of pregnancy. As soon as they arrived, Margot cornered Antonia. "Why didn't you tell me you were going to have a baby at Christmas, when I told you about my baby?"

The two pregnant women stood close as Antonia whispered her confession. "Because I was not totally sure at Christmas."

With that reply, Margot's confidence in her friend was restored, and then Antonia changed the subject. "Come see the presents we have for all of you! This was all Vaclav's doing." The gifts were met with astonishment, joy, and heartfelt thanks.

Two hours later, Antonia and Vaclav announced they had to get back to Morrisania and the children. Yet they continued to sit at the table. Neither of them knew how to deliver their news about moving to Nebraska.

Peter and Johann seemed aware of their uneasiness and refused to let Vaclav leave without an explanation. It took a concerted effort by husband and wife to stumble through their news, and it diminished much of the joy everyone had felt throughout the afternoon. It was harder than Antonia or Vaclav had imagined it would be, telling these dear people they were leaving. With each glance, they realized that soon they would say goodbye. And it would probably be forever. It was a sadness they knew all too well.

Preparing for Travel

Maria and Grandmother Wolff made several trips to Morrisania during the next two weeks to help Antonia prepare her family for the journey. At every opportunity, Maria implored them to wait until after their child was born before setting out for Nebraska. The Karellas steadfastly refused to delay their departure from New York and had to explain more than once that they had waited years for this moment. Nothing was going to stop them from moving to Nebraska.

Antonia alleviated her friends' fears by disclosing they would travel comfortably by train all the way to Madison. She also assured them that she would have good medical help available all along the route to Nebraska. Despite those assurances, Maria said, "If you need to stop or layover in a town along the way for your health or the health of your baby, please promise me you will take all the time you need to be safe." Antonia reassured her friend with a tight hug and promised to do whatever was necessary to keep everyone safe.

Departure day finally arrived. Nearly overwhelmed by emotion and tears, Antonia looked at her friends and said, "I promise I will be careful. Now, I am asking you for a promise in exchange. Will you all come see us once Vaclav and I get settled? Will you do that for us?" Her friends nodded, unable to speak. They left after hugging Antonia one last time. Saying goodbye saddened everyone, and no one wanted to linger and make it worse than it already was.

Spring of 1878, the Karellas Stop in Colfax County, Nebraska, for the Birth of Their Baby

After the goodbyes were finally over, what remained was exhilaration as the Karellas boarded the train during the last week of April 1878. The well-appointed train car belonged to the Union Pacific Railroad, and the conductor came through the Karella's car shouting for attention, "This train is ready for departure. Please take your seats. This train is headed for Nebraska."

Vaclav motioned to the conductor who stopped to see what his passenger needed. "Sir, how far is it was to Madison, Nebraska?" Vaclav asked.

"That Nebraska town is approximately 1,330 miles from New York." The conductor spoke with pride in his voice. "The passengers of this train are about to experience the marvel of the steam locomotive. We will be traveling at the fantastic speed of 20 miles per hour." Finishing his statement, the conductor headed toward the car door when Vaclav volleyed one last question.

"How long will it take in travel time to reach Madison?"

Smiling at the nervousness that came through his passenger's voice, the conductor replied, "It will take approximately four days to reach Madison, Nebraska. That timetable includes the mail and freight stop in Omaha, where you will change trains to reach your final destination."

The train trip from New York was exciting and interesting. The Karellas were in awe of traveling at such speed across the new and wild land of America. They were living their dream! They could hardly believe that soon they would be in Nebraska.

Circumstances That Change Everything

Even best laid plans can change. A change of plans came for the Karellas when the conductor noted Antonia was in labor. He reported her condition to the train engineer. As soon as they made the water stop in Colfax, Nebraska, a runner was sent to fetch the doctor and a stretcher to convey the expectant mother to the doctor's office.

Antonia's labor pains had begun much earlier than she expected. Madison was only an hour or so away, but her unborn child refused to wait. The Colfax doctor had converted his house into an office and small infirmary, choosing to live above the space where he worked. Thankfully, it was also only a short distance from the train station.

The Karellas followed the men carrying Antonia from the train on a stretcher. Dr. Chris Paul met them at the front door of his office. Taking charge, the doctor sent Vaclav off to the boarding house with his children, and directed the men carrying the woman into the infirmary.

Pleased to be in the doctor's infirmary Antonia was relieved she would not give birth in a hotel room. She did not want her children standing outside the door worrying, Antonia gratefully accepted the nurse's help removing her clothing. In a quiet voice, the nurse asked Antonia to raise her hands and then she slipped a nightdress over Antonia's head and guided her to the bed. Antonia made an effort to relax, letting the gentle woman continue to fuss over her. After washing Antonia's face and hands with a warm cloth, she told Antonia to try and rest between contractions. Vaguely aware of her surroundings, Antonia did not remember when the nurse began using cool water on her forehead. However, it felt wonderful when the next contractions weren't racked her body.

A Son Is Born

Once Vaclav relinquished Antonia's care to the doctor, he took his children over to the Shell Creek Station Boarding House where the conductor had sent their luggage. After making arrangements for a room and supper, he left the children in Anton's care. Vaclav told Anton to send word to him at Dr. Paul's infirmary if he needed anything. On the walk back and during his wait at the doctor's office, Vaclav had time to think. He still hoped that once his child was born, he and his family could move on to Madison. Many hours later, Antonia gave birth to their third son, Emil John, on May 1, 1878.

"Congratulations, Mr. Karella! You have a healthy son. Your wife and baby are sleeping at the moment, and I would not recommend disturbing them."

After the long labor and difficult delivery, Dr. Paul needed to explain the reality of the situation to Antonia's husband. "Mr. Karella, I don't want to alarm you, but it is important that you realize your wife is going to need a good, long rest."

Concerned, Vaclav replied, "How long do you think she will need to rest before she and the baby are ready to travel?" Dr. Paul removed his glasses and cleaned them, thinking about his answer. Putting his glasses back on, he replied, "Mr. Karella, it could take several months before she is ready to travel anywhere."

After making his point about the seriousness of the situation, Dr. Paul told Vaclav about his friends, Carl and Lillian Babcock. Their children were all grown and gone, leaving the elderly couple with a large, empty farmhouse. The doctor suggested Vaclav could rent a few rooms from the Babcocks at a much more affordable rate than the boarding house charged. Staying with the Babcocks would give his wife time to regain her strength. Dr. Paul promised to send a note to the Babcock's immediately. He would explain the situation so they would be expecting Mr. Karella to call on them. Vaclav thanked the doctor for his help and went back to the boarding house.

The Babcocks of Colfax

Setting a time for his visit with the Babcocks, at the last minute, Vaclav decided to take Anton, Stanislaus, and Little Anna with him. Based on the older couple's reaction to his family, Vaclav could see Carl and Lillian loved children. That knowledge eased Vaclav's doubts about staying in Colfax, and he struck a bargain for three rooms for the next seven days. He told the Babcocks he and his family would return with their belongings around sunset. At the boarding house, Vaclav set Anton the task of packing up the family's things while he went to see his new son and give Antonia the good news about the Babcocks.

Little Emil John was sleeping soundly when his papa entered the room. Vaclav did not need to be a physician to see the depth of Antonia's exhaustion. Although he did not want to admit it, he was frightened to see how weak his wife appeared. Even though he made the decision without her consent, Vaclav felt relieved they would stay a little longer in Colfax so Antonia could regain her strength.

Picking up his infant son, he walked over and sat down on the edge of his wife's bed, cradling Emil close to his chest. Not wanting to wake the baby, he whispered, "How are you feeling, My Heart?" Placing one hand on his wife's cheek, he waited for her answer.

In a fatigued voice, she replied, "I must admit I am more tired than I remember being with any of our other children. But other than being sore and weary, there is nothing to worry about. I am fine."

He sat looking at his brave wife for a moment and then whispered, "Now, I want you to listen to me. Please do not say a word until I have finished what I have to say. Will you agree to do this for me?" Antonia nodded slowly. "Dr. Paul does not want us traveling for a while."

"I have decided this is a good idea. While you and the baby rest, I will have the time to go to Madison ahead of the family and prepare a home for us. I have been busy reworking our plans, and I have some wonderful news."

He could tell she was going to protest, so he put his finger on her lips to stop her and nodded his head toward the sleeping baby. She made a face at him, and for a moment, he thought she might bite his finger. He also knew she would not want to wake Emil, giving him the advantage he needed to continue his explanation without interruption.

Vaclav raised his eyebrows and removed his finger from her lips. Antonia smiled and nodded for him to continue. She could tell he was pleased with her for resisting the urge to argue against his decision to delay their move to Madison.

"Darling, I have been introduced to an elderly couple, Carl and Lillian Babcock. They are good friends of Dr. Paul's, and I have rented three rooms for us in their house here in Colfax. We shall live with the Babcocks until Dr. Paul says you and Emil can travel." Looking down at his son, he continued, "Carl and Lillian have met Emil's brothers and his sister and are eager to have us stay with them. They are similar in age to our parents and have missed their own children who have grown up and moved away. Since we do not know exactly when the doctor will give you permission to travel, I have also set up an appointment to enroll our children in school for the winter."

He knew his wife would not be able to be quiet the whole time. He was impressed she let him go on so long without saying anything. However, the last bit about the doctor restricting their travel and putting the children into school alarmed her. "Wenceslaus, it is just turning from May to June. What makes you believe we will be in Colfax long enough for our children to go to school?" Calling him Wenceslaus and not Vaclav indicated she was much more upset with the news than she let show.

"Hush now, My Heart, please let me finish!" With big eyes and silent lips, she nodded, indicating he should continue. "Dr. Paul says that having Emil was harder on your body than you realize. I will not risk additional harm to you or our son by hurrying off to unknown territory and more work than you are capable of at the moment. So, I am asking you to rest and regain your strength. Enjoy the baby and let me, Carl, and Lillian help with the children. Please, will you do this for me because you love me?"

A large tear rolled down her cheek, and he leaned over and caught it as he kissed her gently. "Let me take care of you until you are strong again. Then, we will continue our journey. For the present, why don't you think of our time here as a long holiday?"

Emil woke and began to fuss, which abruptly ended their conversation. Relieved the baby had ended a budding dispute, Vaclav felt sure once Antonia thought about it, she would no longer resist this necessary delay. Two days later with the help of Dr. Paul, Vaclav moved Antonia and baby Emil into the Babcock's home.

Over coffee the next morning, Lillian Babcock directed Vaclav to get in touch with the school's principal, Mr. Sprecher, saying, "This man can tell you what the children will need for school and when the school session will begin for this year. I can take care of anything else that the children might need for the coming winter season while you go over to Madison and have a look around."

Overwhelmed with gratitude, Vaclav accepted the help offered by Mrs. Babcock. "Thank you, Lillian. I am grateful for anything you can do for the benefit of my children."

Then, Carl asked, "Father Ryan is our local Catholic priest, and he is a good friend. Do you think Antonia would like him to come by for a visit?"

"How thoughtful of you, Carl, to think of Antonia. I know she would be happy to meet Father Ryan and have him visit. It's a great comfort to know there is a Catholic community in town. Once Antonia is strong enough to get back on her feet, it will be wonderful to attend Mass as a family again."

1800s Madison Train Depot with horse-drawn delivery wagons © Madison County Historical Museum, Madison, Nebraska, Curator Carol Robertson

Within three weeks of Emil's birth, the Babcock's place felt like home, and Vaclav and Antonia were amazed at how quickly the elderly American couple had become like grandparents to their children. It seemed inconceivable they had known each other for weeks and not years.

While Lillian spent a great deal of time with Antonia, Emil, and Little Anna, the older Karella boys preferred to accompany Carl around the barnyard. The boys vied for the honor of feeding the horses and chickens each day.

On weekdays when Vaclav was at the Babcock home, the mornings began with the same ritual. There were two different newspapers published and distributed in town. Carl took a walk before breakfast each day to pick up the papers and coincidently came home with a pocket full of peppermints. Carl would never admit that was part of the reason he went to the store every morning, but he thoroughly enjoyed the happy ruckus the candy caused with the kids.

After breakfast while Vaclav and Carl drank their coffee, if Carl read the Sun, which generally gave the news from a Republican position, and Vaclav read the Schuyler Herald offering the Democrat's point of view on most of the same subjects. After drinking about two cups of coffee, they enjoyed debating the news.

Reviewing local events and debating the news turned out to be a good way to learn about Vaclav's new home state, including its politics. Some of the articles explained why everyone was so relieved and happy with the rain that had been pelting the county for a month. In fact, people he met were rather superstitious about it and seemed to dread complaining in any measure about the rain for fear it would stop. The newspaper published an article that explained Nebraska had been suffering from a serious drought for years. Then, a plague of grasshoppers descended on the area decimating what little had survived the drought. That all changed in the spring of 1877 when the rain returned. Wisely, Vaclav ceased complaining about the rain too.

Madison, Nebraska—Vaclav Learns About Homestead Land Grants

Antonia's recuperation was slow, and Vaclav did not want her to feel anxious. He encouraged her to enjoy this time after the years of hard work she had been through and said, "Let me take care of you, Antonia. While you rest, I'll go to Madison to have a look around. Let me get a feel for the town. Maybe we will decide that Colfax is a better place for us now that we have friends here." Antonia started to protest, and Vaclav chuckled before he said, "I did not say we are changing our plans, Antonia, only that I would like to go and see Madison and talk to some of the people there. Let me bring back that information, and together, we will decide what our next step will be. Please rest and let me do this for us?" Antonia smiled up at her husband and nodded, and Vaclav leaned down and kissed his wife and then went downstairs to talk to Carl.

Vaclav took a couple of months to look around and liked Madison. Selecting a property near the edge of town with a house and barn, he had his Cobbler equipment delivered and was ready to get his workshop set up. Stopping by the post office, Vaclav wanted to see if there was a listing of local businesses, and while he looked at the posting board, Vaclav overheard bits of a conversation between the postmistress and a couple of men. He heard the words … Homestead Act of 1862 … land available for homestead land grants in Nebraska … any adult man could apply … never taken up arms against the government of the United States … even women could get a land grant … had to be eligible for citizenship … two years in America … Vaclav strained to catch as much information as possible; the little bit Vaclav heard made hopeful excitement rush through his body. He had to know more about what these people were talking about. Taking advantage of a break in the conversation, he introduced himself. "Excuse me. I'm Vaclav Karella, and I plan to move my family here after getting my business set up and running. I did not mean to listen in on your conversation but what I did hear was very interesting. Would you mind explaining this homestead land grant act to me, please?"

"No harm done, Vaclav," Postmistress Penny said. "Let me introduce you. This is Joseph Kuchar, and that man there is Frederick Maxell."

Then, Maxell asked, "What kind of business are you setting up, Mr. Karella?"

"Please call me Vaclav. I am a Master Cobbler by trade. In addition to shoes and boots, I can design and craft anything made from leather—clothing, harness, or even a blacksmith's bellows."

"Welcome, Vaclav. My wife, Katherina, and I live in the Schoolcraft Precinct of Madison. Where are you from?" Kuchar asked.

"Right now, from Colfax—we've been staying with friends in Colfax for about two months. We are originally from Bohemia and came by steamship to New York City first. We lived and worked there about a year before we started our journey west to Nebraska," Vaclav explained.

Kuchar smiled and replied, "My family is from Bohemia as well, and my wife's sister, Mary, and her husband, Jacob Holy, are coming from Bohemia soon to live with us. We'll make room for them and their children until they can get a place of their own."

"That's what a good family does, helps each other!" Maxell said as he extended his hand to Vaclav for a handshake. The calluses on Maxell's hand indicated he was no stranger to hard work. "My family is from Germany, and we have a homestead just south east of Madison. We've lived in Madison almost as long as my friend, Joseph, here. What has it been now? Almost 20 years, Joseph?" Maxell asked. Joseph nodded his head in agreement, indicating Maxell's guess was correct.

"Now then, you asked about land grants and homesteads?" Maxell reiterated.

"Yes," Vaclav replied eagerly.

Maxell launched into an explanation of what it took to be eligible to apply for a homestead like his. "How long of you been in America?" Maxell asked.

"I have been in America a little over a year, but my wife has been in America over three years now," Vaclav replied.

Postmistress Penny knew all about homestead applications, too, and jumped into the conversation, "Well, your wife could apply right now, and you would be eligible in another year. You need to fill out the right paperwork and send it in. Then, you wait for a review. As long as you meet their criteria, you should get your land grant," Penny said.

"That's when your work really begins, Vaclav," Maxell added. "I know those rules very well. If your land grant homestead goes through, I can tell you all about what you have to do to keep it."

After another 45 minutes of questions and answers, Vaclav could not wait to get back to Colfax to tell Antonia what he had learned. If they could get a land grant homestead, they would not have to use the money they had saved to buy the land! Only live on it, work the land, and pay the land taxes. Then, they would own the land and be able to pass it on to their children! He could not believe their good fortune to have moved to America and the opportunity to be given land! It was almost too much to comprehend!

Colfax, Nebraska

Antonia was as enthusiastic about the possibility of getting a land grant homestead as he was. "I know we have grown comfortable here in Colfax with the Babcocks, but I believe God is showing us our path with this news. Madison is the right place for us," Antonia said. "And we must get those papers and fill them out as soon as possible."

Vaclav nodded his head, indicating he felt the same way. "Penny is sending away for the applications we need. In the meantime, I have already had my equipment delivered to the property I rented for us. I'll get the equipment set up and get the business going."

Postmistress Penny knew everyone around Madison and quickly spread the word about the new leather worker who was moving to town. The Karella property on the edge of Madison had a good-sized house with plenty of rooms for his family, a big yard with an old chicken coop, and most importantly, it had a secondary building on the land where he set up his workshop and began advertising that he made shoes and all manner of leather goods.

Vaclav established a routine leaving Colfax on Mondays, stayed at the Madison house, and worked at his shop through Thursdays and returned to Colfax on the noon train on Fridays. Although his commute was an hour by train to Madison, the same journey took half a day by horse and wagon. The travel time saved was a good justification for spending the train fare. It also gave him more time with his family at the Babcocks. One day, several months after setting up his workshop in Madison, the homestead paperwork came in, and Postmistress Penny made a trip over to the cobbler shop to deliver it. At least that was her excuse to see the shop and look at Vaclav's work.

Vaclav and Antonia filled out the applications and sent them in to the government office listed on the document within a week. From that day on, he and Antonia prayed for God's blessing on their application and their hopes for a land grant homestead.

The School Year Ends, and Vaclav Readies His Family for Their Move

Colfax felt so much like home, and the Babcocks felt so much like family that no one really thought about time passing until baby Emil was turning two years old. Although Antonia and the baby had been declared healthy and ready to travel by Christmas of 1879, Vaclav said it was important that there be no interruption in his children's schooling. Actually, Antonia knew he did not want to leave the Babcocks any more than she did. It was going to be hard to say goodbye to them. The Babcocks happily encouraged the Karellas not to relocate to Madison until the spring of 1880.

As the school year in Colfax drew to a close, Antonia contemplated the change in her children. They had grown up so fast.

Anton was now a mature 12-year-old; Stanislaus a precocious 11-year-old; and little seven-year-old Anna acted like a second mommy with her two-year-old baby brother Emil. For the three older children, the school session would end for the summer in two weeks.

Antonia sat talking with Lillian in the kitchen as she held her squirming son. "I missed so much with my other children, and now they have become so independent it actually hurts when they tell me they don't need my help."

Lillian smiled, remembering she had felt the same about her own children. Reaching out, she shook a wooden rattle in front of Emil, one that Carl had made for the baby. While Emil concentrated on trying to grab the toy, he quit fighting his mama's hold on him, and Lillian replied, "I know exactly what you are saying, Antonia. I think every mother goes through those hurt feelings when their children no longer depend on them. In fact, I know I am going to feel that way when all of you leave in a few weeks for Madison. I hope you know how much Carl and I have grown to love all of you."

Antonia reached out and gently took hold of Lillian's hand. "You have been a wonderful mama to me and Vaclav and a terrific grandmother to our children. We can never thank you enough for taking us into your home and for the love you've showered on us." Lillian sat, fighting the tears threatening to fall from her eyes and nodded her head.

Carl walked into the kitchen with a big basket of eggs and set them on the counter by the kitchen sink. Emil squealed with delight, pumping his arms up and down in excitement as Carl walked across the room. The elderly man scooped the boy out of his mother's arms and tossed him into the air, catching him safely as Emil's baby giggles bubbled over and filled the room with warmth.

Carl's presence helped Lillian get her emotions back under control, and she wiped her damp eyes on her apron while Carl was enthralled with Emil. Continuing to play with the boy, Carl said, "I'm hungry, woman. What have you got for your starving man to eat?"

The Karellas Make the Move to Madison, Nebraska

To put off saying goodbye, the Babcocks announced they wanted to drive the Karella family to Madison in their freight wagon. Anton and Stanislaus were so excited with this idea that Vaclav and Antonia did not have the heart to refuse. Lillian packed half a dozen picnic baskets full of food for the trip. When Antonia saw them, she said, "It looks like you packed enough food to feed a cavalry of horse soldiers."

Lillian giggled like a young girl. "Can't have my children going hungry, can I? Besides, you haven't stocked the larder in your new house yet, so the extra food will come in handy until you can go to the mercantile." Mrs. Babcock was right, of course.

Antonia smiled and hugged the dear woman. "You are so kind and thoughtful. Thank you."

Meanwhile, Carl presented Stanislaus with three cages. The first two cages contained a young rooster and in the second one was a hen and her brood of baby chicks, which Stanislaus had watched hatch. "Do you remember everything I taught you about raising and taking care of chickens, Stanislaus?" Carl asked.

With sparkling eyes, Stanislaus replied, "Yes, Grandpa Carl. I will take good care of them, and I will start a business with them, just like you did."

The third cage contained three baby rabbits. These animals were pets Carl had given to the three older children, and he convinced Vaclav not to leave them behind. The children squealed with delight when they found out they could take their pets with them.

Vaclav placed the food baskets under the driver's bench seat on the left side of the wagon and put the chickens and rabbits in the same area on the right side. Next, the men piled the wagon bed high with soft mounds of straw, which made the ride delightfully smooth for Lillian and Antonia. Yet it was the children who were in heaven playing in, under, and on top of the fluffy stuff. Emil slept like a log most of the way.

Even after stopping and taking an hour break for lunch, the Babcock wagon pulled into Madison at two o'clock in the afternoon. Lillian shared Antonia's delight as they investigated her new house for the first time while Vaclav showed Carl around the barn and outbuilding where he had his workshop.

As much as the Karellas wanted the Babcocks to stay overnight, they refused. Carl reassured everyone by saying, "Don't you worry. Lillian and I will be making regular trips to Madison to visit with you folks and our grandchildren." With his wonderful promise, the loving hugs they exchanged did not hurt. Happy the Babcocks would remain a vital part of the Karellas' lives, no one felt sad as they waved goodbye.

Madison, Nebraska, Feels Like Home

Since Lillian assured Antonia there was enough food in the picnic baskets to last at least a couple of days, she did not feel an urgent need to go the mercantile right away. It pleased her to see that Vaclav now spent his full workday in his shop and no longer hovered over her like she was an invalid. Only in Antonia's heart would she admit she still felt a little weak. She doubted she would ever regain the strength and stamina she had before Emil was born. Antonia knew her Vaclav needed to believe she was fully recovered so he would not worry. That morning when Vaclav kissed her before leaving for his shop, he seemed happier than she had seen him in a long while. That wonderful smile solidified her determination never to admit she felt unwell ever again.

On the way to his shop, Vaclav reflected on how satisfied he felt. There were several reasons for this newfound peace. Praise God, his Antonia had recovered from the ordeal of childbirth and was full of energy again. His wife and children were adjusting well to their new home. He and Antonia were still fairly young, only turning 41 years old, and over the last two years, he had succeeded in laying a solid foundation for their future. Now, his planning and hard work was beginning to pay off. A steady stream of regular shoe customers and harness work kept him busy most days, and he was able to eat lunch with his family every day. Lunches were especially fun with his children.

Antonia spent the first couple of days getting used to her new home and meeting her neighbors. But now there were a few errands she had to attend to, which included stopping by the church, the school, the post office, and then the mercantile. Making her list of the grocery items she needed, she mentioned her errands the next morning at breakfast. After finishing his food, Anton went to fetch his mother's marketing satchels. When he returned with the satchels, Anton insisted he was old enough to be put in charge of his brothers and sister in her absence.

St. Leonard's Catholic Church, original location and building—1870s, Madison, Nebraska. (Photo supplied courtesy of Father Greg Carl, from church history archives, St. Leonard's parish, Madison, Nebraska, 2018)

Antonia did not answer immediately and thought, *I agreed if it's just the baby, but I doubt he is ready to manage his other two siblings at the same time.* Trying not to hurt Anton's feelings, she set Stanislaus to the task of cleaning out the old chicken coop. It was time to get his chickens out of the small cages they had been transported in. *That chore ought to keep Stanislaus busy while I'm away*, Antonia thought.

Still worried that watching the baby would be too much for Anton with any other distraction, Antonia said, "Little Anna, I'm going to walk into town. Would you like to go to the mercantile with me?"

Little Anna nodded quickly and replied, "Oh yes, Mama, and I'm going to bring along my basket too. I want to help carry the things we buy." Antonia smiled, holding out her hand to Little Anna and thought, *Now, Anton can focus on the baby.*

Stopping at St. Leonard's church first, mother and daughter met Father Cyprian Banscheid. Antonia learned he only visited the Madison parish every other weekend, arriving on Fridays and staying through Mondays. She had been fortunate to catch him at the church. Antonia asked if he would come bless her new home on his next weekend in town and extended an invitation for supper. Father Banscheid accepted the request and invitation, and after giving Antonia his schedule for the month, Antonia asked for directions to the school. Father Cyprian directed her to Principal Krimmer's home instead.

Antonia spent the next several hours accomplishing most of her planned tasks. She got the three oldest children enrolled in school, which would start in September, then visited the post office. She and Little Anna had a nice chat with Postmistress Penny about Madison and the people who lived in and around town. Penny gave them directions to the hardware store, and mother and daughter strolled in and out of shops along the way. Antonia found a few items for the kitchen, and storeowners offered Little Anna treats, which she politely accepted. It was remarkable how many people guessed Antonia was Vaclav's wife even before she introduced herself. Everyone had something nice to say about her husband. Madison's people put her in mind of Kutna Hora and also began to remind her of their old neighborhood in Morrisania. The warmth of their welcome felt wonderful.

Within a couple of weeks, Antonia felt satisfied that her new home was finally in order. Her children had established a good routine. They learned that if they got their chores completed quickly after breakfast, they earned uninterrupted playtime until lunch. Rarely did she have to call them. Anton kept an eye on the time, and despite the children's chatter and teasing, they were always washed and sitting at the table when their papa appeared.

The children had grown very close to their papa during the two years they had spent away from their mama. They knew him well and remembered what he had taught them about the importance of time, and lunch was a special time for all of them. The children cherished the playfulness they shared with him during their meals.

Vaclav arrived in the kitchen at the same time every day—12:30 sharp. Today, when he sat down, rather than his usual playful banter, he announced he had a letter from Bohemia he wanted to share with everyone. He smiled at the four sets of eyes fastened on him and the letter he held as he read the words.

Dearest Antonia, Wenceslaus, and   Bohemia, July 1880
our wonderful grandchildren,

Antonia, thank you for your letter. We cannot express how excited we are to hear the whole family is now living in Madison in your own home. Your father and I could not be prouder of all that you have accomplished as a family. We visit with Vaclav's parents every other Sunday and share any news we have had from you about America and your life there.

Antonia, your father and I are so happy to hear that you are baking for your parish socials. You are carrying on family traditions and keeping our special recipes alive. We miss you, dear girl, and miss the time when you did your baking here with us. Though we cannot be there, you know we are with you in spirit.

Please write how the children are doing in school. My goodness, it is hard to believe Anna has grown up so much. We still recall the huge celebration we had at her baptism, and it seems impossible that she is already old enough to attend school.

We are in good health, though we are slowing down and have more aches and pains than we'd like to admit. I know I told you that your father took on an apprentice when you left home. Well, the boy made Journeyman two years ago and has just made Master. He now has an apprentice of his own, and the two of them run the bakery for your father. He still makes a few special breads for us on Saturdays, but Journeyman Fritz with Apprentice Max do a good job managing the rest of the work.

Well, that is all of our news for now. We love you all very much. Please give a hug and kiss from us to each of the children.

God Bless you all, Grandma and Grandpa Nemec

Putting the letter aside, Vaclav's stomach grumbled loudly, and everyone laughed. "I'm hungry—who's ready to eat?" Vaclav asked.

Everyone replied together, "We are, Papa."

Madison, Nebraska, September 1886 — A Bohemian Dream Comes True

Six years after moving to Madison, the Karellas finally received an important letter from the Federal Government of the United States. After twelve years of utter commitment, toil, and sacrifice, the Karellas' Bohemian dream was about to come true.

Vaclav and Antonia sat at the desk of the recorder at the Antelope Company Land Office in Neligh, Nebraska. Outwardly calm, on the inside, their hearts were racing as Vaclav paid the recording fee for their land grant. The receipt stated that on the 13th day of September 1886, a land grant for a 160-acre homestead, which included 60 acres of forest, located 2 miles North and 2½ miles East of Madison County, Nebraska, had been issued in the name of Wenceslaus Vaclav Karella.

Wenceslaus and Antonia sat side-by-side smiling as they looked at the small document held between them. It represented the fulfillment of a seemingly impossible dream. They owned land—the land they had dreamt of owning! A dream that inspired them and sustained them through many hardships had finally become reality.

"We must make the house big enough for Anton and Stanislaus to have families when they are old enough," said Vaclav.

"Yes," whispered Antonia, "I have daydreamed about grand-children living with us."

"I look forward to the day when Anton is ready to take over the farm," said Vaclav. "That is when our Bohemian dream truly bears fruit. Now, each of our children will have the opportunity to create an American dream of their own.

1886–1887, Preparing for Life on the Karellas' Nebraska Homestead

Although the Karellas acquired their land through a United States land grant program and only had to pay the fee for recording the deed for the acreage, it did not guarantee they could keep the land. To do that, the Karellas had to live on the land, work the land, and pay the land tax each year. They did have a grace period before they had to prove they had fulfilled the land grant requirements, but they needed to be living on the land within a year of the recorded deed.

As the Karellas had done in the old days in Bohemia, Vaclav and Antonia spent many hours planning their next move and estimating how much money they needed by the following spring to build a house, a barn, rent the farm equipment to prepare the land, buy seed, and schedule the time to sow the crops. The savings Vaclav and Antonia had set aside to buy the land could now be used to order lumber and other supplies. However, it would not be enough for everything they needed. Holding a family meeting, Vaclav and Antonia asked Anton and Stanislaus for their ideas.

The winter of 1886 and 1887, the whole Karella family worked relentlessly to earn the extra money needed for the homestead. Vaclav spent long hours in his shop, and 18-year-old Anton started assisting Vaclav making leather goods. They set up a delivery service with Vaclav's clients when the customers placed their orders.

For a fee, once the orders were finished, Anton would deliver the items. Stanislaus had turned 17 and decided to sell eggs and meat from his chicken flock. Antonia began baking sweet breads and wholesaled them to the local bakery shop. With 13-year-old Anna's help, Antonia was able to double the quantity of baked goods made in the Karella kitchen for sale. Emil John, who was eight years-old, was still considered the baby of the family. Consequently, everyone voted he should focus on his schoolwork. Emil happily complied because he loved school.

Anton worked well with his brothers and sister and had demonstrated the maturity and diligence of a natural leader all his life. He graduated high school in the spring of 1886 just before his parents found out about their land grant. Stanislaus completed high school the following year. The two young men shared their parents' goals for the family and were just as keen about the homestead.

In the spring of 1887, the Karellas worked feverishly to organize the labor needed to build the farmhouse. Once they had the contracted labor, Vaclav took over supervising the construction of the farmhouse while his two older sons focused on turning a few acres of homestead land into fields and getting them planted. With those two projects completed, the Karella men moved the big furniture from the old house in Madison to the farm. Then, the men turned their attention to building a barn while the Karella women with Emil's help made trips between the old house and the new, moving all the rest of their belongings one wagonload at a time.

Anton proved he had a good head for business while they were raising money to build the farm. Stanislaus proved his knack for farming when they were preparing the land and planting. Turning the farm business over to them was logical and allowed Vaclav to focus on his shoe business. It would continue to provide an income for the family until the farm started producing enough money to pay for its operation and feed everyone.

Emil John Karella turned nine years old during the summer of 1887. Then, in early September, the Babcocks traveled to

Madison to help the Karellas celebrate the blessing of their new house on the homestead. When Father Banscheid came to bless the farmhouse, he reminded the Karellas they still had a son who needed baptizing. Somewhat embarrassed by such a long delay, Vaclav and Antonia made arrangements, and their son, Emil John, was baptized at St. Leonard's on September 25, 1887. For Catholics, having a child baptized so many years after the child's birth is unusual. In the letter that announced Emil's baptism to the boy's grandparents in Caslav and Nechanice, Vaclav felt he should provide a good explanation for such a breach in faith protocol. Hoping for their understanding, he explained how nine years had elapsed so quickly between the boy's birth and his baptism.

Karella Nebraska homestead, original photo from Anna Plouzek Karella, wife of Stanislaus Karella. *People in photo from left to right:* Grandmother Anastasia, daughters Mary, Martha, Helen, son Frank, Grandfather Anton, Great-Grandfather Vaclav, Ambrose (Rusty), and Uncle Emil

A Bohemian Dream

America

Dearest Mother and Father,   *Madison, Nebraska, 1887*

*Antonia and I realize that Emil's baptismal announcement
may come as a bit of a shock to you since your grandson has
already turned nine years old. You may also say that Antonia
and I were taught better and should have done this long ago.
However, I would ask you to consider how concerned I was
for Antonia's and the baby's general health when he was born
in 1878. All other considerations were secondary. Even after
moving in with the Babcocks, I realized it would take longer
than originally planned for Antonia to recuperate, and we did
not belong to a parish at that time.*

*I had to concentrate on getting our children enrolled in school
in Colfax before I started traveling to Madison to set up my
business. That way, I could support my family once I did move
them to Madison.*

*It took a while to find a good home for us, and then I concen-
trated on launching my shoe business. Yet even after I moved
the family to Madison, we were all very busy settling into our
new home, getting the kids into their new school, and becoming part of our new community and parish.*

*America is a very large place with immense expanses of unset-
tled land. There are not enough priests for every community to
have a full-time pastor. We share our priest with three other
communities right now, and he only comes to our town twice
a month. Can you imagine how busy he is? Or how easy it has
been to lose track of time with everything else going on?*

*My dear father and father-in-law, I want to you know I have
not been idle or irresponsible. Your grandchildren are strong,*

healthy, and happy, and every one of them is now a baptized child of God.

We send our love to all of you and want you to know we miss you all very much.

Your children and grandchildren always,

Vaclav, Antonia, Anton, Stanislaus, Anna, and young Emil

Madison, Nebraska—Letters from Family in Bohemia

Over the years, the American Karellas made it a point to regularly write to their relatives who remained in Bohemia. Through return letters from family, Vaclav and Antonia kept abreast of the radical changes occurring throughout the old country. The news sounded more than a little frightening. It was hard not to worry about the family still living there as Vaclav's father wrote about the nearby town of Oshkosh and its troubles.

Dear Wenceslaus, Antonia, and our　　*June 1888*
wonderful grandchildren,

First, let us say how very happy we are to hear that you are now landowners! Such a magnificent accomplishment, and it took both of you to make such a glorious dream come true. We are so proud of you. We are also happy to hear you have moved to your homestead and that the family is together under your own roof. It sounds like the children are excited to have a bigger area for their pets too. Grandpapa wants to know if you bought that horse for Anton yet?

Wenceslaus, your father is particularly pleased that you write about your shoe business. He always said you would do well. It makes us proud to hear Anton is showing interest in learning to work leather as well.

Antonia, you have written about how wonderful your friends, the Babcocks were and how comfortable life was in Colfax. But now, you own land and your own home! You must admit there is nothing better than organizing your own home. We are delighted that you and the children are finally able to unpack for the last time and truly settle in.

Perhaps someday we will get a chance to meet our newest grandson and see first-hand how the others have grown. I can admit that the sacrifice you made in leaving your husband and children for two years was worth it. For us, just knowing that our grandchildren are safe and that they have a promising future ahead of them eases our hearts. This knowledge gives us more comfort than you could possibly know. Goodness me—it makes me emotional.

I suppose it's largely due to what is happening here in Bohemia with the continuing industrialization. First, it was the cloth factories that closed the small weaver shops. Now, our cousins believe the wood workers are next. I do not know if you heard what has been happening in Oshkosh at the Paine Lumber Company? It is shameful. Did you know they operate seven large factories now? Your father says no company is producing more doors, sashes, or blinds than they are. They are also the largest match producer as well as one of the largest carriage- and wagon-producing centers in the world. Yet, despite this great success, they refuse to share even the smallest amount of their wealth to give the woodworkers a decent wage.

With continuing wage cuts and bad work conditions, the woodworkers in our family are talking about leaving Bohemia too. I wish I had better news. I don't want to worry you, but I thought you would want to know.

Though we miss all of you terribly, we are lighter of heart knowing your family's future is no longer tied to Bohemia. We are proud of you, Antonia, and of you, my son, for what you both have been able to accomplish in 11 short years. May God continue to bless your footsteps, and we send this note filled with our love and ask that you give each of our grandchildren a hug and kiss from us. We are so proud of you, and so is the rest of the family in Bohemia.

Your devoted mother and loving father,
Grandpa and Grandma Karella

Vaclav put down the letter from his father and spoke softly to Antonia. "It is so hard to read about what is happening back in the old country. People losing their trades! How can people live on such poor wages in those overcrowded factory towns? No wonder we have been meeting so many Czechs and Bohemians in the last couple of years. I can hear the worry in Mama's words. My Heart, no matter what we have been through, it was worth it to make this new life for us and our children." Antonia nodded, knowing in her heart every word her husband said was true. "It's just as my father predicted so long ago when I first began my apprenticeship. A community will always welcome the addition of a good cobbler." Wenceslaus believed his papa's words as a boy. As a man, he found his father's wisdom proved to be as true in Kutna Hora as it had been in New York and now again in Madison.

The years of separation from their parents had taken its toll on both Vaclav and Antonia. Thinking out loud, he whispered, "I miss Papa so much." Suddenly realizing what he said, he looked over at his wife and saw her eyes filling with tears. Antonia had lived with the pain of being separated from her parents longer than he had. He quickly pulled her close and said, "I'm sorry, darling." Placing his cheek near her ear, he whispered, "America has been a blessing. We might not miss the land of our birth, but we will never forget our parents or our family that stayed behind.

Thousands of miles may separate us, but part of our hearts will always remain in Bohemia with them."

Antonia nodded, unable to speak. She knew they both feared they would never see their parents again in this life. They were already of greater age than many relatives who had died much younger. It hurt to admit such mortality in people who stood next to the saints in their minds and hearts. The accolades were endless—wonderful, loving parents; strong mentors; and impeccable role models. There was no need for words as Vaclav and Antonia sat together in front of the fire holding each other swimming in warm memories of their childhoods. Their dreams later that night would be filled with visions of Mama and Papa kissing them goodnight and keeping them safe.

Vaclav Remembers His Father's Guidance and Advice

The Karella children were off to school for the day, so Vaclav finished his lunch surrounded by an unusual silence around his dining table. Antonia bustled about cleaning up the kitchen, so his thoughts drifted into daydreams. *Papa was an exceptional teacher. He never allowed second-rate items to leave his shop. Such dedication to detail and craftsmanship earned him a loyal clientele over the years, creating longevity and success in his business.* He could hear his father's voice. "If you truly perfect your skill, it will render you a good living. As long as there are people with money, they will need footwear and will not mind paying the price for quality boots and shoes."

A more mature Vaclav remembered how he had clung to those words during two long years of separation when all he could do was write to his courageous wife in New York. He had sworn to himself that once he and Antonia were reunited, she would never want for anything again. He worked hard to perfect his skills and knew he could live up to his promise.

His commitment to the future was reinforced every time he had to soothe the tears of his children because they missed their mother. "We will do fine when we reach your mama in America. I will work making shoes, boots, saddles, and many other wonderful leather things so that I can take care of all of you. We will be happy. "Remember what your grandfather always says—just as it is true in the villages of Bohemia, so everyone in America will need shoes too." Wenceslaus could always feel the faith his children had in him. He knew they believed in their grandfather's wisdom as well when they heard those simple, but powerful words. They always nodded bravely and stopped crying. He remembered hugging them and thanking God for their trust and belief in him.

Antonia sat down next to Vaclav and asked if he was all right, which brought him out of his contemplation. Standing up from the table, he pulled his wife into his arms and whispered into her ear, "Our life is perfect. As long as we have each other and our children, I could never want for more. That is unless you would like to make more children?" He leaned back so she could see the look in his eyes and think about what he was asking. When she smiled up at him, he pulled her close and put his lips near her ear and whispered again, "It would make me very happy to make more children with you."

Those words made a tingle of excitement rise up from the pit of her stomach. Antonia leaned into his embrace and replied for his ears alone, "My darling, shall we try to make another one tonight?" Antonia pulled away from his chest to glance up into her husband's face. She held a lovely promise in the twinkle of her eyes, and Vaclav sucked in his breath. *What a woman I am married to*, he thought. He knew if he did not leave for his shop immediately, he would be taking his wife to their bedroom. "Tonight," he whispered and scorched her earlobe with an intense kiss of promise. He left the kitchen before he had time to change his mind; Antonia's husky laugh followed him out the door. Smiling, Antonia gazed at Vaclav's retreating back and thought, *I'll never get enough of that man.*

The Karellas of America Are Home with A Future Full of Promise

Vaclav and Antonia Karella moved to Madison, Nebraska, 16 years after the first Arbor Day and benefited from millions of trees already producing a local source of lumber for its settlers. The Karella family had hoped the land of Nebraska would feel like home, and upon seeing it with their own eyes—fertile rolling plains, young forests, and lush fields—they saw a land more beautiful than anything they had dreamed of.

Nebraska's familiar climate, as well as the farming, livestock, and lumber industries, did mirror life in Bohemia. The brochures had been right all those years ago. Vaclav and Antonia's American land felt like the land of their birth, which they now lovingly referred to as the old country. Vaclav and Antonia fell deeply in love with their adopted country of America, and their desire to be Americans helped them feel like they belonged there.

By the age of 47, through self-sacrifice and dedication, Antonia and Vaclav secured a future for their children in America. Yet having achieved their Bohemian dream in America, this land would become the foundation of new dreams. The future would be guided by the American dreams of their children.

Between 1889–1897, Antonia bore six more children—two sets of twins and two single births. Sadly, none of those babies lived very long. With each additional pregnancy, Antonia's body began to grow weaker, although at first, she could hide it. As time went on, and with each additional death, Antonia's mind grew a little more wearied. Her heart began to long for peace without aching for little souls she never got to see grow up.

1870s Madison, Nebraska—seed and feed store,
Madison Historical Society, GKM 2017

Karella Family—1st documented generation

Above: Wenceslaus
Vaclav Karella
Below: Antonia Karella

Parents Miklaus Jerome, Eliska
Ambrosia Karella, son
Wenceslaus Vaclav Karella

Born Bohemia 1839 Died in
Nebraska 1922

Anton (Anthony) Born
Bohemia 1868

Stanislaus (remaining twin)
Born Bohemia 1869

Parents Nicolas Stanislaus,
Marketa Ivana Nemec daughter
Antonia Nemec -Karella

Born Bohemia 1839 Died in
Nebraska 1900

Anna M.
Born Bohemia 1873

Emil John
Born America 1878

Parents
Wencelaus Vaclav Karella
Anontia Nemec Karella

Parents
Jacob Holy
Mary Koryta Holy

Anton
Karella

Anastasia Holy
marries Anton Karella in 1895

CHAPTER 7

The Bohemian's Dream Continues in Nebraska

1890 –1894

Letters Written Between Sister Margaret Mary and Her Cousin, Andy Karella

Dear Sister Margaret Mary,

Here is the Karella story to date; I hope you like how I have written it using the genealogy names, dates, and facts you sent to me along with my own research. Thank you for the photos of Wenceslaus and Antonia; they are wonderful.

Like you suggested, I am following the Karella name, and the storyline follows the first-born male Karella of each generation in our family line.

Now we are at the first big transition where I introduce new names. This is where I write about people related to Anastasia Holy and her marriage to Anton Karella.

I look forward to receiving anything else you have on the Kuchars and Holy families.

Hope you are having as much fun as I am.

Sincerely, Andy

Dear Andy,

I love how you have molded the Karella facts into the information you found on Bohemia and American history. It is becoming an adventure story through time as our ancestors leave Bohemia and continue their journey in America.

I must say I fall in love with Vaclav and Antonia every time I read what you have written about their lives. It is so real to me that I feel I am right there with them living their story as it is happening. Thank you for that experience!

In regard to the next part of the story, I've enclosed everything I have collected on the Kuchars and Holys. I suggest as the story moves from one family group to the next, we put in a family chart showing the connection to the Karella lineage. I will make more charts like the one we have for Antonia, Vaclav, and their children because it will make the relationships easy to see.

*Andy, keep sending me the pages as you get them done. If I
have any additional information you might need, I can send
it. I am currently preparing a packet with everything I have
on Stanislaus and his wife, Anna Plouzek, on Emil John who
married Emily, part of the Chicago Karellas, and on Little
Anna who married Anton Kratochvil from California.*

I am enjoying this adventure,

God Bless, Sister Margaret Mary

The Karella Children Grow Up

Hitching up the horse to the family buggy, Vaclav went into
Madison early, excited to buy three copies of the Nebraska State
Gazetteer. This business directory, which had recently been
published for the year 1890
to 1891, should contain his
son's name. Vaclav intended
to keep one directory and send
the other copies to family in
Bohemia.

Arriving at the mercantile
at the same time as the owner,
Vaclav had an opportunity to
catch up on the news with the
man while he opened up his
store. As soon as it felt polite,
Vaclav requested the booklets,
added a few sketching pencils
to his purchase for Emil, and
returned to the homestead.

NEBRASKA STATE GAZETTEER,

Business Directory and Farmers List
FOR
1890-91
EMBRACING
A GENERAL DESCRIPTION OF NEBRASKA, ITS
PRODUCTIONS, SOIL,
CLIMATE, NATURAL ADVANTAGES, EDUCATIONAL.
RAILROAD
FACILITIES, NAMES OF STATE, CITY AND COUNTY OFFI-
CIALS, POST OFFICES, NEWSPAPERS, POPULATION
OF TOWNS, AND A COMPLETE CLASSIFIED
BUSINESS DIRECTORY OF ALL BUS-
INESS HOUSES AND PRO-
FESSIONAL MEN.
ALSO, GIVING THE NAMES AND P. O. ADDRESS OF ALL
FARMERS IN THE STATE.

Cover of Nebraska State Gazetteer,
1890–91

Walking into the quiet
house, Vaclav figured most of the family was busy with farm work
or had gone to the mill. Vaclav gave Emil the new pencils, and
his son went out to the porch with his sketchpad. Appreciating

the peace and solitude he found in the kitchen, Vaclav poured himself a cup of coffee and sat down to read the Gazetteer.

1890–1891, Anton Karella, the Man

Turning the pages until he found what he was looking for, Vaclav's eyes stopped searching the columns. There on the printed page was his name, Vaclav Karella, and his son's name, Anton Karella, noted as two of Madison County's farmers and landowners.

Overwhelmed with pride, Vaclav's eyes got teary and he wiped them quickly almost as if he didn't want to be caught revealing such emotions. *What a ridiculous reaction,* he thought and laughed at such a silly response to something so wonderful.

Looking at the clock, he knew his Antonia still slept but would awaken soon. He had resumed cooking breakfast for his family when Antonia's health began to fail as she neared her 50th birthday. His beloved wife did not have the strength she once had and needed more sleep in the mornings. Looking at his pocket watch, he got up to prepare tea before she came downstairs. It was difficult to contain his excitement. When she saw the business directory, she would be as thrilled as he was to see their son's name in the business publication. This little booklet was a priceless affirmation of a Bohemian dream they had carried in their hearts all their married life.

Anton Karella, son of Vaclav and Antonia Karella

The only thing that could possibly make this moment sweeter would be sharing it with their parents back in Bohemia. Grimacing, Vaclav conceded that was an impossible wish. His and Antonia's parents were nearing their seventies. He closed his eyes, envisioning their faces beaming with joy at their family's accomplishment and thought, *Mama and Papa, thank you for supporting our dreams.*

The Enterprising Karella Brothers

Vaclav's grown sons no longer needed supervision running the family businesses; they only required his advice now and then. To stay productive, Vaclav worked his leather business using one of the outbuildings on the farm, but he worked at a more leisurely pace.

Proud of both of his sons, Vaclav thought back to when his two oldest boys started asserting their independence. They learned how hard life could be at a very young age. They lived through the pain of their family being split up for two years. At the same time, Anton also understood his Mama and Papa had to do what was best for the family and helped his little brother and sister understand too.

Vaclav smiled sadly as he reminisced about lost time. *Anton grew up too fast when his mama left for America. He matured beyond his years during that time. I am sad that he lost his childhood along the way, but I could never have done so much or taken care of the family so well without my little man, Anton. Those experiences did play a big part in turning him into the sensitive, strong, and resourceful man he is today. Anton has worked with me since he could drive the wagon by himself. He showed no hesitation about learning the farming business. I know him to be an exceptional son, and exemplary brother. Anton can do anything he puts his mind to.*

Vaclav's thoughts shifted to Stanislaus. *I think Stanislaus made his transition from a boy into a businessman when he got his first rooster and hen from the Babcocks. He applied everything he learned from Grandpa Carl concerning how to raise chickens. Once we moved to Madison, he built a poultry and egg business ... in two years ... all on his own. Stanislaus' calm and conservative mind is thriving with the orderly planning and operation of the farm. I think he has found the security he needs. His organized attention to detail helps him avoid problems with the livestock or with the crops*

... it's clear Stanislaus loves the farm despite the daily backbreaking work it takes to keep it running smoothly.

I'm so relieved there has never been any competition between them. I'm glad to see Anton appreciates his brother's strengths and opinions. He also trusts Stanislaus' insight and leaves most of the decision concerning the farm to him. But I can also see Anton is restless. His active mind will never be satisfied with the predictable rhythm of farming. No, my Anton requires a different kind of challenge, and I'm sure he will find one soon enough. Vaclav was drawn out of his thoughts as he heard Antonia coming down the stairs. He got up to pour her some tea and couldn't wait to show her the Gazetteer.

1800s Nebraska, Around the Town of Madison

Madison Nebraska, Anton Karella

By the time everything was running smoothly on the farm, Anton was ready for a new challenge and had settled on a new idea for an additional family business. Taking the initiative, Anton surveyed the 60 acres of forested land attached to the farm. Thinking of the forest as a renewable resource, he carefully worked out a business plan for a sawmill to process raw timber and sell the finished lumber. He would only rely on Karella trees until he had other farmers who would bring their trees to the sawmill for processing. Then the mill would sell their lumber. Once the sawmill was generating enough profit from other sources, he would no longer harvest Karella trees or use family money.

253

Anton presented the plan to his father and asked permission to develop the sawmill. He received his father's consent to proceed with the new business. Anton had permission to log a limited amount of the homestead's forest to get the business started on one condition. He had to secure contracts with other landowners who had timber to process to support the sawmill.

"Papa, I get the idea. I know what you mean." Anton said, "I could have the contracts stipulate that the landowners would receive payment for the raw trees only after their milled lumber had been sold. I will need family money to buy the equipment, build the sawmill, pay for cutting and transporting of our trees to the mill, and the maintenance of the mill until the new contracts start generating cash to cover operating expenses."

Anton's quick mind made Vaclav smile, and he said, "Yes. You have a good plan, son. You may get started immediately."

After receiving his father's approval for the new business, Anton encouraged Stanislaus to take over the farm management and crop sales completely. Stanislaus accepted the honor and responsibility of running the farm business. Anton quickly secured the contracts he needed to operate the sawmill and ordered the machinery. Construction of the sawmill began in the spring, and within six months of opening the sawmill, Anton no longer needed family trees or family money to support the mill's operation.

During the first harvest under Stanislaus' management, he realized there was a serious shortage of threshing machines around Madison. One night over dinner, Stanislaus said, "Papa, we could use more than one threshing machine. One machine takes too long to remove the seed grain from the dried stalks and husks after we harvest the fields. If we bought a second thresher, we could rent both of them once we finish our work. All the farmers need them before they can sell their grain, and not many farmers can afford to buy the equipment outright.

"We could make contracts with the farmers like the ones we have for the trees at the sawmill. Just as the suppliers do not get paid until the lumber is sold, the farmers could rent a threshing machine during harvest for a guaranteed percentage of their grain sales. The equipment would be producing a profit all season and pay for itself." Vaclav and Anton were impressed with the idea and agreed to do as Stanislaus suggested. Stanislaus' investment idea turned out to be a good and profitable one.

The Karella Family Children Begin Lives of Their Own

Karellas always looked forward to Sundays, which they observed as a day of worship and rest. This was a day to enjoy attending Sunday Mass as a family, visit with other farming families around Madison, and participate in the church-sponsored picnics held after Mass during the summers. Once a month, St. Leonard's sponsored a dance for the young adults. Church socials created a healthy and chaperoned environment for girls and boys of the community to meet and have some fun. Anton and Stanislaus began attending the church socials when the turned 19 and 18, which was long before Anna even liked boys.

Vaclav and Antonia were actually relieved their only daughter was not in a rush to meet a boy, marry and move away. They felt the opposite about the single status of their two eldest sons. They wished Anton and Stanislaus would find nice Catholic girls, marry, and start having children. As Anna grew close to graduating from high school, her interest in church socials changed dramatically.

Even Emil no longer acted like a little boy. After finishing his farm work, he would be found on the porch sketching or over at the church helping Father Cyprian or Father Jerome with the new phonograph they used for the church socials. Music excited Emil, and he volunteered whenever the Church elders needed help with the music at the picnics or the monthly dances. Father Cyprian was getting on in years. Emil got along well with the younger priest, Father Jerome, who would eventually take over at St. Leonard's. Father Jerome had been responsible for getting the donations to buy a phonograph. He told Emil about another priest, a friend of his, who ran a large parish in Omaha. They planned to exchange the new records they purchased for the

phonographs each month. Father Jerome started using the phonograph for the music at the monthly church socials so the local
parishioners who played instruments could take turns entertaining
at the church picnics.

Full of excitement, Emil told everyone at breakfast, "Father
Jerome will play two new waltzes by Johann Strauss at the social
this month."

Anton smiled and said, "Good! We need new music. Father
Jerome had a great idea about setting up a special donation box
to regularly buy music records. Playing new music will make the
socials more fun and encourage couples to dance."

Antonia and Vaclav were happy to see Anton and Emil had
a deep connection through music and art.

A Mother with Marriage and Grandchildren on Her Mind

At 23 years old, Anton had not spent much time with girls who
were not Karellas. If the subject came up, Anton shrugged it off,
saying, "I'll have time for that later. I'm too busy to look for a
wife right now." And Stanislaus always followed his brother's lead.

While the family had been building the homestead and getting
the farm started, Antonia's boys were too busy to think about
getting married. Yet she thought once the farm was up and running, her boys would settle down, find wives, and start families.
Instead, Anton turned over the farming business to Stanislaus,
leaving him no free time while Anton put all of his effort into
building up the sawmill business.

Antonia believed her sons were everything a girl could want
in a husband. *I'll admit,* Antonia thought, *Anton can be a bit cool
and aloof, but he is also handsome, smart, organized, and successful
in anything he puts his mind to. If he took a little time off from
work, he could have his business, and a family! He is so much like
his father! Anton seems unaware that years are passing him by, while
he builds businesses, fulfills his responsibilities as a big brother, and*

looks after us! I thank God he enjoys attending the church socials. I just wish he would meet a special girl.

Stanislaus at 22 Years Old

Antonia's thoughts moved to her second son. *Now, Stanislaus is handsome, charming, and easy to talk to. In general, people find him warm, spontaneous, and everyone loves him or would ... if he gave them a chance. If he spent even a tiny bit of his energy looking for a wife, I'd already have grandchildren!*

Stanislaus is just like his father and brother ... he takes his responsibilities so seriously it is hard for him to make time for anything else. First, the farm has to bring in a stable income; then, he has to get the best price for the Karella grain, and in the middle of all that, he has to supervise Emil's work.

I'm glad Emil is learning the poultry business. He might do well with the farm equipment rentals too. It's a good time for him to be earning a wage. He needs to get a feel for the kind of work he wants to do in the future.

Vaclav walked into the room and brought Antonia out of her deep reverie, and she said, "Vaclav, I am proud the farm is doing well under Stanislaus' supervision, but don't you think he could do that *and* find a wife? I believe if he put a little effort into it, he could run this farm and have a family too! But he won't talk to me about it, so will you please talk to him?"

"The last time you asked me to do this, you included Anton. What has changed?"

"Vaclav, it is not about what has changed with Anton. It is about what *never changes* with him. 'Business comes first, Mama. I'll have time for all that later, Mama. Please don't worry, Mama. I'm too busy, Mama!'" Antonia mimicked Anton's patient tone. The one he used to deliver news she didn't want to hear. "Every time I ask either of them about girls, they ignore me or leave because they suddenly remember something they forgot to do."

Vaclav laughed as he pulled his irritated wife into his arms and said, "Don't worry My Heart, they are good boys and good businessmen. Those attributes are going to be very important to the wives they pick. And yes, I will have a talk with both of them. I guess we are both ready to be grandparents. I dream of having youngsters around the farmhouse again too".

Despite her obsession regarding wives for her sons, Antonia and Vaclav maintained a good relationship with their children. The whole family still lived under the same roof and generally ate breakfast and dinner together. Conversations over meals made it easy to keep up with most of what was happening in their day-to-day lives.

1892, A Special Birthday Present for Emil

Emil was allowed to enjoy his personal time, develop his interests, and see his friends, but he did not see that his freedoms were supported by his brother's or his father's endless hard work. He enjoyed a type of freedom from responsibility that his older brothers never had.

When Emil Karella turned 14 years old, the Karellas celebrated the birthday of the *baby of the family*. Looking around the room, Emil decided no one seemed to notice he was not a baby anymore. He felt a distance growing between him and his older brothers. He could still talk to them when they had time, but their days were very busy. He and Little Anna used to have more in common until she started getting interested in her suitors. He loved his parents. Yet the more he was drawn to the modern world and its inventions, the more they clung to the old ways of doing things or thinking about things. They didn't want to change with the times. Emil believed they didn't even notice he had grown up. Despite the laughter and conversation going on around him, as the family celebrated his birthday, Emil stood quietly by his cake. He felt one of his moods coming on and became lost in thought …

Do any of them understand me? Anton spends most of his time at the sawmill these days; Stanislaus thinks about little else besides running the family farm. Now that Anna is 19, she likes different things than I do. Papa is just getting old and really doesn't notice what is happening to anybody accept Mama ... I guess Anton and I do share a love of art, literature, and music. When he is home, we talk about technology and modern inventions in the big cities. Like the first telephone exchange they built in New Haven Connecticut in 1878. We have a standing bet about how long it will take to get telephone service into Madison. Omaha got their telephone exchange only a year after Connecticut. ... Papa prefers to talk about his old shoe business... or the family's current businesses ... and If it's not about the Karellas' business... then Papa starts telling old stories about Bohemia and people I never knew. He never talks about the progress in America or places beyond the state of Nebraska. He's not even interested in hearing about the first transcontinental railroad and the land it opened up in 1869, because it's not about Nebraska. Mama thinks about little else except getting Anton and Stanislaus married and having grandchildren. If anyone bothered to ask me, I'd say, we have enough people in this house ... who needs more kids around? No one seems to have time for the one that still lives here.

Even when Emil was depressed, he did not let it show. Staying true to his nature, he politely kept all his thoughts to himself.

Suddenly, a hand tapping him on the shoulder jerked him out of his pitiful thoughts. Emil focused his eyes on his brother standing next to him. "Emil, did you hear what I said?" Anton asked, concerned by the woebegone look on Emil's face. Seeing his brother's concern, Emil turned pinked-cheeked with embarrassment over what he'd been thinking about his family. "Sorry, Anton, I was thinking about other... things... I didn't hear you talking to me. What was it you said?"

Emil's skin had gone back to its normal shade as he answered Anton and reached out to accept the large, rolled paper Anton held out to him.

"I wanted you to take a look at this advertisement I found. I thought the art was interesting and figured you'd appreciated it as much as I did. It reminded me of the artwork you did on that lumber sign for me a couple of months ago."

Curious, Emil carefully unrolled the poster and his eyes went wide. A huge smile spread across his face. It was easy to see Emil did appreciate the exciting words, bright colors, amazing images of exotic animals, and beautiful costumed people that filled the paper as it captured his artist's eye.

"I had many adventures before I was your age and can appreciate that you want them too. Emil, we are more alike than you think. I still like adventure. But I must balance that desire with my responsibilities. However, since The Barnum and Baily Circus is going to be in Omaha in September... and that's just a little over five hours by train... I thought we should go. It seemed like a birthday present you'd like that we can experience together. So, what do you say? Shall we take a train ride?" Anton asked. Anticipating his baby brother's reaction, Anton just smiled, waiting for the whole idea to sink in.

"Are you serious? You really mean it, Anton? You'd take time away from work to do this? Just you and me?" When his brother gave an affirmative nod, Emil yelled, "Yes! Of course, I'd love to go to Omaha to see the circus with you!"

While Emil and Anton were in Omaha, they spent two days at the circus, and also visited the University of Nebraska to watch a Bugeaters football game. The brothers walked through Buffalo Bill's Wild West Rocky Mountain and Prairie Exhibition and then took a tour of the Omaha World Harold Newspaper headquarters. While they were at the newspaper, Emil paid for a subscription so the World Harold newspaper would be mailed to him in Madison.

Emil enjoyed long talks with Anton while they traveled on the trains, and as they neared Madison, he looked at his brother and said, "Thank you, Anton. I loved my birthday present. I am glad you are my brother, and I'll never forget this trip with you."

"Thank you, Emil, I will never forget it, either," Anton replied with a soft smile.

1891, Madison, Nebraska: Little Anna turns 19 Years Old

As a young girl, Anna had been totally fascinated and preoccupied with her studies. Serious about science, she had talked about becoming a doctor or a nurse throughout her sophomore year of high school. In her senior year, as Anna's graduation drew near, Antonia noticed a change in her daughter. Anna's personality and respectful intelligence had been drawing men's attention for the last several years, yet she had seemed unaware of it. By 18, Anna had begun to notice her effect on men, and by 19, she was actually enjoying the attention she was receiving. Proud of the young woman her daughter had matured into, Antonia understood why Anna found it easy to talk to men and sway their thinking. She had been practicing on her father and brothers for years. *My daughter will make an impressive wife and business partner with the right man,* Antonia thought.

Having attended St. Leonard's church socials for two years, Little Anna enjoyed the dancing. The boys who had the courage to ask her to dance were not the ones she found interesting. They were the bold ones who hung around her brothers and talked about crops and business. Though her brothers' friends were fun, and she enjoyed matching wits or shocking them with her political opinions, she wasn't really interested in any of them.

Little Anna's laughter and ease with everyone who socialized with her brothers, made girls request to stand by her at the socials. She knew most of them were trying to gain the attention of one of her handsome brothers or their friends. That ploy rarely worked. Eventually, most of them began to feel invisible, and when that happened, they would stomp away disappointed and frustrated.

In her opinion, Anton was cordially social and polite with everyone at first, and eventually, he would turn a bit serious and aloof. Stanislaus was the opposite. He charmed all the ladies while showing none of them any particular favor. Both her brothers seemed unaffected by the constant attention they received from girls.

Anna knew her Mama hoped that when she began attending the socials, she would be able to find out which girls her brothers liked. Her Mama stopped asking her questions because Anna's answers were always the same. "Sorry, Mama, they don't seem to like any of those girls very much."

As for herself, Anna had recently taken note of a new boy at church. At first, she assumed he was quiet because he was shy. After watching him at a couple of the church picnics and the last church social, she decided he was just reserved like her brother Anton and liked that about him.

At the next church picnic, Little Anna found Father Jerome as he was filling his plate and asked, "Excuse me, Father, do you know that young man standing over there near Melissa Throck and Tina Blaha? Do you know who he is?"

Father Jerome smiled and replied, "Who? Oh yes, I see who you are talking about. His name is Anton Kratochvil, and he is in town visiting family." Anna smiled and thanked the priest for the information. As she walked back to the table where her parents sat, her mind was busy trying to figure out how to introduce herself to Mr. Kratochvil. Anna did not realize how infatuated she had become with young Mr. Kratochvil until Father Jerome made an announcement at Mass.

St. Leonard's Holds a Lady's Choice Church Social Dance

Excitement coursed through Anna as Father Jerome publicized a change in the upcoming church social schedule at Sunday Mass, "I am pleased to announce our invitation to several new parishes has been accepted. The next church social and dance hosted by St. Leonard's will include young adults from three neighboring parishes. And ... this will be a *lady's choice dance*. In case there is any confusion about the rules of this dance, I will reiterate; the ladies may ask any young man they wish, to dance." A positive murmur ran through the congregation, and heads nodded in approval. Feminine giggles of excitement were heard around the church. There was no doubt about how the ladies felt about choosing whom they wanted to dance with.

Anna, unlike the tittering girls sitting behind her, did not make a sound or show outwardly how her heart leaped with exhilaration at the idea of being able to ask Anton Kratochvil to dance. Anna leaned up against her mother's side and whispered, "Mama, could you help me make a new dress for the lady's choice dance in two weeks?" Antonia smiled and squeezed her daughter's hand, nodding that she could.

The evening of the lady's choice dance finally arrived. Anton and Stanislaus were dressed in their Sunday clothes and handsome as ever as they waited for their sister. Exceptionally attractive in her new dress, Anna had twisted and pinned her hair in soft waves on her head and let pretty ringlets fall down her back. "Little sister, you look … nice," said Anton with a brotherly smile.

Stanislaus shoved Anton's shoulder and rolled his eyes before saying, "Anna, you look lovely! I'd be honored to take your arm if you're ready to go." His charming compliment put a radiant smile on his little sister's face.

At the Lady's Choice Dance

By the time the Karellas arrived, there was quite a crowd in the church hall. "Anton, why don't we take a stroll around the outside of this crowd and have a good look around before we settle in one place?" Stanislaus suggested.

"Good thinking. Come on Little Anna, hold on to our arms as we walk around the dance floor," Anton suggested.

Anna felt like a queen being escorted by her two handsome brothers and knew everyone was looking at them. But nothing could compare to her excitement when she spotted Anton Kratochvil. *I'm going to finally meet him!* Anna thought. After making one circuit around the floor, Anna pointed Anton Kratochvil out to her brothers, and the three of them walked over to stand in front of the young man. Anton introduced his party, "Excuse me, may I introduce myself? I am Anton Karella, this is my brother, Stanislaus, and this is our little sister, Anna."

"I am pleased to meet you. My name is Anton Kratochvil. I am here in Madison visiting family, though my parents live in California."

"Anton, since you are new around here, I'm not sure you are aware of the rules concerning tonight's social. This is a lady's choice dance," Anton informed the younger man, "and my sister, Anna, would like to dance with you."

Smiling directly at Anna, young Anton Kratochvil replied, "It would be my honor and pleasure to accept your invitation, Anna." Holding out his hand to her, he said, "Miss Anna, may I escort you to the dance floor?" She took his hand, and the smiling couple disappeared into the crowd, waltzing on the dance floor.

As Anton and Stanislaus watched them walk away, Anton felt a bit impressed. "That was smoothly done of Kratochvil, wouldn't you say, brother?" Before Stanislaus could reply, he felt a soft tap on his arm. He turned to his right and looked down into the sweet eyes of an attractive young lady who blushed now that she had his attention.

Charming as ever, Stanislaus smiled and whispered, "Go ahead and ask. I won't bite."

With a sigh of relief, the young woman replied, "Stanislaus, I'm not sure you remember me. My name is Anna Plouzek, and we went to school together. Would you like to dance?" Stanislaus' eyes lit up with surprise. He did remember her name, *but she definitely had not looked like this ... in school.*

Stanislaus had been silent so long in appreciation of Anna's lovely face that she grew embarrassed and started to turn away, thinking he did not want to dance with her. Snapping to attention, Stanislaus hastily extended his hand, touching her gently on the shoulder to stop her retreat, and replied, "Forgive me, Anna. I was momentarily speechless because you look so lovely. I would be honored to dance with you." Extending his hand, he continued, "May I lead you to the dance floor?" Nodding, pink-cheeked, and smiling with pleasure, Anna placed her hand in his, and they walked toward the dance floor. Anton watched them go and then looked around for Alfred Jenks. He had an idea to discuss that Alfred might find interesting.

Typical of Anton, as dancers whirled waltzing happily around the floor, he spent his time engaged in a conversation about lumber. That is until Alfred and two other men who had joined their conversation stopped talking and were staring at a point somewhere across the room. A little miffed that they were not paying attention, Anton turned to locate what had distracted them.

Instantly captured by what he saw, he whispered, "Who... is... that?" The striking young woman across the dance floor was standing next to Father Jerome, his sister, and that young man—Anton—that his sister had been dancing with. Anton Karella did not say a word to the other men. He just walked straight through the crowd of dancers on the floor and stopped in front of Father Jerome, and said, "Good evening, Father." He nodded at Anna's dance partner, saying, "Anton," and then looked at his sister and said, "Anna, my dear little sister, would you please introduce me to this beautiful young lady?"

Anna nearly laughed out loud. Her brother, Anton, was the last person she expected to react like this, but it was a good thing he had. The crowd of men around them had grown rapidly, and they all wanted an introduction to her beautiful new friend. None of them stood a chance now that Anton had got there first.

Little Anna made the introduction quickly, "Anastasia, this is my eldest brother, Anton. Anton, this is Anastasia Holy. Her family lives in the School Craft Precinct." Knowing she was now in the way and her brother had everything under his control, Anna turned to her young man and asked, "Would you like to dance again, Anton?" Smiling, he replied with a nod and placed her hand on his arm as they walked away.

Anton neatly pinned Anastasia between Father Jerome and himself successfully keeping all his potential rivals from getting too close. Then, in a husky voice, he almost did not recognize as his own, Anton said, "Excuse me, Father Jerome. I know you said this is a lady's choice dance. But would you give me permission to break that procedure and ask for the honor to partner Anastasia in the next dance?" Father Jerome looked at Anastasia and asked, "Would you like to dance with Anton?" Anastasia nodded her head and replied, "Yes, I would very much enjoy dancing with Anton. Thank you, Father, for keeping me company." Anastasia turned to Anton and laid her hand on his arm, and they walked into the crowd to join the waltz in progress.

The carriage ride back to the Karella homestead was a quiet one. Anton, Stanislaus, and Anna were reliving their wonderful evening. Each had shared a magical night partnered with an exceptional person, and each of them had received a promise there'd be more nights like this one to come. It was an evening that would change the course of their lives. But none of the siblings were ready to say out loud what their hearts had already decided for them. These new feelings were still too private to talk about.

Little Anna was the first of her siblings to recognize the true depth of the feelings each had experienced with the new people they had met.

Once Anna decided Mr. Kratochvil was the man she wanted for her husband, she began seeking him out at church functions. Two years quickly passed as they spent as much time together as possible and began to dream about their future.

Stanislaus recognized his affection for Anna Plouzek shortly after his sister decided she was in love with Anton Kratochvil. However, Stanislaus was a thinker and needed a lot more time to plan. The idea of getting married was such a momentous decision that it overwhelmed

Anton Kratochvil and Little Anna Karella three years before marriage

Stanislaus. The idea of marriage made him worry about things that he had never considered before. *I am a second son. Since I must assume the farm is going to be Anton's, I have to consider the money I need before I feel comfortable taking on the responsibility of a wife ... and then I must consider our children ... what will I need to provide for them?* All that thinking, worrying, and planning occupied his thoughts when he wasn't busy with the farm. However, his preoccupation with long-range plans did not mean Stanislaus was unaware of the competition other men might create.

Stanislaus made a visit to meet Anna Plouzeks family. He liked her father, Frantisek Aloysis, and her mother, Marie Philomena, and got along well with Anna's siblings, Mathew, Mary, Frank, and Emma.

Once a week, the Plouzek family welcomed Stanislaus to share their Saturday night meal. He also received her parents' permission to begin sitting with Anna at church on Sundays. Each month, Stanislaus made sure Anna attended the church socials exclusively with him, or he monopolized his Anna's attention at the socials, so no other man had a chance to interfere. Eventually, Stanislaus felt his life was organized and settled enough to formally request permission to be engaged and to court the Plouzek's daughter.

For a long time, Anton did not recognize his attraction to Anastasia for what it was. All he knew was that he enjoyed spending time with her. He felt comfortable, and she was easy to talk to. Everything Anastasia said was interesting. Their connection had been instant and only grew deeper each time they were together. After discovering Anastasia was of Bohemian descent, he was even more excited to learn as much as possible about her, and her relatives who lived in the Schoolcraft Precinct of Madison County.

Though they did not formally attend the church socials together at first, they always ended up together. Every time they saw each other, it was like no one else existed. The two of them would sit and talk or dance all evening, and only after the last dance of the social did Anton wonder where his brother and sister were.

The Beginning of Real Change in the Karella Household

Although the Karellas had busy schedules during workdays, they always gathered in the evenings. Conversations held at Vaclav and Antonia's dinner table were particularly fruitful for picking up odd bits of news such as when Anton began to repeatedly mention a girl named Anastasia. The differences in Stanislaus and Anna's conversations were not as clear because Anna kept talking about Anton, and Stanislaus kept talking about Anna. Consequently, those new relationships went undetected a little longer than Anton's budding romance with Anastasia.

Antonia listened intently to every detail Anton mentioned about Miss Anastasia Holy and was determined to find out as much as she could about the girl and her family. Antonia was sure Anton was serious about Anastasia long before her son acknowledged it himself. Those feelings were confirmed when Anton introduced Anastasia to his mother and father as they held hands at a church picnic.

Just like his father had done, Anton mistook the beginnings of love between him and Miss Holy as only friendship. As Antonia watched them together, something about Anastasia made it clear she would help Anton figure out the truth, instead of waiting for him to figure it out on his own.

Vaclav and Antonia ask Father Jerome About What He Knows

After Antonia convinced Vaclav that Anton was serious about Anastasia, Vaclav became as curious about the young lady and her family as Antonia. They sought out Father Jerome at the next church picnic. When he was alone, they asked him what he knew about the Holys. Father Jerome remembered the night of the lady's choice social when he helped introduce Anton Karella to Anastasia Holy. He approved of the attachment forming between

Anton and Miss Holy, and decided the situation justified sharing the information he knew with Mr. and Mrs. Karella.

"Anastasia's parents, Jacob Holy and his wife, Mary, recently filled out a family record for our community census. So, I happen to know a good deal about them as well as her aunt and uncle, Katharina and Joseph Kuchar, who live in the Schoolcraft Precinct."

"Say, I know Joseph Kuchar," Vaclav said. "We met when I first moved to Madison. We see each other at the Feed & Seed in town and generally talk about crops. So that's Anastasia's uncle? I do recall he said his wife's sister and husband were coming to live with them from Bohemia. I don't remember him mentioning children, but he might have—it was a long time ago."

"Jacob Holy did come from Bohemia and was born in 1849 in the village of Duby Hora Kraj Pirel."

Antonia whispered, "Her father is ten years younger than we are."

Vaclav hushed his wife, saying, "Please let our priest tell his story."

"Thank you, Vaclav. Now then, Jacobs's wife's family name is Koryta, and Mary was born in 1853 in the village of Kozli. They married in 1872, in Radobia, Bohemia."

"They were married nine years after we were," Antonia whispered, and Vaclav rolled his eyes and prayed for patience.

"My Heart, please let Father continue."

Father Jerome took a breath and began again, "Jacob and Mary were married three years when they had their first child Mary in 1875."

Antonia leaned toward Vaclav and whispered, "By 1875, we already had three children and made the decision to go to America. I left for New York in 1875!"

Vaclav was having a hard time figuring out if Antonia was talking to him or to herself. *If Antonia doesn't quit interrupting, this is going to be a very long story,* Vaclav thought. Then, politely ignoring Antonia's comment, Vaclav said, "Father, please go on."

Nodding, Father Jerome began again, "The Holy's second daughter is Anastasia, and she was born in 1877. And—" Father Jerome suddenly changed tactics, cutting off another of Antonia's observations. "Yes, I know, Antonia. That was the year you told me Vaclav and the children joined you in New York."

Antonia blushed, grumbling beneath her breath so only Vaclav could hear and said, "Our priest has a mind like a trap ... never seems to forget anything."

Father Jerome had excellent hearing, too, and responded with a smile, knowing she had not meant for him to hear her comment. "It is good of you to notice, Mrs. Karella. I possess the gift of total recall. I remember everything I have ever read or heard like it was written in a book in front of my eyes."

Antonia's blush deepened, but she remained silent for the moment. Father Jerome tried to finish his story as fast as possible. "Jacob and Mary had a third baby girl, Bessie, in 1879. Three years later, Anna was born in 1882. Two years after that, they had their first son, Frank, in 1884. Then, Mary gave birth to Josephine in 1886."

Antonia couldn't help herself. She took hold of Vaclav's hand and interrupted again, "Oh my goodness, 1886? That was the year we recorded the title on our homestead."

Trying one last trick to silence the woman, Father Jerome said, "It is also the year this country celebrated the building of Liberty Island and the installation of the Statue of Liberty in New York Harbor." Father Jerome's unrelated comment took Vaclav and Antonia so completely by surprise it silenced them both. Tickled his plan worked, Father Jerome grinned and said, "I do love history, don't you? I also find it amusing when I speak of the Holy family in School Craft, some people literally think I'm talking about Mary, Joseph, and Jesus, *The Holy Family*." Father's eyes twinkled with humor until he realized it was lost on the couple staring at him with blank expressions. *Best finish the rest of my Holy family story as quickly as possible,* Father Jerome thought.

"Mary and her sister, Katharina, had been writing to each other since Katharina and her husband Joseph Kuchar were married. Mary's sister and her family had already immigrated to America and were living in Madison. After the birth of Josephine, Katharina pleaded with Mary to come to America. "The Holy's had already purchased tickets to America when Mary discovered she was pregnant. At the time of their departure from Bohemia, Mary was eight months along in her pregnancy. Jacob and Mary decided they could not wait for the child to be born and boarded the steamship Alba. The Holy family arrived in America in the spring of 1888 and then traveled

Joseph and Katharina Kuchar and daughter

by train to Colfax, Nebraska, where they would meet the Kuchars. Upon reaching Colfax, Nebraska, Mary went into labor and had her baby there."

Holding up his hand to stave off another interruption, the priest said, "Yes, Antonia, just like when you had Emil. Mary Holy's seventh child, Katherine, was born in July of 1888 in Colfax. The Holys eventually moved in with the Kuchars, and that's the whole story as I know it," Father Jerome concluded.

"Father, can you believe all the similarities between Anastasia's family and ours?" Antonia asked.

Before Father Jerome could answer, Vaclav said, "I like the fact that she is Bohemian and that her parents had similar dreams."

The priest nodded his head in silent agreement, then excusing himself, left the table to visit with more of his parishioners.

Vaclav shook his head thinking, *So, Anastasia's family arrived in the spring of 1888 ... I remember that winter! It wasn't near as bad here as it was further north ... the snow and wind ... it came on so fast ... temperatures plunged to 30 and 40 below ... 100 adults and children died … now when a winter storm is coming, we always say, "I hope it won't be as bad as the Blizzard of 1888."*

Antonia tapped Vaclav on the arm. "Are you alright, darling? I've been talking to you, and I don't think you've heard a word I said."

Vaclav's face cleared as he replied, "My Heart, I apologize. I was just remembering the winter of 1888 because Father mentioned it." Antonia frowned and whispered, "Yes … that's the year … all those children died."

Vaclav regretted bringing up anything that reminded Antonia of children dying. Taking her by the hand, he whispered, "I'm sorry, My Heart, that's all in the past. Please don't think about it." The lunch bell clanged, and everyone around them began to move toward the picnic tables full of food. Vaclav grinned, saying, "I'm starving! Let's hurry so we don't have to wait in line!"

Laughing at his eagerness to eat, Antonia forgot her heartaches for the moment and followed her husband to the food.

Father Jerome Remembers Meeting the Kuchars and the Holys

After leaving the company of the Karellas, Father Jerome kept thinking about the Kuchars and the Holys. While he ate his food, he recalled his first visit with them at their home. He made that visit shortly before the Schoolcraft Precinct built their new church.

When he accepted Mrs. Kuchar's invitation, he deliberately chose to go late on a Saturday afternoon, hoping the family would not feel obligated to share a meal with him. Visiting the members of his congregation at their homes allowed him to learn a lot about his parishioners and their lives.

Walking up to the door of the dugout, he had been amazed to discover two families lived together in that tiny space. Of course, he was familiar with this type of housing. Dugouts were used extensively in areas where lumber was unavailable or too expensive for the people settling the plains. Many were built in the 1700s, and that construction continued into the mid 1800s in Nebraska. The Kuchars had literally dug into the hillside and built most of their house underground. The part above ground at the front of the dwelling was connected to an outer wall. Very little wood was used except for framing the window and doorway. The rest of the house was constructed from a collection of sod grass, bricks, and field stones.

American style dugout house, Kuchars, 1800s

Katharina Kuchar greeted him at the door, saying, "Good afternoon, Father Jerome. Please take the chair under the shade tree, and I'll bring out some cooled tea."

With joyful noise, children poured out of the house and sat on the ground around him. Mrs. Holy came out of the house carrying a large plate of cookies followed by a toddler struggling to hang onto her skirt. Right behind them was Mrs. Kuchar carrying a pitcher of tea, and two of the older girls carried cups.

Bessie and Josephine Holy, 1800s, Madison, NE

Father Jerome's Conversations with Little Bessie Holy, 1894

Katherina Kuchar introduced her sister, Mary Holy, and then named the children settled at his feet. Katherina's teenaged niece,

273

Anastasia, poured the tea, and her sister Mary, passed out the filled cups. Warm afternoon sunbeams filtered through the leaves above as the children sat listening. That is until little Bessie Holy decided to explain to him why they had so many children living together.

Bessie stood up in front of him tapping him on the knee for attention. When he looked at her, she informed him, "I'm Bessie, and I was almost ten years old when we came here. I remember Auntie Katharina and Uncle Joseph had six kids, and we had six kids, and then Mama had our new baby. We all started living together. That's why there are so many of us," said Bessie, nodding her head for emphasis.

He had thought she was finished, but then Bessie continued. "Oh, and Mama said this little dugout would be warm and safe. I heard her tell Auntie Katharina that she didn't know how we would have made it without them and their little house."

He remembered smiling at Bessie and thanking her for her fine explanation. Pleased by his praise, the little girl decided to add more information. "Oh, and Mama said we came here to live with Auntie Katarina and Uncle Joseph because they hoped life would be better in America."

Mrs. Holy blushed with embarrassment with Bessie's last statement, and young Anastasia seemed somewhat embarrassed as well, and said, "Mama, I'll take the children over to the stock shed. It's time we fed the chickens."

Her mother and aunt sighed in relief as Anastasia gathered up the children. Obviously, the mothers were glad to have the little ones preoccupied before any of the others decided to enlighten him with more stories. He recalled the scene with approval, remembering how gentle and patient the two mothers had been with their combined brood of 14 -children. He also remembered how observant, respectful, and well-spoken Anastasia had been.

Coming back to the present, he looked around the picnic area and spotted Anton and Anastasia eating together. Father Jerome thought, *Yes, Anastasia Holy has grown up into a fine young woman and would make a good wife for Anton Karella when the time comes.*

Holy Family Tree

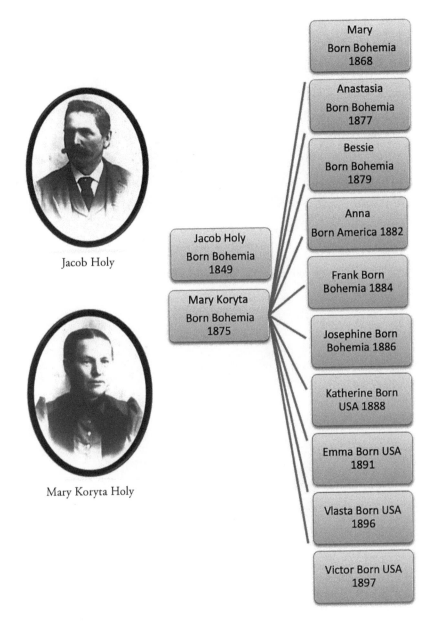

Jacob Holy

Mary Koryta Holy

Jacob Holy
Born Bohemia
1849

Mary Koryta
Born Bohemia
1875

Mary
Born Bohemia
1868

Anastasia
Born Bohemia
1877

Bessie
Born Bohemia
1879

Anna
Born America 1882

Frank Born
Bohemia 1884

Josephine Born
Bohemia 1886

Katherine Born
USA 1888

Emma Born USA
1891

Vlasta Born USA
1896

Victor Born USA
1897

Left to right back row: Mary, Josephine, Anna, Bessie, Frank,
Victor, Anastasia, and Catherine
Left to right front row: Husband Jacob Holy,
Grandmother Koryta, Jacob's wife, Mary Koryta Holy

Anastasia Holy, future wife of Anton Karella

The New Generation of Karellas Learn About Falling in Love

There was nothing careless or disorganized about the way the Karella men planned and worked to build their businesses. Perhaps it was their habit of looking at a plan from every angle before making a decision that made them slow to distinguish between friendship and love. Or when it came time to move from engagement to marriage. This was not the case with the women who set their sights on Karella men. These strong women and the women born into the Karella family were quick to recognize what they wanted in a man and did not easily give up on what they wanted.

Karella Engagements

Sundays became the highlight of Anton's week. He left the farm early so he could pick up Anastasia and go to Mass with her family or his. He and Anastasia went to all the Schoolcraft parish events and attended the St. Leonard's church social every month; the same as Little Anna was doing with Anton Kratochvil, and Stanislaus with Anna Plouzek. One evening almost two years after Little Anna met her Anton, she asked her eldest brother to take a walk with her and confided, "Anton, I am going to keep Anton Kratochvil, and I am going to marry him."

"When did all this happen?" Anton asked.

"I knew almost from the beginning that he was the one. But it has taken time to get my Anton to see that we are ready to be engaged." Then, Anna asked, "Have you talked to Anastasia about getting engaged yet?"

Anton shook his head. "I think it's too soon to think that way Little Anna. Anastasia is great, I really like her company, and we have lots of fun together… but I don't want to assume she is thinking about anything permanent," Anton replied.

"Anton! It has been two years since you started seeing her. I think there is a lot more than friendship between you two. You might try asking her what she thinks about it. Open your eyes, brother, before she gets tired of waiting for you to figure it out."

During the harvest season of 1893, Little Anna asked permission to bring her young Anton to a Karella family picnic. Anna had secretly become engaged to Anton Kratochvil at the mid-summer church social. It was time to talk to her parents and make their engagement official so they could set a wedding date. Holding hands, young Kratochvil asked Vaclav and Antonia to sit with them for a private conversation.

"Mr. and Mrs. Karella, I love your daughter, and I ask your permission to marry Anna," Anton said.

Little Anna jumped in before her father or mother could say a word, "Mama, Papa, I want you to know I have already agreed to this engagement. Anton and I … we … want to get married next spring."

Vaclav gazed directly at his daughter, not young Anton, took hold of Antonia's hand, and replied; "My daughter, it appears we have no say in this."

"Papa, you and Mama taught me to know what I want and to go after it. I want Anton, and he wants me. We want your approval, and we are asking for your blessing on our choice."

Vaclav and Antonia Karella looked at Anton Kratochvil and asked, "Anton, how do you plan to take care of my daughter, and where do you plan to live?"

"Mr. Karella, my father's family lives in California, but Anna and I would like to stay here in Madison after we get married. I am looking for work and plan to have enough money set aside to allow Anna and I to marry by next summer."

"What kind of work do you know how to do?" Vaclav asked.

"I can learn anything, and I am willing to work hard," Anton replied.

Vaclav could feel the young man's honesty regarding his daughter. Looking at his wife, Antonia gave a slight nod. Vaclav gave permission, with the family's blessing, to the engaged couple to marry when Mr. Kratochvil could support a wife.

Little Anna squeezed Anton's hand and whispered, "It is not entirely yes. But it is not a *no*, either. We will get his full blessing soon—you will see."

"Anton," Vaclav said, "go see Stanislaus about work. I believe he could use help on the farm. Anna is our only daughter. Her mother and I do not want to see her leave us or to be unhappy, so this is what we propose. We would like you two to live here with us on the farm after you marry, until you can afford a place of your own."

"I am humbled by your offer," replied Kratochvil, "I accept. I shall seek out Stanislaus right away." As Little Anna and her Anton walked away holding hands, Anna, bursting with excitement, said, "I told you it would be all right! We will make it work. Oh, and do not worry that you will feel uncomfortable at the homestead when we get married. I have the largest bedroom in the house! We will do just fine together."

1894, The First Wedding of Vaclav and Antonia's Children

Anton Karella could not believe his Little Anna, his baby sister, had turned 21 years old and was now a married woman. As he hugged and congratulated her, she giggled and whispered in his ear, "Brother, get off your slowpoke-plow and ask Anastasia to marry you!"

He stiffened up a moment, then relaxed and whispered back, "Do you really believe she wants to?"

Amazed her older brother had to ask such a thing, she realized he was less confident than

Anna Karella Kratochvil and husband Anton Kratochvil, wedding

he let on. Happy to help, she whispered back, "Of course she does. You've been seeing her as long as I have been seeing my Anton. Three years has been more than enough time to decide you're the one she wants. Besides, she told me she wishes you would ask her. But if you don't get moving, Mike Miles is going to ask her first." Anna let go of her handsome older brother and smiled up at him. She watched the expression on his face go from a look of surprise, to competitive awareness, and then to one of determination as he walked away.

Another guest tapped her on the shoulder, and although Little Anna continued to receive and give hugs, her mind remained preoccupied with Anton and Anastasia. She smiled and thought, *Now, that bit of news ought to get my slowcoach brother moving! I can't wait to talk with Anastasia or to call her my sister!* Little Anna and her brother, Anton, had grown close over the last three years, and she wanted him to be as happy as she was.

As if summoned by Little Anna's thoughts, Anastasia was suddenly in front of her enveloping her in a warm hug and wishing her love and happiness. Anna returned the hug enthusiastically and whispered in Anastasia's ear, "I believe my brother has something he wants to ask you. But you must promise to act surprised when he does."

Anastasia stepped back and looked her friend in the eyes. Wearing a radiant smile, she whispered breathlessly, "*Truly?*" Anna nodded her head excitedly, and Anastasia whispered, "Thank you dear sister. I promise to act surprised."

By the time Anton told his parents he planned to ask Anastasia to marry him, he had been unofficially courting Anastasia for three years. Vaclav and Antonia were thrilled with Anton's decision. After giving him their blessing to marry, they also gave him a special heirloom. The Karellas' first born son received his great, great, great grandmother Nemec's Bohemian garnet wedding ring to grace the finger of his bride.

Anton had been carrying around the heirloom his parents had given to him for weeks. He was having difficulty deciding when and where to ask Anastasia to marry him. As he drove the carriage out to pick her up for the monthly social at St. Leonard's, he kept wondering what he should do. When Anastasia answered the door, she was so lovely that she took his breath away. Warmth wrapped around his heart. He instantly knew it was the right time and the right place as he stepped through the doorway.

"Anastasia, could you please tell your parents I'd like to talk with them?" Anastasia turned and passed the request to her parents, Jacob and Mary. As the Holys joined Anton and their daughter by the door, Joseph and Katherina gathered the rest of the family and moved to the other side of the room.

Anastasia stood by Anton's side, placing her hand on his arm, and he covered it with his hand. Anastasia's father greeted Anton, and he replied, "Good evening Mr. Holy … Mrs. Holy … I am in love with Anastasia, and I ask for your permission to marry your daughter."

Jacob and Mary had always liked Anton and now respected him for formally asking their permission to marry their daughter. Jacob, looking at his daughter, could see the love she had for Anton by the way she looked at him.

He and his wife had questioned Anastasia over the years about her feelings for the Karella boy, especially when she began to see Anton exclusively.

"Anastasia, do you want to marry the Karella boy?" Her mother had asked.

Anastasia was always emphatic in her reply. "Mama, I am in love with him, and Anton Karella is the only boy I want to marry!"

As Mr. Holy stood in front of the handsome couple, he looked at his wife, Mary. Upon receiving her slight nod, he turned to Anton and replied, "Anton, you have our permission and our blessing to ask our daughter if she wants to marry you."

Anastasia looked at her papa with love. He was giving her the honor of making her own decision. Speaking from her heart, she replied, "Thank you, Papa."

Anton knelt down on one knee in front of the entire Holy-Kuchar family gathered in that small space and asked, "Anastasia, will you honor me by becoming my wife? With an open heart for all to see, he whispered a second time, "Will you marry me?"

With tears of joy filling her eyes and wearing an enchanting smile, she replied, "Yes, my dearest Anton, I will marry you! I will love you forever."

As Anton stood up to embrace her, Mr. Kuchar opened a bottle of homemade cordial and called for a toast.

Anton took a small ornate wooden box from his jacket pocket and opened it. Anastasia gasped at the beautiful gold and garnet ring lying within. With a trembling hand, she picked it up and slipped it onto her finger.

Mary and Joseph Holy, Anastasia Holy's parents.

Anton leaned close to Anastasia's ear and whispered, "My papa gave it to my mama when he asked her to marry him. It was my great, great, great grandmother's ring, and they handed it down to me for you, my love."

Holding hands, the engaged couple held up their glasses and accepted the family's toast of love and happiness. Anton and Anastasia smiled at each other feeling lightheaded and giddy as the sweet and spicy liquid slipped down their throats warming them to their toes. It was a feeling they would never forget.

The Karellas Put an Addition on the Homestead House

As soon as the announcement of Anton's engagement was printed in the newspaper, he began preparation for married life. Anton had lumber sent to the homestead for a two-room addition. Anastasia wanted their rooms on the main floor, so Anton built the additional space for him and his family off the kitchen side of the farmhouse.

Karella homestead house, front-door view

Only four short years after Anton's printed debut in the Nebraska State Gazetteer, and one year after Little Anna Karella married Anton Kratochvil, 18 year old Anastasia Holy was getting dressed for her wedding.

"Little Anna, how do I look?" whispered the bride waiting to walk down the aisle.

"My dear sister, you are going to take my brother's breath away!" Little Anna said as she hugged Anastasia.

As Anastasia walked up the aisle, she held onto her father's arm tightly. *Little Anna is wrong. I'm the one who is breathless,* Anastasia thought as she saw the handsome 27-year-old Anton Karella waiting for her with a brilliant smile on his face. "Papa," Anastasia whispered, "I'm marrying the most wonderful man in the world."

Madison Daily Herald Wedding Announcements for April 30, 1895

Anton Karella entered into matrimony in Battle Creek, Nebraska, with Anastasia Holy. Anton Karella is the eldest son of Wenceslaus (Vaclav) Karella and Antonia Nemec Karella who reside in Madison, Nebraska. Anastasia Holy is the second-born daughter of Jacob Holy and Mary Koryta Holy from the precinct of Schoolcraft in Madison, Nebraska. Anastasia and Anton Karella were married before Reverend Domino Clemens, rector of the Schoolcraft Catholic Church, on the 30th day of April 1895.

Anton Karella and Anastasia Holy-Karella wedding, 1895

CHAPTER 8

Karella Weddings, Births, and a New Century

1895–1900

Dear Sister Margaret Mary,

Thank you for the interview notes and stories you've collected in Nebraska from Anton and Anastasia's children, Helen, Frank, Martha, and Mary. I've gathered the stories from their other two brothers here in Alaska, my dad (Ambrose Jerome) and dad's youngest brother, Uncle Shorty (Anastas Leonard). I agree that the family charts you are making are the best way to keep the family connections clear and organized. Please send a chart for each family to put into the pages.

*At the beginning of this next section, we come to the year
1900. There will be big changes within the family during
these next five years, and it is time for me to give a summary
on each of Antonia's remaining children.*

*I could use anything specific you have about Stanislaus, Emil,
and Little Anna as they marry and all the information you
have on their children, the third generation of American
Karellas.*

*After I've finished these summaries, the story will mostly fol-
low Anton's life as the first-born son of his generation.*

Much love cousin, Andy

Dear Andy,

*I approve of the way you've been molding a historical view
of the world and the facts concerning the Karella family into
a touching story about the lives of Vaclav, Antonia, and their
children, Anton, Stanislaus, Anna, and Emil John.*

*I have enclosed the rest of what I found on Anton and his sib-
lings and also what I have on Anton and Anastasia's children.
Please note the new branches on the Karella family tree in this
section will include Helen Karella, who married into the Bean
family, Martha Karella, who married into the Pojar family,
and Mary Karella, who married into the Voborny family.*

*I included the information I have on the three Karella boys as
well—Ambrose Jerome, Frank, and Anastas.*

*In addition, I have sent copies of the research notes and doc-
umentation collected by Florence Karella Roggenbach, Mary
Karella Voborny, and myself. See copies of the records we found*

at St. Leonard's Catholic Church and the county public records office. It is quite a pile of dates, names, facts, and events.

Looking forward to your next letter and the next batch of story pages,

God Bless cousin and good luck,

Sister Margaret Mary

June 1895, Nebraska Homestead: Stanislaus Has an Announcement

These days the Karella family took up two whole pews at St. Leonards during mass. Most often there were seven adults that included Vaclav and Antonia, the newlyweds, Anton and Anastasia, Little Anna, her husband, Anton, and Emil John. But sometimes it was nine, when Stanislaus brought Miss Plouzek to sit with the family.

Father Jerome had finished his homily, and then added, "Sorry, one more thing. The Lady's Guild wants me to remined everyone that the first parish picnic of the summer will be held after Mass today. Everyone is encouraged to bring a little extra money to buy a raffle ticket for the music quilt. The proceeds will go toward buying new music records for the Church Socials." Smiling at the excitement his announcement caused among the young adults, he said, "It is a good cause, and your participation will be appreciated."

The warm sunshine felt good as parishioners unloaded baskets of food from the wagons and carried them to the picnic tables. As the Karellas walked to the picnic area, Stanislaus pulled his older brother aside and whispered urgently, "I've got news!"

Instantly curious, Anton said, "Anastasia please go on ahead. I'll be there shortly." Turning toward his brother he couldn't help wondering what had caused the amazing smile on Stanislaus' face. "What is it?" Anton asked quietly.

Stanislaus announced enthusiastically, "By June of next year, I'll be a married man too! Anna has agreed!"

Anton hugged Stanislaus and replied, "Congratulations brother! Anastasia will be thrilled when I tell her she's going to have another sister in the house."

"Oh, please don't say anything to anyone yet. Not even Anastasia. Anna and I plan to surprise Mama and Papa during the Christmas gathering."

"Stanislaus! That is over six months away." Anton complained.

"I know. But Anna and I need time to work out the details. Please do this for me Anton." Stanislaus asked.

Anton rolled his eyes and finally agreed to keep silent. However, what he thought was, *Only Stanislaus would tell me something like this, and then expect me to keep it a secret for six months! I can't believe they need over six months to think about something they have already decided to do. This gives a whole new meaning to being called a slowcoach!*

Christmas 1895, Karella Homestead

Christmas Eve day 1895 would never be forgotten. Antonia hummed with happiness as the Karella men brought in an evergreen tree and set it up in the living room. Pine sap and the fragrant tang of evergreen boughs filled the room. The scent instantly filled Antonia's mind with memories of Christmases passed. Vaclav found all the old, handmade tree ornaments the night before in preparation for setting up the tree. The afternoon of Christmas Eve overflowed with fun and delightful decorating activities. Antonia felt wonderful and so full of energy she pulled out the Nemec family recipes and baked rohlikys and berry-filled kolaches. Inspired by his wife, Vaclav began preparing hot chocolate while three of their grown children, along with Anton's new wife Anastasia and Stanislauses' Anna, decorated the Christmas tree. Laughter filled the room. Each time one of the older Karella boys hung an ornament they told a favorite story about their first Christmas in America. Emil took over the conversation and added stories about Christmas at the Babcocks. As the afternoon progressed Anton kept watching the door, waiting for Little Anna and Kratochvil to get back from town. They were bringing a surprise.

View of Karella homestead from a distance

When the door finally opened a cold fog billowed into the room. Anna's eldest brother rushed to help her take off her coat, and she handed him a package. Grinning, he opened it knowing what he would find. After Little Anna and Kratochvil joined the group by the Christmas tree, Anton distributed peppermint candies to everyone.

When Kratochvil started to open one to put in his mouth, Anton said, "No, don't eat them. You must tie them on the tree. They are part of our Christmas tradition! Little Anna show your husband how to do it." As Little Anna demonstrated how to tie the candies on the tree, she explained, "You see, it was thrilling to discover St. Nicholas had found us, even after we moved away from home in Bohemia. We found our pepermints, tied just like this on our first Christmas tree in America in 1877. Of course they did not appear until Christmas morning after we opened our presents. That is when we noticed the odd packets on the tree branches."

Smiling at the memory his sister had shared, Stanislaus added. "Mama and Papa let us eat all the candies we could find even after we ate that huge Christmas dinner, remember?"

Anton laughed and replied, "Yes I do remember that! I also remember we all got tummy aches from eating so much candy. And, we did not tell Mama because we knew she would never let us have treats again." As Anton finished his story he looked to see if their mama had been listening. Although she appeared to be concentrating on her baking, her smile indicated she had heard all the stories and was enjoying them.

With the decorating finished, the family sat around the table drinking hot chocolate and eating rohlikys. Stanislaus told Kratochvil, Anastasia, and Anna Plouzek all about their first Thanksgiving turkey in Morrisania with the Wolff and Kraus families. Anton gave his rendition of how at age nine, he thought St. Nicholas had magically found them in America, so he could put presents under their tree. Antonia and Vaclav told stories about the twelve days of Christmas celebrations in Morrisania with their friends. Then, Anton reminisced about the Christmases the Karellas shared with the Babcocks in Colfax when Emil was a baby.

Sitting down to a late supper Christmas Eve, Vaclav told Antonia to lead the prayer circle, and he would finish the blessing. She nodded and said, "Let us join hands and thank God for our blessings. Dear Lord, thank you for your love and all the blessings you have bestowed on this family, and for the bounty we are about to receive at this table."

Anton took over and said, "Thank you, dear Lord, for my wife, Anastasia, and for the baby you are sending us in the spring." Anton and Anastasia had not told anyone this news, and he could feel his Papa's grip of excitement tighten on his hand as they prayed.

Before Antonia could say anything, Stanislaus took over quickly, saying,"And dear Lord, thank you for guiding me to my dear Anna, and because Anna has agreed to become my wife this coming summer."

Filled with delight, Antonia thought, *God, please forgive this interruption in our prayers, but I can't keep quiet a moment longer!* Antonia uttered a loud, "Amen," then said, "Anastasia! Stanislaus! Thank you, my darlings! I could not have received anything more wonderful for Christmas." The rapid *Amen* from his wife made Vaclav laugh and he said, "Antonia, God has quite a sense of humor. You Just thanked him for the blessings He has bestowed on this family, and look at the jubilation this wonderful news has caused." Antonia had everyone stand up from the table so hugs of congratulations could be shared and the room overflowed with happiness.

Anton turned to Emil John who seemed a little stoic considering the exciting news. Hugging his 18-year-old brother Anton said, "Congratulations, little brother, you are going to be an uncle! This is great news ... so be happy!"

Christmas morning started early with kolaches, hot chocolate and Christmas presents, followed by the tradition of selecting a peperment from the tree. Then everyone dressed warmly for the wagon ride into Madison for 12 o'clock Christmas Mass.

On the ride home, there was an unusual amount of enthusiasm running through the conversations. Preoccupied and enjoying the ride despite the frosty air, Antonia did not catch the undercurrent of anticipation shared by her family.

The warmth of the house came as a lovely relief from the chill Antonia had begun to feel at the end of the wagon ride. The family quickly shed their winter coats and went to the living room. Vaclav helped Antonia with her heavy coat and then asked her to sit next to him near the fireplace. "The family has a surprise present for you," Vaclav whispered. Once Antonia was seated she gazed around the living room. Next to the tree was a beautiful wooden contraption that she had never seen before.

Vaclav nodded his head toward Emil, and the young man proudly opened the wooden lid of the box. "It's the latest thing from the city Mama, it is a phonograph. The best I have seen, better than the one we use at the church socials." Emil held up a black disc as he spoke, "this is a music record," and then placed the disc on the device inside the polished wooden box with the large fluted horn. "Merry Christmas Mama, we hope you like it," Emil said sweetly, as the rest of the family murmured "Merry Christmas Mama."

The matriarch of the Karella family smiled the moment the music filled the room. Overwhelmed with emotion, Antonia was transported to another time when she and Wenceslaus sat in the great cathedral. They were young. Just married and setting up their home in Kutna Hora. A stringed quartet played this tune as they sat next to Abbott Ansell. She turned to look at her husband. The years fell away from his face. It was her young Wenceslaus who held out his hand to her, and whispered, "My Heart, will you dance with me?"

As Antonia took his hand, she whispered back, "Forever, my darling." The music created an enchanted world, where a young Antonia danced a waltz with the love of her life, as though they were the only two people in the room. When the music died away Antonia blushed in her husbands arms. Only Vaclav could see it as their grown children clapped and cheered complimenting their parents on how beautifully they had danced.

A Night for Memories

That evening as Anton and Anastasia lay in bed, she asked, "Anton, what happened tonight? It was so lovely … the dance between your parents. But there was something more to it … can you tell me about their lives when they were young?"

Anton settled his wife on his shoulder and pulled her close to his side and said,

"Oh, Anastasia. Their world was so different when they were young. On Saturday evenings in Kutna Hora, Mama and Papa would take me and Stanislaus to the market square to watch the puppet show. While we ate Kolaches and sipped on tea, street minstrels played wonderful Bohemian gypsy music, and Mama and Papa would dance. You may find it hard to believe, but when I was a child, I lived in a place where kings, princes, and kaisers were real. Counts and royal guardsmen purchased custom boots from Papa's shop. My city was nothing like these frontier towns in America, not even New York. I remember tall, elegant buildings made of cream-colored, ornately carved stone, mosaic floors … royal palaces and cobbled streets.

"Count Chotek ... he was the governer of Bohemia *and* my papa's most important customer. The royal families came to Kutna Hora during the summers and held beautiful parties and balls. Their musicians practiced at Abbot Ansell's cathedral on Friday nights before they performed at the palaces.

"The abbot and Count Chotek's steward would invite Papa and our family to hear the music at the church. There were violins, pipes, and harpsicords and many other fantastic stringed instruments and woodwinds ... such beautiful music, Anastasia."

"Do you miss it?" Anastasia asked in a soft voice.

Hugging her, he replied, "My wonderful wife, I am in love with you and our future together here. This is where I belong and where I am happy. These are only memories. I admit I do miss the beauty of the cathedral. It is like nothing you've ever seen. Stained-glass windows, fresco-painted walls, gilded white marble altars, and candelabras lighting the vaulted ceilings. And then there was the music—so beautiful. They played an enormous pipe organ on Sundays during Mass. The vibration of its warm tones used to run straight through my heart. I remember that feeling as I prayed for my baby sister, Antonia. It felt ..." He closed his eyes and looked inward for a moment and then said, "Like my sister was letting me feel what heaven ... felt ... like ... to her." Anton's voice faded away. Anastasia slowly looked up from his shoulder, and as she suspected, her wonderful husband had fallen to sleep. He was smiling.

Grandmother and Granddaughter Meet for the First Time

Two months after the new year, the whole family gathered to celebrate the birth of the first Karella grandchild born on March 1, 1896. Anton and Anastasia named their little girl Helen Agnes.

Anton walked beside his mother and seated her comfortably in a chair he had set in corner of his and Anastasia's bedroom.

Anastasia looked lovely sitting up in bed dressed in a soft pink nightgown holding their new baby. Anton picked up his sleeping child and walked over to his mother. As he set his daughter in his mother's arms, he saw in her eyes, the mama he remembered from his childhood. His papa did not seem changed much by the years, but the bright spirit of the mother he had known as a child, had practically disappeared. Yet his tiny baby girl had done what no one else could. Little Helen was reawakening her grandmother's spirit and rekindling her joy. As his eyes filled with tears of happiness Anton thought, *Thank you, Lord.*

Returning to the edge of the bed, Anton sat next to his wife filled with peace as he watched his 60-year-old mother, hold her grandchild. He whispered to Anastasia, "Papa said as soon as Mama heard Helen's wail after her birth, Mama's mind cleared and she asked, 'When can I see my grandchild?'"

Loving tears filled Anton's eyes as he gently squeezed Anastasia's hand in gratitude. Leaning over, he kissed her and said softly, "Thank you for this amazing little girl you brought into our world my love. And for the joy this baby girl has reawakened in her grandma." Anton looked at his papa watching his mama. The devotion written on his face spoke to Anton's soul. It spoke of truth and about what true love and commitment is. His papa's love for his mama had never dimmed over the years. It had only grown stronger, and now her joy was his joy too.

A New Secret

Little Anna held her niece, Helen, in her arms and said, "I can't believe Helen is six months old already. She still looks so tiny. Anastasia, I want you to be the first to know. I'm going to have a baby too," she confided with a smile.

"Oh, Anna, I am so happy for you. When are you going to tell Papa and Mama?" Anastasia asked.

"Soon," she replied. Little Anna and Anastasia had enjoyed a close bond of friendship for years. They loved being sisters and confidants, and now they would share motherhood as well.

Vaclav took great pleasure in writing letters to the Karella and Nemec grandparents in Bohemia announcing the arrival of their first great grandchild and the news that a second great grandchild would join the first one in the summer of 1897. He smiled thinking about the party the Bohemians would hold celebrating these wonderful events.

Sad News Breaks Antonia's Heart

In the midst of all the happy and emotional flurry caused by Little Anna's announcement that she was going to have a baby, and Stanislaus' wedding plans set for June, the Karellas received sad news. Their maternal Nemec grandparents in Bohemia had contracted an influenza and passed away.

Despite the advanced age of Anton's grandparents, the sorrow caused by their deaths cut deeply into his heart. As a child in Bohemia, he had been very close to both his Karella and Nemec grandparents and missed them. Closing his eyes, Anton could still see their faces the night they had said goodbye in Kutna Hora. He had always held hope in his heart that he would see them again. Now the Nemecs were gone. With sadness Anton faced the fact that his Karella grandparents were also in their late 70s. He would never see them again either. Resigned to that knowledge, he thought, *Time is so precious. When I was young, I never considered that when I said goodbye it would be forever.*

Antonia took the news of her parents passing extremely hard. After Vaclav gave Antonia the devastating news, her fragile state of health deteriorated rapidly. In concern for his wife's swiftly declining condition, Vaclav decided it was time for him and Antonia to move back into Madison.

When his sons tried to change his mind, Vaclav shook his head and replied, "Stanislaus, you will be married soon. Little Anna and Kratochvil are getting ready to have a child. Anton, you and Anastasia will have more children too. So, eventually you will all need the room here on the farm. It is a good time for Mama and me to move into Madison.

Vaclav received hugs of acceptance from Stanislaus and Anton. Responding to his sons' concern, he said, "Don't fret about it.

Let's get the move done by next month. Then, we can paint and fix up the room upstairs before the wedding. Stanislaus' new bride will have a fresh-looking home to move into. How would that be, Stanislaus?"

Returning his Papa's smile, Stanislaus replied, "That would be very nice, thank you, Papa."

During the month of April, Vaclav and Anton hunted for a house in town and found one located near the doctor's home, which was also near the fairgrounds. When Vaclav chose the house, he told Anton he would enjoy walking to the harvest fairs that would be held nearby. "One day, I'll take my grandchildren to the fair. I think they would enjoy seeing all the animals. Maybe I'll even enter some of my flowers in the gardening competitions." Anton was proud of his Papa, knowing the strength it took to think positively about the future while he was so worried about Mama.

Wenceslaus (Vaclav) Karella, 60 years old, at his house in Madison, Nebraska

"Yes, Papa. The farm will miss your gardening skills. Although you taught me how to plant flowers, they don't grow for me, like they grow for you. The perennial flowers and trees you planted around the farmhouse and down our road will always make the farm beautiful. I would love to help you plant flowers at the Madison house, and go to the fair with you, too," Anton replied.

Vaclav grinned, hearing the voice of a much younger Anton from the days when they lived in Kutna Hora. Looking at his grown son, he recalled, "Yes, you always did love flowers didn't you? Son, I am so proud of you. It will be wonderful to go to the fair with you, and my grandchildren."

The new Madison house was not as large as the one Vaclav had moved his family into when they first came to Madison in 1880. It did have a large well-maintained barn, and with his son's help, Vaclav set up his leatherworking equipment. *I'm only 60 years old,* Vaclav thought; *I still have time to pass on my Master Cobbler knowledge. Perhaps one of my sons will give me a grandson to train. A little boy to love and utilize skills that have served me so well during my lifetime. Knowledge will always have value.*

Coming out of his personal reflections, he said, "Thank you, Anton. It will be nice to use the workshop for my projects. Now, the paint in the bedroom was almost dry when we started setting up this equipment. Will you help me carry the linen boxes into the house and make up the bed? Then we can go back to the farm, pack up Mama, and get her settled in her new home."

A Decision to Be Made

Emil John Karella was torn by conflicting emotions after being told he was going to be moving into Madison with his parents. Although he was 19 years old, he had never thought of how he would support himself on his own. His family had always taken care of him. He worked around the farm and made a wage for managing the poultry business for Stanislaus. That gave him plenty of spending money. After he completed his chores, he was free to do as he pleased. His older brothers encouraged him to enjoy his childhood. They were happy he had the freedom to spend time with friends.

Now that his mother and father had decided to move into Madison things would change for him. He had to figure out what he wanted. Emil frowned. Something didn't feel right. He had to rethink everything. What did he want?

With sudden clarity Emil knew what he did not want. He did not want to watch his mother getting sicker ... and ... even in his mind, he could not admit that his mama might be dying. *No! I've got to talk with Anton. I don't want to move into Madison.*

Anton will understand ... he'll let me stay and work on the farm ... at least, I hope he will.

A Week Before Vaclav and Antonia Move Back to Madison

Emil waited for Anton to come home. As soon as he showed up, Emil asked, "Anton, can we take a walk outside?" Once they were out of hearing distance, Emil explained, "Anton, I don't want to move away from the farm. Please let me stay here with you and Stanislaus. I can do more chores. I could take over the rental business, too, after I finish the poultry deliveries. I know I could be of more help here, and I promise to work hard."

The center of Anton's brow wrinkled, showing he felt confused. "I thought you'd be happy to be in town. You have lots of friends there," Anton replied.

"No! I mean, yes, I do have friends there. But I don't need to move into Madison to see them. Living out here has never stopped me from enjoying my friends or hindered me in any way. Please, I want to stay with you. You've always been more like a father to me ... actually more than ... Papa has. Honestly, I don't even think he'll miss me. He spends all his time with Mama." Emil was looking at the ground as the last of his private thoughts spilled from his lips.

Anton almost gasped when he heard what Emil said, and in a controlled no-nonsense voice, he replied, "Rule number one, little brother. Don't let me ever hear you say anything like that again. Papa has been as good a father to you as he has been with any of us! I know you don't understand, but Papa needs to spend time with Mama, especially now."

Emil looked dejected and continued to stare at the ground even as he nodded his head in acceptance of what Anton said. Anton wanted to help his brother but needed time to think about what should be done. "I need to talk to Stanislaus. Then we will see what we can do about this. You keep quiet, Emil, until he and I have a chance to figure this out." Emil looked up at his eldest brother with hope, he nodded in agreement and then trotted back to the house.

The supper bell had not rung yet, so Anton went out to the barn. He found Stanislaus working on a hay rake. "Brother, can I talk to you? It's important."

It was the tone in Anton's voice that caused Stanislaus to turn immediately to look at his brother and ask, "What is going on?"

"Emil does not want to stay with Mama and Papa when they move into Madison. He just asked me for permission to stay here on the farm."

"Did he give you a reason why?" Stanislaus asked.

Anton shook his head. He would not repeat the words he had heard. Instead, Anton replied, "Not exactly. I think he is having a hard time accepting the fact that Mama and Papa are getting old. He doesn't seem to have the same relationship with them as we did at his age."

Frustrated, Anton went on to say, "We know he can be difficult. Emil even has issues with me and you sometimes, and we are only nine years older than he is."

Stanislaus nodded in agreement. "If he is willing to follow our rules and do his work without argument, I don't see why he can't stay. But we are going to have to talk to Papa about it first and get him to agree."

Anton nodded at his brother, dropping into deep thought. *How do I approach Papa? That's the question—the boy does not comprehend that it is because of Mama's sacrifice that we have this life in America. It's Mama's turn to come first. Emil never went through hard times with Mama and Papa, not like the rest of us did. Maybe he feels forgotten with all the changes happening now. It hurts all of us, it feels like we are losing both Mama and Papa right now.*

Coming out of his deep reflections, Anton said, "Staying here on the farm is probably better for Emil. Otherwise, he might run away from us and from what is happening to Mama. Stanislaus, we must talk to Papa about this tomorrow."

After lunch the next day, Anton and Stanislaus waited until it was just the three of them in the kitchen. Stanislaus poured coffee, and Anton passed the cups around the table, saying, "Papa, we have a matter to discuss." Vaclav listened, as his two eldest sons suggested that their baby brother stay on the farm instead of moving into Madison.

Stanislaus and Anton could not see the frown forming on Vaclav's mouth hidden as it was under his huge mustache. However, they could see their Papa's brow wrinkled in thought as they waited for an answer.

Obviously, both my grown sons agree this is the right thing to do for Emil. They have good judgment, and I'll have one less worry. The boy will have proper supervision, and if his brothers need my help with him, they will let me know. Vaclav looked first at Anton and then Stanislaus and gave a nod of acceptance, granting the permission Emil wanted so desperately.

Anton and Stanislaus glanced at each other. Both were relieved their little brother had not been in the room to witness this future-altering decision. Their papa had decided Emil's living arrangements without saying a word.

Still sitting at the table with Anton and Stanislaus, their father's mind returned to his preoccupation with Antonia's condition. He murmured to himself, "I know I will feel less anxious once we are in town, and the doctor is nearby."

Anton watched his father with sadness, gleaning two important things from what had just happened. First, his papa was so preoccupied with their mama, he spoke as if no one else was in the room. And second, having the doctor close by was not only important for his mama, but for his papa too.

Vaclav's grown children understood their father had no delusions about their mother's health; it would only grow worse. Anton and Stanislaus didn't like having their parents move away, but they agreed with their father's reasons for doing so. Out of respect, they never brought up the subject of Emil or their mama's health again while their papa and mama were still living at the homestead.

Vaclav's unspoken motives for moving away from the farm were perhaps even more important than the one he gave his sons.

There would be sadness ahead. He had to focus on Antonia now. Vaclav could sense Antonia didn't have a lot of time left in this life. He needed every remaining moment there was, to really be with his wife. At the same time his children and grandchildren needed the farm to be a place of peace and happiness.

June 1896, A Third Karella Wedding

Little Anna was taking care of her baby niece, Helen, while her mother was busy. It was now a week before Stanislaus's wedding and the bride-to-be, Anna Plouzek, and her sister-in-law, Anastasia, were busy cleaning the master bedroom, which had been Vaclav's and Antonia's old room.

After completely rearranging the furniture, painting the walls, and making up the bed with beautiful linens—an early wedding gift

Stanislaus Karella, son of Vaclav and Antonia Karella

from Anton and Anastasia—the room looked remarkably different and fresh.

Anastasia squeezed Anna's hand and said, "Now this room is perfect for the new bride who is to become the next Mrs. Karella!"

Anna returned the squeeze with gratitude, replying, "Are you sure? This should actually be your room. Anton is the eldest."

"No, Anna," Anastasia replied shaking her head. Anton and I are happy where we are. He built those rooms for me, and they are just

Anna Plouzek Karella, wife of Stanislaus Karella

what I wanted. Besides, the baby has the room next to us, which makes it perfect. Don't fret. We are content, and I am thrilled Stanislaus is bringing me another sister to live in this house."

The farmyard looked appealing with bright young leaves fluttering in the trees and the lilac bushes that Vaclav had planted had begun to bloom. Enthusiastically, the Karellas completed preparations for the wedding feast. Emil showed Anastasia a beautiful plaque he painted, which read, -Welcome home, Mr. & Mrs. Stanislaus Karella- and then went to attach it to the wall by the front door. Little Anna and Anastasia made small bouquets of flowers for the tables, and then made a few more with bows and ribbons wrapped around the stems to decorate the wedding coach. Emil and his friends would attach the flowers to the horse's harness and bridle while the ceremony was taking place. At the last minute, Emil also tied some old horseshoes on twine to drag behind the carriage for good luck.

The perfect weather added to the excitement. The wedding ceremony could not have been lovelier and was followed by a receiving line outside the church. Family and friends poured out of the building into the sunshine, and each guest got a chance to extend their best wishes to the newlyweds.

"We look forward to seeing all of you at the farm for the wedding feast this afternoon," Stanislaus announced. Turning to his new wife, he asked, "Shall we head home, Mrs. Karella?"

Smiling up at her handsome husband, she replied, "Yes Mr. Karella, I can't wait to ride in that beautifully decorated coach." Anna smiled as she made her compliment loud enough for Emil to hear, and her brother-in-law broke into a grin from ear to ear.

Honoring Family Names Can Get Confusing

Despite how well the Karellas knew one another, now that Stanislaus was married to his Anna, they discovered having two Antons and two Annas in the same household made for some confusing conversations. However, if this was confusing for the family, one could only imagine how it was for friends and neighbors.

After one particularly confusing day, Stanislaus and Anton decided everyone should always refer to their sister, the original Anna Karella, as Little Anna. It was their pet name for her growing up. Then everyone could call Stanislaus's wife Mrs. Anna. It was a solution that suited both women perfectly.

Anton, as the eldest Karella living in the household, asked Anton Kratochvil if he minded just being called by his last name to reduce the confusion. "Brother, I know it's been confusing around here with both of us being named Anton, so, yes, please call me Kratochvil."

1897–1898 Three Grandsons Are Born

Vaclav and Antonia's move into Madison did make more room for the families living at the farm. However, babies began filling up that space sooner than anyone anticipated. Five months after the wedding of Stanislaus and Anna, happy news rang out for the Kratochvil and Karella clans. Little Anna gave birth to the first Kratochvil grandson in 1897, and they named him Louis. Shortly after Louis' birth Anastasia announced she was going to have another baby sometime in January. At 21 years old, Anastasia gave birth to the first Karella grandson of his generation, Ambrose Jerome, born on January 5, 1898.

Little Anna quickly gave Ambrose Jerome another cousin, and her baby, Joseph Kratochvil, was also born in 1898. The farm was filling up fast. The seven adults living at the farm had many sleepless nights trying to

Ambrose Jerome (Rusty) Karella, born 1898

303

keep up with an active toddler and three small babies. If one of the boys started crying, the other two babies generally joined in, and no one got any sleep.

Grandparents in Madison

Grandpa Vaclav waited to celebrate each of his grandson's births until they were old enough to make the trip into Madison. These days Grandma Antonia was not strong enough to make the long ride out to the home-stead anymore, and he would not leave her.

Anastasia Holy Karella and Anton Karella, parents of Ambrose Jerome (Rusty) Karella

Anton and Kratochvil worked out schedules as the babies grew old enough to travel. The parents let no more than a week pass without bringing the grandchildren to see their grandparents.

While Vaclav entertained Louis, Ambrose, and Joseph, Antonia developed her relation-ship with two-year-old Helen. The calm and quiet child loved to snuggle with her grandma. She had learned to talk early and held remarkable conversations for one so young. Little Helen was nearly the only person who could raise Antonia's spirits as her vitality continued to diminish.

After Vaclav mentioned Antonia's reaction to the toddler, Anton brought Helen over to spend afternoons with her grandma every Sunday after mass. Blissfully happy with his sweet grand-daughter, and three inquisitive grandsons, Vaclav spent many satisfying hours in his shop, making tiny shoes and leather toys for each of them. Vaclav planned something new to teach his grandchildren each week and marveled at how quickly their per-sonalities were changing and developing. As the weather warmed up, he looked forward to teaching his grandchildren how to work in the garden with him.

An Anniversary to Remember, September 28,1898

Summer had finally arrived, and with the warmer weather, Antonia began to feel a little better. She had even made a few trips to the farm with Vaclav and enjoyed sitting outside watching her grandchildren play.

With the improvement in their mother's health, Anton, Stanislaus and their wives asked Vaclav to let them throw a surprise party for his and Antonia's 35th wedding anniversary. Vaclav had been thinking out loud and said thoughtfully, "Perhaps a party would be good for Antonia."

That comment was all it took. The party planning began immediately, and everyone wanted to help with the anniversary celebration. Father Jerome said, "I'll reserve St. Leonard's church hall for, September 28th, and I'll supply the music." All the families would bring food and between the Karellas, Plouzeks, Kratochvils, Holys and Kuchars there would be enough to feed an army.

When the family explained all the plans that had been made for the 35th wedding celebration, Vaclav felt blessed to have so much attention from so many family members. He did not expect anyone to take his comment so seriously, so what could he say? Smiling, he nodded and said, "It's going to be a wonderful party. Antonia and I will enjoy this celebration held in our honor, and this fun surprise will be good for your mama."

The Day of the Surprise Party Arrives

"Mama, let us help you get ready. You will not be able to manage all those buttons by yourself." Little Anna was a little miffed because her mama was not cooperating with them, and none of the girls wanted to spoil the surprise by telling her why they wanted to make her look her best.

Antonia did not want the girls making such a fuss over her, yet they persisted, and she finally decided it took too much effort to make the girls stop, so she let them have their way.

Antonia's three daughters had collaborated to make a new gown for her anniversary present. Antonia didn't know why they were making such a commotion over getting her all gussied up. It was just going to be a family gathering at the farm to celebrate her and Vaclav's wedding anniversary. When they asked her about her favorite color and the kind of fabric she liked, she told them not to waste the money. But none of them had listened to her.

Now, as Mrs. Anna buttoned up the back of the dress, Antonia had to admit she did like the color. The fabric was very soft, and she said, "Thank you, girls, the fabric you picked is wonderful. I love it, though I'm sure you could have spent the money on something more important." Yet even as she made that statement, Antonia continued to run her hand over the soft fabric in appreciation.

Little Anna chided, "Mama, this is not a time to be frugal. It is your 35th wedding anniversary. You deserve a nice present after all the years of looking after us." Then, Little Anna added softly and sincerely, "And for the sacrifices you made so that we could be happy."

With the dressing finished, Anastasia asked her mother-in-law to sit in the chair by her nightstand. Anastasia was the best at doing hair styles and with ease she twisted and pinned Antonia's silver tresses into fashionable soft waves on the top of her head. The girl's enthusiasm was contagious. Suddenly, Antonia felt tickled by all the fuss. It had been a long time since she felt this good and began to enjoy all the attention her girls were bestowing on her.

Finished, the three young women smiled at what they had accomplished. Little Anna said, "Mama, look in the mirror." Antonia stood up and turned, not expecting much and was astonished as she looked at her reflection. "Mama, you look beautiful. Papa is going to love seeing you like this."

The Coach Takes a Wrong Turn

"Where are we going?" Antonia asked. But no one answered her. Thinking they didn't hear her questions, she said louder, "Excuse me, Anton, where are we going? The turn out to the farm was back there." Titters of laughter came from Anastasia's direction. Confused by such a reaction to her question, Antonia turned to look at her and thought, *Something is going on here, though for the life of me, I don't know what it is.* "Vaclav, do you know where we are going?" she asked.

"No, I don't," he replied, glad he could keep a straight face as he told that white lie.

Anton made the excuse that he had to pick up something from Father Jerome at the church. "Mama, will you and Papa come with me and hold the door open. Anastasia needs to stay with the children. The two men walked on either side of Antonia, and when they got to the church hall door, they opened it for her.

Light poured through the doorway, and she heard many voices yelling, "*Surprise*! Happy Anniversary!" Antonia's family and friends caught her completely by surprise! She was overwhelmed by their love and their attention.

When Vaclav removed the large overcoat, Antonia's breath caught in her throat, as she thought, *My Vaclav makes an impressive sight dressed in that fine new suit.* She had thought it was a bit warm out for such a heavy overcoat when they left the house. Now, she realized Vaclav had been hiding his clothing. *I feel like a queen,* she thought, holding on to Vaclav's arm as they walked among the huge gathering in the church hall. It was a revelation, seeing how many members formed this American branch of the Karella family. In her heart, she suddenly knew her family would keep prospering in this land of promise.

Drawn out of her thoughts by lilting music, her handsome husband asked her to dance. Smiling, Antonia accepted the invitation, and Vaclav took her in to his arms as they stepped onto the dance floor.

The matriarch and patriarch of the Karella family made a handsome couple as they waltzed around the church hall. They were both 59 years old, had been married for 35 years, but had been friends and playmates since childhood. As Vaclav led his wife through the waltz, he whispered, "My Heart, you are a lovely sight." Antonia smiled up at her husband. He could still make her heart flutter with his complements. Although his hair and mustache had turned silver, Vaclav stood straight and tall, and he was handsomer than ever.

"Thank you, my darling. It was the girls who got me all gussied up. They said you would like it."

"They were right," he replied.

As the dance ended, the anniversary couple received a round of applause from friends and family, and Vaclav whispered, "Antonia, look, we are surrounded by our family. Did you ever dream a day like this would come?"

"My darling, I always hoped a day like this would come. But I always believed in our dreams and that you would help me make a family like this to love."

1899, Kratochvils Move Away

After the birth of his son, Joseph, Kratochvil saw a billboard notice at the feed store about a farm for rent in Pierce, Nebraska. Taking a day off, he went to see the property and came back with exciting news to share with Little Anna. The opportunity was too good to pass up. It was time to have a place of their own. Leaving their three sons with Mrs. Anna, they went for a meeting at the land office in Pierce. Little Anna and her husband Anton signed a rental agreement for the house and a plot of farmland, and they moved their family to Pierce in the summer of 1899. Just a few months after the Kratochvils moved to Pierce, Anastasia gave birth to her third child, Martha Genevieve, on October 30, 1899.

Time Moves On

Although Anton had not worked with his father for years, except for gardening together on summer evenings, he still missed seeing his papa and discussing the news over a cup of coffee each morning. At the same time, Anton also experienced a deep satisfaction with his independence as a grown man. Anton and Stanislaus had divided up the responsibility for the family businesses, and now they enjoyed a deeper bond as men. They discussed business as equals and found great satisfaction in their chosen work. Yet work was not what made Anton happy.

Anton cherished poignant memories of his father, which had taught him what happiness is or should be, and how to keep his priorities straight. He admired his father. Vividly Anton recalled images from his childhood in Bohemia. His papa made happiness part of everything he did. When his papa came in from the workshop in Kutna Hora, despite what might have happened with work, he smiled when he greeted his family. He teased and played with them over lunches and dinners and encouraged his sisters Julie and Masy to put on puppet shows. His papa had helped developed their imaginations and he laughed with them.

Those were the kind of memories he wanted to make with his own little ones who were already developing unique personalities. Being able to take care of his family made work worth the effort. Yet he had no problem leaving his work behind. Anton looked forward to going home to Anastasia and his little Helen, his son Ambrose, and baby Martha. His children made every day memorable and he loved the happy chaos they created.

It made him sad to see the Kratochvils move away. He would miss his little sister and her family. At the same time, he wished them all the best as they started their new life in a home of their own.

Karella Homestead, Brothers

Anastasia had a good relationship with Stanislaus and his wife. The two women shared the work in the household, which made doing the laundry, cooking, cleaning and looking after the children much easier. However, the ladies did look forward to five o'clock in the afternoon when their husbands returned home. Then it became the brothers' responsibility to watch Helen and the babies. Giving Anastasia and Anna time to freshen up and prepare supper.

Anton never tired of playing with his children. Anastasia would be drawn from the kitchen to the living room by precious giggles and baby laughter. Fascinated, she would watch her husband and his brother crawl around on the floor playing with two-year-old Helen and the two babies, keeping the children busy until the food was ready.

"Anastasia, I got a letter from Little Anna today." Anton called out around the little hand, which his son had stuffed into his papa's mouth. Laughing as he removed the little fist, Anton continued, "She and Kratochvil are going to have another child in the spring. If it's a boy, guess what they are going to name him?"

The silly grin on her husband's face gave away the surprise. Anastasia replied, "She's going to name him Anton?"

Laughing at how silly it was going to be with three Antons at the Karella picnics, he replied, "I know, Anastasia. But I love that my little sister's baby boy will be named after me."

Anastasia shook her head, grinning, not saying a word about what she was thinking. *I guess he's forgetting the child's father is named Anton too. Funny that he did not think of that.*

Nebraska 1899–1900

With so many babies and toddlers to manage, Karella family traditions began to change. It was far easier to invite all the Karellas, Plouzeks, Kratochvils, Holys and Kuchars in the area to gather at the farm once a month, rather than packing up all the children each Sunday to visit in different places. The monthly gatherings became a potluck picnic. Each woman or family brought a dish of food to share. It became an entire day of food, and playful chaos where everyone enjoyed fresh air outside the house and catching up on family news.

Emil John

At 22 years old, Emil John felt like he had fallen into a rut. His set routine was driving him crazy. He took care of his responsibilities at the homestead without complaint. He made the deliveries into Madison for the poultry business during the winter and summer, and in the spring, he helped with the farm planting. He got his first bit of relief from boredom during the summer growing season and would not return to a regular farm schedule until harvest.

During the summer, Emil met up with a group of buddies at church picnics and was the first to know everything about the intrigues emerging after each church social. In his free time, he also searched for every scrap of news about the world outside Nebraska. Madison had one newspaper, and his papa let him have the old newspapers their cousins sent from Chicago. When Emil listened to his brothers tell old stories at home, he felt irked that he had never lived in New York and even envied his sister Little Anna when she and her husband and their children moved to Pierce, Nebraska.

Emil John Karella, youngest son of Vaclav and Antonia Karella

When he tried to explain his dreams to the family, it felt like they never took him seriously. He had even heard Stanislaus say, "No harm in daydreaming. Emil's just passing through an unsettled period; he'll settle down soon." Emil thought, *They cannot understand me or what I want because they are happy with farm life, marriage, and children. But that is not the life for me; it is not what I want.*

Looking at Emil from His Brother's Point of View

Every once in a while, when Emil seemed a little more agitated than normal, Anton and Stanislaus felt they might be partially to blame for his restlessness. "You know, Anton, maybe it's the old stories about the early days in New York and Morrisania that spark these ideas in Emil. I'm talking about the daydreams he has about wanting to travel and live in a big city."

Anton shook his head and replied, "No, Emil has always had different interests than us. Learning about new places and especially about new technology has always been important to him. He loves geography as long as it is about any place other than Nebraska. Where we were quiet and serious, he loves to talk and laugh. Emil has always been comfortable with girls. He enjoys going to church functions and brags about dancing with all the prettiest women in town. We both know that unlike us, at 22, he seems to fall in and out of love as often as he meets someone new. Sometimes the differences I see between us worries me. Even though Emil has more freedom than we had at his age, it does not seem to be enough for him. I know he loves this family, but I can tell he yearns to be free to go his own way. Stanislaus, I am sure Emil is going to leave home, and when he decides to go, nothing is going to hold him back."

Turn of a Century and the Dawn of 1900

Vaclav set down the newspaper, shaking his head. He had been reading a story about the turning of the century, or as the article had stated, "The end of an era." *Could the 1800s really be coming to a close?* Vaclav wondered. *It doesn't sound possible to me. The turning of a century ... how remarkable it is that Antonia and I should live to see such an event.* Vaclav got up from his chair and went into Antonia's room. Sitting on the bed next to her, he watched her sleep. "Time is running away from us, My Heart," he whispered softly. Gently, he placed his hand on her brow, blinking back tears. He did not want to wake her, but still, he wanted to be close to her. "I am so sorry," he whispered softly. "I needed to believe you regained your strength after Emil John was born. I was wrong. I'm sorry I made life harder for you. I'm sorry that your other babies did not live, despite all the strength and hope you poured into bringing them into the world. Our little angels wait for us, and I will always be here for you. Thank you for all you did for us. Without you, there would have been no family, no dream, and I would never have known what love could mean."

Antonia opened her eyes. He could see she had heard every word he said. She moved over in the bed, and he laid down beside her and wrapped his arms around her. Laying her head on his shoulder, she whispered, "My dearest husband, we made this dream together. Without you, I would have had no children. I do not regret the work, the pain, or the loneliness of the past. My family has brought me joy, and you gave me the gift of your love."

September 1, 1900, Grandpa Vaclav Turns 64

"Happy birthday, Grandpa," shouted happy voices from the porch. As Vaclav held the front door open, Stanislaus and Anton carried in the two baby boys, and the wives and little Helen carried in picnic baskets exuding wonderful aromas.

"I smell fried chicken," Grandma Antonia said from her chair by the fire.

Four-year-old Helen excitedly announced, "Grandma, we brought kolaches and rohliky too! Mama let me help put the poppy seeds on-um!"

Vaclav laughed and asked, "Well, My Heart, do you think they are as good as the ones you make?"

Anastasia and Mrs. Anna both chimed in with a reply, "They certainly are! Mama did teach us how to make them from the family recipes!"

Vaclav smiled, happy to be celebrating turning 64 years old surrounded by his family. Antonia would turn 64 in three months and he was looking forward to celebrating like this again.

December 1, 1900 Grandma Antonia Turns 64

It was Saturday and snowing at the moment. More than 20 inches had accumulated overnight. The weather seemed to be warming up, and Anton pulled Stanislaus out of bed early to help him wax the runners on the sleigh. Both brothers were determined to celebrate their mama's 64th birthday despite the snow. Their wives had packed nearly all the food the night before and set it on the porch. This morning the women focused on getting the children ready for the cold ride into town.

Anton said, "Stanislaus, I'll go get extra blankets. Can you hitch up the horses without me?"

Stanislaus laughed over that question and teasingly replied," Exactly who is the old man here? Furthermore, as I recall, you are the only one who ever had trouble hitching up a team of horses by yourself."

Anton chuckled and replied," Ok, you have me there! You've always been better with wagon animals and farm equipment. But give me a good saddle horse and we'll see who wins the race."

The brothers continued to tease one another while they loaded the food and made sure everyone was covered with a warm blanket. Restless, the horses whinnied, tossing their heads. Stanislaus snapped the reins on their rumps and the bells on the harnesses jingled as the horses pulled the sleigh smoothly through the snow headed to the Madison house.

Grandpa Vaclav had been watching for their arrival. Laughing and red cheeked, four-year-old Helen had been the first one to scramble out of the wagon. She caught hold of Ambrose as he was set on the ground and Anton held the baby in his arms. The rest of the adults brought in the food baskets.

Helen began dragging the two-year-old behind her. She had Ambrose by the hand, pulling him through the snow, up the stairs, over the porch, and tugged him through the door her grandpa held open for her. The little boy had refused to be carried, so Helen had been put in charge of getting him into the house.

As soon as she got through the door Helen shouted, "Happy Birthday Grandma!" Ambrose was trying to get his hand out of Helen's grasp and looked like he was going to bite her. She yelled, "Don't you dare bite me Ambrose! I'll tell Grandpa on you... you little hunyuck!"

Ambrose had a full set of teeth now. When his temper was up, he sometimes tried to use them on his sister. Grandpa had been working on that problem. Regrettably, he had not been fully successful in discouraging the two-year-old in regard to biting when he got frustrated.

Grandma intervened before any biting or fighting could start, saying, "Helen dear, please let your little brother go. He is not one of your dolls."

Looking outside, Vaclav noticed it had stopped snowing; the sun was shining, and the weather was holding at about 10 above zero. Vaclav was thinking, *The snow should be just sticky enough to make a good snowman.* To distract grownups and children alike, he asked, "Who wants to go outside and build a snowman?"

Squealing with delight, Helen yelled, "I do, Grandpa!" Ambrose liked to squeal, too, and mimicked his sister, making an ear-piercing, high-pitched sound that made everyone laugh.

Anton chimed in with "me, too, Papa!"

Then, Stanislaus announced, "And me! you are not leaving me out of this fun!"

Anastasia, Grandma Antonia, and Mrs. Anna looked up from their food preparations periodically. They enjoyed watching Grandpa Vaclav directing his grown sons and granddaughter on how to make a snowman. After building a respectable snowman, the brothers turned the outing into a snowball fight. Helen giggled when she got hit with a snowball, but Ambrose started crying when Helen dumped a hand full of snow on his head, and the cold stuff began to melt on his face.

Anastasia called from the front door, "Come in, all of you! It's time for lunch, and then we will have Grandma's birthday dessert."

Sitting down around the table surrounded by her children and grandchildren, Antonia began the prayer of thanks, "My Dear Lord, thank you for all the blessings You have given us. Thank you for this joyful birthday celebration." Just as Antonia was about to continue, she heard a rather loud whisper coming from her granddaughter.

"Can we eat now, Papa? I'm really hungry!" Helen whispered loudly.

Whispering back loud enough for his mother to hear, Anton replied, "When Grandma says Amen, then you can eat." He wore a cheeky grin, and his comment was followed by feminine giggles and deep chuckles.

Laughing out loud, Grandma Antonia gave in quickly and said, "*Amen.*"

Little Helen replied immediately, "Thank goodness, I'm starving." Her comment sounded remarkably like something her Grandpa Vaclav was fond of saying. Everyone recognized that fact and laughed again.

The End of a Wonderful Visit

It was getting late and growing colder by the time the adults began to bundle up the children for the long ride home. Antonia kissed and hugged each one quickly before they started complaining about being hot. "You are the best gifts I could ever get for my birthday. You are my fondest dreams come to life. I love each one of you. Off you go now and stay warm!" Vaclav stood by Antonia's side as they watched the sleigh disappear down the lane. Antonia had enjoyed herself immensely.

December 5, 1900

Antonia breathed her last breath and lay still in his arms. Vaclav's hand rested on her chest; he could no longer feel the beat of her heart. It felt as though his heart stopped beating too. Emptiness filled him as he thought, *My Heart, must you leave now? It's only been four days since we celebrated your birthday. You were so happy surrounded by our children and grandchildren. You told them they were all your best dreams come true. You were so full of life when you hugged and kissed each one goodnight.*

Vaclav could not bring himself to let her go. He knew Anton and Stanislaus waited outside the door with the doctor, but he did not have the will to leave her. "My Heart," he whispered, "you have gone ahead of me again. I know you are with all our tiny guardian angels in heaven, that you are not alone. But I am lost without you." He sobbed quietly.

Pierce, Nebraska

When Little Anna received the news about her mother's death, she went over to the church to sit and pray. Almost numb, she realized her best memories of her mother were from the years they spent with the Babcocks in Colfax and the first couple of years in Madison. Her mother had been strong and happy then, and they used to do all kinds of things together.

Although tears ran down Little Anna's face, she smiled. She remembered baking cookies and rohlikys ... closing her eyes, Anna could hear laughter and smell fresh bread right before it was ready to come out of the oven. She remembered wonderful lunches shared with her father. He had been so playful; he never stopped teasing them, and they had so much fun together.

The memories continued to warm her heart. In her mind, she saw her brothers standing by her papa as he lifted her up to hang an ornament on the Christmas tree. She could taste peppermint on her tongue and saw her mama smile and hand her a hot rohliky, saying, "Careful, sweetheart, it's hot." Silently, a new flood of tears rolled down her cheeks.

Quietly, her dear Anton came into the church and found his sweet Anna hunched over and sobbing. He sat down in the pew next to her, putting his arm around her, and she laid her head on his shoulder. Both her heart and her voice broke as she whispered, "I think Mama died a long time ago, and now finally her body followed her heart. She lost herself a little at a time—that's what I think. Starting with the death of my eldest sister and then a little more with the deaths of my other sisters and brothers."

For Little Anna, the family's guardian angel story made a lasting impression, and she made a point to remember the baby brothers and sisters who didn't live. None of the Karella's guardian angels would ever be forgotten as long as she remembered the infants that had been born. Little Anna talked to her husband in a sad voice. "I felt the change in Mama as she lost more of her vitality with each pregnancy and a little more of her heart with each child's death. Did you know for two of those pregnancies she bore twins?"

Her husband shook his head but did not say a word. "One set of boys and one set of girls, and there were also two single births. By the last baby's death, Mama had grown distant and constantly sad. You were there at the farm and saw it, too, didn't you?"

"Yes, my love, I did see that," replied Kratochvil quietly. "But there were a few good times over the past years as well. You must remember those moments too."

"You are right, Anton, although I'm glad I can still remember Mama when she was younger and happy. When she remembered the rest of us who

Anna Karella Kratochvil, 1873–1966

318

were still living. I am grateful she lived long enough to see three of her children happily married and had a chance to hold five of her grandchildren." Looking up at her husband, she added, "Thank you, Anton. You have brought such joy into my life, and I'm glad Mama got to play with our children."

When his wife fell silent, Anton spoke, softly saying, "Sweetheart, she is in heaven watching over us and our children. She loves them, and she will always love you." Little Anna suddenly felt alert and filled with anxiety, feeling that something was missing. Kratochvil guessed what had upset his wife and said, "Don't worry, my love. I left our babies with my mother. I knew you needed me more right now."

Little Anna Recounts Her Mother's Life

Steeped in grief over their mother's passing, Anton did not allow the local newspaper to speak with Vaclav or interview the family. Instead, he waited for Little Anna to arrive from Pierce. Anton asked Little Anna to take care of what should be given to the newspaper about their mama and the family. She accepted the solemn duty and felt she was prepared to honor her papa, mama, and all her siblings, both those who had grown up and those who had died. It was hard for her to be interviewed by the man from the newspaper, yet she was content that she had spared her brothers and her papa such a hardship.

—Births and Deaths for December 1900—

Mrs. Antonia Nemec Karella of Madison, Nebraska, died December 5, 1900. She is survived by her husband, Wenceslaus Vaclav Karella, their four children, and five grandchildren. Antonia left her parent's home to marry at the age of 24, moving to the city of Kutna Hora with her husband and had her first child at age 29. She bore fraternal twins at age 30; the boy lived, and the girl died. At 34, she gave birth to another daughter and then came as a vanguard for her family to America at age 36. She earned the money to send for her family in Bohemia and was reunited with them in America at age 38. Antonia bore another son at age 39, and he became the first Karella child born as a naturalized American citizen in 1878. Antonia and her family moved to Madison from Colfax, Nebraska, after she turned 41. At the age of 47, Antonia and her husband recorded the deed for their 160-acre Nebraska homestead. According to their only daughter, Anna, her parents shared the satisfaction of knowing they had actually accomplished their dream of owning land and creating a better life for their children. The Karellas' first four children thrived in America, and at the age of 56, Antonia and Vaclav witnessed the marriage of their eldest son, Anton, to a Bohemian girl, Anastasia Holy, from the Schoolcraft Precinct here in Madison in 1895. Antonia lived to see three of her children married and witnessed the birth of three grandchildren from these unions. According to her only surviving daughter, Anna Karella Kratochvil, her mother gave birth to 11 children during her life, five boys and six girls, and five of the babies who died were twins. An upstanding citizen of the Madison community, this good woman will be missed.

The Funeral Mass for Antonia

Everyone sat down and waited for Father Jerome to begin his sermon. But as Father Jerome looked at the congregation and the Karellas who mourned the loss of their matriarch, he felt a need to talk about faith, courage, and hope for the future.

"The newspaper wrote, 'Antonia Nemec Karella passed away four days ago on the fifth of December shortly after her 64th birthday.' While those are the facts, they do not give any insight into the soul of this amazing woman whom I had the honor of knowing.

"Her family is an important part of our community and would not be here if it were it not for her sacrifices, hard work, courage, fortitude, and let us not forget her *faith*.

"Think about what it took to come to America and start a new life alone. Antonia became a pioneer and fearlessly journeyed to the unknown for love … for her family …

"Everything she did was to help fulfill the dream she and her husband held in their hearts … for the safety, security, and future of their family. Through the grace of God, after two years of separation, she reunited her family against near insurmountable odds.

"Let us not dwell on tears … let us rejoice! Honor this good woman's example of faith! Trust that God listens and gives us the courage we need to go on hoping and dreaming. God will grant us the fortitude to bear up under the sacrifices it takes to achieve impossible dreams! Let us pray for the Karella children and grandchildren.

"Lord, help them live each new day feeling Antonia's spirit as she encourages them to embrace the opportunities they have in America … to keep believing that beautiful dreams can come true … and that they appreciate the life Antonia and Vaclav built together here in Madison to give them a good future … Amen."

St. Leonard's Cemetery, Madison,
Nebraska

1839–1900 gravestone,
Antonia Nemec Karella

Antonia Nemec Karella,
1839–1900

The Historic Cemetery at the Original Location of St. Leonards Church in Madison
Nebraska, and the Karella Ancestor's Plot with Individual Gravestones.

CHAPTER 9

A New Era for the Nebraska Karellas

Nebraska, 1901

Anton and Stanislaus worried about their father; for years the focal point of his life had been devoted to taking care of their mother. Now that she was gone, they wondered if he would have the heart to go on himself. Gradually Vaclav began to look forward to church on Sundays when he sat with his family and friends in the Madison community. In less than a year of losing Antonia, God blessed the family with joy. Little Anna gave birth to a third son whom they named Anton. All remaining fear for their father was swept away as Vaclav's grandchildren brought sweet joy into his life and helped mend his broken heart.

Summertime on the Farm

Grandpa Vaclav eagerly waited for the weekends. He cherished all of his grandchildren in Nebraska, but he lived for the four grandchildren that resided close to him. These young souls drew him back to the homestead every Saturday during the warm months for family picnics. The children revived his heart with their joyful chaos and vigor returned to his body. As he played with his grandchildren the years of grief fell away from his face.

Vaclav marveled at each child as they developed unique personalities and talents. He had grown particularly fond of three-year-old Ambrose Jerome. The youngster learned to walk and talk quickly, and the boy loved the smell of leather.

"Papa, it is impossible for me to give away any of those old toys you made for him. Ambrose throws a fit if I even suggest giving any of them away!" Anastasia complained. Vaclav only smile and thought, *A little man who takes after my own heart.*

If Ambrose heard his grandpa's voice the boy came running and wanted to be held. "Grandpa tell me a story! Pease tell me a story," Ambrose would beg. Of course, Vaclav would happily sit for hours telling him one tale after another. When Vaclav discovered Ambrose never tired of sitting and listening to him, a secret hope began to bloom in his heart. Just maybe Ambrose Jerome would be the child who would want to learn what he dearly wanted to teach. Maybe Ambrose would become his apprentice.

Whenever Vaclav visited the homestead, he could most often be found sitting on a blanket under the shade tree in the yard surrounded by his grandchildren. He would hold one of the youngsters on his lap while the rest crowded in as close as they could get. Vaclav kept the children occupied for hours telling them about the amazing adventures of Grandma Antonia in Bohemia and America. After lunch when the mothers began to worry because the children were too quiet, they would find the children all cuddled up with their grandfather napping under the tree.

Wintertime in Madison

Wintertime was worrisome when it grew too cold for Vaclav to drive his buggy to the homestead. Anton made a point to visit his father several times a week. One cold November day after closing the lumber mill Anton stopped by to see his papa before heading home. Walking into the house he surveyed the quiet room. He noticed that fresh coal on the fire was just turning from black to red among the burning logs. Vaclav was lightly snoring asleep in his chair with a blanket over his knees in front of the fireplace. Anton smiled, relieved to find his father resting. He noticed a letter lying on the floor by his Papa's feet. Picking it up, intending to set it on his father's lap, he recognized his father's handwriting. Without thinking he read the words on the page.

My Dearest Heart,

I see your smile in the faces of our children and now I hear your joy in our grandchildren's laughter. Anton is a marvel and so much like you. He has your inner strength. I confess my weakness. You were always the stronger one. Each morning I wonder how I am to face the days to come without you and then I see our grandchildren and they make me glad that I am here to see them grow. But I still miss you… so much… every day.

The vision of you waiting for me with little Antonia by your side and all our baby girls and boys playing at your feet does ease my heart. It gives me peace to know our little angels were there to meet you, and I want you to know I have not forgotten any of them.

Antonia you have earned your rest in the Lord, yet I cannot grasp that you are now where I cannot yet follow. You were ever an amazement, a pillar of strength and courage facing so many uncertainties for the love of our family.

*So please let me pretend you are just an ocean away and I will
write to you and dream as we did before. Soon we will be
together again. I beg the Lord's forgiveness for this pretense.
My heart is not capable of saying goodbye to you yet, and
probably never will be. I pray to see you in my dreams.*

Your loving and devoted husband, Wenceslaus

Tears ran down Anton's face as he finished reading his father's
words. He set the letter gently on his Papa's lap careful not to
disturb him. Inspired by his parents' devotion, they had lived
their whole life in love with each other. During all their years
together, his parents taught him to have faith in the love of God.
They gave him an example to live by and showed him how to
honor and nurture the love God bestows on husbands and wives.
Through words, actions and commitment they proved there was
a kind of love that would not fade over time. He ached to be
with his wife and children and hurried home.

Pierce Nebraska, Little Anna Kratochvil

Little Anna Karella Kratochvil and her big brother Anton wrote
to each other often and through that correspondence they kept up
on family news. Although they only lived 30 miles apart, between
work, children and day-to-day responsibilities, her brothers felt
much farther away than a day's journey.

The letters between the Karella siblings overflowed with
information about everyone's children and the list of cousins kept
growing. Little Anna read some of her letters to her children in
hopes of making them feel a little closer to their Madison cousins.
Sometimes after reading letters Anna would think, *I would never
change my life or give up one day with my husband or my children,
but I do wish my sister –in-laws lived with me like we did when
we first got married.*

A BOHEMIAN DREAM

Dear Little Anna,   Nebraska 1901

*We miss seeing you and your children every day and hope all is
well with your family. Everything is fine here at the farm and
in Madison. I believe Emil will be the next family member to
move away. He always talks about you and admires you for
making your life in a new place. He is especially proud of you
for knowing what you wanted, and not being afraid to take
the risk of moving. He can be a little dramatic, but he does
remind me of Mama with his big dreams.*

*Stanislaus and Anna are in good health and they still love the
homestead. Anastasia and I are doing well, and the children
are growing like weeds. My dear Anastasia is due to deliver
our new baby anytime now. I only wish your family was closer
so all the little cousins could play together as they used to.*

*Papa is not as strong as he once was. He used to come to share
his news with us at the homestead on Saturdays. These days
at least once a month we get together at the homestead or in
Madison, and during the summer we still try to gather once a
week.*

*The biggest news I have is about some new Bohemian Karellas
Papa has been corresponding with. Apparently, they are Papa's
distant relations, which came to America quite a few years
earlier than Mama did. Their people settled in Chicago. Papa
writes to them and dreams of going to see them. I am not sure
that will ever happen. Perhaps they will come here. I know he
has extended an invitation to them.*

*Papa also receives lots of news from the old country. Many of
Papa's old neighbors from Kutna Hora have come to America.
He says many of them are doing what he did, using trade skills
that became obsolete in Bohemia, to build new lives for themselves in America. That kind of news always gives me hope.*

Please keep in touch. I miss you little sister,

Your loving brother always, Anton

Kratochvil Family Back Row: Anton Jr., Rose, Louis, Katherine, and Emil
Front Row: Ed, their father Anton Sr., Ray, Mary, their mother
(Little) Anna Karella Kratochvil

Little Anna Kratochvil gave birth to her daughter, Katherine, in 1901 and shortly after that Anastasia gave birth to her son, Frank Emil, on December 12, 1901. With those healthy births, the family's grief over their mother's passing began to ebb and their worlds returned to a more natural rhythm. The men focused on business and the infants in each household kept everyone else too busy with joy to sink back into sadness. Little Anna relished her close relationship with her sisters-in-law despite living in separate towns. The four women made baby clothes, took turns sewing beautiful linens for infant cradles, and shared baptismal clothing by mailing packages back and forth.

Kratochvil Family Tree

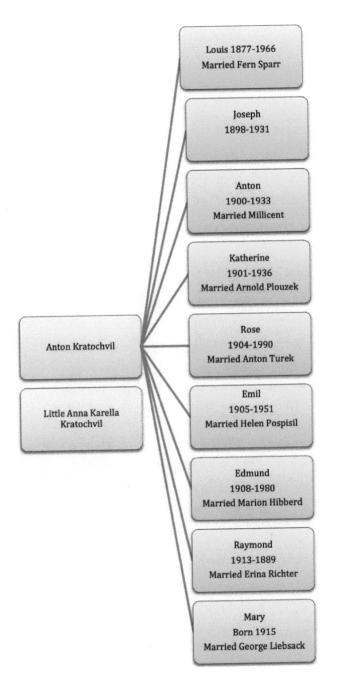

Louis 1877-1966
Married Fern Sparr

Joseph
1898-1931

Anton
1900-1933
Married Millicent

Katherine
1901-1936
Married Arnold Plouzek

Rose
1904-1990
Married Anton Turek

Emil
1905-1951
Married Helen Pospisil

Edmund
1908-1980
Married Marion Hibberd

Raymond
1913-1889
Married Erina Richter

Mary
Born 1915
Married George Liebsack

Anton Kratochvil

Little Anna Karella
Kratochvil

As mothers, Anastasia and Little Anna wrote to each other of hope and looked forward to a day when their children lived close again and could play together as cousins should. However, in 1904 news arrived in Madison which made that hope fade away.

"Anton, did you read Little Anna's last letter?" Anastasia asked.

The tone of her voice alerted Anton that something was amiss. "Not yet. What has happened?"

Giving the good news first Anastasia said, "Little Anna is going to have another baby and she and her family are moving to California." The last part of her statement made Anton put down the newspaper to look at his wife. "Little Anna says although she does not want to live so far away from you and Stanislaus, Grandma and Grandpa Kratochvil want to see their grandchildren before they die. She is going to support her husband's need to be with his parents and so they will move this summer."

Emil John at the Homestead

At age 26, Emil John still lived at the Karella family homestead and worked on the farm. Anastasia and Anton had four children and so far, Stanislaus and Anna didn't have any babies, but that could always change. Emil felt trapped. As a younger son he really had no right to personal space in a house that would eventually belong to his brother. Although his brothers said it was also his home and he had loved growing up there, he yearned for change.

After cleaning his drawing pencils, sticky from being played with by baby fingers, Emil thought, *Why can't five adults keep track of four*

Emil John Karella, youngest son of Vaclav and Antonia Nemec Karella

messy little children? Why do those children always seem to find my things and muck them up? I need change. I have to seriously start looking for an opportunity that will take me away from here.

Anton's Concern for Vaclav Creates Change at the Homestead

There is really only one solution, Anton thought, *it's getting too crowded here at the homestead and I constantly worry about Papa spending so much time alone in town. If I build a house next to the sawmill, it would solve both problems. I'd be close to my work; Anastasia and I would have plenty of space for our children and it would be easy to keep an eye on Papa.*

Ambrose Jerome (Rusty) Karella, elder sister, Helena Karella, first two children born to Anton and Anastasia Holy Karella

When Anton spoke to his brother he said, "Stanislaus, you and Anna could use more room here on the homestead, especially when you start having kids." Stanislaus was going to protest but Anton raised his hand to halt his comments until he'd finished his thought. "Brother, you have to admit the house is getting very crowded. I'd like to move closer to my work at the mill, which will also be closer to Papa. Just think about it please."

Stanislaus's frown reminded Anton of their father and he could tell his brother was initially against the idea of Anton moving his family away from the homestead. After a long pause, Stanislaus replied, "Listen Anton when Papa and Mama moved back into Madison it was hard but necessary. Yet we brothers stuck together. Yes, I'm married now. That does not replace what we have as brothers. We are a family."

Anton and his brother had always shared a special bond and he knew Stanislaus hated change. "Stanislaus, we are not leaving right away, nor am I leaving the town or our family. I'm thinking that in a couple of years I intend to move my family so I can be near the mill and closer to Papa."

Stanislaus realized his brother was right about the space at the farm. Both of their families would need more space eventually and it would reduce the worry they had about their Papa. Finally, Stanislaus nodded his head, saying, "I agree with what you've said. But this won't be for at least two more years, right?"

"Right" Anton replied and both men stood up from the table and hugged one another, reaffirming their love and respect for each other.

Emil John Karella of Madison, Nebraska

Madison Nebraska

During the next four years, Little Anna Karella Kratochvil had two more children. Her daughter, Rose, was born in 1904, and her son, Emil, was born in 1905. Two years later, Little Anna wrote to Anastasia telling her she was going to have another baby in the summer of 1908.

Dear Little Anna,

It is with great joy I tell you that Anastasia is also going to have another baby shortly after you do next year. I only wish we lived closer so I could share this joy with you in person.

Congratulations little sister, you are a wonderful mother. We all miss you!

Much love to you and your family,

Your devoted brother Anton

Little Anna delivered their son Edmund during the summer and Anastasia delivered Mary Cecilia in the fall, on August 15, 1908. Time had gotten away from Anton. The house by the sawmill had been under construction for a year yet still sat unfinished. *Too many project I suppose* thought Anton, *and now we are having another baby at the farm.*

Over recent years babies became a delicate subject around the farm. It worried Anton enough to pull Stanislaus out to the barn to ask him a question, "Stanislaus, can I talk to you about something personal?"

"Of course, what is it?" Stanislaus replied.

"You and Anna have not had children yet. I wanted to ask if it would bother you having a new baby in this house? Do you think it will hurt Anna's feelings having an infant at the farm again?"

Stanislaus was quiet for a long time. His face had gone ashen at hearing the question out loud. Looking Anton in the eye, his face cleared before he replied, "Thank you for thinking of us. We love our nieces and nephews and my Anna has always enjoyed sharing everything with Anastasia. Anna and I will be fine. We are happy for you and Anastasia. Thank you for con-sidering our feelings." With his

Two-year-old Mary Cecilia
Karella, 1911

333

thoughts finished, Stanislaus left the barn and headed toward the house.

Anton's heart ached for his brother. He knew how much they wanted children yet so far God had not blessed them with a baby. *Maybe it is time to finish the house by the mill...maybe after Anastasia is recovered, we will make the move. It might be easier on Stanislaus and Anna. I must speak with Anastasia,* Anton decided.

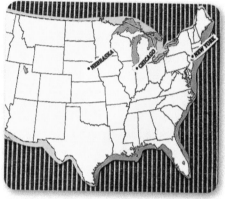

Map showing location of Nebraska's outline and the city of Chicago in relation to New York City

Children always make a household extremely busy, but thankfully, as they get older life feels more orderly. Seven years without an infant in the house left everyone unprepared for Mary Cecilia. She turned the farm upside down with happy chaos. It seemed to take everyone in the household to keep up with her needs.

Anastasia's twelve-year-old daughter Helen assisted her Auntie Anna with household duties, allowing Anastasia to recuperate and focus on the baby. The men and boys took care of everything else.

Emil loved his nieces and nephews well enough, but he was not enjoying this new bout of disorder at the farm. Anton, Stanislaus, and Vaclav understood a young man's need for personal space and came up with a plan that would help everyone. They granted 30-year-old Emil his wish to travel. Emil would take a train to Chicago, Illinois, to visit the Chicago Karellas. Vaclav had been corresponding with them for years and they extended an invitation for a family visitor to stay with them.

After Emil left for Chicago, ten-year-old Ambrose Jerome became Stanislaus's assistant helping with the farm. Ambrose also took charge of nine-year-old Martha and seven-year-old Frank, making sure they did their chores and homework so their

Papa could return to his normal work schedule at the sawmill. Vaclav made trips to the farm as often as he could to help keep the children occupied. Once in a while he stayed overnight in Emil's room. On those nights, he would lay awake listening to the sounds of the house... reliving other times... and remembering other children making the noise.

Emil John Falls in Love

On his way back to Nebraska after an extended visit in Chicago, Emil John found himself in a quandary. He wondered who he should tell about the decisions he had made, and the move he was about to make.

Historical photo of Chicago, Illinois, 1910s

When he accepted the gift of this trip from his father and brothers, the purpose of the trip had been to enjoy seeing places he had only read about. The thought of meeting distant relations on his father's side of the family was nothing compared to the thrill of seeing his first big city. Now, he knew the extraordinary part of this trip had been meeting the love of his life. Emil could see he had been impetuous and foolish about many things when he was young. He had told his brothers he was in love numerous times when he was a boy, yet he had no idea what love was then. He did remember scoffing at their descriptions of what love felt like. Of what they said love was. Now he knew after finding true love for himself, he could admit his brothers were right all along.

The face of love filled his mind, and his love's name was Emily. Bohemian and a Karella, Emily's paternal bloodline was so far removed from his father's bloodline, that the two of them could barely be called cousins. For that blessing, they were exceedingly grateful to God.

The Karellas of Chicago, Illinois

Emily Karella loved Chicago. She never got tired of talking about her city or its history. After meeting her cousin from Nebraska and finding he was interested in everything she wanted to tell him, she volunteered to be his guide. Within weeks they became inseparable.

Commitment to A New Life

Emil John did not feign interest; he found Chicago vibrantly exciting and everything he dreamed a big city would be. As he toured the town, he also looked for job opportunities. Seeing a poster for an opening at a railroad office, Emil set up an appointment for an interview. During the interview, the personnel manager disclosed they were adding a new routing clerk position. Due to Emil's mathematic skills and extensive knowledge of geography, the employment agent offered Emil the position if he was willing to move to Chicago. Everything happened so fast. Emil found himself in love with Emily, in love with Chicago, and thrilled about the job offer. Sitting on a park bench in the sunshine he thought *I have some important decisions to make.*

Emil stayed in Chicago a month longer than originally planned, and before he left for Nebraska, he asked Emily to marry him. She said yes and Emil went to see her father.

The Karellas of Chicago liked Emil right from the start and were further impressed when he asked properly for Emily's hand in marriage. Emil also agreed to marry Emily in Chicago. Any reservations her family had were swept away when Emil explained he had no intentions of taking Emily away to live in Nebraska. He would be moving to Chicago.

With their engagement settled, Emil accepted the routing clerk position with the understanding he had to be on the job before the holiday travel season began. That meant he had a four-month deadline to get moved and settled in the city.

On the Train Headed to Nebraska

Aboard the train the immensity of Emil's decisions and actions he had already set in motion took his breath away. *It is hard to believe everything that has happened. And it all happened so fast! I'm getting the girl I love and the life I have always wanted. But what will the family say? Is it wrong for me to be happy? I need this and I want this.* Shaking his head from side to side he continued to think, *but how do I make them understand that I am going after the life I want on my own without them?*

Emil found himself at a loss trying to figure out how tell his family about his future. *What should I tell them about my marriage plans?* He thought as he laid his head back on the seat and closed his eyes, hoping an answer would come. But his thoughts kept returning to Emily and skipping over his problems, without producing any answers. Slowly his mind drifted off to sleep.

Madison Nebraska

The whole Karella clan knew Emil was home and looked forward to the next Saturday family picnic so they could hear all about his trip. When Saturday arrived, before the rest of the family got to the homestead, Emil pulled his two brothers aside and told them he was in love.

Laughing, thinking Emil was going to tell them about another one of his infatuations, Anton and Stanislaus decided to heckle him a bit. "Oh, did you meet this love of your life on the train or at the depot? Or is this a new girl in town you met on the way home? How long have you known her? A couple of hours or a couple of days?" Emil remembered all the times he had told his brothers he had fallen in love, and to be fair, Anton and Stanislaus had no reason to believe this time was any different.

Holding up his hands in mock surrender, Emil said, "Ok, I'll admit I have told you I was in love quite a few times in the past. But never during all those other romances did I actually think of marrying the girl. Remember I always found myself bored with the relationship before it got that far. This time it is different; I've already asked my girl to marry me. She has accepted and her family has given us their blessing."

Emil never thought a moment like this would ever happen between him and his older brothers. He had shocked them into total silence. *Maybe this will be fun after all!* Emil thought. Emil talked briefly about the Chicago Karellas and shared some of his excitement regarding the railroad station job, he had been offered but did not say he had already accepted the position. Every one of Emil's topics led back to Emily. How she had taken him sight-seeing around Chicago, escorted him to the opera, showed him the museums and art galleries, and how they had gone walking in the parks. Every time he spoke of Emily, he noticed Stanislaus and Anton's expression change.

As Anton and Stanislaus listened to Emil go on and on about Emily Karella, both of them could hear the love and admiration in their brother's voice. Emil sounded like they had when they talked about their wives. For that reason, they believed their little brother had truly fallen in love.

Emil's two sisters-in-law joined the group as he told one of his favorite stories learned from the Chicago Karellas. "…I'll confess, I only call him Papa Chicago around Emily, but then I also refer to our papa, as Papa Nebraska. It can get real confusing with both families sharing the same last name." The group listening chuckled, nodding in understanding having dealt with name confusion in the same household for years.

"We've all heard our Papa's stories about arriving in New York and heading west to Nebraska. Well Papa Chicago has stories too, but they are quite different from ours because his branch of the family came over to America in the mid-1700s, almost 100 years earlier than our group did."

"What was so different about it?" Stanislaus asked.

Anton hushed his brother saying, "Let Emil talk."

The experience of having both his older brothers raptly listening to him for a change, not to mention the rest of the family, was exhilarating. Smiling, Emil replied, "To answer your question, they did not have trains to travel on. Those Karellas left New York in buckboards, ox carts, and covered wagons to journey west in wagon trains. Mama Chicago said her great-grandmother had to check the children's pockets each night to be sure they did not have anything poisonous in there."

Multiple gasps from the mothers listening broke the silence. "What kind of poison? And why would children think to put anything like that in their pockets?" Anastasia asked.

"Snakes," Emil replied. "Some of the boys were picking up baby rattlesnakes and playing with them as they walked along the trail, and would keep them in their pockets. While snakes can be deadly, the real problem they faced was sickness. Papa Chicago said it was an outbreak of cholera that killed a good portion of the men, women, and children in their

Wagon and horse team, Photo by GKM

wagon train. The Karellas traveling with that train lost a couple of adults and at least one child to cholera by the time their party reached Illinois. When they got to the Chicago area, they left the wagon train. From New York, they traveled just under 800 miles. Taking them almost two months. It had been hard going despite good weather and having plenty of grazing for the livestock. Papa Chicago explained wagon trains started west in the spring, stopped when winter hit and continued west again once the snows melted and the land was dry enough to travel across. The Chicago Karella ancestors decided they had lost too many family members by the time they reached Illinois, and chose to stay in the Chicago area when the wagon train continued west. In the 1700s the town of Chicago was a lot smaller, but according to Papa Chicago's ancestors, the land was good. Four generations of his family has prospered there."

By the end of the story Emil's audience had grown to include everyone at the picnic. Encouraged by Anton and Stanislaus, Emil repeated the beginning of the story about meeting and falling in love with Emily and the news of their engagement.

Emil received congratulations from not only his brothers again, but from their wives and his father as well. In the excitement and flurry of all the well-wishing, it was easy for Emil to omit the rest of his news. He avoided answering the big questions, like when did the family get to meet his Emily? And when was he getting married? His general responses to those sticky questions, was that he was going back to Chicago soon to finalize everything. Emil continued to dig a deeper hole for himself during the next six weeks by being vague about all of his plans.

Time to Leave

Anton watched as Emil completed his packing and helped him ship off his belongings to Chicago without asking any questions. He knew Emil better than anyone and suspected his baby brother had not been entirely open about his future. Emil had sidestepped all the family's questions about when he and Emily might set a wedding date or even when the family would get to meet her. Wanting to get to the bottom of the issue, Anton volunteered to take Emil to the train station.

Accepting his brother's offer, Emil hoped he would have the courage to be honest, at least with Anton, before he left town.

Anton wanted to give his brother every chance to tell him what was really going on, which is why he picked Emil up an hour early. The quiet ride to the station was exactly what Emil needed. Once he started his explanation Anton let him finish without saying a word. Not at all surprised by Emil's decisions, at 30-years-old, Anton knew Emil needed a life that would fulfill him as a man. Anton had always known this day would come. But the idea that Emil had no plans to bring Emily home for a visit was truly harsh. That would hurt the whole family.

At the train depot, Emil looked at Anton with relief. His brother had not been angry with him, nor did he criticize him for his decisions. *Anton will know the best way to break this news to the family for me* Emil thought.

Recognizing the look in Emil's eyes, Anton shook his head at his youngest brother. That action stopped Emil in his tracks. Emil had to ask, but he was afraid he already knew the answer. "Why are you shaking your head at me?"

Looking his little brother in the eyes, Anton replied, "I will not do your dirty work for you. You and Emily will have to send word of your news to the family yourselves and that includes Papa. I will try to soothe the hurt feelings your choices will cause. This is part of being a man and a husband. You'll have to accept the consequences of your actions and decisions."

Madison train depot, early 1900s, original from Madison County Historical Museum, curator Carol Robinson

Having said his peace, Anton hugged his brother and delivered what he hoped were a few encouraging words. "I think you underestimate your family. They would have been happy for you. I cannot say they won't be hurt to learn of your plans after the fact, but that is your choice. We will always love you and hopefully you will bring your wife to meet us one day. You might consider inviting Papa to come to your wedding. You know he would enjoy meeting the relatives he's been writing to all these years. Let

Papa have the joy of watching his youngest son marry. Please, just think about it. I wish you and Emily a good and blessed future. You and your family will always be remembered in my prayers, brother. I love you. We all do."

Wedding in Chicago of Emily Karella of Chicago Karella clan and Emil John of the Nebraska Karella's

With those parting words, Emil boarded the train back to Illinois and back to the girl and the city that had stolen his heart. As the train pulled out of the Madison Depot, Emil was hit with a sadness he could not explain. As he watched the familiar buildings disappear, he realized the sadness came from not knowing when he would see his papa or his brothers again.

1909, Nebraska—Mr. Edmund Shoe Comes to Visit his Karella Cousins in America

In 1909, Mr. Edmund Shoe traveled from France to visit his American relatives in Nebraska. What he knew about the American Karellas, came from old French stories. He had heard those French stories from his grandfather about his brother and his brother's wife, whom they had called their gypsy Karella girl. The old French-Bohemian stories about his great uncle and aunt fascinated him as a child. After he became a grown man and served his time in the French Foreign Legion, he made a visit to Prague. That city played an important role in the stories he heard about Bohemia. He wanted to see the places where the gypsy Karella girl had come from. While visiting in the town of Caslav, he met Karellas that still lived in the area and they told him he had relatives living in America. Edmund wanted to meet his distant cousins in America. He had no idea they would become very close friends.

The bond was instant when they met. Anton invited Edmund to stay at the farm and moved him into Emil's old room. He became Uncle Ed to Anton's young children. Before long all the Nebraskans referred to Edmund Shoe as Uncle Ed.

Slightly younger than Anton and Stanislaus, they all thought alike and soon Ed felt like one of the brothers working side by side with Stanislaus on the farm. He also learned the basics of the sawmill operation from Anton. During the winter months when farming was nearly at a standstill and the other Karella children were in school, Uncle Ed helped keep an eye on Anastasia's two-year-old toddler, Mary Cecilia.

United States Census, 1910

1-1 of 1 results for >Name: **Anton Karella**, Gender: **Male**, Marital status, **Married**, Event: **Residence**, Place: **Madison Nebraska**

Number of results to show: 20 | 50 | 75

Name	Birth	Parents	Spouse	Children	Other	Residence	Events			Relationships	
Anton Karella Head United States Census, 1910	1868 Germany		Annastasia Karella	Helene Karella, Ambrose Karella, Martha Karella, Frank Karella, Mary Karella	Edmund Shoe	Fairview, Madison, Nebraska, United States	birth:	1868	Germany	spouse:	Annastasia Karella
							residence:	1910	Fairview, Madison, Nebraska, United States	children:	Helene Karella, Ambrose Karella, Martha Karella, Frank Karella, Mary Karella
			Name		Parents	Spouse	Children	United States		other:	Edmund Shoe
							immigration:	1870			

1-1 of 1 results

United States 1910 census sheet for Anton Karella and family and Mr. Edmund Shoe

During the busy summer of 1910 the United States held a national census. Anton and Anastasia met with the census taker and described each adult living in the household. Along with Anton and Anastasia, the census taker listed their five children—Helen, Ambrose, Martha, Frank, and Mary and a distant relative, a forty-year-old Frenchman who was living with them by the name of Edmund Shoe.

1910, Ambrose Becomes His Grandfather's Apprentice

When it was warm, 71-year-old Vaclav like to drive his buggy out to the farm in the mornings to visit with his sons and Uncle Ed. As they discussed business and the news, the Frenchman noted twelve-year-old Ambrose listening intently. The boy looked like he had opinions he wanted to share. One morning Uncle Ed turned to Ambrose and offered, "Why don't you join the conversation?" Looking at his Grandfather for permission, Vaclav aksed, "What's on your mind Ambrose?"

"Scientists are using cameras to understand space. They have taken pictures of the night sky, even Halley's Comet. The newspapers have been filled with stories about Halley's Comet since May, when we first saw it, remember?" The men all nodded that they did. "Now the newspapers say people are panicking about the earth passing through the tail of the comet. From what I've read, it is too far away to be a danger to earth. So, I am wondering why people are panicking?"

Ambrose's subject and observations took everyone a bit by surprise. Anastasia could not help feeling impressed by her son's intelligent question. The men looked at each other and Uncle Ed replied, "I think science and astronomy are subjects many people don't understand or know very little about. Their lack of knowledge makes them afraid."

"Exactly!" Ambrose replied, "That is why I like to know things. I don't like being afraid."

"Well said, Ambrose." was their response.

When the men went off to work, Ambrose sat with his mother a little longer. "Mama, I'm glad Uncle Ed came to live with us. These talks remind me of listening to Papa and Grandpa Babcock discussing things. Now I get to ask questions too. I am particularly interested about what is going on in America and in the old country. I want to know what Papa and the Uncles are learning from the letters they receive from Bohemia and France." His mother nodded solemnly, pleased with her son's maturity.

What Ambrose did not tell his mother was that he was aware of the volatile political situation spreading across Europe. He had discussed the subject with Uncle Ed. Then Uncle Ed advised, "Ambrose, try not to worry too much about what princes and monarchs are fighting over in other countries across the ocean." But those things still kept him awake at night.

The winter months were always busy, but they had gotten even more so since Ambrose's twelfth birthday when Grandpa Vaclav accepted him as his apprentice. Now Ambrose went to the Madison house for several hours each day after school. On Saturdays he went to the sawmill with his father, and Sundays was for church and family events out at the homestead.

Vaclav felt invigorated as he buttoned his vest, thinking, *I may be seventy-one, I do get a little tired in the afternoons, but my mind is as sharp as it has ever been.* "Thank you, Lord, for blessing me with a grandson that wants to share my knowledge," he whispered. With a spring in his step Vaclav left his bedroom headed toward the kitchen to make a cup of coffee and plan the day's lessons.

Everyone knew Grandpa Vaclav was keen on education, and Ambrose never tried to shirk his schoolwork. As a reward after his homework was completed, his grandfather let him choose what they worked on. Sometimes it was leather and sometimes it was some other project that needed doing. While they worked, Ambrose asked questions about things he saw and talked about things he read.

Inspired by Ambrose's curious and creative thinking, Vaclav began to add various tools and parts to his shop inventory guided by the different subjects and projects that interested both of them. Ambrose soaked up the mechanics of leather working and developed the skills to use that knowledge quickly. As a result, Vaclav encouraged Ambrose to study whatever caught his attention.

The newspapers were bursting with information on the latest inventions and technologies being introduced in America and Europe. Those articles stimulated many creative conversations between grandfather and grandson and were proof that the industrial revolution continued to change the world around them.

Excited by invention, the two were inspired to create tools to make tasks easier, and loved to work on any kind of electrical device they could lay their hands on.

Fascinated with clocks, Ambrose began his quest to understand their workings by taking functioning clocks apart. Too often in the early days, there were leftover parts when he put the clocks back together. Consequently, his mother put a stop to Ambrose fixing her clocks until he could prove he could do it properly. That challenge only drove Ambrose to work harder to find solutions. Before long Ambrose could take apart, fix and properly reassemble any type of equipment on the farm or at the mill.

The only person Ambrose consulted when faced with a unique problem was his grandfather and they would decide what action to take. On a new project, they would decide if it could be done and if so, how to do it.

With the onset of summer, Ambrose's schedule changed because family priorities shifted to the homestead. Ambrose helped his uncles with spring planting. He worked on motors, farm equipment, and every electrical and steam gadget that was part of their daily life. As he grew in proficiency, he was trusted to do vital repairs at the sawmill as well. Even after his return to school in September, harvest work had to be done before and after school until the crops were in.

After harvest Ambrose resumed his lessons with his grandfather. Despite his age, and the intense demands on his time, he loved it. When Ambrose's father and uncles asked him about his jobs and what kind of work, he liked the best, Ambrose always replied, "I love inventing things with Grandpa Vaclav. I know I'm busy, but I wouldn't change any of it. I love working with all of you." The men smiled proudly at him and reply, "Well said Ambrose, we like working with you too."

1911, Anastasia Announces They are Going to Have Another Child

Anton sat in his office at the sawmill. Early that morning his wife had given him the news with her head on the pillow and her eyes closed, "My darling we are going to have another baby. I am exhausted this morning. Is it alright if I sleep in?" Anastasia had taken him by surprise. He was thrilled with the news and leaned down to kiss her, saying, "Thank you my sweet wife, please rest. Thank you for that wonderful surprise." His sleepy wife opened her eyes briefly, returned his smile and a kiss, and then went back to sleep.

Anton pulled out the time sheets planning to work on them. As he sat there thinking his mind switched subjects. *Time and living space have slipped away from me again. Our sixth child! I suppose it is time I get the house here at the sawmill finished.* Suddenly the buzzer in his office went off. That was the signal that his crew needed him out on the cutting floor. Anton got up from his desk immediately. Leaving his office, he promptly forgot everything else he had been thinking about, again.

1911, Uncle Ed Helps Out Where He Can

September 9, 1911 Anastasia gave birth to a little boy and they named him Anastas Leonard. The needs of an unruly infant, added to the havoc caused by little two-year-old Mary Cecilia, took a lot of patience on everyone's part. The toddler was not merely walking, she was running by the time Anastas began to crawl and both children loved to trail after Uncle Ed.

Uncle Ed insisted he did not mind being shadowed by the children. He missed his nieces and nephews in France and never tired of entertaining the Karella's two youngest children. Anastasia gratefully accepted his help and appreciated the extra set of adult eyes keeping track of her curious two-year old toddler and her active baby son.

Invention that Inspires a Discussion between Ambrose, Vaclav, Uncle Ed, and Anton

"Ambrose, all this invention and progress in the newspapers, is part of the same industrial revolution that began years before I left Bohemia." Vaclav remarked.

"That's what makes it so exciting and interesting Grandpa. It's always moving forward. Everyday there is something new and different coming to the forefront. It feels like whatever a person can think up, can be done," replied thirteen-year-old Ambrose.

"For those living in America, I think your statement is accurate." Vaclav replied thoughtfully.

"It's like that story about George Eastman," Ambrose said, "he is the man who invented the Kodak Brownie I camera in 1900. Eastman didn't stop inventing just because he introduced the black and white model and successfully sold that camera. I have read he will introduce a model that can take color photographs too.

By the way Grandpa, Jeff Potter had a broken Brownie I that he threw out. I fixed it.
Kodiak Camera "Brownie 2"
Now I can take black and white photographs for the family. We don't have to hire a professional photographer anymore." "Nice work Ambrose," Vaclav replied.

"Son, I'd like to go back to what you were saying about Eastman. In my opinion the man thinks strategically." Anton added, "Eastman is anticipating what people want! People like being able to take their own pictures. However, once people use film, they also need to get the film developed into photographs. Selling the Brownie camera for $1.00 is only the first step of a three-step business plan. Once you have a camera, you need film. Once you use film, you need to get it developed. Eastman anticipated this would happen. He is a good businessman." Anton finished.

"Ambrose, I read that article. Eastman's new generation camera will be released sometime this year." Added Uncle Ed. "This new one will take color pictures and will be called the Brownie 2. Eastman is selling the color camera for $2.50 a unit. That's more than double the price of the first-generation camera. I believe people who don't think they can afford the color Brownie; will buy the black and white Brownie because it is so much cheaper. Either way Eastman will generate sales for both models, rather than one becoming obsolete because of the new one. The concept is brilliant." Uncle Ed concluded.

Ambrose Admires Inventors and Scientists

Ambrose saw something new and exciting on the front page of the newspapers every day. Glenn Curtiss invents an airplane that can land on the water! Thomas Edison and Nicola Tesla work with electricity to light up cities! Alexander Gram Bell demonstrates his telephone! Cyrus McCormick's mechanical harvesting machines change farming forever!

When Ambrose would get frustrated with one of his projects his grandpa would say, "Do not give up on that idea. The list of inventions gets longer every day and none of those inventions happened overnight. Those inventors you read about spent vast quantities of time learning from failed experiments before they

1914- Wenceslaus Vaclav Karella age 75 and grandson Ambrose Jerome Karella- at age 16-

achieved success. Let their hard work and dedication inspire your creative ideas." Vaclav suggested.

Ambrose did not quit learning, and the practice he got repairing mechanical equipment and farm engines naturally drew him to automobiles. At first, he was only allowed to study his father's automobile engine. The questions he had about combustion engines led Ambrose to examine the work of mechanics like Charles Kettering who built an electric automotive ignition. *That makes good sense* thought Ambrose, *It makes the process so much simpler using an electric spark from inside an automobile to start the engine, rather than requiring a second person to use a hand crank from outside the auto.* Despite Ambrose's knowledge, dedication and skill, it took years before Anton asked, "Ambrose can you take a look at the Model T, please? It keeps backfiring and I don't know the reason." Ambrose smiled at having finally won over his father's confidence enough to let him work on the Ford.

1913, A Serious Son

Anton worried about his fifteen-year-old son. *Ambrose is obsessed with his work, projects, and studies. I'm also proud that he is committed to his faith, being a good brother, son and grandson but he has no free time. I work hard so my children can enjoy their childhoods. I must have a talk with Ambrose about this.*

Anton's mind had been preoccupied with this worry the day Ambrose stopped by the sawmill to work on one of the steam engines that had stopped running. After observing his son had finished his task, he motioned for Ambrose to come to his office. As Ambrose reached the office doorway, he said, "Papa the engine is running fine now."

"Thank you, son. Please come in and sit down for a minute. I'd like to ask you a personal question if you don't mind."

Ambrose's thoughts had already moved on to his next project. However, in response to his father's request he nodded and sat down, only mildly curious.

Anton decided to be direct and asked, "Son, why don't you ever ask for free time to spend with your friends?"

Surprised by the unexpected question Ambrose replied, "Papa, I will have plenty of time for that later. I want to open my own business someday and right now I have a lot to learn to be able to achieve that goal."

"What kind of business are you interested in? Anton asked. "I enjoy the blacksmith and leather work I do with Grandpa. I can do anything with horses tack and harness. I have the skill to offer repair service associated with mechanical farm equipment too. I think a business like that would allow me to use most of the skills I've learned from Grandpa. I also think it would be a good business that would do well here in Madison." Ambrose replied.

Ambrose Jerome (Rusty) Karella and mechanical tractor

Being a man of action himself, Anton could not fault his son for this logic. At the same age he had felt the same way. After a minute of silence, Ambrose brought Anton out of his reverie by asking, "Will that be all, Papa?" Anton waved him out of the office, saying, "Yes, and by the way, all those are good ideas son. Have a good day." He heard a -thank you- float over his son's shoulder as Ambrose rose quickly and was gone. Staring after the young man Anton thought, *He makes me proud. With that kind of determination my son will be a man who can accomplish anything he sets his mind to.*

Uncle Ed, Anastas and the Gypsy Karella Girl

Like a puppy, two-year-old Anastas dogged Uncle Ed's footsteps relentlessly demanding to know the -why- of everything. As Mary and Anastas grew a little older they loved to have Uncle Ed tell them stories. Anastas would pull his sister Mary down to sit on the floor beside him; they would fold their hands and wait quietly for Uncle Ed to say, "Do you want to hear about the gypsy Karella girl?" And the children would reply, "Oh yes please, tell the story about Karina!"

Laughing, Ed realized the children probably knew the story better than he did, because he had told it so many times. "Well Karina and her family were Bohemian just like you two. She and her family lived in Bohemia a long, long time ago in the 1700s.

When I was a small boy like you Anastas, I listened to my great-uncle Lucca tell stories about the Karella girl who married his brother, that was my grandfather, and his name was Philippe. He remembered when Philippe met Karina and when

Figure 12 148 Old Bohemian gypsy style traveling wagon, 1700s

then fell in love. 'They was good times Uncle Lucca would say. My brother Philippe called Karina his gypsy Karella girl and taught her to speak French. Karina lived in a wagon in the Bohemian Quarter in Paris...."

... "And you were born in Paris right Uncle Ed?" said Anastas.

Nodding he answered, "Yes Anastas, I was born and raised in Paris and when Karina lived in Paris, she taught everyone who would listen how to speak Bohemian."

"That's why you call us hunyuks, right Uncle Ed, because Karina taught you?" Anastas asked.

"Well yes, hunyuk is a Bohemian term for someone who gets into mischief. And yes, Karina taught it to Uncle Lucca, and he taught it to me. So you see, you have also learned something from the gypsy Karella girl too. Shall we get back to the story?"

The children nodded and Ed continued… "Now Karina and her family came to France in a beautiful wooden wagon. This was no ordinary wagon. Not at all like the one we use to go to Madison. The Karella's wagon had a roof and walls and inside there were wooden cupboards painted with beautiful flowers in bright colors. This house on wheels was pulled by an enormous horse."

… "With hoofs bigger than a dinner plate!" Anastas added excitedly….

Smiling Uncle Ed nodded and replied, "Yes, that's right Anastas! Now Karina and her family came to France because they were afraid…" …Frowning Anastas jumped in to add, "because of the bad soldiers marching through Bohemia."

… nodding Uncle Ed replied, "Yes that is true Anastas. Now then, one day a letter came, and it said the bad soldiers were gone and the Karellas could go home to Bohemia. Karina's family was happy," …. Anastas broke in to say softly… "But your Grandpa Philippe was sad, wasn't he Uncle Ed."

"Yes, he was sad. You see, Grandpa Philippe did not want his gypsy Karella girl to leave. He was in love with her. Because he was in love with her, he asked her to marry him. Karina said yes and they did get married."

Anastas jumped up from the floor to hug Uncle Ed, and finished the story by saying proudly, "And that is why you are our uncle! I'm glad Karina made you my uncle!" Uncle Ed returned his hug and smiling softly he said, "I am happy she made me your uncle too!"

As Anastas grew older he could most often be found sitting quietly listening to Uncle Ed telling stories about their distant relatives who still lived in Europe. The other stories Anastas loved were about Uncle Ed when he served in the French Foreign Legion and about his adventures in Greece, Africa, Morocco and Egypt. These stories had a profound influence on his young mind and how he viewed his responsibilities to the world he was a part of.

1914, Disturbing News from Europe

Vaclav put down the newspaper. The headlines of late were filled with descriptions of rising tensions in Europe. He looked around the breakfast table at Uncle Ed, Anton, Stanislaus and Ambrose saying, "These escalating political clashes in Europe could explode into real trouble. I recall Count Chotek and his steward telling me about other times like these. Only then it was two royal houses battling against one another. Most of the time it was the Austrian and German aristocrats fighting. It worries me when all this royalty from so many royal houses get involved in one fight. That kind of trouble means real dangerous times for the working classes."

Prelude to World War I

Vaclav's concerns were well founded. Soon the newspaper headlines read, "Royal Assassination. While visiting Sarajevo, Archduke Franz Ferdinand of Austria, heir to the throne of the Austro-Hungarian Empire, was assassinated."

It was not long before the papers published information about the assassins from Serbia. The Austro-Hungarian Empire issued an ultimatum to the King of Serbia to turn over the assassins. That ultimatum was rejected and so the Austro-Hungarian Empire declared war. Following that declaration of war, allies on both sides were forced to declare their support and join the war. The ongoing conflicts and battles continued to escalate across Europe during 1915 and 1916.

1917 The United States Enters World War I

Vaclav's blood ran cold as he read the headlines on the front page of the morning newspaper. "April 6, 1917 The United States Senate has issued a declaration of war against Germany. President Woodrow Wilson, originally opposed to U.S. involvement in the

European wars, has been forced to respond as German submarines are attacking U.S. shipping lines and sinking U.S. ships."

Every citizen across America worried as they speculated what would happen next. It did not take long to find out. The United States began issuing WWI draft registration cards to men born between 1872 and 1899 in all the American states and territories.

Not all registered men would be called into active duty with the armed services. The government draft program known as *NARA M1509* required the men to register with the government on June 5, 1917.

The resulting draft pool included men from ages twenty-one through thirty-one. If selected from the draft pool, that man would be informed when and where to report by a letter issued from the office of the provost marshal general in Washington D.C.

Because they were too old Vaclav, Anton, Stanislaus and Uncle Ed were not affected by the draft. Reading the published age restrictions, the men discovered 19-year-old Ambrose was too young to be drafted as well. However, Emil was thirty and might be called into active service. Vaclav wrote to his son in Chicago and let him know the whole family was praying for his safety, especially if he got called into active duty to fight in the war.

Heart of a Patriot

Uncle Ed and Vaclav sat together talking quietly. "It seems war has caught up to us again. Are we doomed to live with the same fears our families lived with for generations in Europe?" Uncle Ed asked.

"No, this problem is very different," Vaclav, replied.

"How so?" Ed asked. "Before in Europe it was all *the royal's* land. The royals never cared about us. It did not matter whether it was France or Bohemia. They took anything they wanted. Our families suffered when their armies marched across land our ancestors worked. But this," Vaclav pointed to the ground under his feet, "this is our land. They think I'm too old to fight, but I would fight. It might not be the country of my birth, but America is the country I have chosen to be my country. I would fight for America and to protect what America has given to me and my family."

Life Moves On in Nebraska

Although a World War raged in Europe throughout 1918 and affected many people in America, life went on normally for most of the Karellas in Nebraska. For the Nebraskan Karellas life was governed by the annual rhythms of farming, the sawmill operation and their children's education. Each person had responsibilities and worked hard, long hours. As the harvest ended and winter set in, everyone

Joseph Alvinus (Alvin) Bean, husband of Helen Karella Bean

looked forward to the slower pace of life. They cherished the wonderful family gatherings held throughout the holidays.

But the spring of 1918 was filled with excitement. The Karella, Holy and Bean families celebrated with Anton and Anastasia as their eldest daughter, 22-year-old Helen Agnes Karella, married Joseph Alvinus Bean on April 9th at St. Leonard's in Madison.

After the spring planting was completed, Anton and Anastasia took part in another census. The Madison County's Genealogical Society sponsored a census much like St. Leonard's parish census had done a few years prior. The new census listed each businessman of the area, their occupation or trade, and their family members. The booklet listed Anton

Helen Karella Bean, wife of Alvin Bean, wedding day

Karella as a farm owner, a dealer in lumber and threshing machines as well as a sawmill operator. It also listed his wife Anastasia, their six children—Helen, Ambrose Jerome, Martha, Frank, Mary, and Anastas—plus Mr. Edmund Shoe.

With teary eyes, Vaclav read the Madison County census murmuring quietly to himself, "Antonia my darling just look at what we have accomplished. This was our Bohemian dream. Our son is not only listed as a farm owner; he is recognized as a businessman. We did this my love. Together we created opportunities that our children have embraced. Now it is our children's turn to go on and create an American dream."

Madison, Nebraska, photo called mulberry time—Vaclav Karella standing, grandson Ambrose Jerome (Rusty) Karella sitting at his feet; *Girls left to right*: Helen Karella, Jenny Pojar, and Martha Karella

Vaclav walked down to the mercantile thinking to pick up two more copies of the census to send to relatives in Bohemia. As he walked through the mercantile door and the bell jingled, he suddenly remembered both his and Antonia's parents were gone. Trying to shake off his sad feelings, Vaclav turned around and walked home empty-handed, thinking, *Antonia My Heart, I never imagined how much our world was going to change. At least our parents lived long enough to see the Gazetteer from 1890, and* the U.S. census booklet from 1910. The Karella's will continue to prosper here in America. Walking into his house Vaclav picked up the tiny portrait of Antonia that sat on his desk and spoke to it softly, "Because of you My Heart our Bohemian ancestors will live on through our children and their children."

In the late summer of 1918, Anton finally finished the house by the sawmill and moved his family. Vaclav had turned 79-years old and though he would not admit it, Anton and Stanislaus could see their Papa's hands had grown too weak, most days, to hitch up the horse to the buggy by himself. Now that Anton was living close by, he had coffee with his father each morning at the Madison house. He brought his father to the farm whenever there was a family gathering or picnic. Vaclav went to church with Anton and the family. He enjoyed the sermons given by young Father Clemens, who took over the parish from Father Jerome.

Martha Karella

1919 Madison

A year after Helen Karella Bean and Alvin Bean's wedding, Vaclav celebrated with great joy as his first great grandson was born. Helen and Alvin name their little boy, Francis.

Not long after Helen's baby was born, the Karella, Holy, and Pojar families celebrated the wedding of Anton and Anastasia's 20-year-old daughter Martha. Martha Karella married Rudolf Pojar and they lived in Madison.

By 1920, when Francis was a toddler, his mother Helen gave birth to his little sister. Helen and Alvin named their little girl Margaret Mary.

During the early years of their marriage Helen's husband Alvin Bean was employed on a construction crew that helped build the early state highway system throughout Nebraska. Work kept Alvin away from home for long periods of time. That is, until he figured out a way to make a house on wheels. After creating a little house on an old tractor frame, Alvin pulled the trailer house behind his car. The whole family went on the road with Alvin while little Francis and Margaret Mary were still too young to go to school.

In 1922 only four of Anastasia and Anton's children still lived at home; 24-year-old Ambrose, 21-year-old Frank, 14-year old Mary and 11-year-old Anastas. When Helen and her sister Martha got married and moved to their own homes, it left an empty room in their parent's home. Anastasia had seen an article in the newspaper about the new teacher moving to town. The Karella's decided to rent that empty room to the young woman who would be teaching at District-School #66, located across the road from their home. The teacher's name was Agnes

Martha Karella Pojar with husband
Rudolph (Rudy) Pojar,
wedding photo 1919

Moore. She moved in to the Karella home in July of 1921 with plenty of time to prepare her curriculum before her first school term began.

Within in a couple of months Miss Moore felt like a member of the Karella family. The Karella's youngest daughter Mary

Cecilia and her younger brother Anastas were two of Miss More's students. Sharing their home Miss More developed a special bond with Mary Cecilia and had a keen appreciation for Anastas' questioning mind.

1922, First Week of April Madison Nebraska

April was unseasonably cold for Madison, hovering around 25 degrees at night and climbing to 48 degrees during the day. With the fluctuation in temperature it was easy to get the sniffles. One Friday evening in early April Anastasia told everyone she didn't feel well and went to bed early. The whole family believed she would feel better in the morning and thought no more about it.

Anastasia rested in bed with a cough and a slight fever believing she had a minor illness and all she needed was a good night's rest. However, she felt much worse the following morning and she had not been able to shake the fever.

Anton felt worried because Anastasia never got sick. His worry changed to alarm when he discovered she felt worse, and he did not go to the sawmill. After telling Ambrose and Frank to go to work, he told them he planned to wait at home until lunchtime to see how their mother felt. By 11:30 Anastasia was doing much worse and Anton insisted on fetching the doctor.

Agnes More sat with Mary and Anastas, feeling just as concerned about Mrs. Karella as her children while they waited for the doctor's report.

Anastasia Holy Karella with youngest son Anastas (Shorty) Karella at the homestead feeding chickens

Anton and the doctor emerged from Anastasia's sickroom stone-faced. Neither said a word as they went straight to the water closet to wash their hands. When the doctor and Anton came down to the living room the doctor delivered his diagnosis and it terrified everyone.

"Anastasia has contracted *Scarlet Fever*. It is a highly contagious disease that is often fatal. Should a patient recover from this fever they frequently die later from organ damage or infections." Staring directly at the young boy in the room, the doctor continued, "Anton this disease is particularly perilous for young children. It is my recommendation that your young son be sent away immediately. He should stay away until Anastasia is no longer contagious." Staring at the young women in the room the doctor

Ambrose Jerome (Rusty) Karella with mother Anastasia Holy Karella

went on to say, "Young ladies, that room on the second floor of this house is forbidden to all but me and Anton. I must go and make some arrangements, but I will return very soon."

White-faced, Anton wrote a quick note to Vaclav, gave it to Mary and sent her running to fetch her grandfather. As his daughter left the house, Agnes asked, "Mr. Karella, what can I do to help?"

"Will you please keep Anastas with you? When my father arrives please ask him to find Ambrose and Frank." Agnes nodded and Anton left the room to pack his son's things. Anton decided to send Anastas to his sister Martha's home. Finishing his task quickly he returned to the living room just as Vaclav arrived with Mary, his face deeply etched with concern. "Papa we must get

Anastas over to Martha and Rudy's place and he must stay with them until the doctor says it is safe for him to come home." The doctor walked into the house as Anton finished talking, and so he asked the physician to explain the situation to Vaclav in detail.

Though telephones were rapidly becoming a household convenience, not every Karella home had one yet. Anton's did, but he wanted to get Anastas out of the house quickly and so he asked his father to make the calls to the family from his office over at the sawmill.

Vaclav understood and said, "I will take Anastas with me now and see that he gets to Martha's house. I'll have Martha call her brothers. She will make sure the rest of the family at the homestead knows what is happening as well. I'll get a message off to Helen and Alvin myself."

"Thank you, Papa," he said as he watched his father walk out of the house holding his son's hand and carrying the boy's suitcase. With Anastas safely away Anton looked around for Mary and found her standing next to Miss Moore for comfort. "You are fourteen so I will let you choose. You may stay here or go with your brother to Martha's."

"I would rather stay here and help you and Agnes take care of Mama."

Mary watched her papa closely while his mouth pulled down in a worried frown and then finally, he nodded in agreement. Immediately and fiercely he added, "Only I can be exposed to your Mama, since it's already done. You must promise never to enter her room!"

"I promise," Mary whispered in a frightened voice, which normally won a hug of comfort from her papa, but not today. Today her papa only

Wenceslaus (Vaclav) Karella
73 years old

stared at her as if he was angry. After a moment he firmly nodded his head and then turned without a backward glance to climbed the stairs leading back to Anastasia's bedroom.

"Miss More, is Papa mad at me because I wanted to stay?" Mary asked in a frightened voice. "No Mary, your Papa is not angry. He is worried and scared for your Mama." Agnes replied as she watched Mr. Karella climb the stair.

Days Without Relief From Fear

The fever burned in Anastasia for days. Hour after hour it climbed higher and hotter, and nothing the doctor nor Anton did could bring the fever down. Mary and Agnes felt helpless as they sat and waited while the weather outside turned bitterly cold during the nights. All they could do was pray and wait as Anastasia's fever raged on.

During a break from the sick room the doctor told Agnes he had informed the school principal of Mrs. Karella's condition. Because of the contagious nature of the illness, until he could verify that she had not been infected by exposure to scarlet fever, her classes at the school were canceled.

As Miss More was quarantined in the Karella home, she offered to help in any way she could. Agnes worked with Mary, and made sure she and Anton ate, answered the telephone and also passed information to the family when they sent notes or called.

On Sunday April 16th, 1922, Anton sent for the doctor again and asked the girls to watch for him. Then he disappeared into Anastasia's room once more. Fear had been clutching at Mary's stomach since her mama fell ill a week ago.

It was freezing cold down in the kitchen, but Anton had asked Agnes and Mary to stay there and watch for the doctor. The windows were half-frosted over making it hard to see, especially as the afternoon light got dim. Only the very center of the glass pane was clear enough to see through. Mary's papa did not leave her mama when the doctor came. When the doctor arrived, he reminded the two girls he knew the way and said for them to remain in the kitchen.

After the doctor went upstairs, Agnes built up the fire in the stove and put on the teakettle to make hot water.

Agnes and Mary whispered to each other as they sat at the kitchen table while the doctor was upstairs. For some reason it did not feel right to talk out loud. After a long spell of silence Agnes looked around and said, "It feels almost as if your house knows its mistress is dying."

Agnes was the first one to say out loud what Mary feared most. Mary could not stop the sob that escaped from her throat. Agnes put her arms around Mary as the tears ran down both of their faces and Agnes whispered to her. "Honey girl this is a time you must be brave and realize this is how life can be. If this is your Mama's time to go to heaven, ask God for the safe passage of her soul and to go without pain."

Mary nodded and whispered that she would try, as new tears slipped down her face. Even after what Agnes said, Mary was still unprepared when the doctor came downstairs and announced Anastasia had died. Mary looked at Agnes hoping she would say the doctor was wrong, but Agnes shook her head.

More tears slipped down Mary's face as the doctor asked Agnes to watch for the undertaker. That is when Mary noticed the kitchen windows had frozen over completely. The frost was so thick that she and Agnes had to use the steam from the teakettle to melt enough ice off the glass to be able to watch for the people coming with the casket.

After the undertakers arrived and then carried Mrs. Karella's body away, Agnes sat quietly with Mary for a moment. While they were alone in the kitchen, Mary whispered, "I think Mama went to her final resting place dressed in only her nightie. Do you think God minded?" Agnes hugged Mary laying her cheek against the young girl's hair and whispered back, "No, dear one. I think God was happy to welcome your Mama back home to heaven just as she was."

A Family's Time of Grief

Vaclav was the first to arrive at the house after the doctor left to complete the death certificate. He embraced his son. The shoulders of both men shook from the grief welling up inside. "Papa she's gone. It all happened so fast. I'm not even sure Anastasia knew I was there beside her the whole time."

Vaclav's throat was so tight he could barely reply without sobbing himself. "Son, she knew you were there, and I know your mama and Little Antonia were there too." Vaclav continued to comfort his son and mentally he spoke to his wife. *Antonia My Heart, perhaps this is why you were supposed to go before me. I needed to wait here to help our son. I know this is my duty. I just never imagined I would be doing anything like this without you by my side. It is so hard to watch our son go through this, please stay close to me. Together we will help Anton be strong and get the family through this.*

And to God Vaclav said, *Dear Lord thank you for letting me know that my Antonia is still with me. Please grant my children peace.*

A week following Anastasia's passing all the children were out at the homestead with Uncle Ed and Auntie Anna. The rest of the adults were helping Anton cleanse his house. They used lye soap and a disinfectant the doctor recommended on every surface. All the bedding and towels from the sickroom were burned and the doctor recommended destroying the objects Anastasia had used or touched. After the cleansing was completed Anton allowed his children to return home.

The first night that everyone was home together Father Clemens paid the family a visit. The priest hoped the arrangements he had come to talk about would comfort the family. At times like this, God's greater plan was hard to understand with grief-stricken hearts. Despite the Karella's strong faith, Anton had lost his wife and the children had lost their mother. He had to be careful with what he said to them.

Father Clemens sat in front of the fireplace with Anton and spoke quietly "Anton, may I make a few suggestions?" Anton had been staring at the fire but at Father's words he looked up and nodded.

"Please don't take this the wrong way," Father Clemens said, careful to keep his voice soft. "While it could be weeks yet, before the weather permits us to bury Anastasia, what do you think if we hold her funeral mass this coming Sunday? I believe this would allow the family to gather and help them begin to release some of their grief."

Anton sat silent for a long time staring at the flames. Father Clemens thought Anton might not have heard him and was about to repeat his suggestion when Anton looked up and replied, "Yes Father I do think that would help everyone."

Last Week of April, Funeral Mass for Anastasia

After the funeral mass for Anastasia, the Karella family agreed to hold a family wake at the homestead on the following weekend. Vaclav asked Anton and Stanislaus to be available before the gathering started to discuss some family business. On the day of the wake the weather warmed considerably and despite the aches and pains in his hands, and legs Vaclav enjoyed being alone on his horse and buggy ride out to the homestead.

Greeted warmly upon his arrival Stanislaus helped Vaclav remove his heavy winter coat and handed him a hot mug of coffee. Minutes later Anton walked into the kitchen to say hello and Vaclav seized the moment to ask, "Boys, could we have our private talk now?"

The brothers looked at each other nodding in agreement and Stanislaus said, "Let's go upstairs." And led the way to his little office and closed the door behind them. The brothers waited for their papa to tell them what was on his mind.

"My sons it's time for me to officially pass on the ownership of Karella land and businesses." Anton and Stanislaus looked at each other and wondered why their papa felt a need to do this today?

"Anton there has never been a question that the sawmill should be yours, and today I make it official. Stanislaus you have always loved the homestead and have taken good care of it. I want you to continue the management of the farm for as long as you feel up to it. We all know it is very hard work that will only get harder with time. For your future, I want you to have my house and property in town. When you and Anna are ready, you can move into the Madison house and be near Anton.

Your mother and I always intended that our homestead land would be handed down through the generations of our family. I have decided to bequeath the homestead to your youngest brother Emil. I am asking you to guild him as you have always done. However, I do not want you to tell him of this inheritance until he decides to come home on his own. I have prepared information needed to transfer the deeds, which I would like the three of us to do soon. I want to set an appointment in May to record these changes before spring planting begins. My mind will rest easier knowing all of these arrangements are finalized." He paused and hearing no objections from his sons, Vaclav said, "It's time to join the family and remember our dear Anastasia."

Vaclav returned to his home in Madison after the wake for his daughter-in-law feeling more tired than he had ever felt. As was his habit he built up the fire in the fireplace and sat down at his desk to write a letter to his Antonia about the day.

Antonia, My Heart,   *April 1922*

The wake for Anastasia was emotional. Everyone remembered so many wonderful moments they had shared with her. I am worried for Anton though; he is so young to lose his wife. I know what it feels like when a man loses his heart. You always talked to my soul reminding me that I had to live for our children. I hope that motivation is enough for Anton.

My darling, today I officially passed on the fruit of our Bohemian dream to our sons. Now they can begin building their own American dreams. I know they did not understand why I needed to deal with the ownership of the land right now, but they have agreed to go with me next week and register the transfer of deeds. You would have been very proud of them. Of course, they were thrilled to know which land would be theirs. But they were also glad for Emil. They believe as I do, that owning the homestead will make him feel like an independent man instead of a younger son living off the generosity of others.

When the time comes to give him the deed, perhaps he will truly want to come back to his family and be happy to make Nebraska his home.

We have good children my dearest Antonia; they take after their brave Mama. My love, I am very tired tonight. I look forward to seeing you in my dreams. Please give your parents and mine a hug and kiss from me.

I might be seeing you very soon, I think.

Your loving husband always,

Vaclav

Slowly Vaclav set his pen in its holder, waiting for the ink to dry on the paper. Staring into the flames of the fire he felt his eyes getting heavy. Carefully folding the letter he had written, he placed it in the drawer with the others he had lovingly penned to his wife. Vaclav walked to the fireplace, put the screen in front of it so sparks would not fly into the room while the fire burned down, then turned down the flame in the gas lamps and went to bed.

Middle of May 1922

All of Anton and Anastasia's children were in Madison the week their mother took ill and died, except for their eldest daughter Helen Karella Bean. Helen could not afford to come home when her mother died so suddenly. She and the children were still living in their trailer house near Alvin's road construction site and moved with the crew throughout Nebraska as they extended the highway. Helen and Alvin did receive mail through the construction company and so they kept up on what was happening at home through letters she received from her brothers and sisters.

Surviving Grief

Time slipped away from Anton after Anastasia's death. He managed his normal routines without hardly any thought. Anton could wake up and eat when necessary; he stopped by his father's house several times a week to talk over a cup of coffee and went to work every day. Going to work gave him something to focus on other than the pain that filled him. Anton did not see or comprehend the sense of abandonment his detachment was causing his children. Overwhelmed with thoughts he could not run away from; Anton did not hear the

Frank Karella, second-born son of Anton and Anastasia Holy Karella

silence around him nor realize he had stopped talking.

Anton's children, led by Ambrose, pulled together and did what they could to keep their home life in some kind of order. Their married sister Martha spent as much time as possible helping 14-year-old Mary with the cooking and housework. Frank wrote to Helen explaining what was going on at home and asked what she thought they should do. Ambrose spent as much time as he could with their youngest brother Anastas. Despite having full time jobs Ambrose and Frank also took turns checking on their father at work.

July 30th Appointment to Record the Karella Land Deeds

Though Stanislas and Anton had every intention of setting the land appointment in May, it did not happen. July was almost over when Stanislaus called Anton and told him he had set the appointment for the 30th of July.

Anton had recently purchased a Model T Ford Automobile for the sawmill, and it made travel between Madison, the sawmill, and the farm much faster. Vaclav still preferred to ride in a horse drawn carriage when it was warm enough, but under the circumstances Stanislaus suggested it would be better to make their trip to the land office in the Model T, and Anton agreed.

As Anton prepared the Ford for the trip, he automatically thought, *Anastasia would have loved riding in this.* Thoughts of Anastasia were a mixture of pleasure and pain which he could not control. *Could it actually be three months since my Anastasia passed?* wondered Anton as he drove over to pick up his father.

Anton Karella with automobile at Karella homestead, Madison, Nebraska

Vaclav waited by the door of his house. Anton helped him into the auto and soon they were on their way to the homestead to pick up Stanislaus. After the three men finished their greetings they fell into a comfortable silence during the drive.

Upon reaching the Antelope Land office in Neligh, Nebraska, the clerk was ready and waiting for them. Vaclav had prepared everything properly and the deeds were executed swiftly. The clerk handed Anton the receipt for the sawmill and its parcel of land, then handed Stanislaus the receipt for the house and property in Madison. The final receipt concerning the 160-acre homestead was given to Vaclav to keep with his will. The paperwork required to change and reissue the land titles took less time than it had to drive to the office. With the business concluded, the Karella men drove back to the homestead and Stanislaus's wife made lunch.

Sitting around the table filled everyone with sweet memories of happier years when they had lived together at the homestead. Their Papa sat at the head of the table where he had sat for years. Stanislaus and Anton took their familiar seats to their papa's right and left while Stanislaus's wife Anna and Uncle Ed filled the other two chairs.

Surrounded by his family, Vaclav's eyes filled with tears of pride and he said, "let us join hands and thank God for His blessings. Dear Heavenly Father thank you for this magnificent land. I thank you for this family and the bounty and blessings you have showered upon us through your great love."

Anton deferred to Stanislaus as master of his house, and Stanislaus said, "Dear Lord, we thank you for always watching over us. Thank you for giving us a wonderful Papa and Mama whose love and devotion prepared a future for us." Stanislaus was so overcome with emotion he had to stop talking.

Anton took over, saying, "Dear Creator of Life and all that is good, you gave our Mama and Papa selfless hearts filled with love and courage that have no equal. I thank you on behalf of this family for giving us such loving and extraordinary examples of how to live our lives in faith with you. Please continue to bless us and provide our daily bread. Amen."

Uncle Ed surprised everyone when he spoke up, saying, "Dear Lord, thank you for guiding me to my family in America. I have never had a wife to love and lose. I did not know what joy children could be until you brought Mary and Anastas into my life. Thank you for this family that took me in and gave me brothers and sisters to love."

When it was time to take Vaclav home, Stanislaus embraced his father warmly and whispered, "Thank you Papa for your constant love, for the sacrifices you made for me, and for what you did today for Anna and me. I love you, Papa."

Uncle Ed hugged Vaclav and said, "Thank you for giving me a family and a place to belong in America."

The drive to town went quickly and quietly. Anton helped his father into the house and automatically built a fire in the fireplace as Vaclav lit the lamps in the room. The flames eagerly ate at the dry wood as Anton turned and hugged his father gently. *Papa feels so small and frail in my arms,* thought Anton. That realization came as a shock to him.

Whispering into his father's ear, he said, "Papa, you have always shown me what a good man and father should be. The love you had for Mama taught me how life should be between a husband and wife. You've been the guide that shaped the man I am now. The gift you gave me today to secure my family's future fills me with deep gratitude. Papa, I want you to be proud of me! I promise to always be the man you taught me to be."

"My son, I am very proud of you. God has placed a heavy burden on your shoulders, but I know you are strong enough. You must do as your Mama reminded me to do. You must be strong for your children. Open your mind and your heart to them, and they will lead you back into life. Always remember your Mama and I love you dearly."

"I will Papa, I will be there for my children and grandchildren, I promise." Anton replied.

Details of a Long Life

Vaclav sat at his desk staring at the flames in the fireplace. The sun was setting, and he felt great relief at what had been accomplished in the months since Anastasia's passing. Seeing the land deeds change hands had been an extraordinary moment. He would never forget the smiles on his son's faces as they were handed their deeds. Smiling Vaclav had one more thing to accomplish, something for Ambrose.

Ambrose Consults His Grandfather

Ambrose had worked for the past year with an old blacksmith in Norfolk while he saved money to set up his own business. When he reviewed what he had saved he thought that had enough to set up shop in Madison, but he wanted his grandfather's advice before he chose his location. "Grandpa, I think I'm ready to open my own business and I need to choose a location in town. What do you think?" Ambrose asked.

"I think the time is right if in your heart you feel up to the challenge. Look for a central location with plenty of room around it to make it easy for customers to leave things to be worked on. What services will you offer?" Vaclav asked.

"I plan to do standard metal work with horseshoeing and harness. I will offer leather design and assembly of saddles, bridles and the like. I was hoping you'd let me borrow your tools until I can afford to buy my own."

Smiling with pride and a heart bursting with love, Vaclav replied, "My dear apprentice, I give you all my tools and leather working equipment. I cannot tell you how much it means to me and how much it would have meant to your great grandfather to know another Karella is carrying on the family tradition." Suddenly, his grandson was hugging him, and both shed tears of joy as they laughed and lived those precious moments.

September, 1922

Vaclav no longer brooded over things that needed to be finished. Today, when Stanislaus stopped by his house, Vaclav was able to finalize the last thing he wanted settled.

Antonia, I am so proud of our Stanislaus. He agreed to let Ambrose keep the barn on the property here in Madison as his workshop for as long as he wants or needs it. Stanislaus will tell Ambrose about this when Ambrose is ready or needs it. Yes, my dearest Antonia, I have finished our list. I am ready for a new adventure, My Heart.

Vaclav walked across the room and moved his chair closer to the fire. He sat down and covered his knees with a blanket. As the logs in the fireplace hissed and snapped, the familiar sounds helped Vaclav relax. A vision of Antonia floated in his mind, and he talked to her. "Our Bohemian dream for our children has come true, Antonia. It took a lifetime, but we did it!"

Wenceslaus (Vaclav) Karella, 1839–1922, died at 83

He rested his head on the back of his chair. A soft smile spread across his face, and he closed his eyes, feeling at peace. *How nice I feel right now,* he thought ... *that terrible ache in my chest is gone ... and the pain in my hands and legs too ... I think I'll get some good rest tonight ...* In the quiet, he thought he heard Antonia's voice calling to him. Vaclav's heart leapt with joy at the wonderful sound. He opened his eyes, and there she stood in front of him surrounded by a radiant light.

"Oh, My Heart," he whispered, "It is so good to see you! Oh, how I have missed you! Please don't leave me again."

Antonia smiled and held out her hand to him, saying, "I will never leave you again. Come with me, my darling, there are souls who have been waiting to meet you."

The Patriarch Has Passed

It was Stanislaus who called their little sister Anna in California and Emil in Chicago when Anastasia had passed away. Now, it was Stanislaus again who took on the responsibility to call Little Anna and Emil to tell them that their papa had also passed on.

Little Anna was pregnant and too far away to come home and it broke her heart not to be with her brothers at this sad time. Shaken to his core, Emil had replied in a broken voice,

"Stanislaus, I'm coming home immediately! I will bring my family with me." When Emil arrived in Madison with Emily and their son, Raymond, Stanislaus and his wife, Anna, welcomed them warmly and had them move directly into the homestead.

A Second Funeral Mass

Anton and Stanislaus sat side by side in the church; strain and grief showed in the dark circles under their red eyes. Anton whispered to his brother, "Do you think Papa knew he was going to die when he talked to us before Anastasia's wake?"

Stanislaus leaned close and answered Anton's question with another question. "Did you ever notice Papa had a way of knowing things before they happened?"

Anton nodded and whispered back, "So, you are saying that in his own way, he did know. It would explain why he was so adamant we get those documents registered."

Stanislaus choked on his next words. "All he and Mama ever wanted was for us was to be healthy and have the opportunity to have good futures. I miss Mama every day and I miss Papa so much my heart is breaking."

Tears ran down Anton's face as he replied, "Me too brother."

A Time to Say Goodbye

Anton stared at the trestle table draped in black. It had been placed by the altar and would soon hold Papa's casket during

Mass. Anton spoke to Vaclav in his mind, *Papa when I saw you sitting in front of the cold fireplace, I knew you were gone. But when I knelt down to look at your face, I thought for a moment that I was wrong. I thought maybe you only sleeping because you were smiling. I understand why you were smiling. You are reunited with Mama. Yet right now that thought does little to ease the pain of living in this world without the two of you... I miss you Papa.*

Knowing Stanislaus needed this time with his brother, his wife, Anna, helped Martha with her children and asked Mary and Anastas to sit on the other side of the youngsters.

As Vaclav's casket was carried to the front of the church, Anastas asked Mary about something he overheard, and it worried him.

"I heard Auntie Anna say Grandpa died of a broken heart. She said he's been sad since Grandma died, and he grew sadder when Mama died. So sad that he did not want to live anymore." Anastas asked his next question in a scared whisper. "Do you think Papa is going to die now too?"

Mary was frightened at that possibility and whispered back, "I don't know, but I hope not."

Anastas leaned even closer to his sister, whispering his next question, "What did happen to Mama? No one will tell me."

With heads touching, Mary whispered that she and Agnes had listened to the doctor talk to the undertakers the night their Mama died. "It was so cold in the kitchen the windows iced over completely, but the doctor told Agnes and me to watch for the people coming from the funeral parlor. When they got to our house they brought in the casket for Mama. The doctor gave the people rules to follow about Mama and though we were not supposed to be listening we couldn't help it. Agnes and I needed to know what was happening. The doctor said that just before Mama died her temperature was so high it broke the thermometer and that the mercury inside separated because her body was so hot. The people listening to him were shaking their heads and seemed scared and the doctor told them they had to wear masks and gloves to put Mama's body in the casket. Once Mama's body was sealed in the casket, they could make one stop at the church but Father Clemens would have to bless the sealed casket because he forbid them to open it for any reason. After Father Clemens was through, he told them to take the casket to storage so they could keep Mama frozen until they could dig her a grave."

Both Anastas and Mary were crying by the time she finished her story. Mary put her arm around her brother and said, "Agnes said not to be sad because Mama is in heaven with God and Grandma and Grandpa. She is happy and would not want us to be sad." Anastas nodded. He wanted to obey his Mama's wishes, but he still missed her and could not help feeling very sad about that. As brother and sister sat holding hands, feeling alone in a church full of people, suddenly everyone stood up.

Father Clemens began to pray loudly somewhere in the middle of church and Mary and Anastas stood up too. "In the name of the Father and the Son and the Holy Ghost." chanted Father Clemens. Everyone made the sign of the cross and prayed The Lord's Prayer together.

Father Clemens took a deep breath, then said, "Please be seated." Looking at Anton and the Karella family, he began his homily, "Saying goodbye is never easy. Losing a mother, wife, father, or a child breaks the heart and it feels like you will never recover, but you can. God is with you and does not expect you to carry such burdens alone.

"The people who are left behind feel pain and loss. Yet if they truly believe in Jesus's promise and the glorious life that awaits those who believe in Him, then you know Souls that have gone home to heaven still live. They have gained their reward and are happy beyond imagining. If we stop living our life because they have gone home? Are we feeling sorry for them, or are we feeling sorry for ourselves?

"It is the nature of human beings to feel immortal when we are young, or at least until someone we love dies. When that happens, it feels unfair. It is hard for us to comprehend or fathom that no one, at any age, is guaranteed a tomorrow.

"It is my job as a Shepherd of the Lord's people to remind my flock that each day is a gift and every moment we live, is precious. God does not want you to look back, and say, if I had only known I would have told them I loved them; or why didn't I say I had already forgiven them when I had the time? Move on today, don't waste the time you have, don't wait until you can't change things, do not be haunted with regrets.

"Live each day as though you know it will be your last day. Let your faith in action inspire hope. Accept God's unconditional love and let him help heal your hurts and bring peace to your hearts. Love each person that is yours to love, today. We may not be able to physically hug the ones who have gone home to heaven, but if you look with the eyes of your soul, you'll see they are not gone. You will realize you can feel their spirit living in every beat of your heart."

Later at the Karella Farm

The family gathered at the Karella farm for Vaclav's wake. Struggling with tears, everyone looked to Anton to speak first. But Anton's heart was still too broken from losing his wife and his Papa so close together that his throat closed on the words, and he shook his head, unable to speak. Ambrose Jerome had been watching his father struggle with emotions. Ambrose could also see the look of expectation on the faces of Uncle Stanislaus, Uncle Emil, Mrs. Anna, and the rest of the family.

Suddenly, it felt as if his grandfather tapped him on the shoulder as a sign that this was his duty. His grandfather had always said he was the firstborn son of his generation and would need to lead the family someday. A feeling inside told him this was the day to start leading. He had to help his family ease their grieving and keep their dreams alive.

Standing slowly, Ambrose straightened his shoulders as everyone's eyes turned to him. He began to speak in a clear, strong voice that sounded remarkably like his grandfather's and something inspiring took place. "If and when a person is blessed to find their soul mate like Grandpa did and as my Papa did, then that person has been given a gift. As human beings we do not know how long we get to keep our gifts. Yet I believe even if we knew the time would be short, we would not change our mind, we would still want those gifts for however long they were ours.

"I just know that without Grandpa, Grandma, and Mama we would have no family. We would never have come to this great land of promise and none of us children would be here to celebrate three of the most special people who ever lived.

"Like Father Clemens said, we must cherish the gifts we have, and the time we have with them, and always remember no one is guaranteed a tomorrow. Mama and Grandpa would not want us to waste our lives in sadness. They want us to remember we are blessed. We are a family, we are strong, and we have a future to live for.

"I know their spirits are close to our hearts encouraging us to live every moment of life we have. They want us to embrace the fruit of their Bohemian dream. But that is not enough. We must go on and build our dreams, an American Dream that is right for each of us. God never promised having dreams would be easy, nor would it be simple to make those dreams come true. Just look at the examples God gave to guide us toward our dreams. I miss my Mama and Grandpa, but what they taught me and the love they gave me is still here,"

Ambrose laid his hand over his heart as he spoke. He continued, "That is how I go on. It is how we keep believing, and why we keep hoping, and how we find happiness in each day. They want all of us to go on and make them proud. We must honor their belief in us. We will build our American Dreams. We are the family born in the Land of Promise, and our American Dreams will be built on the foundation they built with their Bohemian dream."

Inspired, Ambrose's father Anton stood up and hugged his son. "I am so proud of you," he whispered. Stanislaus hugged Ambrose next and then each family member waited for a chance to thank him for expressing what was in all their hearts.

Sitting around the dinner table, the family prayed the Our Father, the Hail Mary, and the Glory Be. With open hearts, each had a chance to express their love and gratitude for their good life. "I thank God for giving us our Mama and Papa and my Anastasia and for the love they shared."

Anton looked to Stanislaus to continue, and he added, "I thank God for my brothers and sister and for this family Mama and Papa created with their faith, love, and fortitude."

Stanislaus looked to Emil to speak next. "I thank God for showing me what love means. And for this family who has shown that love to me, my wife, and my son. I am grateful to be part of this family." Emil finished speaking and then looked at Mrs. Anna who would read a letter Little Anna had sent for this moment.

"Little Anna wishes me to read her thoughts to all of you as part of this prayer.

"'Dear Lord thank you for bringing Mama and Papa safely to this new land, where each of their children have found husbands and wives and now are bringing more children into the world. I know all my family is gathered there and with them I say, Mama and Papa thank you for making us Americans and teaching us how to dream and showing us how to make our Dreams come true.'"

To be continued...

*This concludes A **Bohemian Dream,** book one of a trilogy called A **Family Born in the Land of Promise.** This family story continues with **American Dreams** … the continuing saga of Ambrose Jerome Karella and his family … see a sneak preview from American Dreams in the following pages …*

Sneak preview
American Dreams
Sequel to A Bohemian Dream, A Family Born in the Land of Promise

American Dreams...
A Family Born in the Land of Promise Trilogy

Prologue, 1941—Karella home in Norfolk, Nebraska

Ambrose Jerome Karella (also known as Rusty) is now a grown man with a wife and eight children. He has two teenaged sons Ambrose James (known as Andy or AJ) and Charles Dale (known as Charlie) who have been planning to join the Marines and Army Air Corps ever since the conflict broke out in Europe and war was declared against Germany in 1939.

After the Japanese attack on Pearl Harbor in 1941, the United States joined the rest of the world at war.

Rusty now faces the day he had hoped would never come. He must live up to the agreement he made with his son Andy who had turned 17-years-old. Signing

Karella Kids: *Back to front boys:* Andy, Charlie, Lloyd and Pete
Back to front Girls: Florence, Marcella, Millie, and Sharon

the papers in his hand to permit early enlistment he would send his eldest into the battles of World War II …

1943, January, Norfolk, Nebraska

"How could he do it?" Charlie shouted as he ran his hands through his hair in frustration. Charlie resented the agreement his eldest brother Andy had been able to ring out of their father. His Dad had actually agreed to let his eldest son and namesake enlist in the Marine Corps once he turned 17.

That's just dandy for him!! Thought Charlie, *but how could Andy move ahead with his plans to join the Marines without including me? We were going to do this together. Andy was going to join the Marines and I was going to join the Army Air Corps! How could my own brother leave me behind?*

"Well, it doesn't matter!" Charlie shouted aloud although there was no one around to hear him. "I'm still gonna leave and get into the sky. I'll get an equal deal from Dad or else... That threat hung in the air and Charlie spoke again through gritted teeth. "I'll do it one-way or another! No one is going to stop me from joining up and flying for my country!"

A Father's Dilemma

Rusty felt boxed into a corner by Charlie and the boy's mother, Delora. His wife foolishly believed she could actually stop their second born son from joining the Army Air Corps by refusing to let him go. In reality, Rusty knew nothing was going to stop their boy from flying and fighting for America. Not even being almost two years younger than his older brother Andy. Rusty's only hope was to convince Charlie to wait as his brother had, until he was 17 to join up. At the same time Rusty feared if Charlie hit any resistance, he would take matters into his own hands.

Andy Leaves for Bootcamp and Charlie Goes Ballistic

In January of 1944 after Andy left for Marine bootcamp, Rusty tried to neutralize the rising tensions at home by proposing the same bargain for early enlistment to Charlie as he had for Andy. If Charlie would wait until he was 17, Rusty would sign early enlistment papers for him. Getting an equal deal seemed to satisfy his son, and Charlie agreed to wait until he was 17.

Unfortunately, the boy's mother heard what Rusty had said and all hell broke loose. "Rusty, *I refuse* to give my consent for any more early enlistments! Do you hear me? I will not allow Charlie to join the Army Air Corps! He is not even 16 yet!"

Trying to calm her down by being reasonable, Rusty replied, "Delora please! Charlie has agreed to wait until he is 17, like his brother did."

Rusty's redheaded wife was blistering mad and refused to be reasonable. Her blue-blue eyes looked cold as ice at the moment, and she barked her one-word reply, "NO!"

Charlie disappeared the next day.

Bitter Worry and War

"Rusty, you have to go after him!" Delora shouted.

"Where do I start looking, Delora? Even if I knew how to find him, what good do you think it would do if I dragged Charles Dale back here? Do you think that will work? I don't. You must know as I do, he'll just run away again. Please leave it alone! Hopefully, if we don't chase him he'll contact us after he has gotten into the service. The Army Air Corp might not take him. But if they do, I believe he will contact us after he gets settled. Just like Anastas did after he ran off to join the French Foreign Legion."

Before Rusty had even finished his statement, he knew he should not have brought that sensitive subject up. To be honest Anastas was a true patriot. But even as a boy, his decisions had been a source of anxiety for the Karella family. He had run away at 14 to become a soldier. Because of Anastas's past choices, his wife had decided Rusty's youngest brother was not the best influence on her sons.

"Rusty, don't even try to defend Anastas's actions. It is bad enough that he ran off to war when he was fourteen *and* enlisted in the French Foreign Legion *and* caused the family horrible worry and heartache! Now he's running off again. Only this time he is leaving his new wife to join the army and go to another war! Don't tell me that you think that is right!" Delora fumed.

As his wife glared at him, Rusty regretted mentioning his youngest brother. He knew Delora's anger actually had nothing to do with Anastas. His baby brother was a wonderful person. His wife was worried about her sons, and needed a target to vent her anger and frustration, and Anastas made a good target.

"Delora, please believe me, I'm as concerned as you are about Charlie being gone. We at least know *where* he planned to go." he said softly. When Delora stormed out of the kitchen without a word, Rusty knew it would be a while before his wife would see reason.

Ambrose Jerome (Rusty) Karella and wife Delora (Bitty) Holt Karella

A Father's Prayer

Alone in the quiet house, Rusty rested his elbows on his knees and put his face in his hands as he prayed silently, *Dear Lord, my trust is in you. Please watch over my brother and my two sons. Heavenly Father, their future is in your hands. Please bring them home safely from war. I humbly pray this request be in alignment with Your Divine will, and may Thy will be done.*

With this final thought Rusty closed his eyes as tears ran down his face. He hoped and prayed that none would be lost, and that World War II would end soon.

St. Leonard's Grave Plot of the Ancestral Karellas in Madison, Nebraska

Original cross gravestone for the Karella plot, engraved with Antonia's name and date of her death, 1900

And the individual grave markers embedded in the ground for Antonia, Anastasia, and Vaclav Karella at St. Leonard's cemetery, Madison, Nebraska

Complete Outline on Historical Bohemia

The Karellas' Homeland, Part of the Czech Republic

The oldest documented patriarch of the Karella Clan in this story originated in Bohemia in 1839. Today, a person might have heard the word Bohemia as a brand of beer or the term *bohemian,* indicating a person's offbeat lifestyle.

However, Bohemia was a small, very old and important kingdom in central Europe. The Bohemian lands included lower Lusatia, Moravia, and Silesia and this region spoke dialects of Czech. Bohemia covered approximately 52,750 sq. km, which is two-thirds of today's Czech Republic. Prague is the capital city of the Czech Republic and was also the capital city of the Kingdom of Bohemia. Bohemia had a short existence as an independent kingdom. Powerful kingdoms surrounding it fought for control of the rich and strategic Bohemian lands.

Bohemia was discovered and named by the Roman Empire in the 1st century. It became an independent kingdom ruled by Bohemian kings in the 9th century, and Bohemia was ruled by the Holy Roman Empire in the 11th century. When the Holy Roman Empire ended in 1806, Bohemia became a possession of the Habsburg Hungarian Empire. In 1867, Bohemia was reduced to a crown land of the Austro-Hungarian Empire and was split equally between the rulers of Austria and Hungary. Bohemia ceased to exist by name when its land became part of Czechoslovakia in the 19th century after the end of World War I.

Historical facts regarding Roman and Bohemian History

The Roman Empire had three phases in its development. The first phase began with emperor Augustus Caesar, 27 BC – 98 AD.

Bohemia was discovered and named by Roman legion mapmakers during this first period of expansion.

The second phase of the Roman Empire emerged under the leadership of Emperor Trajan in 98 AD. Ruled by several different emperors, this period lasted until 284 AD. During this time, the Roman Empire reached its territorial peak.

The third phase of the Roman Empire began with Emperor Diocletian 284 AD and lasted until 305 AD. The people of the Roman Empire worshiped the gods and goddesses of Greek and Roman mythology. During the rule of Diocletian, Romans aggressively persecuted the followers of Jesus Christ of Nazareth who called themselves Christians. Diocletian's successor was Emperor Constantine.

When Constantine came to power, he split the total lands of his empire into the Eastern Roman Empire and the Western Roman Empire, and he ruled from the city of Constantinople. Constantine was the first Roman Emperor to be converted to Christianity in approximately 313AD. He and his mother helped end the persecution of Christians throughout the Roman Empire. During its existence, the Roman Empire used several forms of government—autocracy, absolute monarchy, and theocracy. The Roman Empire ended in 476 AD.

Middle Ages—Fifth Century to the Fifteenth Century

The Middle Ages took place in central Europe after the fall of the Western Roman Empire in the 5th century and lasted until the Renaissance period beginning in the 15th century. After the disbanding of the Roman Empire, groups of barbarian invaders, which included various Germanic peoples, formed new kingdoms throughout the land that had been the Western Roman Empire. Also, during this time,

Royal Crest of
King Wenceslaus I

388

period Pope Urban II, of the Roman Catholic Church, began to preach about a crusade using military force to regain control of the Holy Lands from the Muslims. Middle Ages were marked by calamities that included famine, plague, and war. One of the most terrifying plagues was called the Black Death, and it claimed approximately one-third of the European population between 1347-1350.

The Holy Roman Empire

The Holy Roman Empire emerged during the Middle Ages in the 9th century and lasted until the 19th century. The largest territory left after the fall of the first Roman Empire was the Kingdom of Germany ruled by Charlemagne. King Charlemagne's lands included Germany, the Kingdom of Bohemia, the Kingdom of Burgundy, the Kingdom of Italy, and numerous other territories. In 800 AD, Pope Leo III crowned King Charlemagne Emperor, reviving the use of the title in Western Europe after three centuries. Charlemagne was considered the first new age emperor to succeed directly from the first Roman emperors.

The title of emperor was revived again in 962 when Otto I was crowned as the successor to Charlemagne. During the reign of Emperor Otto I, he assumed not only the role of emperor he also claimed the imperial title for the Holy Roman Empire.

The term Holy Roman Empire distinguishes it from the ancient Roman Empire, though this title was not used until the 13th century. When Emperor Otto I began using this title, he sought to legitimize his claim to call his empire, the Holy Roman Empire, by promoting the principle of direct succession. He claimed his right to rule was received directly from Charlemagne, who received his authority directly from the old Roman Emperors. Based on that line of succession, Otto I maintained that as the Emperor of the Holy Roman Empire he inherited his powers and title from the original Roman Emperors.

A point of clarification: the office of Holy Roman Emperor was generally elective. The German prince-electors (highest ranking noblemen of the German Empire) elected one of their peers, naming him King of the Romans, and then the Pope of the Catholic Church would crown that king emperor. Papal coronations ceased in the 16th century.

Emperor Francis II was the last Holy Roman Emperor, and he dissolved the Holy Roman Empire in 1806. During its existence, the Holy Roman Empire had no single language, the religion of the empire was Roman Catholicism or Protestantism, and the government was an Elective Monarchy, which also ordained Emperors.

27BC – 98 AD

When the Roman legion of Augustus Caesar found this central European region and named it Bohemia, Slavs inhabited the land, and it was also being invaded by nomadic Celts. The Slavs eventually ousted the invaders.

Bohemia is Converted to Catholicism in the Eighth Century AD

Neighboring Avars conquered Slavic Bohemia between the 1st and 5th centuries AD. In 658, Slavs won their freedom from the Avars. Within the next one hundred years, Bohemia became part of the Moravian Empire. During this period, two Byzantine-Christian missionary brothers from Constantinople, Cyril, and Methodius introduced Catholicism and converted the population of Bohemia to the Catholic faith in the 8th century.

Bohemian Becomes an Independent Principality

Wenceslaus I was the first native-born Bohemian leader to emerge in the 9th century. Also known as Good King Wenceslaus, he played an instrumental role in freeing Bohemia from Moravian control.

After the establishment of the Wenceslaus I dynasty, his line ruled Bohemia for several hundred years. His crest was a lion standing on his hind feet with two tails intertwined over its back. The Bohemian people considered Wenceslaus a King, but the neighboring kingdoms did not. During the reign of Wenceslaus, I (907 to 935), Bohemia was recognized as an independent principality by the surrounding kingdoms, and the kings of those kingdoms recognized Wenceslaus as a prince and his brothers as Dukes of Bohemia. During the reign of Wenceslaus, I, he successfully rebuffed a Germanic invasion force.

After blatant invasion failed, individual Germans secretly began infiltrating the Bohemian government. Those Germans began to fill important positions, and their influence in government grew stronger as more towns were established, and trade routes were developed between neighboring countries. The political power shift within the country was subtle, and the change went unnoticed until it was too late. By the time the danger was recognized, Germans were in control of all strategic policy-making positions within the Bohemian government.

King Wenceslaus I, 907-935

Though ethnically Germans were the minority culture in Bohemia, it was the German administrators that introduced governmental guidelines and prejudicial laws blatantly detrimental to most of the Bohemian population.

In 935, King Wenceslaus I was assassinated by his brother, Bolesav the Cruel. Under the reign of Bolesav, Bohemia became part of the Holy Roman Empire when he pledged Bohemia's allegiance to Holy Roman Emperor Otto I in 950. In return for

Bolesav's pledge, Bohemia was allowed to retain autonomy for internal affairs but lost its status as an independent principality.

Bohemia, Part of the Holy Roman Empire of 1152–1198

It wasn't until after 962 that the territory controlled by the Holy Roman Empire included the kingdoms of Germany, Bohemia, Burgundy, and Italy as well as numerous other annexed territories.

Also, during this era, Pope Urban II began his holy wars, calling them crusades. The first of those battles took place in 1095 against the Turks, and the last was the Siege of Acre in 1291. During those years crusade battles were fought in Palestine, Lebanon, Syria, Egypt, Constantinople and in both the Latin Empire and in the Kingdom of Jerusalem. By 1198, the Holy Roman Empire had grown to encompass Germany, Netherlands, Belgium, Luxembourg, Switzerland, Austria, the Czech and Slovak Republics, as well as parts of eastern France, northern Italy, Slovenia, and western Poland.

Bohemia ceases to be known as a principality and becomes a kingdom

In 1200, Holy Roman Emperor Otto IV and Pope Innocent II anointed the Bohemian leader, Ottokar, with the important title of hereditary King of Bohemia.

Once he was officially recognized as a King, Ottokar also gained independence for his Bohemian kingdom, which still swore allegiance to Holy Roman Emperor Otto IV and was strategically, politically, and financially allied with Otto IV's Holy Roman Empire.

In 1211, the Royal Bohemian house of Ottokar announced the birth of Princess Agnes. As the daughter of King Ottokar I of Bohemia, the princess was considered an important political pawn. Ottokar planned a strategic alliance and betrothed his daughter at eight years old to Henry, son of the Holy Roman Emperor

Frederick II. At that time, Henry was ten years old and had been crowned king of Germany. However, due to political intrigue, this marriage was prevented. Once again in 1226, King Ottokar planned to marry Agnes to Henry III of England. Unexpectedly, the thirty-two-year old Holy Roman Emperor Frederick II canceled this second potential alliance with England because he wanted to marry Princess Agnes himself. However, Agnes, now fifteen years old, refused to be used for political gain and chose instead to enter a convent and devote herself to God and a life of prayer. In 1236 at twenty-five, Princess Agnes joined the religious order of Poor Clares where she spent the rest of her life.

Even without the strategic alliances he might have had through his daughter, Bohemian King Ottokar I still brought his country to its height in landmass and political power through conquest and material acquisition between the years 1253 and 1258.

The next big change for Bohemia took place almost fifty years later when Holy Roman Emperor Henry VII arranged the marriage of his eldest son John (Count of Luxembourg) to Elizabeth, niece of the deceased King Wenceslaus III of Bohemia. The hereditary bloodline of Bohemian kings descended from Ottokar I ended with Elizabeth's marriage. The royal house passed to John, Count of Luxembourg, when he was crowned King of Bohemia in 1306, and his son Charles IV was crowned after him.

Bohemia's Golden Age Within the Holy Roman Empire, 1355–1419

Bohemia experienced its golden age when King John's son, Charles IV king of Bohemia, was also elected Emperor of the Holy Roman Empire in 1355. Charles IV loved the beautiful city of Prague so much that he made it the capital of the country of Bohemia and then made Prague the seat of the Holy Roman Empire. Successors to Charles IV were emperors Wenceslaus IV and his brother, Sigismund.

Bohemia and the Hussite Wars, 1419 -1434

At the beginning of the 15th century, a Christian reformist group called the Hussites started a religious and political rebellion in Bohemia against the Holy Roman Empire during the reign of Sigismund. The Hussite-led wars commenced in 1419 and raged across Bohemia and Moravia. Three main issues spawned these conflicts. The first issue was a religious freedom struggle between the Hussite Christians and the Roman Catholic Church. The second issue was a political struggle between the Bohemian population and the Germanic minority in control of the government. The third issue was a socioeconomic battle between the landed aristocracy and the peasant classes. After fifteen years of brutal war, the Roman Catholic Church and the Hussite leadership established a compromise to end the conflict. The Hussites agreed to end their religious rebellion, and in exchange, the Roman Catholic Church gave them dispensation to retain and practice their own religious rites.

Bohemia, the House of Habsburg and the Habsburg Hungarian Empire 1471-1749

The Habsburgs began as Counts of Germany and Switzerland prior to Rudolph Habsburg, who was crowned King of Germany. After this event, men of the Habsburg bloodline continuously occupied the throne of the Holy Roman Empire between 1434 and 1740. During this same time period, the House of Habsburg also produced kings that ruled in Bohemia, England, France, Germany, Hungary, Croatia, Ireland, Portugal, and Habsburg Spain. They also produced Emperors for the Empires of Russia and Second Mexican Empire as well as rulers for several Dutch and Italian principalities. In 1471, the kingdom of Bohemia became a possession of the Habsburgs of Hungary.

By 1487, the noble classes of Bohemia had learned to profit from the fighting going on between surrounding monarchs of neighboring countries. In exchange for food and material support to foreign troops crossing Bohemian lands, the aristocracy of Bohemia secured vast privileges for themselves growing richer. But it was the Bohemian people working the land that supplied the food and labor to support these armies. With little to no compensation, the Bohemian people were reduced to serfdom and treated like slaves by Bohemian land barons.

During this time in history, the royal house of Bohemian monarchs existed in name only, and a battle for control of the Bohemian land raged between the Habsburgs of Hungary and the monarchy of Austria. In 1526, the Habsburgs of Hungary won complete control of Bohemia.

In 1627, the Habsburg Empire renounced the existence of the royal house of Bohemia and reduced the country of Bohemia to the status of imperial land. This meant the Habsburgs considered Bohemia as a geographic property held within their private estate holdings. These two fundamental insults against the Bohemian people fueled thirty years of civil unrest.

The civil unrest rose to new heights in 1648 when oppressive taxation pushed most of the Bohemian population into abject poverty. On the heels of grave financial despair, additional cultural oppression was imposed. In 1749 by governmental mandate, the German language was decreed to be the sole official language of Bohemia. This edict ignited a deep hatred and bitter hostility against the entire German population within the borders of Bohemia.

Dawn of the 1800s in Central Europe

During the 1800s, political strife ran ramped across Europe, and the Bohemians were constantly victimized by military troops crossing Bohemian land.

France, Austria, Hungary, Russia, and Germany kept the population of Bohemia in chaos. The monarchs of these countries battled with each other over national sovereignty, land borders, religious identity, and relentlessly inflicted their own cultural and ethnic prejudices on their neighbors through military threat or physical occupation.

The Bohemian countryside housed armies from at least one foreign nation constantly throughout the 1800s. For example, in December 1799, Austria was in dispute with Russia. Russia displayed its power by moving its armies from Switzerland into Bohemia under the guise of resting the troops. The first Russian corps stayed in Central Bohemia, the second Russian Corps stayed in Western Bohemia, and the third Russian Corps stayed in southern Bohemia. This formidable invasion force was deployed as a pressure tactic to make Austria acquiesce. Caught in the middle of this constant aggression, it was Bohemian land and its people that dealt with the needs and demands of all those military troops.

War

European history is fraught with two kinds of war. There are wars generated by human rights issues, which create civil unrest within a country. There is also a second type of war waged between monarchies and nations that crush everything in its path to gain title, land, resources, or power.

Wars also tend to affect bordering nations not actually at war with the key players. These countries fall into fringe battles, drawn into conflict as a preemptive measure to protect land they possessed. For example, in August of 1813, border strife erupted when Austria declared war on France. Immediately, Russian and Prussian armies move from Silesia and Moravia into Bohemia to ensure the protection of Russian territory. The following year Napoleon is removed as emperor and imprisoned on the isle of Elba, which ends the Napoleonic wars, but that peace was shattered within a year when Russian armies moved back and forth through Bohemia as they marched against France in a new conflict.

Neighboring kingdoms continuously coveted Bohemia for its natural resources, which included forests, abundant fresh water, fish, potatoes, rye, barley and wheat, and for its livestock, beer breweries, and precious metal and gem mines.

Regardless of this natural wealth, the average Bohemian citizen did not believe in building or maintaining an army. The small military guard that existed within the country was stationed in Prague, and their job was to protect the royals. They did nothing to protect the land or its people from foreign forces or aggression.

What Bohemians believed in was education and investing money in schools, literature, art, and music. The average Bohemian strove to make beauty a part of their daily life. Bohemians satisfied this requirement in simple ways such as painting doors, lids, and window casings with bouquets of flowers. Bohemians tended to be marvelous woodworkers who carved beautiful lintels, storage chests, wardrobes, and even decorated the inside of kitchen cupboard doors. Bohemians were also known for building intricately carved and painted wooden house wagons for traveling. During troubled times, some Bohemians would load their families into these wagons and drive to neighboring countries where they remained until receiving word it was safe to return home.

Legend of the First Gypsies and the Bohemian District of Paris

These traveling caravans of wandering Bohemians and Hungarians are thought to be the first Gypsies. Specifically, the legends referred to bands of people that crossed Europe in house wagons searching for peaceful places to stay during times of trouble in their homelands. The city of Paris, France, was one of their destinations. Many Bohemians found sanctuary within districts of the sprawling city of Paris. Even today, there is still an area within Paris, France, referred to as the Bohemian District, and on Parisian

1700s – 1800s traditional Bohemian style Traveling wagon—i.e. Gypsy legend

397

maps, it is found in 6éme, St. Germain. The area is known for its art museums, book markets, street musicians, poets, and the best antique shops.

The Bohemian District of 1800s Paris was the meeting place for traveling Bohemians. Over time, the area and the name Bohemian became synonymous with the radical types who lived there. Like many Bohemians who visited the city, the occupants of the district tended to be artists, musicians, intellectuals, poets, and avant-garde thinkers. Parisians who felt strongly about the arts, or freedom of speech also gravitated to this area. As time passed, those living in this district were considered to live as Bohemians did as non-conformist citizens who did not abide by the morays of aristocratic society and did not abide strictly by government regulation.

1800s Brings Great Change to Bohemians

Even as far back as the 1400s, Bohemians were passionate about education. In an era when many of the peasants of European countries were illiterate, the average Bohemian peasant used mathematics and could read and write.

Bohemians were traditionally freethinkers and not above rebellion to retain and protect their unique heritage and personal identity. Throughout Bohemian history, that quest for knowledge led adult Bohemians to form an assortment of reading clubs. Within these clubs, they studied and discussed poetry, read newspapers from major European cities, and debated the ramifications of that news. Even when the news was outdated, these groups still deliberated over political views, discussed religion, and reflected on the changing conditions within bordering countries. When Napoleon Bonaparte came to power in France, he captured the attention of the Bohemian people with his revolutionary ideas.

Bohemians and Napoleon's Code of Law

In 1804, Napoleon Bonaparte became the Emperor of France and began to shake the foundation of European aristocracy with his radical Code of Law, and consequently, most of the aristocracy across Europe denounced Napoleon as an anarchist.

This Code of Law incorporated principles such as equality of aristocracy and the peasant classes before the law. It also outlined the following concepts: careers open to talent, freedom of religion, and protection of private property. The law also forced a shift in power. By moving state matters into civil management, this Code of Law abolished serfdom.

"Serfdom by definition is categorized as a form of slavery. A person or persons in a condition of servitude required to render services to a lord, commonly attached to the lord's land and transferred with it from one owner to another."

Though Napoleon's Code of Law introduced the beginning of change for the peasant classes, it was still flawed in many respects. The same document denied workers collective bargaining, outlawed trade unions, and required the institution of labor passports, which permitted the government to track all workers. But the most infamous section of this same Code of Law dealt with women and children. Napoleon Bonaparte's Code of Law declared women were inferior to men, and children had no rights at all. Yet regardless of the flawed thinking concerning women and children, this Code of Law stimulated courage in minority cultures and ethnic groups living in every country across Europe, particularly those who found themselves at odds with the landed aristocracy.

Bohemia Education in the 1800s

One of the few positive movements that took place in Bohemia in the 1800s was the educational reform of 1805. The Bohemian government made school attendance compulsory for all children between the ages of six and twelve. In reality, this schooling regulation for older children was seldom enforced when every-day survival required all family members to work to keep the family fed.

The End of the Holy Roman Empire

The last emperor, Francis II, dissolved the Holy Roman Empire in 1806. Following the demise of the Holy Roman Empire, Francis II declared himself Emperor of Austria (changing his name to Franz I or Francis I).

As Austrian King Francis I, he made a deal with the Habsburgs of Hungary. While they agreed to stand united against the rest of Europe to control as much land as possible, they continued to fight privately between themselves for material acquisition and dominance. However, their alliance allowed Austria and Hungary to become the new ultimate power in Europe.

By 1806, the Bohemian population was a diverse mixture of Bohemians, Jews, Poles, Russians, Austrians, Hungarians, and Englishmen and Germans. Germans were the minority race in the country, and yet they held the most powerful government positions in the country. The German politicians used their authority to confine the rest of the Bohemian population to a lower class of treatment.

Inspired by the concepts in Napoleon's Code of Law, the Bohemian population believed they deserved civil rights. When they were denied those rights by the German controlled govern-ment, the rest of the ethnic groups united in rebellion against those injustices forced upon them. This strife catapulted Bohemia and its diverse population into an age of civil unrest.

King Francis I of Austria and his henchmen, Prince Klemens Wenzel von Metternich

In a time when the Bohemian people loathed aristocrats, there was one man who was universally hated across the whole of the Austro-Hungarian Empire, and his name was Metternich. The man had been appointed Chancellor of the Austro-Hungarian Empire in 1809 by King Francis I and then also received the title of Office of Foreign Minister of the Austro-Hungarian Empire in 1821.

Acting on behalf of paranoid King Francis I, Metternich instituted a series of controls and surveillance to spy on and control the working classes of the Austro-Hungarian Empire. Metternich was directly responsible for the empire's most corrupt issues and practices.

King Francis authorized Metternich to implement his tyrannical policies through a network of spies and secret police. This network reported directly to Metternich, and he alone bore the initial contempt of the people.

The population of the Austro-Hungarian Empire appealed to their governments for change, attempting to bypass Metternich. When change did not take place in Bohemia, Hungary, or Austria, anger and rebellion grew to new heights, and the people's animosity spread to include King Francis. Metternich continued unchecked, and the discontent increased dramatically throughout all the lands of the Austro-Hungarian Empire. When the stranglehold of governmental intrigues began to affect even the Germans living in Austria, they finally joined the revolution. For the first time, German voices merged with the peasant classes. United as the working classes of the Austro-Hungarian Empire, they were demanding essential and fundamental change to end the oppressive bureaucracy of King Francis I.

The concepts within the Napoleonic Code of Law transformed the fundamental way the working classes looked at themselves. These radical ideas infused the suppressed minorities across central Europe with a determination to fight for control over their futures. This thinking was particularly strong in Bohemia among citizens of non-Germanic heritage.

In 1818 despite the turmoil rampant in the empire, a remarkable Bohemian project was approved. A national museum was founded in Prague and commissioned with a charter to support and preserve cultural diversity and its initial focus centered on natural science, art, and music, and would eventually include literature.

The first president of the Society of the Patriotic Museum was Count Sternberk, a botanist, mineralogist, and eminent Phyto-paleontologist. The importance of this museum was not in its exhibits but in the establishment of the museum itself that signaled an intellectual shift in Bohemia.

Prior to this project, German aristocrats and nobility dominated political, scholarly, and scientific groups and believed that knowledge was their exclusive domain. The National Museum created to serve all the inhabitants of Bohemia helped eliminate that age-old myth.

Increased support was generated for the project when historian F. Palacky suggested a break in tradition. Normally, the museum only published its scientific journals in German. Palacky proposed the museum publish a second set of journals in Czech and took on this project himself. Within a few years, German journals ceased to be printed due to a lack of interest. However, the Czech journals were in demand for more than a century after Palacky created this policy change. This movement of tolerance and cultural respect began to spread throughout the country and grew into dominance over the next twenty years in Bohemia.

The Industrial Revolution

Practically overnight, an unprecedented form of change dominated the world's future. The 1830s introduced the beginning of the Industrial Revolution. Though some momentum toward automation began to appear in the late 1760s, it took a dramatic leap in 1820s, 1830s, and again in the 1840s across many industries and in equipment design and transportation.

For example, production procedure was changing from human to machine, and new chemical manufacturing was introduced to process iron and brass. There were equipment upgrades that used waterpower to run silk mills, brass mills, cotton spinning, and textile mills, and new invention in tools that used steam power to mechanized agricultural equipment.

Technology had begun to reinvent many types of businesses in England and in the northeastern parts of America long before it began to make its way into central Europe. The first Bohemian industry converted to mechanized manufacturing was textiles, and with its success, the lives of working-class Bohemians changed forever.

Traditional Trades and Craftsmanship

Prior to the dawn of the 1800s, the industries of Bohemia and nearby German Bavaria were primarily farming and woodworking. Bohemia's manufactured goods were made by hand, and in some cases, men used simple mechanical devices and water wheels for limited power. The production of most commodities took place in villages scattered across the countryside, and individuals sold them. There were a few bigger towns and cities where select groups of craftsmen and artisans belonged to associations called guilds. These associations controlled the standards of their craft within the towns, set prices, and sold the guilds'-finished products in guild stores.

Industrialization began to spread rapidly across Central Europe and then gradually into Bohemia. As companies-built factories, management needed employees to operate the equipment. By centralizing employment opportunities, the factories slowly began to draw fathers and young adults away from their ancestral homes in rural areas. Eventually, factory-produced goods began to erode traditional handcrafted markets. Within a short span of time, mechanical production was cheaper and faster than hand-craftsmanship, and the traditional Bohemian lifestyle soon became obsolete. Desperation emptied the countryside as people moved to towns where factories promised jobs.

1839, Wenceslaus Karella is born

The oldest Karella ancestor of this story first appears in 1839. His name was Wenceslaus (Vaclav) Karella, and this Karella son was born into a time of political, and social unrest raging across Europe and would grow up during the unsettling introduction of factories with mechanical technology inspired by the Industrial Revolution in Europe and America.

Seven years after Wenceslaus' birth, the people of Bohemia were already suffering from industry change and were about to receive another shock from their government. To stop the cultural diversity movement spreading across Bohemia, the empire sanctioned a law in 1844 to mandate German be spoken as the only language in Bohemia. This law outraged minority groups within the Bohemian regions of the Austro-Hungarian Empire, uniting them against the German authority. Though citizens were forced to comply publicly, secretly Bohemian women went underground to train children in Czech dialects ensuring the survival of their native languages and traditions.

Bohemia and the Austro-Hungarian Compromise of 1867

The civil unrest was extensive across all the Austro-Hungarian Empire as Metternich continued to serve as both chancellor and foreign minister. He went unchecked in his activities until 1848, when out of self-preservation, King Francis I expelled Metternich from office for his repressive policies. King Francis met with the Habsburgs of Hungary and claimed that Metternich acted alone and was the sole underlying cause of the civil rioting plaguing the empire.

From 1848 through the middle of the next century, the main political issue in Bohemia and Moravia was mounting tension between the Czech populations and the Germans living in the industrialized regions of Bohemia. Bohemia went through another radical change nineteen years later in 1867 when the Austrian and

Hungarian monarchs agreed to a compromise. Rather than fight each other for total land control, they agreed to rule Bohemia as co-equals. On a map of Bohemia, they created boundaries that split the land into two equal parts.

From Prague to Bohemia's western border, the area would be ruled by Austria. On the opposite side, from Prague to Bohemia's eastern border, the land would be ruled by Hungary. With two different governments dictating to the Bohemian population as well as making more demands, it was only natural that escalating civil unrest would follow.

History Sources

History on the first Empire—https://www.ancient.eu/Roman_
  Empire/
History of Bohemia—https://en.wikipedia.org/wiki/Bohemia
List_of_Bohemian_monarchs
https://simple.wikipedia.org/wiki/Austria-Hungary
https://eudocs.lib.byu.edu/index.php/Kingdom_of_Bohemia_
  in_Holy_Roman_Empire_1212-1806
https://www.britannica.com/place/Bohemia
https://www.butterfield.com/blog/2017/03/22/deep-brief-history-
  bohemia/
https://www.czechtourism.com/a/north-bohemia/
http://www.historyworld.net/wrldhis/PlainTextHistories.
  asp?historyid=ac40

Final Notes on Bohemia

As for the common Bohemian, they might not know all the names and locations of the myriad hamlets or villages within their country's borders, but each citizen knew how to find Prague. Directions could be provided to anywhere in relationship to the golden city.

Therefore, it was common for Bohemians to described where they lived in relation to the distance and direction from Prague, the capital city of Bohemia. By now one may have come to realize most towns in Bohemia are small and referred to as villages. However, the capital of Bohemia, Prague, was and remains to this day, an extremely grand and beautiful city. This jewel flourished in the 14th century in the reign of the Holy Roman Emperor, Charles IV. As the stories go, he loved the city so much that Prague became the seat from which this emperor ruled his entire empire.

By the 1900s, the Karellas' European homeland was technically called the Protectorate of Bohemia. The Bohemian kingdom ceased to exist in 1918 when the land became the property of the Czechoslovak Republic. However, Prague, the jewel of Bohemia, survived and still thrives.

Samples of research conducted by Sister Margaret Mary Bean and Andy Karella

Letter written by Andy Karella in 1987, the year before he died, acknowledging the work Sister Margaret Mary had done to accumulate the family data. At this time, Darlene Helinski Cipra and her family traveled to Czechoslovakia, and while on vacation visiting her husband's relatives, undertook verification of research at Catholic Church arch dioceses. They also visited civil record halls of several cities, including Kutna Hora, in an attempt to establish more corroborating evidence regarding the lives of our Karella and Nemec ancestors in Bohemia.

Fairbanks, Alaska
May 31, 1988

WENCESLAUS (VACLAV) KARELLA and ANTONIA NEMECZ

After many years and much work by many persons, particularly Sister Margaret Mary Bean, I think I may be able to compile a whole lot of information into some readable chronological order. There are so many related facts gathered by so many persons over the years that it is going to be difficult to keep in order.

Sister Margaret is a teaching Benedictine missionary, and she must have literally squeezed in the vast amount of time to gather so much information. Her mother was Helen Karella Bean, my father's eldest sister, and like myself, she is a great-grandchild of Vaclav and Antonia.

Within two weeks of the above date, my very dear friend Paul Cipra is returning for a visit to his former home, Czechoslovakia, after 20 years, with his wife Darlene and their two daughters, Jeanne and Dianne. Paul intends to track down our ancestry further back than Vaclav and Antonia, if it is possible. Also, there are at least four persons living in our mutual "neighborhood" around Caslav that he will attempt to interview in our behalf. There will be at least foot-notes concerning this trip at the end of this Wenceslaus trunk of our family tree. As you will see, Paul's father, Olda, has already done a great deal of leg work for us.

Benedictine Sisters to the Mission

(l.) Sister Antionette, Principal, Sister Margaret Mary, Sister Margaret ... r and Sister Ann.

Paul, Darlene, Diane and

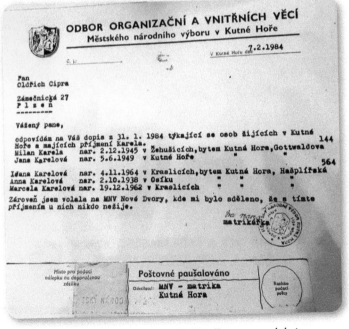

Copy of handwritten church ledger from Bohemia, recording Wenceslaus Karella's birth in 1839 and marriage to Antonia Nemec in 1863 and Antonia Nemec's birth (1839) and her wedding to Wenceslaus Karella in Bohemia. Below: Czech report received by Darlene Cipra on Karellas who lived around Kutna Hora 1984. These are just two samples from a packet of documents the Cipras bought back for Andy Karella.

1988, Original note from Andy Karella on research being Conducted by family on a trip to Czechoslovakia

409

Here is one of the personal notes from Sister Margaret Mary Bean regarding the portraits she collected from the Karella family, of ancestress Anastasia Holy Karella and notes from interviews with family members.

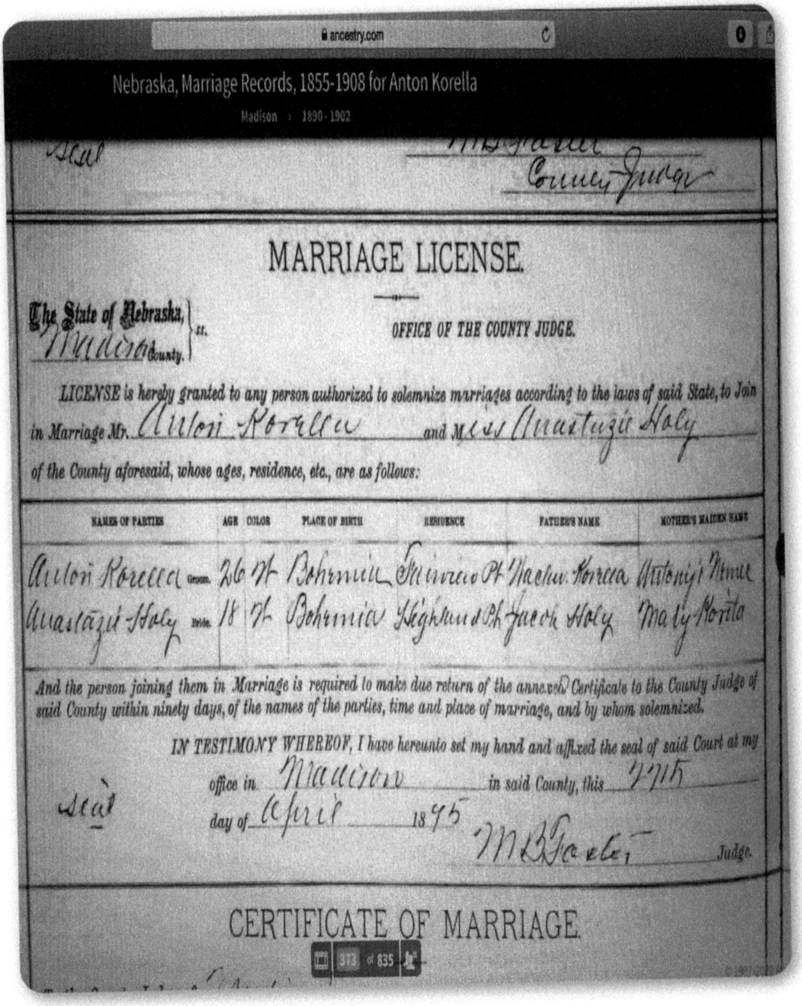
ancestry.com

Nebraska, Marriage Records, 1855-1908 for Anton Korella

Madison : 1890-1902

County Judge

MARRIAGE LICENSE.

The State of Nebraska, Madison County. } ss.

OFFICE OF THE COUNTY JUDGE.

LICENSE is hereby granted to any person authorized to solemnize marriages according to the laws of said State, to Join in Marriage Mr. Anton Korella *and* Miss Anastazie Holy *of the County aforesaid, whose ages, residence, etc., are as follows:*

NAMES OF PARTIES		AGE	COLOR	PLACE OF BIRTH	RESIDENCE	FATHER'S NAME	MOTHER'S MAIDEN NAME
Anton Korella	Groom	26	W	Bohemia	Meridian Pt	Vaclav Korella	Antonie Nemec
Anastazie Holy	Bride	18	W	Bohemia	Highland Pt	Jacob Holy	Maly Korita

And the person joining them in Marriage is required to make due return of the annexed Certificate to the County Judge of said County within ninety days, of the names of the parties, time and place of marriage, and by whom solemnized.

IN TESTIMONY WHEREOF, I have hereunto set my hand and affixed the seal of said Court at my office in Madison *in said County, this* 17th *day of* April *18*95

Seal

M B Foster *Judge.*

CERTIFICATE OF MARRIAGE.

373 of 835

Genealogy Records Covering Generations 1, 2, 3; The Births of the 4th Generation of Karellas; and Nebraska Family Groupings

Vaclav and Antonia Nemec Karella Family Tree

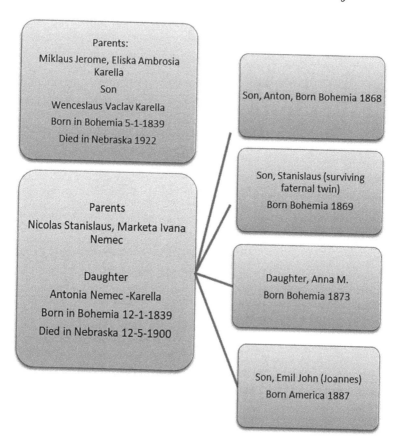

Parents:
Miklaus Jerome, Eliska Ambrosia Karella

Son
Wenceslaus Vaclav Karella
Born in Bohemia 5-1-1839
Died in Nebraska 1922

Parents
Nicolas Stanislaus, Marketa Ivana Nemec

Daughter
Antonia Nemec -Karella
Born in Bohemia 12-1-1839
Died in Nebraska 12-5-1900

Son, Anton, Born Bohemia 1868

Son, Stanislaus (surviving faternal twin)
Born Bohemia 1869

Daughter, Anna M.
Born Bohemia 1873

Son, Emil John (Joannes)
Born America 1887

Anton Karella Family Tree

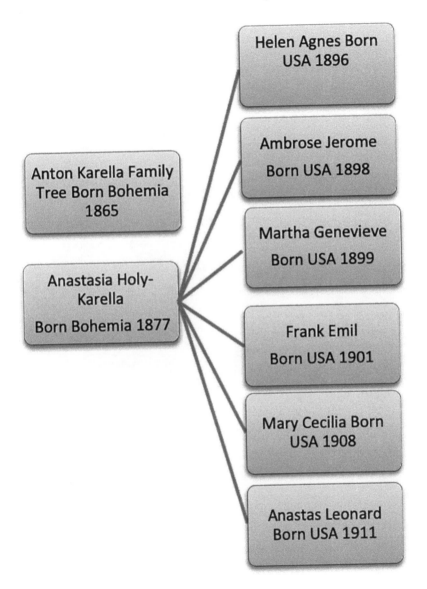

Jacob Holy and Mary Koryta Family Tree

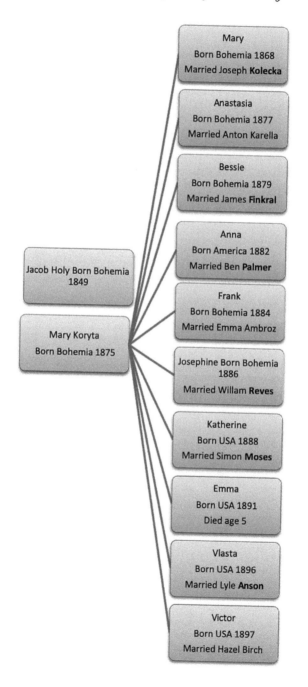

Jacob Holy Born Bohemia 1849

Mary Koryta Born Bohemia 1875

Mary
Born Bohemia 1868
Married Joseph **Kolecka**

Anastasia
Born Bohemia 1877
Married Anton Karella

Bessie
Born Bohemia 1879
Married James **Finkral**

Anna
Born America 1882
Married Ben **Palmer**

Frank
Born Bohemia 1884
Married Emma Ambroz

Josephine Born Bohemia 1886
Married Willam **Reves**

Katherine
Born USA 1888
Married Simon **Moses**

Emma
Born USA 1891
Died age 5

Vlasta
Born USA 1896
Married Lyle **Anson**

Victor
Born USA 1897
Married Hazel Birch

Joseph and Katharina Koryta-Kuchar Family Tree

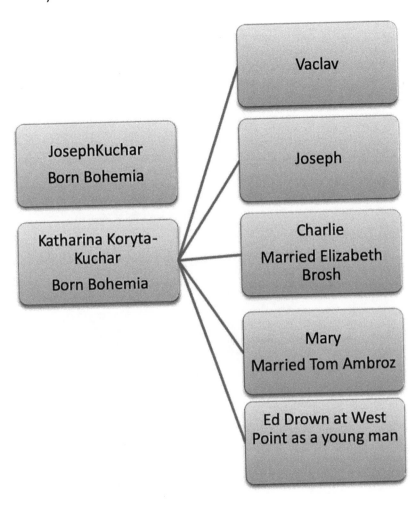

JosephKuchar
Born Bohemia

Katharina Koryta-Kuchar
Born Bohemia

Vaclav

Joseph

Charlie
Married Elizabeth Brosh

Mary
Married Tom Ambroz

Ed Drown at West Point as a young man

Little Anna Karella & Anton Kratochvil Family Tree

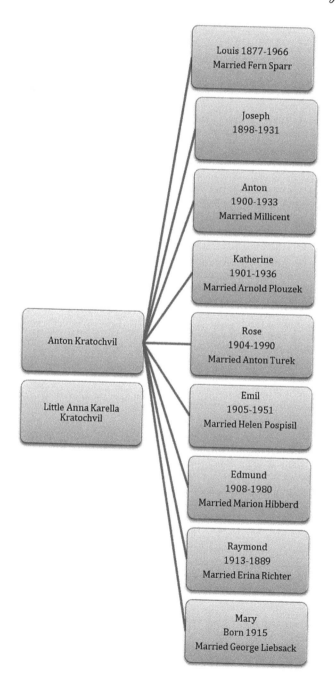

Karella Family Tree part 1

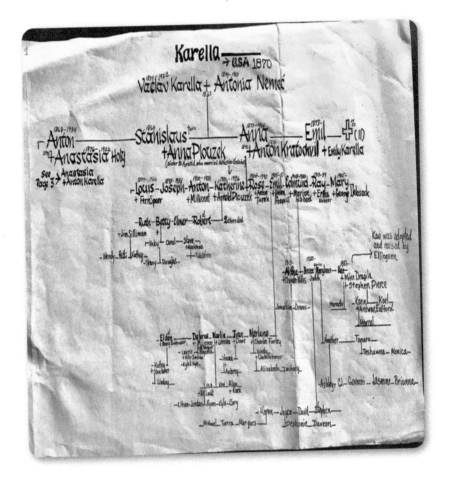

Karella Family Tree part 2

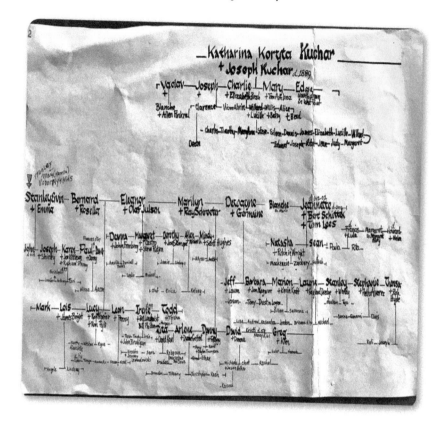

Karella Family Tree part 3

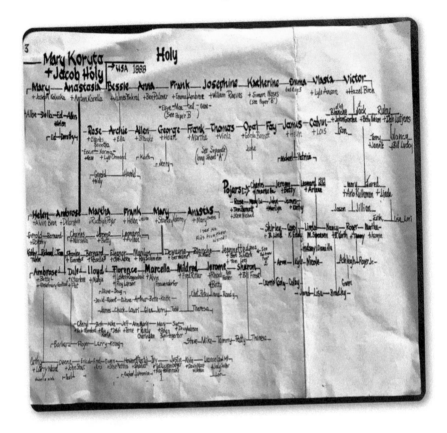

Additional Clan Tree Part A

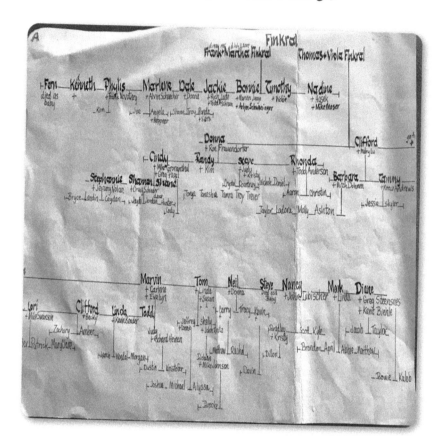

Additional Clan Tree part B

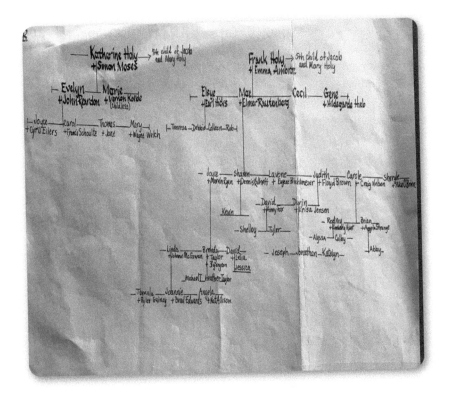

APPENDIX 3

Important Note: Bohemian names have different spellings when designating a woman or a man. Example: on a grave marker you might see Nemec or Nemecova (adding OVA to the last names, indicating it was a woman).

Example: Anna Nemecova and Josef Nemec are family members and are buried in the same grave plot.

Personal Notes from Researchers, Interviewers, and Facts That Are Part of This Book

Regarding Betmann's Archives

It is one of the world's great libraries, used all over the world by publishers and educators. Bettmann created his little fact book to counter the impression created by overly romanticized images from Antonia's era. It shows how contrary to reality that impression is. Bettmann's facts have allowed us to better understand what Antonia Karella faced in terms of living expenses once she arrived in America.

Research with Bettmann, a Glimpse of the Slums of New York

Here is an eye opener for those who think it is bad sharing a bedroom. Bettmann describes a cross section of a New York tenement house as follows. "Between 1868 and 1875 an estimated

500,000 people lived in New York's slums, about half the city's population. As many as eight persons shared a living room that was 10 feet by 12 feet and one bedroom 6 feet by 8 feet. In one tenement building on the Lower East Side, it was recorded to house 101 adults and 91 children."

Research with Bettmann on the Meaning of Subsistence Wages

"Subsistence wages were negotiated at a rate significantly less than the $2 per day gross income, used as an example, in Bettmann's monetary compensation for New York City, during the 1800s. This data was printed in a book by Otto Bettmann, founder of the famed Bettmann Archives in New York."

Research Referenced for food, rental costs and conditions in New York 1875

Credits: Research study of Bettmann's cost and wage data, regarding 1800s New York: **Bettmann** sold the **archive** to the Kraus Thomson Organization. In 1995, the **archive** was sold to Corbis, a digital stock photography **company** founded by Bill Gates

Bettmann Archive, Conditions and Costs in New York 1875
https://libraryguides.missouri.edu/pricesandwages/1860-1869
https://www.immigrantentrepreneurship.org/entry.php?rec=71

"Contrary to popular belief, $2 a day in the 1870s was not a lot of money. Except for native New Yorkers where rents were lower, (immigrants were not considered New Yorkers) rent took at least 10 to 15 percent of an average wage that might cover dismal accommodations and certain foods, which could be bought reasonably. Statistics show that food generally absorbed 50 percent of low incomes. For example, in 1882, a Boston bookmaker with a family of five that made $660 as a yearly income spent $120 on rent and $319.29 on groceries. When measured against $2 a day salary, considered an acceptable wage for the times, the average prices for foods per pound, went like this: butter 19 cents small 4oz pot, bacon 10 cents lbs., 1 fowl 10 to 15 cents, and eggs 15 cents a dozen. As can be seen, food costs were quite high. Many families had only $1 a day to spend for food and if they made $2 per day, surviving day to day was a desperate hardship." Bettmann notes, "Many of these people often lived on bread alone, with no meat, for weeks."

Credits: Corbis to acquire **Bettmann Archive**. BELLEVUE, Wash., Oct. 10 -- **Corbis** Corp., founded six years ago by computer billionaire Bill Gates, announced Tuesday it will buy the **Bettmann Archive**, one of the world's largest photo libraries, for an undisclosed price from the Kraus Organization Ltd. Oct 10, 1995

Regarding facts about Morrisania in letters from Sister Dorothy, a native of New York, who relayed the following personal information to Sister Margaret Mary Bean

"Dear Sister Margaret Mary, at first, when you said your ancestor Antonia worked in a cigar factory in New York, I had been quite frightened about what she might have gone through. You see, originally the immigrants in Antonia's era lived in cold-water flats (meaning no hot water unless you boiled it yourself), and in the city these buildings were five stories high. They were stacked like railroad cars with windows on the inside walls and built with two apartments per floor with one toilet to share between them in the middle of the hallway. They were really dank and dark places, and whenever there was a cholera or yellow fever epidemic, thousands died.

"However, later after you wrote and told me Antonia lived in an area called Morrisania, I was much relieved, and so this is what I remember. The area called Morrisania was named after Governor Morris.

"I include this description so you can visualize where this community was. The province of New York had twelve original counties. The territory contained within County Bronx was originally part of County Westchester and parts of the towns of Yonkers, Eastchester, and Pelham. In 1846, the division of Westchester created the new town of West Farms; then in 1855, the town of Morrisania was created from West Farms.

"In Antonia's early days in America, Morrisania was a small village on the mainland of the state, East of the Harlem River and across from the Willis Bridge. The Willis Bridge extended from First Avenue and East 124th Street in Manhattan to Willis Avenue and East 134th Street in the Bronx. This bridge was a gate-lift that allowed barges and tall chimney-stacked ships to pass up the river. In 1874, the villages of Morrisania, West Farms, and Kingsbridge became part of New York City, when the city annexed these three large villages. In 1880, all the communities surrounding New York City were merged into one great metropolis. That was when the city's five boroughs were formed, and New York City proper was split to form the boroughs of the Bronx and Manhattan. Sister Margaret Mary, when I was a child, one could take a trolley across Willis Bridge into the Bronx or to 156th Street and Amsterdam Avenue, into New York City, or into the Bronx/Morrisania areas. The Third Ave EL (elevated train system) also ran into these areas as well. Sister Bean, I hope these old memories have helped in your investigations, God Bless you my friend, yours truly, Sister Brooks"

Regarding the Cigar Industry of 1875 — Data and Facts from the Cigar Industry Museum

In 1875, hand-rolling cigars for twelve hours, six days a week, was typical of factory work in America, and according to their data, in 1875, there were one hundred mid-size and two large cigar factories operating right in Morrisania. There were 123 medium and twelve large cigar factories operating right in the heart of New York.

The museum had a few other interesting statistics as well, such as the factories of New York State manufacturing six to eight billion cigars, making it the cigar capital of the world. As it happens, it was also the state that produced the most cigars during Antonia's era, followed by Pennsylvania, and then Illinois.

The museum made note of an early challenge faced by the American Cigar Makers' Union regarding a new system of manufacture established between 1870 and 1871. Many companies feared they would be forced to adopt the new system to stay competitive. However, stalling for time yielded an unexpected solution to the factory's dilemma. Throughout 1872, a substantial wave of immigrants from Bohemia arrived in New York, which provided these cigar manufacturers a ready source of low-cost labor. Factory management not only avoided investing in new manufacturing changes, but they also reduced their production costs by hiring from this new pool of desperate immigrant labor. Men and women flooding the city were willing to work for subsistence wages. This type of wage was negotiated at significantly less than the $2 per day gross income, used as an example, in Bettmann's monetary compensation data for this time period.

Final Note on Average Life Expectancy of Men and Women in the 1800s

Reference chapter 3—Antonia and Wenceslaus were childless until 1868, and according to life expectancy age data in the UK from 1700 to the mid-1800s, average adult lifespan was fifty to sixty years.

Having a Child Baptized So Late in Life Is Highly Unusual for Catholics.

Yet considering all the circumstances surrounding Emil's birth, the unsettled state of the families living conditions and how Emil's birth had weakened Antonia, this writer can make a few assumptions regarding the nine years that passed between the boy's

426

birth and his formal baptism. At first the, primary concerns had to be for Antonia's and the baby's general health. With Antonia recuperating, school for the older children became the next priority. When you consider that Vaclav was traveling weekly to establish a new business and their permanent home in another town, the next two years passed rapidly. Then, they moved to Madison, settled into a new house and community, and their parish only had services twice a month. In those circumstances, one can understand how a formal baptismal ceremony came years after it normally would have.

Regarding Madison, Nebraska, in the 1880s

Nebraska state history confirms that by the time the Karella's arrived in Madison, which was eight years after the first Arbor Day. Millions of trees were already producing a local source of lumber for settlers. The Karellas believed Nebraska would be similar to Bohemia. The fertile rolling plains, young forests, and lush fields as well as the climate, and the industries of farming, livestock, and lumber reminded them of what had been good in their homeland of Bohemia. Once they moved to America, they lovingly referred to Bohemia as the old country. The similarities between Bohemia and America helped them form a bond with their new country, and the Karella's flourished, and a clan was born in America.

Researching Historical Records at the Antelope Co. Land Office, Located in Neligh, Nebraska

This land office covered all the area around Madison, Nebraska. Florence Karella Roggenbach, a 30-year reporter and column writer for the Norfolk Daily Newspapers, and Sister Margaret Mary visited this office and found records that showed a paid receipt recorded on September 13, 1886. It was issued for the Karella family homestead of 160 acres in Madison County, Nebraska. The land of the original homestead of Vaclav Karella is located 2 miles north, and 2 ½ miles east of Madison. In the year 2010, the family farm of Mildred Karella Ridder was, and still is, located only a few miles away from this historic Karella homestead site.

Regarding Research in St. Leonard's Parish Records

In the spring of 1880, St. Leonard's Parish was established to serve the Catholic community of Madison, Nebraska. Its pastor, a Franciscan Monk, Father Cyprian Banscheid, also worked for two other parishes, St. Bernard's and the Lindsay parish in nearby towns.

By the time the Karellas became residents of Madison, Father Banscheid was saying mass for St. Leonard's parishioners twice a month. One of the first tasks accomplished by this monk was creating a record system for St. Leonard's. He asked each family of the parish to fill out a family history document, and with that information, he started a formal Parish archive.

In Father Banscheid's first parish census, it listed the head of each household, the man's occupation, and his family members. Wenceslaus Vaclav Karella was listed as a shoemaker, and his family included his wife, Antonia, and their four children, Anton, Stanislaus, Anna, and Emil. In addition to the census, St. Leonards' has many old church photographs and records of major events of their parishioners by name, date, and event, i.e. births, baptisms, confirmations, weddings, and deaths.

According to several verbal accounts Sister Margaret Mary Bean recorded, Vaclav and Antonia Karella had eleven children during their life together. Among those children were three sets of twins. However, the only documented children to grow to adulthood were Anton, Stanislaus (who was a fraternal twin), Anna, and Emil, who are the children this writer has written about by name.

There was a photocopy of a newspaper obituary in the documents forwarded by Mildred Karella Ridder written for Antonia Karella on Friday May 11, 1900, commemorating her life at her passing. In this article, it also stated Vaclav and Antonia had given life to eleven children during their marriage—five boys and six girls. Sadly, the seven children that must have died very young were never named. There were no birth announcements or death certificates to indicate when they were born or what they died from. At the time of Antonia's death, the article indicated her daughter, little Anna, still lived close by. She was married and Anna and her family lived in Pierce, Nebraska.

During her life she and her husband Anton had nine children—seven boys and two girls—and was known as Anna Kratochvil. Anton Kratochvil's family was from California. Though this book is focused on Karella lineage, in recent years, descendants of Anna Karella Kratochvil, one young man who is a flight attendant, introduced himself to another flight attendant with the last name of Karella. After a short conversation, it was established that they were related to the Nebraska and Alaska Karellas through his grandmother Anna Karella Kratochvil, and his family still lives in California.

Anastasia is the daughter of Jacob Holy and Mary Holy. Jacob Holy came from a Bohemian town, fifty miles northeast of Prague, born January 9, 1849, in the village of Duby Hora Kraj Pirel, Bohemia. Jacobs's wife's family name is Koryta, and Mary was born August 15, 1853, in the village of Kozli. Mary and Jacob were married in 1872 in the village of Radobia, Bohemia. Jacob and Mary lived in the village of Piscek after their wedding, and three years later they had their first child whom they named Mary in September of 1875."

Jacob and Mary had a second daughter, Anastasia, born in Piscek on February 24, 1877. After 1878 Jacob moved his family back to Duby Hora to be near the children's grandparents. They had a third baby girl, Bessie, on April 27, 1879. Three years after that a fourth daughter Anna was born on July 24, 1882. But that year trade and industry issues were causing instability in Bohemia and the family moved again to find work. Two years later, just when the couple thought everything was getting easier, they had their first son Frank. He was born on January 13, 1884. Then barely a year after that Mary gave birth to their fifth daughter, Josephine, on April 14, 1886.

Mary Holy had been writing to her sister Katharina who had immigrated to America with her husband Joseph and were already living in Madison, Nebraska. In Mary's letter she confided that she feared it would be impossible to find good husbands for her daughters in Bohemia. After the birth of Josephine Katharina wrote begging Mary to come to America and that she and her husband would help them. While Katharina and Joseph didn't have much, they did believe with hard work there was hope for a better future for all of them in America. Mary convinced Jacob to move to America then discovered she was pregnant again.

"The couple still felt they could not afford to wait. Even though Mary's pregnancy was advanced they boarded the steam-ship Alba and arrived in America in May of 1888. Thankfully, Mrs. Holy had no complications during the sea voyage and disembarked from the Alba two months before her baby was due. Katharina had written to Jacob recommending the family catch the train out of New York to Colfax, Nebraska. Colfax is an hour away from Madison by train. However, it was easier to get to the Kuchar's place by wagon. Mr. Kuchar met the Holy family as planned but only carried them as far as the doctor in West Point in County Colfax. Mary went into labor and could go no further. Their seventh child Katherine was born on July 30, 1888 and Mary required a month of rest before she could continue on to her sister's home.

Regarding Karella Artifacts at the Nebraska Museum in Madison

For those who would like to see some antique memorabilia, it can be found at the Madison County Historical Museum and Archival Library, located in Madison, Nebraska. The Madison County Historical Museum is under the direction of Carol Robertson, and the Museum was founded in 1969 under the direction of Bob and Florence Cumming of Madison. This museum is an incredibly valuable resource for those researching the pioneers who settled the Madison, Nebraska, area. Uncounted citizens have donated and/or loaned amazing antiques, photographs, and family histories and heirlooms, which are preserved and displayed. They have a working, turn-of-the-century switchboard and paid telephone booth that school children can see and use to demonstrate the advancement of technology. They have a whole building dedicated to the history of trains. It is quite unique, and they have built an entire miniature town that has working trains, and that town fills a whole building. It is well worth making a trip to see it and help to support it. The amazing curators have a wealth of local knowledge, and the research materials I gained by making several visits to this museum added a remarkable amount of historical evidence to what is contained in this book. There are extensive displays, and many include items from many branches of the Karella clan and their cousins from other family clans that are wonderful to look at and appreciate.

Regarding the Church of St. Leonard's in Madison

Father Greg Carl is the name of the priest at St. Leonard's parish who let Millie Karella Ridder and Gwen Karella Mathis look through the archives in the church basement. This is where we found the old history on the original St. Leonard's church that had been built by the historical cemetery where the Karella ancestors are buried.

Regarding Additional Facts about the Holy and Kuchar Families

Bessie Holy-Finkral, Jacob and Mary's third child, was ninety-three years old in 1970 when she was interviewed by Mary Voborny and Sister Margaret Mary Bean. To the younger women's delight, Great Aunt Bessie recalled firsthand coming to America. The interviewers noted, "We will never forget that visit with Great Aunt Bessie. In her soft-spoken way, she answered all our questions in regard to what she remembered about those first years in America. 'I was almost ten years old then,' said Bessie, 'and here we came. Auntie Katharina and Uncle Joseph had six kids, and we had six kids and Mama had the new baby too. There we lived all together in their little old one-room dugout. I don't know how we did it.' This one-room dugout Bessie describes, where sixteen family members plus a one-month-old baby lived, was located west of Madison in the Schoolcraft Precinct."

Sister Margaret Mary went on to say, "Bessie also recalled the reason their family moved to America. 'It was because Mama and Papa hoped life would be easier in this new land.' Given that thought, it is hard to imagine the situation the two families found themselves in, was considered better, or easier, than what they had come from. Yet the fondness that could be felt during the interview with Bessie as she recalled those long-ago days was undeniable. Consequently, it could not have been as bad as it sounded to us, and there was no doubt that it was a home full of love. Clearly, the four adults were committed to making ends meet, and they all managed to survive. Bessie also said that Jacob and Joseph became fast friends and shared the workload."

The family investigators eventually learned the two families saved enough money to better their condition. Documentation and family records showed Jacob and Mary Holy had a total of ten children. Please note Katherine

American style dugout house, Kuchar's, 1800s

was born shorty after they arrived; then Emma was born April 1, 1891; Vlasta was born November 20, 1896; and the second son and 10th child, Victor, was born April 27, 1897. According to the records, the last three children were all born in Madison, Nebraska.

Recap of Handwritten Notes Recorded on the Holy Family Birth Records

This writer recounted a few specific memories handwritten by a grandchild that read, "Grandma and Grandpa Holy lived in Meadow Grove after leaving the farm. They lived in a little square, one-story house near a few large trees. Whenever us grandchildren visited them, we were warmly greeted and allowed to climb up and sit on our grandparents' laps. We were also encouraged to go outside and play. We loved to pick the Rosemary herb that grew outside at their house and carry it around with us because it smelled so good.

Bessie Holy Finkral and Jim Finkral

In the middle of the afternoon, we would all troop into the house for lunch. We always had fresh, home-baked rye bread with cheese that was the equivalent in smell to Limburger. It was actually ripe homemade cottage cheese, but us kids called it stink-cheese. These visits were always happy times. Mother used to tell us about how Grandpa and Grandma had lost all their savings during the bank crash of the 1920s. But Grandma was always a joyful person, and she dearly loved to play cards. Mamma told us how she used to provoke Aunt Vlasta. She would mark the score from each hand she won on the back of a chair when she couldn't find a piece of paper handy. There was also a story about how frugal Grandma was. Because she had lost all her money she learned to save and be thrifty. So, instead of buying expensive yarn, she would buy less expensive string to darn the holes in Grandpa's socks. This would hurt Grandpa's feet, and so he would be grumpy and ask our Mamma to talk to Grandma about it."

Final Facts Regarding the Holy Family

Mary Holy died March 7, 1935, at eighty-two and was buried in Iowa Valley Cemetery ten miles west of Madison, Nebraska. Jacob Holy died March 12, 1944, at ninety-two in the home of his youngest son, Victor (Vic), and was buried next to his wife, Mary, in the Iowa Valley Cemetery.

Final Facts about the Kuchar Family

In the Madison County land records, Mary Voborny and Sister Margaret Mary found information that establishes the Kuchar family eventually owned the land where they lived in the dugout. Located two miles north and three miles west of the Schoolcraft Catholic Church, this land was not a homestead. The deed recorded for it lists the land as purchased from another owner.

This land is held by Willard Kuchar, and according to an interview with him in the year 1969, the old original prairie dugout still stands on this same property. He also said that the farmhouse that sits on the property today—a white wooden farmhouse—1 ½ stories high, standard to the style built in the WW1 era of 1914 to 1918, was built by Grandfather Holy. Currently, one of Willard's sons farms the land, but Willard still lives on this property.

Regarding U.S. Census of 1910 and Madison County Genealogical Society Records for 1918

Eventually, nineteen years later, we were able to pick up Anton and Anastasia's trail once again in 1910. This was a year when Anton and Anastasia took part in a national census. In this United States census, each adult living in the household was identified, and the census taker not only listed Anton and his wife Anastasia, but also listed a distant relative living with them by the name of Edmund Shoe. The census described the man as forty years of age and that he was born and raised in France. Eight years later, Anton and Anastasia reappear in another listing. This time, the information is found in the Madison County Genealogical Society record for 1918. In this listing, it declares Anton Karella is a farmer, dealer in lumber, threshing machines, and a sawmill operator. It also listed his wife Anastasia and their first five children—Helen, Ambrose Jerome, Martha, Frank, Mary, and one other adult, Mr. Edmund Shoe.

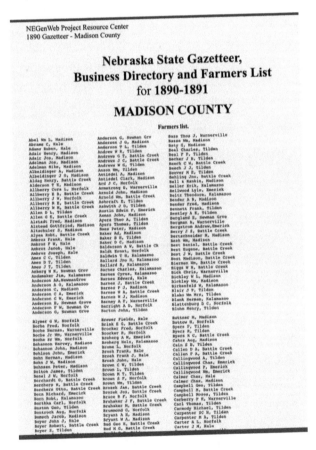

A memory about Vaclav Karella by a Daughter and Granddaughter

Sister Margaret Mary interviews her mother, Helen Agnes Karella. Helen was born in 1896 and remembers her Grandfather Vaclav personally. Helen began her story this way. Margaret Mary's mother, Helen Bean, told them that Great Grandfather Vaclav never permitted anyone to take his picture unless he had on a proper suit. Helen went on to say, "My father, Anton, grew up the same way. Consequently, you will never see a candid photograph of either of them. If a person did not give these men time to change into a suit, there was no picture. Unfortunately, that means there never were many photographs.

```
Juckett Wm H, Emerick
Jung John, Madison
Kalmer Jacob, Kalamazoo
Kampe Anton, Emerick
Kampe Joseph, Emerick
Kamrath Fred, Kalamazoo
Kamrath Wm, Kalamazoo
Kane C F, Madison
Kaufman H, Kalamazoo
Kaufman J D, Emerick
Karm Aug, Norfolk
Karabel Alois, Tilden
Karabel Jos, Tilden
Karelia Anton, Madison
Karella W, Madison
Karge Jos, Tilden
Karmpe Frank, Emerick
Karth Herm, Norfolk

Larson Andrew, Kalamazoo
```

Even fewer survived through the years. That is why the one below is so precious, and one of my most prized treasures. This photo of grandfather Vaclav never fails to amuse me. The scene is supposed to appear as a relaxed afternoon picnic but just take a good look. In the background is Grandfather's house, and he stands at the edge of a blanket that lies on the grass under a mulberry tree. Sitting on the blanket to the far left is me (Helen Karella) then Jenny Pojar, who is sitting next to my sister, Martha Karella, and sitting next to Martha is our brother, Ambrose Jerome Karella. I call this picture 'Mulberry Time.' Grandfather Vaclav is standing straight as an arrow yet is supposedly casually eating mulberries during a picnic with his grandchildren in his side yard. They even took the time to set a vase of flowers in the middle of the blanket for the final photo—now that is real style.

Madison, NE, photo called mulberry time—Vaclav Karella standing, grandson Ambrose Jerome (Rusty) Karella sitting at his feet; Girls left to right: Helen Karella, Jenny Pojar and Martha Karella

"The subject of this photo brings back fond memories too. For anyone who never grew up with Nebraskan mulberries, they can't imagine what they have missed! These berries are succulent when ripe, which readily falls from the trees when one shakes the branches. The berry turns a rich blue-black color at harvest time, and it's delightful juice stains fabric and skin equally with ease.

Yet, regardless of the dark marks that must wear off with time, the delectably sweet fruit can make the gatherer a trifle careless and greedy when one is in a hurry to eat them."

A Note about Vaclav's Homestead by Sister Margaret Mary

"The family investigators found documents in the old Madison courthouse files describing Great Grandfather Vaclav's homestead of 160 acres. Amazingly, sixty of those acres were covered in timber and had been part of the original tree-planting initiative of 1872 sponsored by J. Sterling Morton, the founder of Nebraska's Arbor Day." The documents also recorded Vaclav's statement bequeathing the homestead, and the acreage to his youngest son, Emil John, "For the sum of "$1.00 and much love and affection."

1922, Remembering the Death of Anastasia Karella by her Daughters, Helen and Mary

"In the winter of 1921-22, the Karellas had an empty bedroom to rent. One of their daughters had married, which left an extra room open. The family rented the empty room to a young woman teaching at the District School # 66, located right across the road from our house. The teacher's name was Agnes Moore, and she moved in with us the summer before the new school term began.

"Mary was present when Anastasia Karella was diagnosed with scarlet fever, a highly contagious and deadly disease. The doctor said most patients' die, and should they recover, frequently died later from damaged kidneys related to high fevers and bacterial infections. The doctor recommended Anastas be sent away immediately until Anastasia was no longer contagious. Our father sent him to our sister, Martha who was married to Rudy Pojar. But the doctor said since Mary was thirteen, she could stay. However, I was not allowed to see mother," Helen finished.

"The fever raged in Mama for days, and nothing the doctor or Papa did could bring it down. The weather turned bitterly cold during the worst of Mamma's fever, and then on the afternoon July 16, 1922, Agnes and I stood watch for the doctor once more. It was very cold down in the kitchen, but Papa pleaded with Agnes and me to stay in there and watch for the doctor. The windows were half-frosted over, making it hard to see. In fact, only the very center of the glass pane was clear enough to see through. Papa did not leave Mamma when the doctor came. The doctor went upstairs; Agnes built up the fire in the stove and put on the teakettle to make hot water," Mary said.

"It was still a shock when the doctor came downstairs and announced my Mother had died. That was when Agnes and I saw the kitchen windows had frozen over completely with ice so thick we had to use the steam from the teakettle to melt it enough to watch for the undertakers.

"He told us that just before Mama died, 'Her temperature was so high the thermometer topped out at 110 degrees, and then the mercury inside separated from the heat of her body.' The people listening to him were shaking their heads and seemed afraid. Then, the doctor explained that due to the virulent nature of Scarlet Fever, they were to wear masks and gloves while they were in contact with the body, and the body was to be placed in the casket immediately. The doctor gave further instructions, 'Once the body is sealed in the casket, you may make a brief stop at the church, but the priest will have to bless the sealed casket. It is *not*, I repeat *not* to be opened for any reason. Then, take it to the burial storage. It will remain there, frozen, until the ground is soft enough to dig a grave. I will be along later with the death certificate.'"

Mary sat quietly for a moment, remembering that horrible day as though it had happened yesterday, and then whispered, "My Mamma went to her final resting place dressed in only her nightie. I remember asking Agnes if she thought God minded. Agnes had hugged me and laid her cheek against my hair and then said, 'No, I think God was happy to welcome your Mamma back home to heaven just as she was. I never lost Agnes' friend-ship because she married Joe Pojar, brother-in-law to my sister

Martha's husband, Rudy Pojar and we have remained close friends since Mama's death."

Interview with Helen Karella Bean about when she and her children lived with Anton after Anastasia's Death

Helen explained to her children, "Your papa, Josephus Alvius Bean, who you have heard me call Alvin, worked for a road construction crew when you were very young. His job took him away for long periods of time, and one day he got so lonely for us that he built a house on an old tractor frame. Your Papa literally created a house on wheels that he could pull like a work trailer, to wherever his work was located. That way we could be together. This meant we traveled a lot too and did not see your grandparents very much.

"Then, in 1922, when your Grandma Anastasia Karella got sick and died, four of my siblings were still living at home. My two grown brothers Ambrose and Frank who were still unmarried, and then there were my two youngest siblings, 14-year old Mary and 11-year old Anastas. This was a particularly bad time for our dad because not only had his wife died, his father Vaclav, your Great Grandfather, also died that same year.

"Your Grandfather Anton's grief was too much for him to bear alone so he wrote me a letter, and in it, he begged me to come home. 'Please come home, Helen, come home. For we need one another.' So, your father Alvin and I discussed your grandfather's request. Your papa was very understanding and took us to live with your Grandfather to help him not be lonely.

"Now your Papa continued to travel for his construction jobs, knowing we would be safe and well taken care of, living with your grandfather Anton." Helen always made sure her children understood how kind their Daddy was when he brought them to live with Grandpa Anton.

America History facts about the Statue of Liberty

The construction of *the pedestal for the Statue of Liberty* on Ellis Island in New York harbor preceded the installation of the Statue itself in October of 1886.

The statue, a gift from the French people, originally commemorated the alliance between France and the American colonies during the American Revolution. However, the freedom won in America was a beacon of light to all the citizens of old Europe who still fought the yoke of Governments controlled by Royalty and Aristocrats. This statue was always meant to symbolize *Liberty enlightening the world.*

The actual statue of Liberty, that sits in New York harbor was paid for by the French people. Yet despite their enormous collaborative effort, more money was needed to complete the statue. In the end the sculptor, Bartholdi, charged admission fees to let people see the inside of the unfinished statue and sold souvenirs to enable him to complete the sculpture. Even after the statue was completed, the governments of both the *United States and France* refused to allocate any funding for this project.

According to a story written by Alex Santoso, "Joseph, publisher of the New York World newspaper, outraged by the lack of governmental support for this project, personally launched a campaign to raise the money required to build the correct pedestal for the statue. After two months of non-stop haranguing via newspaper articles, Pulitzer raise $135,750 of the $200,000 needed to build the proper pedestal for the Statue of Liberty. Roughly 125,000 American people contributed to the completion of the pedestal, thanks to Pulitzer's crusade. To show his gratitude, Pulitzer had the New York World newspaper publish the names of each person who contributed, no matter the size of the contribution. Antonia Nemec Karella was the first of her family to set foot on American soil. She made her voyage to New York more than ten years before the immigration facility was built or the *Statue of Liberty* was installed on Ellis Island. From 1855 to 1890 new arrivals coming to New York by ship came through the Castle Garden immigration center gate in Battery Park, New York. It is estimated that approximately eight million European immigrants passed through the Castle Garden gates before the Ellis Island immigration depot was established in 1890.

Facts about New York and Morrisania

"The village was named after one of our Governors, whose name was Morris. During the time of our statehood New York had twelve counties. The territory contained within County Bronx was originally part of County Westchester and parts of the towns of Yonkers, Eastchester and Pelham. In 1846, the division of Westchester created the new town of West Farms; then in 1855, the town of Morrisania was created from West Farms.

APPENDIX 4

Bohemian Recipes

<u>Baker's Directions for Crust</u>

Step 1
Bring chilled dough (see preparation instructions below) to room temperature. Roll dough into a twelve-inch circle, fit into a nine-inch pie tin thinly coated with oil. Fold edges under and press the pie edge with tip of finger one inch apart, around the rim. Bake piecrust at 450 degrees for 10 minutes or until golden brown. Cool completely on rack.

<u>Ingredients for Cream Pie Filling</u>

- Fresh oil

- 1/2 cup sugar

- 1 tablespoon grated lemon rind, hold 1 tsp. aside

- 1/4 cup fresh lemon juice

- 3 tablespoons cornstarch

- 1/4 teaspoon salt

- 2 goose eggs

- 1 1/2 cups milk

- 1/4 cup (2 ounces) cream cheese or soft goat cheese

- 2 tablespoons butter, softened

- 1 1/2 cups whipped cream, stiff

Step 1
Combine sugar, 2 1/2 teaspoons rind, and the next 4 ingredients with eggs in a large bowl, stirring well. Combine milk and cheese in a medium saucepan over heat, never higher than a medium flame. Cook until mixture reaches 180° or until tiny bubbles form around edge. Do not boil. Gradually add the hot milk mixture to sugar mixture, stirring constantly with a whisk. Return milk mixture to pan and cook over medium heat 10 minutes or until thick and bubbly, stirring constantly. Remove from heat. Stir in butter.

Step 2
Cool mixture to room temperature, stirring occasionally. Spoon filling into prepared crust and cover surface of filling with lid. Chill for 3 hours or until stiff and remove lid. Spread whipped topping evenly over chilled pie and sprinkle with 1/2 teaspoon finely grated lemon rind or zest.

Ingredients List for Piecrust

- 2 ½ cups flour
- 1 tablespoon sugar
- 1 teaspoon salt
- 1 cup plus 2 tablespoons butter cut in slices
- 1 tablespoon apple cider vinegar

Baker's Directions and preparation for piecrust

- Mix flour, sugar, and salt in large bowl. Toss butter and flour mixture, working quickly and aggressively with fingers. Blend butter into flour to create a bowl of large and small clumps.

- Combine vinegar and 3 Tbsps. of ice water in a small bowl, then pour slowly over flour mixture, using fingers to distribute the moisture evenly, creating a single lump. Knead lump of dough in the bowl until it starts to come together but still looks dry.

- Drop dough out onto a smooth surface and knead 1 or 2 more times into a single smooth ball. Divide all of dough into 2 pieces and press each part flat until it is about 1" thick. Cover and chill at least 1 hour.

- **Compete this task ahead:** Dough can be made 1-2 days ahead but must be kept chilled.

Nemec Family Recipe for Bohemian Kolache (sweet rolls)

Filling: Prepare a total of 2 cups stewed fruit (or berry) Cherry, prune, and lemon

- Dough Ingredients: for 14 to 16 rolls
- 1/4 ounce active yeast
- 1/4 ounce dry yeast
- 1/2 cup sugar (divided in half)
- 2 cups warm warmed milk, hot to the touch
- 5 3/4 to 6 1/2 cups flour
- 4 large egg yolks
- 1 teaspoon salt
- 1/4 cup butter, softened

Nemec prepares first stage of dough the night before.

Instructions:

- 1 large egg white, beaten in a small bowl
- Dissolve yeast and 1 tablespoon sugar in warm milk. Let stand 10 minutes.
- In large bowl, combine 2 cups flour, remaining sugar, egg yolks, salt, butter, and yeast/milk.
- Mix until smooth. Add enough remaining flour to make stiff dough.
- Drop dough ball onto a floured surface and knead until smooth and elastic, about 6-8 minutes.
- Add additional flour if needed to keep the dough from getting sticky.
- Place dough in greased bowl, turning once to grease top.
- Cover; let rise in a warm place until doubled in bulk, about 1 hour.
- Punch dough down and allow it to rise again.
- On a floured surface, roll flat to 1/2 inch. Thickness.
- Cut with large water glass to form 2 1/2 inch rounds.
- In large greased baking sheets, place the rounds on sheet and let rise until doubled, about 45 minutes.
- Firmly press indentation in center and fill each roll with a heaping tablespoon of compote.
- Brush dough with lightly beaten egg white.
- Bake at 350° for 10-15 minutes or until rolls are light golden brown.

Master Baker Nemec, Rohliky Ingredient List

11) 1 cup milk

12) 1/4 cup sugar

13) 1/4 cup water

14) 2 1/2 teaspoons dry active yeast

15) 1 teaspoon salt

16) 1 (beaten) egg

17) 1/4 cup lard, melted and cooled

18) 3 1/4 – 3 1/2 cups flour and re-measure (sift two times as Papa says it makes them fluffier)

19) Brush with sweet butter while hot and sprinkle with black poppy seeds.

20) Prepare dough, cover in crock, knead once before bed, and let set overnight.

Baking Directions

Roll out dough into thin, flat pieces cut in pie shape angles, roll each slice, and set in crescent moon shape on baking sheet. Bake in oven at 375 degrees for 15-20 minutes until medium golden-brown top center of rohliky. Remove from heat and cool, but while just warm, brush with sweet butter and sprinkle with black poppy seeds. Leave on sheet until cool to touch.

Mildred Karella Ridder and Mary Voborny,
Family history researchers

Build Your Own Family Tree

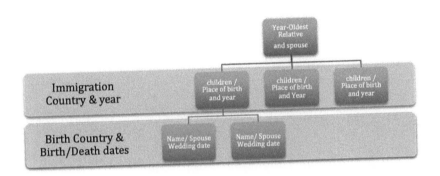

Q. Where do I look for creating a template for my family tree?
A. Computer templates in your current software programs for family charts
   Or computer applications found online, for Mac or PC, for download
Q. Where do I start my data research?
A. Oldest family name, oldest date connected with that name, and place they lived. From this point, you can look at newspaper obituaries, church census and/or event data, and city and state census data.

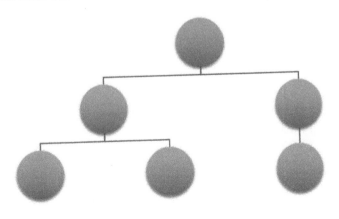

Examples of Genealogy Resources and Places to Begin Your Personal Search for Data

<u>Examples of resources online specializing in genealogy and research</u>

1. AncestorSearch—builds a Google search for you that is optimized to find web pages mentioning your ancestors.

2. Mocavo—launched in March 2011

3. Linkpendium's Genealogical Data Search

4. Geneanet.org

5. Genealogy.com

6. Kin Crawler—Kin Crawler is a genealogy specific search engine

7. https://www.familysearch.org/wiki/en/Search_Engines_for_Genealogical_Research

8. Ancestry.com

9. US Census Records Free

10. *www.zapmeta.ws/search*

11. State and federal listings for land grants, homesteads, and sales

12. State and city office of vital statistics, obituaries, marriages, divorces, and deaths

13. Church records: births, deaths, baptisms, first communions, marriages, and cemetery listings

14. https://www.loc.gov

Note: Local libraries, history_museum_curators and historians are also great resources.

Dear Researchers,

I would begin your quest by establishing everything you can about the oldest relative you are looking for. Keep the stories and facts you learn in a journal—in chronological order. I used a binder that I could add to as I discovered new facts and put copies of my research in those sections. Family conversations can uncover a wealth of data for your research focus. Ask lots of questions, make copies of all the old photos you find, look at any old family records you can find, and take pictures of everything related to your search. When adding data to your journal, list other names, times, and places associated with your research focus. Your goal is to expand your knowledge about your relative. Then, establish additional data surrounding them. Be patient—this is a process that takes time passion and dedication. I wish you the best in your research journeys. Have fun with it.

Dear Family and friends,

Thank you for taking time to read this history. It is a work of love to honor those who came before us. Those who strove with passion and courage to give future generations a better life than perhaps the one they felt they had been born into. Such great examples of faith in action, clearly the Creator was with each of them as most of the children within the generations flourished, in times, where so many did not.

Wherever we are in our personal journeys, the gift is found in learning the lessons embedded within our experiences. I feel a new depth of respect for what our relatives went through for me, providing amazing examples to emulate by their lives and through the lessons they learned. I strived to include all the information: historically documented dates, places, and personal memories collected by family members and sent to me and orally transmitted to me.

Establishing the timeline of the Karella heritage, I followed the firstborn son of each generation to assemble the story. I intend no disrespect to the amazing women or men of our family by using this method to stay focused on the flow of the story. A central character keeps the story grounded. That being said, I made every effort to clarify each child born and the women's maiden name and family who chose to link with a member of the Karella clan.

I hope as you who read this historical human-interest story, you will be inspired to write down more details of your firsthand memories within your extended family groups. Wouldn't it be a grand gift in the years to come to have a library of unique memories for those linked to the Karella clan? Images of where they came from, and inspirations to look to, which help build who they will become. May God bless all your endeavors and grant you the hope, courage, and creativity to sustain you through the years of your life.

Gwen Delora Karella Mathis,
Research period 2010–2019

Printed in the USA
CPSIA information can be obtained
at www.ICGtesting.com
LVHW072023261023
762248LV00029B/332/J

9 781641 844512